Library of
Davidson College

MORE CHAPTERS OF OPERA

ENCORE MUSIC EDITIONS
Reprints of outstanding works on music

THE AUTHOR

MORE CHAPTERS OF OPERA

BEING

HISTORICAL AND CRITICAL OBSERVATIONS
AND RECORDS CONCERNING THE LYRIC
DRAMA IN NEW YORK FROM
1908 TO 1918

BY

HENRY EDWARD KREHBIEL

MUSICAL EDITOR OF "THE NEW YORK TRIBUNE"; AUTHOR OF "HOW TO LISTEN TO
MUSIC," "STUDIES IN THE WAGNERIAN DRAMA," "MUSIC AND MANNERS
IN THE CLASSICAL PERIOD," "THE PIANOFORTE AND ITS MUSIC,"
"A BOOK OF OPERAS," "AFRO-AMERICAN FOLKSONGS,"
ETC, AND "CHAPTERS OF OPERA," TO WHICH
THIS VOLUME IS A SEQUEL

*WITH ILLUSTRATIONS AND TABLES OF PERFORMANCES
WITHIN THE PERIOD DESCRIBED*

HYPERION PRESS, INC.
Westport, Connecticut

Published in 1919 by H. Holt, New York
Hyperion reprint edition 1980
Library of Congress Catalog Number 78-66910
ISBN 0-88355-749-5
Printed in the United States of America

Library of Congress Cataloging in Publication Data
Krehbiel, Henry Edward, 1854-1923.
  More chapters of opera.

  (Encore music editions)
  Principally articles from the New York Tribune.
  Reprint of the 1919 ed. published by H. Holt, New
York.
  1. Opera—New York (City)—History and criticism.
  I. Title. II. Series.
ML1711.8.N3K74 1979   782.1'09747'1   78-66910
ISBN 0-88355-749-5

To

WILLIAM J. HENDERSON, Esq.
*The Author's Colleague and Friend
for a generation*

THE AUTHOR'S ACKNOWLEDGMENTS

PRACTICALLY everything in this book has been printed at one time or another in the columns of the *New York Tribune,* though much of it was written that it might appear in its present form and for reasons which are set forth in the first chapter; the rest was compiled, and to some extent refashioned, from the critical comments contributed by me to that journal at various times in the course of the period 1908-1918. It is therefore meet that I should here make grateful acknowledgment to the Editor and Publishers of *The Tribune,* on the staff of which I have served for nearly forty years, for the privilege of reprinting the remoulded material.

I am also deeply beholden to Mr. Mishkin for his courteous permission to use the great number of photographs which bear the imprint of the Mishkin Studio.

H. E. KREHBIEL.

BLUE HILL, ME., June, 1919.

CONTENTS

Chapter I

INTRODUCTORY OBSERVATIONS

PAGE

Why This Book Was Written—Effect of the World War upon Operatic Conditions—A New Era Predicted—Ten Years of Unparalleled Activity—The Incidents Marshaled—A Frivolous Attitude of the Newspapers Arraigned—New York Today and London Two Centuries Ago—The Cult of the Prima Donna—Criticism Defended—A Critic's Duty to Art, His Conscience, and His Time—Permanency in Artistic Principles . .

Chapter II

OPERATIC CONDITIONS IN THE BEGINNING OF THE DECADE

State of Affairs at the Close of the Season 1907-08—Review of the Preceding Period—Ideals Left by Maurice Grau—The Succession of Mr. Conried in the Management of the Metropolitan Opera House—His Promises and Failures—His Retirement—Engagement of Mr. Gatti-Casazza and Mr. Dippel—Dreams of World Dominion—Death of Heinrich Conried—His Career—Mr. Gatti's Unfortunate Introduction—Wagner's Dramas in Italy—Mr. Gatti's Early Life—Controversy Between the Managers—Singers Intercede for Mr. Dippel—He Is Routed—The New Theater Built and Dedicated—A Beautiful Ideal—A List of the Founders 13

Chapter III

THE FIRST SEASON OF THE DUAL ADMINISTRATION

The Season 1908-09—Emmy Destinn—A Patriotic Prima Donna—Changes Presaged by the War—Signor Toscanini; His Qualities and Triumphs—Reflections on the Season—D'Albert's "Tiefland"—Inter-racialism Rampant—An American School of Composition—Bohemians Object to the Austrian National Hymn—"Le Villi," Puccini's First Opera—Five Generations of Puccinis—Catalani's "La Wally"—The Musical Revolution

ix

CONTENTS

in Italy—Smetana's "Bartered Bride"—Madame Sembrich's Farewell to the Opera Stage—Ceremonies at the Opera House—A Complimentary Banquet—Mr. Henderson's Poem—A Versified Repertory—Retirement of Madame Eames—Her Record at the Metropolitan—Signor Caruso Temporarily Incapacitated . 36

CHAPTER IV

RIVALRY BETWEEN THE MANHATTAN AND METROPOLITAN OPERA HOUSES

An Opera-mad City—Over Two Millions of Dollars Spent on the Entertainment in Ten Months—Mr. Hammerstein's Policies—The Masses Against the Aristocrats—The Lure of French Opera—A House Built in Philadelphia—The Clash of Opposition There—Hammerstein Confesses Failure—Purchase of His Interests and Properties—Agrees to Retire from Opera for Ten Years—Reorganizations and Affiliations—Hammerstein Tries London—Failure There—Attempts to Enter the Field in New York—Builds a Theater in Lexington Avenue—Opera in English—Project of the City Club—Hammerstein Announces His Intention to Evade His Contract—Is Enjoined by the Courts—Mr. Stotesbury and His Loans—Death of Mr. Hammerstein . . . 69

CHAPTER V

LAST SEASONS AT THE MANHATTAN OPERA HOUSE

Mr. Hammerstein's Promises and Performances—Circus Advertising—Special Representations and Prices—Mlle. Labia—Revival of "Samson et Dalila"—"Le Jongleur de Notre Dame"—Engagement of Lina Cavalieri—Miss Garden Resents Her Desire to Appear in Thaïs—Managers and Newspaper-men Come to Blows—Miss Garden Holds the Field—Production of "Salome"—History of the Opera in America—Opéra Comique and Opéra Bouffe—"Princesse d'Auberge"—"Hérodiade"—"Sapho"—Jean de Reszke and Translations — "Tannhäuser" in French — "Grisélidis" — "Elektra" 94

CHAPTER VI

NEW YORK'S ANNUS MIRABILIS

Opera in New York and European Capitals—A Study in Contrasts—The Cost of Opera at the Metropolitan—

CONTENTS

Artistic Doings in the Season of 1909-10—A Season at the New Theater—The Russian Dancers Pavlova and Mordkin—A Large Roster of Singers—Unfulfilled Promises—The Season's Novelties—Lortzing's "Czar und Zimmermann"—Paër's "Le Maitre de Chapelle"—Vicissitudes of Gluck's "Orfeo"—Military Operas—Franchetti's "Germania"—Bruneau's "L'Attaque du Moulin"—Russian Operas in America—"Pique Dame"—Tschaikowsky and Mozart 132

Chapter VII

POPULAR OPERA AT THE CENTURY THEATER

Production of an English Opera—"The Pipe of Desire"—A Versatile Predecessor of This Author—Importance of Operatic Texts—A Fantastic Opera—Jumbling of Mythological and Folklore Elements—English Opera at the Metropolitan—A Prize Competition—"Mona"—Early History of "Natoma"—Agitation Following the Contest—Action by the City Club—Plans for Popular Opera at the Century Theater—A Disastrous Experiment—A Study of Financial Results—The Systems of the Metropolitan and Century Companies Compared—Operatic Translations—The Training Needed by Singers and Composers—National Schools of Music—Musical Idioms—Need of a Forward Man as an Exemplar—Early American Operas 164

Chapter VIII

THE FIRST SEASON UNDER MR. GATTI-CASAZZA ALONE

Opera at the Metropolitan in 1910-11—Reduction of Forces—Failure of an Affiliation with Chicago and Boston—Illness of Signor Caruso—Death of M. Gilibert—Gluck's "Armide"—The Ballets of Lully and Gluck—Rousseau's Sarcasm—Visits of Puccini and Humperdinck—Production of Their New Operas—"La Fanciulla del West"—How Mr. Belasco Trained the Singers to Act—A Failure and Its Cause—"Königskinder"—A "Suffragette" Opera—"Ariane et Barbe-Bleue"—How a Satire was Construed as a Plea for Woman's Suffrage 193

CONTENTS

CHAPTER IX

A VISIT FROM THE CHICAGO-PHILADELPHIA COMPANY

PAGE

Influences of Hammerstein at the Metropolitan—The Decay of French Opera—Hammerstein's Chicago Scheme—Philadelphia Brings Novelties to New York—"Natoma"—Some of Its Predecessors—A Century of American Opera—The Librettist's Poetry—"Il Segreto di Susanna"—A German Opera Sung in Italian—"Quo Vadis?"—Nero the Singer in Opera and History—Story of the Opera, and Comments 224

CHAPTER X

NOVELTIES OF A SEASON AND A PRIZE OPERA

The Interesting Features of 1911-12—Some Excellent Additions to the Metropolitan Forces—Thuille's "Lobetanz"—Characteristics of Matinée Audiences—Use of Wagnerian Materials—Thuille and His Music—Out-of-doors Operatic Festivals—Wolf-Ferrari's "Le Donne Curiose"—A Visit from the Composer—Divided Allegiances, Racially and Musically—"I Giojelli della Madonna"—Visit from the Philadelphia Company—Massenet's "Cendrillon"—Cinderella as an Operatic Heroine—Blech's "Versiegelt"—A Diverting Comedy with Brass Ornaments—Production of the Prize Opera "Mona"—Want of Operatic Suitability in a Strong and Beautiful Dramatic Poem—The Province of Music in a Drama—Obstacles Placed by the Poet to Sympathy for His Heroine—Professor Parker's Music—Earlier Achievements of the Composer—Characterization by Means of Tonality—Themes as Musical Symbols—Monteverde's "Orfeo" 242

CHAPTER XI

AN INCREASE IN TICKET PRICES AND A SCANDAL

The Cost of Seats at the Metropolitan Opera House Advanced—Reason Given in Explanation—Speculation in Theater Tickets in New York—Relation Between Managers and Speculators—Attitude of the Metropolitan Management—Agents Hypothecate Tickets Belonging to Subscribers—Criminal Proceedings Against an

CONTENTS xiii

Agent—Why They Were Not Prosecuted—Cost of Giving Opera in New York—Some Comparative Tables 267

CHAPTER XII

ANOTHER EXPERIMENT WITH ENGLISH OPERA AND A GREAT RUSSIAN WORK

The Season of 1912-13—Additions to the Metropolitan Company—Mabel Garrison, Melanie Kurt, Johannes Sembach, Luca Botta, and Arthur Middleton—Rostand's "Cyrano de Bergerac" Done Into an English Opera—Moussorgsky's "Boris Godounow"—A Visit from the Chicago Opera Company Brings Novelties—Zandonai's "Conchita" and "Les Ranz des Vaches," a German Version of Kienzl's "Kuhreigen" . . . 286

CHAPTER XIII

A SEASON PROLIFIC IN INCIDENTS AND OPERAS

Operas Produced in 1913-14—A Visit from the Chicago-Philadelphia Company—Death of Putnam Griswold—Strauss's "Der Rosenkavalier"—The Theatrical Value of Pruriency—Benelli's Poetical Drama "L'Amore dei tre Re"—Montemezzi's Music—Its Racial Character—Constructive Elements Borrowed from Russia—Signor Ferrari-Fontana—Lucrezia Bori—"Madeleine"—Light French Comedy and Heavy Music—"Don Quichotte"—Cervantes Travestied—Mary Garden and "Monna Vanna"—Charpentier's "Julien"—An Abortive Sequel to "Louise"—A Comedy by Molière Done Into a Delightful Opera—Wolf-Ferrari's "L'Amore Medico"—Death of Mme. Nordica 309

CHAPTER XIV

THE YEARS OF THE NEUTRALITY OF THE UNITED STATES IN THE WAR

Reduction of Expenses Planned—Caruso and Farrar—Phenomenal Activity of the Company—New Singers and Their Débuts—The Season 1914-15—New Operas—"Madame Sans-Gêne"—"L'Oracolo"—"Euryanthe"—Weber and Wagner—The Latter's Debts to the Former—Departure of Alfred Hertz—His Record at the

xiv CONTENTS

Metropolitan—The Loss of Toscanini—Season of 1915-16—Arrival of Mme. Barrientos—"Prince Igor"—"Goyescas"—Spanish Pianoforte Pieces Made Into an Opera—Fate of the Composer—A German Version of "The Taming of the Shrew"—1916-17—Unnatural Activity—"Les Pêcheurs de Perles"—Its American History—Gluck's "Iphigenia auf Tauris"—"The Canterbury Pilgrims"—A Sporadic but Ideal Effort for American Art—The Society of American Singers—Mozart's "Bastien et Bastienne" and "The Impresario" 331

CHAPTER XV

CONCERT MUSIC AND THE OPERA IN WAR-TIME

Gradual Change in Sentiment After the Outbreak of Hostilities—Mr. Bodanzky—A Boycott Declared by Germany Against American Opera Houses—Engaging German Singers in the Olden Time—Draw-poker as an Emollient—First Demonstrations of Patriotic Feeling at the Metropolitan—The Question of Enemy Aliens in the Company—Hans Tauscher and His Wife Mme. Gadski—A Plea for Native Singers—Changes in the Concert-field—Foreign Artists—Kunwald and Muck Interned—A Tax on Entertainments—The Opera Prospectus for 1917-18—Dismissal of German Singers—The Historical Narrative Resumed—A Visit from the Chicago Company—Its Novelties—"Isabeau"—"Azora"—"Le Sauteriot"—Mme. Galli-Curci—New Works at the Metropolitan — "Marôuf" — Saint Elizabeth" — "Lodoletta"—A Revival of "Le Prophète"—"Le Coq d'Or"—"Shanewis"—What of the Future? . . . 376

APPENDIX 421

INDEX 447

LIST OF ILLUSTRATIONS

	FACING PAGE
The Author . . . . *Frontispiece*	
Frances Alda, in "Marôuf"	400
Pasquale Amato, in "La Fanciulla del West" . . .	294
Pasquale Amato, as Cyrano de Bergerac	310
Maria Barrientos, as Lakmé	350
Artur Bodansky, Conductor at the Metropolitan Opera House	378
Lucrezia Bori, in "L'Amore dei tre Re"	318
Sophie Braslau, as Shanewis	412
Charles Wakefield Cadman, Composer of "Shanewis"	392
Enrico Caruso, as Julien	326
Enrico Caruso, in "Samson et Dalila"	330
Enrico Caruso, in "Les Pêcheurs de Perles" . . .	362
Giuseppe de Luca, in "Marôuf"	400
Emmy Destinn	40
Emmy Destinn, in "Die Verkaufte Braut"	40
Adamo Didur, in "Boris Godounow"	296
Andreas Dippel	32
Emma Eames, as Juliet	66
Florence Easton, in "Saint Elizabeth"	404
Geraldine Farrar, in "Königskinder"	214
Amelita Galli-Curci, of the Chicago Opera Company	344
Rosina Galli, in "Le Coq d'Or"	410
Giulio Gatti-Casazza, General Manager of the Metropolitan Opera Company	22
Madame Gerville-Réache, in "Elektra"	118
Charles Gilibert	196
Alma Gluck, as the Blessed Shade in "Orfeo" . . .	144
Oscar Hammerstein's London Opera House	82

LIST OF ILLUSTRATIONS

	FACING PAGE
FRIEDA HEMPEL, IN "DER ROSENKAVALIER"	310
WILLIAM J. HENDERSON, LIBRETTIST OF "CYRANO DE BERGERAC"	288
LOUISE HOMER, IN "MONA"	262
OTTO H. KAHN, MANAGING DIRECTOR OF THE METROPOLITAN OPERA HOUSE	176
MELANIE KURT, IN "FIDELIO"	392
MADAME MAZARIN, IN "ELEKTRA"	118
ITALO MONTEMEZZI, COMPOSER OF "L'AMORE DEI TRE RE"	314
ROBERTO MORANZONI, CONDUCTOR AT THE METROPOLITAN OPERA HOUSE	396
MARGARETE OBER, IN "DER ROSENKAVALIER"	310
HORATIO W. PARKER, COMPOSER OF "MONA"	256
GIACOMO PUCCINI	204
HENRI RABAUD, COMPOSER OF "MAROUF"	398
ROSA RAISA, OF THE CHICAGO OPERA COMPANY, AS AÏDA	394
LÉON ROTHIER, IN "BORIS GODOUNOW"	296
CLARENCE WHITEHILL, AS ESCAMILLO IN "CARMEN"	140
ERMANNO WOLF-FERRARI	234

CHAPTER I

INTRODUCTORY OBSERVATIONS

WHY THIS BOOK WAS WRITTEN—EFFECT OF THE WORLD WAR UPON OPERATIC CONDITIONS—A NEW ERA PREDICTED—TEN YEARS OF UNPARALLELED ACTIVITY—THE INCIDENTS MARSHALED—A FRIVOLOUS ATTITUDE OF THE NEWSPAPERS ARRAIGNED—NEW YORK TODAY AND LONDON TWO CENTURIES AGO—THE CULT OF THE PRIMA DONNA—CRITICISM DEFENDED—A CRITIC'S DUTY TO ART, HIS CONSCIENCE, AND HIS TIME—PERMANENCY IN ARTISTIC PRINCIPLES

WHEN, in the winter months of 1910, I gathered together for book-binder's boards the "Chapters of Opera" which had been published in *The Tribune* during the preceding summer, I sought to justify my historical excursion by the statement that the Metropolitan Opera House, having completed an existence of twenty-five years, was about to enter upon a new régime. The close of the operatic year 1917-18 witnessed no change in management in the institution, but more markedly than its predecessor of the decade before it closed a distinctive era and presaged a change of artistic policy. This change was due to causes vastly different from those which had conspired to bring about the earlier reform, if such it was. The United States had become embroiled in the European war. During three years of the awful conflict, the period of American neutrality, our opera pursued the even tenor of its way without grave concern or great alteration of its aims and methods. Neither did it suffer a loss of prosperity. Its patrons were affluent and their emotions had not been aroused, or if aroused had not been directed against any phase of artistic manifestation. No popular prejudice had been awakened against German music or German musicians. The autumn of 1917, however, witnessed a sudden revolution in this complacent attitude. Incidents in which the Opera was but slightly concerned gave proof that the people who had begun the war had become hateful to the American people and with them their language and their art. To this hatred, which I can not condemn and shall not condone, the directors of the Opera had to give heed unless they wished to have their artistic institution come toppling about their heads. They proceeded gradually and somewhat grudgingly to prepare for a new operatic dispensation whose coming in the season of 1918-19 marked an era at once new and momentous. What it was to bring forth lay on the knees of the gods; but it was obvious to the student of our operatic activities in the past that the institution would have to deal with new forces, new predilections, and possibly be compelled to create new fashions, tastes, and ideals.

It appears, then, that the time was come when the history of opera in New York ought again to be brought down to date. The ten years which have elapsed since I subjected the doings at our local institutions to historical review and critical study were filled wth the most amazing incidents that the annals of the lyric drama have ever recorded in New York or any city of the world. Summing up the record of the preceding quarter of a century I wrote in the summer of 1908:

I have seen the failure of the artistic policy to promote which the magnificent theater was built; the revolution of the stockholders under the leadership of Dr. Leopold Damrosch; the progress of a German régime which did much to develop tastes and create ideals which, till its coming, were little known quantities in American art and life; the overthrow of that régime in obedience to the conmands of fashion; the subsequent dawn and development of the liberal and comprehensive policy which marked the climax of the career of Maurice Grau as an operatic manager. I have witnessed since then many of the fruits of wise endeavor and astute management frittered away by managerial incapacity and greed, and fad and fashion come to rule again where, for a brief but eventful period, serious artistic interest and endeavor had been dominant.

In these words I can not but think there lay a formidable indictment of the Metropolitan management; but the artistic sins of commission and omission of the first twenty-five years were petty peccadillos compared with the follies and scandals which marked the beginning of the lustrum which followed; while in the decade which has passed into history since were grouped such a series of incidents as is contained in no volume of operatic history ever written. There were things admirable and things deplorable in these new occurrences, and whether admirable or deplorable they deserve as much permanency of record as can be gained for them by incorporation in a book.

Among the most noteworthy incidents were the conclusion of the administration of Mr. Heinrich Conried, which was followed by disclosures that brought the business as well as the artistic management of the lessees of the Metropolitan Opera House under popular suspicion; the death of Mr. Conried and the advent of Mr. Gatti-Casazza as General Manager of the opera company which had taken up the enterprise of the Maurice Grau Company; the conflict of authority between Mr. Gatti and Mr. Andreas Dippel, whom the directors of the new company had associated with him under the title of Administrative Manager; the rivalry between the Metropolitan Opera Company and Mr. Oscar Hammerstein, who on his personal responsibility had conducted an interesting and significant operatic venture during the two preceding seasons at the Manhattan Opera House in West Thirty-fourth Street; the ending of the absurd rivalry by the purchased retirement of Mr. Hammerstein and his abortive effort to violate the contract and renew the rivalry in a new theater in Lexington Avenue; the retirement from the operatic stage of Mme. Marcella Sembrich and the magnificent demonstrations made in her honor; the building of the New Theater as a kind of artistic annex to the Metropolitan Opera House; the failure of efforts to habilitate a high type of comic opera as well as grand opera in the vernacular in that beautiful establishment and its reversion to the uses of the modern commercialized drama against which it was conceived as a protest; the competition instituted by the directors of the Metropolitan Opera Company for an original English opera which resulted in the production of Professor Parker's " Mona "; the effect of the European war on the repertory and personnel of the Metropolitan Opera House, culminating in the banishment of the German language from its performances.

That the memory of occurrences of such moment ought to be preserved will scarcely be called into question, though the ability and the methods of the historian will offer a fair subject of controversy. I am aware that I shall not escape the accusation of being an idle, if not a malicious gossip, disposed to chronicle small beer if I set down the narrative of some of the things here catalogued and accompany it with critical comment on the doings of managers and artists as well as the operas which were added to the repertory during the period passing under review. Yet I shall adhere to my purpose for several reasons which I believe to be valid. The historical record is to be a continuation of that contained in the " Chapters of Opera " alluded to in the beginning of this introductory essay. It is therefore proper that in a general way at least the manner of those chapters should be followed. The pertinency of interspersed criticism I shall defend presently on the ground that it is essential to an understanding of the relationship between artistic strivings and achievements, between the protestations of managers and their acts. To an understanding also of the extent to which the managers pandered to tastes which the frivolous attitude of the newspapers encouraged, besides the hero-worship stimulated by managers, artists, and the press alike to such an extent that it worked an estoppal to the creation of a liberal and permanent repertory.

A history of opera during the last ten years would serve little purpose if it did not truthfully set forth the things which shall enable the readers of today, and haply of a future day, to visualize a picture of the social and artistic conditions which prevailed in New York at the end of the first decade of the twentieth century. The picture is presented, though in a diffused state, in those contemporaneous chronicles of the times, the newspapers; and these are in nothing more truthful than in their reflection of the frivolity and folly which obtained then and have endured ever since. This I say with a heavy heart and without the slightest desire to extenuate or defend the profession to which I belong. During the period of which I am writing, even in journals of dignity and scholarly repute the gossip of the foyer and the dressing-rooms of the chorus and ballet stood in higher esteem with the news editors than the comments of conscientious critics. The picture of a comic opera woman or a dancing doll whose sole charm centered in a pretty face or a shapely leg was given more prominence than the judicious discussion by a trained and scholarly critic of the performance of an artist who was one in a hundred thousand; and the chatter of a Mary Garden or Geraldine Farrar about her religion or irreligion, the antithesis of marriage and the artistic temperament, or her taste in dress or undress was editorially viewed as of more consequence than a critical discussion of the new score of a world-renowned composer. And so it came about that no matter how sternly their critics held themselves aloof from the intrigues of the theaters, no matter how punctiliously the reviews confined themselves to the artistic side of the performances and eschewed the internal and private affairs of the managers, the newspapers in their editorial and news columns discoursed upon the wisdom and unwisdom of contracts made or not made, of the bestowal or withholding of rôles from singers whose press agents kept them in the public eye, of honoraria alleged to be paid and remuneration alleged to be deserved. In one case there was a quarrel between two singers for the exclusive privilege of appearing in a rôle whose chief attraction was the chance which it offered for the woman to appear in a costume approaching nearer than any in the operatic wardrobe to that worn by Eve before the fall or Phryne before the court of the heliasts. Here editorial championship went so far that it provoked fisticuffs between journalists and managers not only in the public highway but within the dignified precincts of a court of justice.

> And all for nothing.
> For Hecuba!

What was Thaïs to the pressmen or they to Thaïs, that they should have fought for her?

I am familiar with the journalistic axiom that a newspaper is what the public want it to be. The axiom at the best is little better than a half-truth. In politics, civic morals, literature, and every form of art, except that associated with the theater, newspapers strive to impress their conceptions of right and beauty upon their readers. They do not enter the lists in behalf of bad painters or devote columns of description to their daubs; they do not encourage men to spoil good marble or bronze when they might be carving decent gateposts; they do not seek out illiterate rhymsters and fill columns with their verses. But they play the rôle of stage-door Johnnies to the thousand and one "movie" actresses and comic opera chorus girls who keep publicity agents in their employ. If in this they reflect the taste of their readers, it is a taste which they have instilled and cultivated, for it did not exist before the days of photo-engraving, illustrated supplements, and press agents. Popular interest of an acute and incomprehensible kind we know has always followed the great people of the lyric stage; but never as now (assuming that the newspapers are faithful mirrors) the groundlings. Popular infatuation with stage-people of all kinds is probably as old as the stage itself. No doubt the people of ancient Rome split themselves into parties and quarreled about the merits of gladiators, singers, flautists, kitharists, and dancers two thousand years ago. The phenomenon, inasmuch as it marked the operatic history of the decade of which I am writing, more emphatically than any period within a generation is deserving of study. There can be no opera without prima donnas and, it would seem, no prima donnas without jealousies, squabbles, and rancor. An entertaining and diverting chapter illustrating the truism may be extracted from the history of Italian opera in London. The coming of the prima donna (the Italian lady, of course) had to wait upon the introduction of Italian opera, and so none of the great singers of the seventeenth century who were identified with the first hundred years of the lyric drama were heard in England. Scarcely had the first of the tuneful tribe appeared across the Channel, however, before there arose the rivalries and scandals which have made up a large part of the prima donna's history ever since. The first of record was Margarita de l'Epine; but she sang only in Italian and in concerts and did not get an opportunity in opera until Buononcini's "Almahide" came and provided Addison with a chance to air his delightful wit at the expense of the new style of entertainment and the public that affected to like it. By that time, too, the lady already had an English rival in Mrs. Tofts, whose early success disclosed the innate character of operatic partisans—for her champions hooted and hissed the Italian woman when she sang in Drury Lane in 1740. Knights of the quill, who in that age delighted in satire, carried the warfare into the public prints, and we have preserved for us specimens of the gentle art of satirists who, when they were unable to find fault with the singing of their victims, did not hesitate to descant upon their real or supposed moral imperfections. It was Swift who in his "Journal to Stella" spoke of the Italian lady as "Margarita and her sister and another drab, and a parcel of fiddlers at Windsor"; while an unnamed scribbler, addressing Mrs. Tofts, wrote:

> So bright is thy beauty, so charming thy song,
> That it draws both the beasts and their Orpheus along;
> But such is thy av'rice and such is thy pride,
> That the beasts must have starved and the poet have died.

If one were disposed to look a bit curiously into the rivalries between prima donnas in the eighteenth century and the social feuds to which they gave rise, it would not be very difficult, I fancy, to trace many parallels between London then and New York in 1909. There was a party two centuries ago that espoused the cause of the native English singer against the foreigner and rebuked the public for affecting to like foreign art and foreign artists simply because they were foreign. There was such a party eighty-five years ago in New York (I am writing in the summer of 1918), when the first Italian opera house was built, and there is such a party now. When the great Cuzzoni and Faustina came to London to dispute the popularity of such English singers as Mrs. Tofts, Anastasia Robinson, and Lavinia Fenton, Henry Carey, comparing the second of the English ladies with Cuzzoni, wrote:

> With better voice and fifty times her skill,
> Poor Robinson is always treated ill;
> But such is the good nature of the town
> 'Tis now the mode to cry the English down.

Did we not hear something in like key in 1914 when Mme. Fremstad failed to get a re-engagement at the Metropolitan and it was rumored that Miss Farrar was also going? Dire disaster threatened our opera then in the imagination of some fanatical admirers of these two ladies, but four seasons in some of which the former singer remained wholly and the latter partly away have passed since then and not a brick was displaced in the edifice of homely exterior in upper Broadway. Catastrophes are always impending but never befall. Since I was honored by the invitation which made me a member of the editorial staff of *The New York Tribune* toward the end of 1880, I have seen singers come and go in New York and watched the opera as it weathered many a crisis. I never inquired into the motives of a manager in engaging or neglecting to engage a singer. It was none of my business. I have observed the departure of scores of popular favorites and the coming of as many more artists to take their places. Patti and Nilsson and Gerster went, but Sembrich and Melba came. Nordica and Eames were followed by Farrar and Fremstad and other idols. Materna went, but Lehmann more then took her place. The echoes of Brignoli's silver tones had scarcely died away before Campanini's magnificent voice rang through the old Academy of Music. Jean de Reszke went from us and deep gloom settled upon the Metropolitan, but only to be dispelled by the sun of Caruso. The opera did not collapse when twice Caruso departed from New York before the end of the season. Loss and compensation;—it is Nature's law.

It has been disclosed that criticism will have a part in the historical account which is to follow. The reasons for this have also been set forth. Chastisement will not be its purpose, but, if possible, enlightenment. Should it be said that criticism is ephemeral and therefore valueless I shall not be disturbed in mind. It may at least help to an understanding of the picture which I shall strive to present in the narrative. To the objection constantly urged against musical criticism that progress in the art has uniformly disclosed its fallacy, since one generation of men frequently accepts what a preceding generation has rejected, I reply that no man has a right to an opinion in a question of art who is afraid to express it; and the foolishest course that a critic, lay or professional, can follow is to withhold his judgment for fear that at some future time it may be found that his opinion was erroneous. After that the next most foolish thing is for the critic to sneer at the honest writer of the past from whose views the majority of his successors have turned. The men who could not approve of all that Beethoven wrote were not dishonest fools; nor were they all imbeciles who objected to Schumann, or Wagner, or Brahms. It is not idiocy today to question the artistic validity of every phrase penned by Richard Strauss, or Reger, or Debussy, or Arnold Schönberg. Honest antagonism to innovations is beneficial and necessary to sound progress. It provides the regulative fly-wheel without which the engine would go racing to destruction. It can not stop progress and there never was a critic honestly concerned about his art who wished that it should. There is more cant about everything new being good than there is in the proclamation that old things are good because they are old. The former assertion is too frequently based on cowardice and ignorance. No critic worthy of the name is afraid to speak out his dissent because the history of criticism has taught him that he may be overruled by others tomorrow, or that he may himself change his mind. If he is honest and speaks from conviction there is likely to be something in his verdict which will remain true no matter what the winds and tides of popular favor may do to his utterances or their subject. Beethoven, Schumann, Wagner, and Brahms have won and held their sway over the popular heart; but there was much in the criticism addressed against their creations which was valid when it was spoken and is valid today. That residuum must go down to the credit of the critics. They were brave men and better men than those who sneer at them now. The coward in criticism who has no opinion unfavorable to the artist who is his friend or affects friendship for him, who pronounces everything good which the god of his idolatry admired or admires, screening his ignorance behind an imposing name, will be in no danger of being overruled by posterity, for he will give posterity no reason for remembering him. His influence will stop with his friends or the friends of his friends.

Critics, or rather the critics of critics, sometimes go to an absurd length in their eagerness to discredit their fellows who have condemned the bumptiousness of the self-styled futurists in music. They forget that despite the varying changes in manner of expression and even in the content of art there yet remains permanency in the laws of beauty. I recall an apologia for Schönberg written by an Englishman in which the honest right of an admirer of the "Iliad" also to admire "Paradise Lost" was categorically denied. Can there be found a more striking illustration of the intimate relationship of art-works separated by centuries of time than this writer presented? Is not the beauty which irradiates and vitalizes the Attic tragedians also immanent in Shakespeare? It may be that ancient laws are seeking new manifestations. Of that I do not speak; what ought to be obvious to all, and is obvious to all who know them, is that those laws have always been studied and respected by the masters in art. They are not respected because they are old; they are old because they have always been respected.

It should cause no perturbation of the musical critic's mind that he is compelled to observe that tendencies in the plastic arts are paralleled in music, and that these tendencies give pause to his colleagues. His is the duty to his conscience, to his time, and to art to speak out his opinion about the things that come before the public judgment-seat. The spirit which acclaims everything new is the spirit of ignorance or cowardice. The things which shall be great in the future because they differ from the things that are great now can wait for the future. Better to fail now to hear the future's evangel of beauty than to proclaim that to be beautiful which shall not be recognized as such hereafter. We can not wrong the future; we can wrong the present. How long shall we wait? It is not for us to give heed to time. Speak out the thought of today today and that of tomorrow when tomorrow comes. Be not affrighted by the noise of shouters. He is a very young or an unobservant critic who has not seen as many mediocrities hailed as geniuses as he has seen geniuses fail of appreciation. The forces which are invoking in behalf of the works which are storm-centers now are in many instances personal cults. They reflect the spirit of the times in things sordid and material. This is the age of *réclame*. He is a small composer, indeed, who if he wishes may not have at his beck and back a noisy band of propagandists. The Schmidt, Schulze, and Meyer societies of Germany are numerous and noisy, but they do not make great men of Schmidt, Schulze, and Meyer. All that they accomplish is the corruption of critics and the degradation of art. That is mischief enough, God wot! but it would be worse if they succeeded permanently in influencing public opinion, for that would mean the vitiation of popular taste and the triumph of mediocrity, effrontery, and charlatanism. Music has now its cubists as well as painting. Because of its nature, indeed, it offers an easier field for cubism than do the plastic arts. But "isms" are not likely to triumph over the proven verities of centuries; nor will they long endure.

CHAPTER II

OPERATIC CONDITIONS IN THE BEGINNING OF THE DECADE

STATE OF AFFAIRS AT THE CLOSE OF THE SEASON 1907-08—REVIEW OF THE PRECEDING PERIOD—IDEALS LEFT BY MAURICE GRAU—THE SUCCESSION OF MR. CONRIED IN THE MANAGEMENT OF THE METROPOLITAN OPERA HOUSE—HIS PROMISES AND FAILURES—HIS RETIREMENT—ENGAGEMENT OF MR. GATTI-CASAZZA AND MR. DIPPEL—DREAMS OF WORLD DOMINION—DEATH OF HEINRICH CONRIED—HIS CAREER—MR. GATTI'S UNFORTUNATE INTRODUCTION—WAGNER'S DRAMAS IN ITALY—MR. GATTI'S EARLY LIFE—CONTROVERSY BETWEEN THE MANAGERS—SINGERS INTERCEDE FOR MR. DIPPEL—HE IS ROUTED—THE NEW THEATER BUILT AND DEDICATED—A BEAUTIFUL IDEAL—A LIST OF THE FOUNDERS

THE history of opera in New York, so far as it is directly concerned with the Metropolitan Opera House prior to the period whose incidents I purpose to relate, falls into four eras defined by as many changes in management. To a considerable extent defined also by the same number of policies with reference to the public and to the lyric drama. These preliminary periods were described, their records set forth, and their products discussed in the "Chapters of Opera" published in 1909.* To an understanding of the state of operatic affairs in the American metropolis at the date set for the beginning of this narrative a cursory survey of the preceding quarter of a century may be helpful. In 1883 the time seemed ripe for the amalgamation of the Knickerbocker social régime with a new order of society in New York. The former element

* "Chapters of Opera; being Historical and Critical Observations and Records concerning the Lyric Drama in New York from Its Earliest Days down to the Present Time." By Henry Edward Krehbiel, Musical Editor of *The New York Tribune*, etc. New York: Henry Holt and Company, 1909.

was rooted in old, if not ancient, traditions of birthright and culture; the latter was founded on wealth and the social power which money gives without always commanding rights or privileges. The elements were at one in the conviction that a box at the opera was a more visible, potent, and necessary sign of wealth and social position than a seat in the Stock Exchange or a mansion in Fifth Avenue. The institution which had for nearly a generation been housed at the Academy of Music in Irving Place could no longer accommodate all the representatives of the two elements in the city's fashionable circles. A *rapprochement* of the factions had begun some time before the doors of the Metropolitan Opera House were thrown open in the fall of 1883, but the union was not sealed until a disastrous rivalry between the old and new operatic institutions had taught the lesson, which is as old as opera itself, that no metropolis is large enough to maintain two fashionable opera houses. The distinction indicated by the word fashionable must be kept in mind. If the maintenance of opera were strictly a matter of art, rivalry might be possible and even helpful to progress and success. Opera, however, has always been the toy of fashion, the glass of social " form," and as such it can have but one home in any city. This truth is as frankly confessed by the attitude of the patrons of the box-stalls as it is felt by the occupants of the stockholders' boxes. The Metropolitan Opera House will maintain its present position of splendid isolation only so long as the owners of the building can hold it as the citadel of fashion against the new aristocracy which will be created in time by new accretions of wealth in a new class of the city's population or a wider distribution of the wealth now existing. This fact brings into vision one of the problems which are to be wrought out in the years immediately following the cessation of the war in which the world's peoples are now embroiled, and helps to make the study on which I am engaged pertinent.

The first of the four historic periods was compassed by a single season—that of 1883-84—in which rivalry between the Academy of Music and the Metropolitan Opera House brought disaster to both institutions. Though the new house had been built by vast wealth and had that wealth's powerful backing, neither the director of the new undertaking nor its promoters had a wider outlook than the supporters of the old Academy; they held to the aims and pursued the methods of their rivals, relying on the external glamour of the new establishment and leaving the interest of the public in operas and performers to be divided. The storm of misfortune which overwhelmed their representative, Mr. Henry E. Abbey, threw their bark on a new course which was pursued only because no haven of refuge was open to them. No pilot could be found willing to attempt a second voyage under instructions which had led to shipwreck. The owners of the house had to charter their own ship and sail for ports foreign to their longings and undesirable in their eyes, under the guidance of a master who sought cargo in the land of art instead of the realms of fad and fashion. Thus was inaugurated the second period which endured from 1884 to 1891 and which wrought effects the potency of which has grown with years in spite of the fact that opera house owners and operating companies have time and again tried to set back the clock to the hours which it marked thirty-five years ago. The clock's gong rang disaster after disaster through more than seven lean years while Maurice Grau was assimilating the lessons of his own past and learning how to blend the system which he had developed with the teachings of the seven years of artistic plenty under the German régime inaugurated by Dr. Leopold Damrosch. At the last he succeeded in fusing the principles and practices, the matter and manner of Italian, French, and German opera into a polyglot institution which satisfied the whims of fashion and also met the demands of art. Thus twelve years passed away, two of them in silence because of managerial if not public exhaustion.

The administration of Maurice Grau, begun in company with Henry E. Abbey and John Schoeffel in 1891, was concluded by his retirement from the directorship of the Metropolitan Opera at the end of the season 1902-03. In the last five years of this period the opera reached its apogee of brilliancy. Mr. Grau's associates were a few intimate friends, none of them eminent in wealth or social position, who gave him free hand in the direction of the enterprise and made no protestations of purpose to serve art or the public. Mr. Grau made the opera financially profitable and artistically successful and turned it over to a company organized by Heinrich Conried to which the Metropolitan Real Estate and Opera House Company leased the building in February, 1903.

Here our present story might profitably begin, though the five years of the Conried régime were included in the narrative of ten years ago. But I must do no more than generalize. The new company came into a rich inheritance and the public into the righteous hope of a continuance of the institution on the lines which had brought prosperity to Mr. Grau and gratification to the lovers of art. The public was justified also in an expectation that the late director's programme would be extended and made more perfect; for Mr. Conried had enlisted in his enterprise men of wealth and social position, some of them part-owners of the building, all of them well able to withstand the allurement of money-getting or to sacrifice it for the sake of social prestige and the glory which would attend idealistic strivings. That the majority of them were fired by this lofty ambition is indicated by some of their acts during the Conried lustrum, and these acts it shall be my pleasure to laud; but I can not withstand the conviction that within that lustrum and repeatedly within the ten years which have elapsed since they yielded to the spirit of commercialism which was the inspiration of Conried and also to the clamors of a reactionary element among the boxholders and season subscribers with whom the opera instead of a serious artistic institution was chiefly a social diversion and an occasion for fashionable display.

The opera company was, and still is, a close corporation which takes the public into its confidence only when it is necessary to defend or exploit its own doings or purposes. Nevertheless when Mr. Conried issued the prospectus for his fifth season in the summer of 1908 it was widely known that his policies and methods had caused serious dissensions among the directors of the operating company. Inasmuch as these gentlemen had upheld him in his efforts to introduce "Salome" into the repertory of the Metropolitan Opera House until the owners of the building had exercised the right of censorship and exclusion which they had reserved to themselves in the lease, it seems a fair conclusion that their dissatisfaction with Mr. Conried was due to other than artistic reasons. The knowledge which the gentlemen had of the business methods of opera-giving was in inverse ratio to their knowledge of business methods in general, and in negligible proportion to their social ambitions and zeal for art. They had perforce to learn many things, and some of them were not to their liking. Amongst other things they learned that a system of farming out artists with whom they had contracts which brought emolument only to the Herr Direktor and his factotum in the matter was in operation. Concert-givers who wished to avail themselves of the services of Metropolitan singers learned that they could be more advantageously hired through musical agencies than from the opera company. The cost of production was steadily growing, but there was no corresponding growth in receipts nor obvious reason why performances should cost more than better representations had cost in the past. To answer this Mr. Conried put forth a public statement which was far from convincing. The manager's perquisite of an annual benefit was utilized in a manner which was lowering the artistic standard of the house, Mr. Conried giving performances of German operettas and holding out such lures to the public as the spectacle of all the artists in the company dancing in the ball scene of "Die Fledermaus." The director's benefit which Conried thus degraded into a vulgar sensation was an institution which had come over from the preceding administration; but Mr. Grau refused to make it the basis of a specious appeal for public support and frankly admitted that it was a matter of private agreement between him and the singers whom he engaged. When the reorganized company set to work upon internal reforms in the season 1908-09 they turned the affair into an annual benefit for a pension or "emergency" fund, and such it has remained in name ever since, though how a pension fund can be administered by a corporation whose tenure of existence hangs by so frail a thread as the annual, triennial, or quinquennial renewal of contracts of lease and service is not easily understood. Enough, however, if the employees of the opera company are in any manner the beneficiaries of the annual performances to which all the artists contribute their services without pay and for which the public pours out a largess of patronage without thought of charity.

But if the public was permitted to know little of the business affairs of Mr. Conried's company it was well informed as to the reasons for its discontent with the company's artistic doings; and this discontent, no doubt, had its reaction in the dissension among the directors. Fulfilment followed none of the directors' flamboyant promises. Mr. Conried had said that it was to be his first aim to raise the standard of performances and that no thought of profit was to find lodgment in his mind. The phrase has been repeated *ad nauseam* ever since. He also gave it out that, though he was to gather a galaxy of singers such as had never illumined the operatic firmament before, the "star" system was to be abolished. The old practice of giving opera in

Philadelphia was to be abandoned so that there might be more time for rehearsals in New York and less exhaustion of the forces. We shall see how far the Metropolitan management has departed from this pious but insincere resolve since. The plan of giving all operas in their original tongues was to be pursued and English was to be added to Italian, French, and German. Mr. Grau's high Italian and French standard was to be upheld and German opera lifted to a higher plane. An earnest of this promise was seen by critics and public in the engagement of men eminent in their professions like Mottl, Mahler, Fuchs, and Lautenschläger; but their activities were hampered by Conried's incompetent meddling and their capacity for good nullified. They did not endure. English operas there were none; Italian operas waxed in number but waned in quality, somewhat, I fear, in deference to the personal wishes of some of the directors; French opera was permitted to languish, and this despite the fact that in the last two years of Conried's consulship Mr. Hammerstein built up a dangerous rivalry at the Manhattan Opera House wholly on a French foundation; German opera fell to a low level in the subscription list and was maintained by special performances. The vicissitudes of the various factors in the polyglot scheme during the five years of the Conried administration are illustrated in the following tabulation of performances during the five years:

	Italian	French	German
1903-04	46	10	36
1904-05	41	16	55
1905-06	53	7	49
1906-07	55	15	38
1907-08	77	12	39

The significance of these figures does not appear on their face; otherwise they would indicate little else in respect of a change of policy than a purpose to augment the Italian list, which purpose reflected the wishes of a majority of the directors of the company. The German record must be analyzed. Of the thirty-six performances in the first year eleven were devoted to " Parsifal," whose first production outside the sacrosanct precincts of Bayreuth was the sensation of the season throughout the civilized world. Its attractive power remained without serious impairment in the second year, when it received eight performances. In 1905-06 it had four, in 1906-07 two, and in 1907-08 it was relegated to the special list, where it has remained ever since by virtue of its potency as a getter of money from the multitude. In like manner the novelty of 1905-06, " Hänsel und Gretel," had eleven performances that year and eight in the next, and was made to take the place once occupied by the Christmas pantomimes. Nearly one-quarter of the German representations in the lustrum were devoted to the two sensations of the hour, while the dramas of " The Ring of the Nibelung," which, with " Tristan und Isolde," had been the backbone of the German repertory, had only forty-three performances, and " Tristan " only nineteen in the five years. Moreover, five representations were wasted on " Die Fledermaus," which had been injected into the repertory to enable Conried to put all his singers on show at his benefit, one on " Der Zigeunerbaron," and one on " Salome," with which Conried had hoped to duplicate his profitable " Parsifal " stroke.

Enough of this. It had been decreed before the middle of the fifth season that Mr. Conried must go, and for a space a plausible excuse was found in the fact that he was a sick man, quite incapable of performing his duties in an adequate manner. In the winter of 1908 Rawlins L. Cottenet, one of the directors of his company, was abroad and rumor had it that he was negotiating with Giulio Gatti-Casazza and Arturo Toscanini, respectively director and conductor of the Teatro alla Scala in Milan, with a view to their engagement in the same capacities at the New York establishment. When Mr. Cottenet returned to New York

A SCHEME FOR WORLD CONQUEST

in March he denied all knowledge of the negotiations, but by that time they had been consummated. Mr. Conried also gave out denials designed to conceal the purpose of the company to put the direction of the opera in the hands of foreigners,—a purpose which, when divulged, caused a deal of apprehension on the part of a large and faithful contingent of the institution's patrons who dreaded the introduction of Italian methods no less than Italian ideals. How the directors met these apprehensions by the association of Andreas Dippel with Signor Gatti will presently appear.

Some of the incidents of ten years ago, when viewed in a rearward perspective, seem to indicate that it was not only a desire to be rid of Conried with which the directors were filled but also that they were big with a truly Alexandrine ambition to conquer the spacious operatic world. The suggestion may have come from Grau's assumption of the management of Covent Garden in the summer of 1898, or it may have been prompted by the familiarity of the directors with business enterprises of vast dimensions and international scope; whatever the impulse, they seem to have indulged in day-dreams which recall words like those of Henry IV's wooing: Shall we not between Saint Denis and Saint George compound an opera company, half American, half Italian, that shall go to Constantinople and take the Turk by the beard? Already in October, 1907, the stockholders of the company had elected Henry V. Higgins, managing director of the Royal Opera, Covent Garden, London, and Count San Martino, president of the Royal Conservatory, Rome, members of their directorate. In December, 1908, Eben D. Jordan, of Boston, was also made a director while Mr. Higgins, Count Martino, and James Hazen Hyde, who was gone from New York to live in Paris, were designated a Foreign Committee of the Board. The purpose of the Metropolitan in electing Mr. Jordan, it was surmised, was to protect themselves against the machinations of Mr. Hammerstein in Boston, where Mr.

Jordan was building an opera house and where a company had been founded under the management of Mr. Henry Russell. Mr. Hammerstein had poached upon what the Metropolitan people looked upon as their preserves in Philadelphia, was talking about taking over a theater in Baltimore, and seemed to be contemplating the planting of opera houses in all the large cities of the United States from the Atlantic to the Pacific coast. The Metropolitan Company, instead of cutting out Philadelphia, took Baltimore also into its scheme of performances, affiliated itself with companies organized in Boston and Chicago, and on October 19, 1909, announced a purpose to give seasons of opera in Paris during May and June, 1910, and possibly 1911; a plan which was carried out in respect of the first year. But this belongs to another chapter; *sufficit* that the plans of world conquest came to naught.

Reports of the engagement of Messrs. Gatti and Toscanini came in January, 1908, but were denied by both gentlemen, as cable dispatches told us, and Mr. Conried professed ignorance on the subject. These denials persisted as late as February 8. Meanwhile at a meeting of the Board of Directors of the Metropolitan Opera and Real Estate Company on February 7 Otto H. Kahn and Edmund L. Baylies, directors of the Conried Company, made a request that the period of the lease, which still had three years to run, be extended. The lease had been framed to be operative only during the administration of Mr. Conried; the directors of the Conried Company asked that this restriction be withdrawn. The obvious conclusion from the fact that the matter was discussed for two hours and then laid over was that there was a division in the Conried Company on the question of the retention of the president and managing director. On February 10 it was reported that Conried would resign on the following day, that the resignation would be accepted, and that he would be succeeded by Giulio Gatti-Casazza and Andreas Dippel as joint manag-

GIULIO GATTI-CASAZZA
General Manager of the Metropolitan Opera Company

ing directors. The statement was in accord with the facts. On February 12 the directors of the Conried Company made official announcement that Mr. Conried, on account of the condition of his health and consequent inability to continue in charge of the affairs of the company, would retire as president and director not later than May 1, 1908; that the company, while retaining its corporate entity, would change its title and be known thereafter as the Metropolitan Opera Company; that as such it had leased the house for five years beginning June 1, 1908, and with the approval of the Metropolitan Opera and Real Estate Company had engaged Giulio Gatti-Casazza as general manager and Andreas Dippel as administrative manager. Significant as bearing on the rumors of the real causes of Conried's downfall was the statement that "the traditional system of having the manager share in the profits will be abolished. The managers will receive a fixed salary and neither they nor any employee will have any financial interest in the affairs of the company." It was also proclaimed that Gustav Mahler and Arturo Toscanini had been engaged as "joint musical directors," and Mr. Dippel was described in the words: "At Mr. Gatti's side will be Herr Dippel, already of the Metropolitan Opera House, long known and liked by the New York public as a sterling artist of remarkable musical ability and vast experience, tactful, resourceful, enjoying universal esteem and sympathy as an artist and a gentleman."

With Mr. Dippel the opera-lovers of New York were well acquainted. He had been a member of the Metropolitan forces ever since the last German season directed for the owners of the opera house in 1890-91 and had made himself a popular favorite by his extensive knowledge of operas and his readiness as well as ability to come to the rescue of threatened performances by taking any tenor part on a moment's notice. An amusing newspaper caricature of the day pictured him as sitting in his dressing-room in underwear, an alarm clock at his ear, the costumes of a score of characters hung on pegs within easy reach, awaiting the summons of the call-boy. His appointment, together with the retention of Mahler, had obviously been made in good faith to allay the fears of a large contingent of the opera's patrons that the German branch of the repertory, already in the shadow, was to suffer total eclipse. I shall reach this phase of the story by and by.

The new arrangement was tentative and provisional in character. It was to be tried for a year and then a permanent plan was to be adopted. The owners of the opera house as well as the operators were disposed to be cautious; but in their caution they planted the seeds of inevitable discord. A Janus-faced management could not long endure, and it did not as we shall see. The capital stock of the Conried Metropolitan Company amounted to only $150,000, and on this the owners are said to have received 60 per cent. in dividends. Mr. Conried sold his share in the assets of the company for $90,000 and a member of the board of directors of the reorganized company took over his holdings. The directors, to secure themselves against loss by the termination of their contract with the owners of the opera house, had insured the life of their president. Before the death of Conried legal complications grew out of his contracts of sale and insurance, but were adjusted without public scandal after his death.

During a large part of the season of 1906-07 Mr. Conried had been ill with sciatic neurosis. After his retirement from the management in the spring of 1908 he went to Europe in the hope of regaining his health. He died of apoplexy at Meran, Austrian Tyrol, on April 27, 1909. He was a native of Bielitz, Austria, where he was born in 1855. His father was a weaver and to that trade he was apprenticed, but though little educated he felt early longings for the stage and began a theatrical career as a supernumerary in the Burgtheater in Vienna when he was eighteen years old.

Under the name of Robert Bucholz he was a member of theatrical companies in Leipsic, Berlin, and Bremen. He came to New York in 1878 to be stage-manager at the Germania Theater in Tammany Hall. Mathilde Cottrelly lured him to the Thalia Theater in the Bowery, of which she was director, and to that playhouse, in conjunction with Carl Hermann, he brought von Possart, the first of a number of stage celebrities whom he was instrumental in bringing to this country—among them Sonnenthal, Barnay, Helene Odilion, and Kathi Schratt, the last of whom became the favorite and intimate companion of the Austrian Emperor Franz Josef, who died, as did she, amid the horrors of the war. It was as director of the Irving Place Theater at a later date that Mr. Conried won recognition and attracted the attention of the native American element of the city's population by his production of the German classics and modern comedies. The recognition thus won put him in the line of succession as manager of the Metropolitan Opera House. His only operatic experience before the attainment of that distinction was as stage-manager for Rudolph Aronson at the Casino, where he staged a number of operettas, among them "The Gypsy Baron," to which his thoughts and affections returned when he achieved his ultimate eminence. A large fraction of the financial success of the early years of his Metropolitan management was due to Enrico Caruso, whose services he had acquired under a contract made by Maurice Grau. Geraldine Farrar had also been picked out by Mr. Grau for the Metropolitan, though she did not come to its stage till the third year of the Conried régime.

Mr. Dippel's appointment and Mr. Mahler's retention were obviously made, no doubt in good faith, to allay the fears of a large contingent of the opera's patrons that the German branch of the repertory, already in the shadow as I have said, was to suffer a total eclipse. The manner in which their Italian associate was introduced to the public was not calculated to quiet suspicion. Mr. Kahn invited reporters for the newspapers to the opera house and introduced to them " Count " Centanini, who described the new general manager as a gentleman to whom was due appreciation of Wagner's dramas in Italy, that appreciation having followed his production at the Scala of " Die Meistersinger," " Siegfried," and the entire Nibelung tetralogy. The services of Mr. Gatti in behalf of German art in Milan were incontestable, but the claims advanced in this manner were preposterous. Mr. Gatti had been director of the Milanese theater ten years, but nearly all of Wagner's operas and dramas had been performed in Italy from ten to twenty years before he went to Milan. Thus, " Rienzi " was produced in Venice in 1874, in Bologna in 1876, in Florence in 1877, in Rome in 1880; " The Flying Dutchman " had its first performance in Bologna in 1877, " Tannhäuser " its first representation in the same city in 1872, " Lohengrin " was heard in Bologna in 1871 (the year of its first performance in New York); Florence heard the opera in 1872, Rome in 1878, Genoa in 1880, Venice and Naples in 1881. For the rest the records of La Scala disclose that " Die Meistersinger " had been brought forward on its stage in 1890 and received sixteen performances; " Tannhäuser " in 1893 also receiving the same number of performances. " Lohengrin " was in the repertories of the seasons 1873, 1888, 1889, and 1891, and up to 1898, when Mr. Gatti came, had had forty-eight representations. " Die Walküre " was given fourteen times in 1894, " The Flying Dutchman " eight times in 1893, and " Götterdämmerung " fourteen times in 1897. The Wagnerian drama which Mr. Gatti introduced to Italy was " Das Rheingold " (though as I write I am obsessed with the conviction that Mr. Seidl once told me of the enthusiasm of Italian audiences when he conducted performances of the entire cycle by the Angelo Neumann company). These facts I made public in *The New York Tribune* at the time and their critical point was

CAREER OF MR. GATTI-CASAZZA

not blunted when it became known that " Count " Centanini (" Mr. Centanini is, I believe, a count although he does not flaunt his title," remarked Mr. Kahn to a *Tribune* reporter) was an operatic coach who had been accompanist to some of the singers at the Metropolitan Opera House and was the husband of Mme. Noria (Miss Ludwig), who had sung in Mr. Savage's American company and a peripatetic troupe calling itself the San Carlo Opera Company of which Mr. Centanini had been assistant conductor. Of course he may have been a count for all that, but he became Mr. Gatti's secretary.

Giulio Gatti-Casazza deserved a better sponsor and a less flamboyant introduction. He was born in Udine, Italy, on February 3, 1869; studied mathematics at the universities of Ferrara and Bologna and the Reale Scuolo Superiore at Genoa, and when twenty-two years old obtained the diploma of a naval engineer. His studies in the humanities and music were privately conducted. At the end of 1893 he was called to succeed his father Stefano (who had been one of Garibaldi's " Thousand " and a senator of the kingdom of Italy—he died in May, 1918) in the board of directors of the Teatro Communale in Ferrara and about the same time was made superintendent of the musical institute Frescobaldi in the same city. In 1898 he was made general manager of the Teatro alla Scala, the most famous theater in Italy, and in that position he remained until called to New York.

Mr. Gatti spent the month of May, 1908, in New York acquainting himself with the local situation. In interviews with the newspaper reporters on the day of his coming he bewailed the dearth of good dramatic singers in Europe, a dearth which was so great, he said, that it had created a crisis in the musical world. Ten years before he had organized in a couple of months a company for La Scala the like of which could not possibly be brought together at the time in which he spoke. This plaint has been repeated every year since, and though it no doubt had considerable foundation in fact, it turned up to plague the manager whenever singers of a high order of excellence were heard in the Hammerstein, Boston, and Chicago companies, the most notable cases being those of Mmes. Galli-Curci and Raisa. Touching his own predilections Mr. Gatti said: "In music I am an eclectic. I have no prejudices in favor of the Italian or any other particular school of music. With Toscanini I spent much time and energy with Wagner, so much so in fact that I was severely criticised by the Milanese press. But we also put on 'Louise' and 'Pelléas et Mélisande,' but they did not have the success which they had in this city. The reception of such operas by this country shows that the American public is unprejudiced and open in its views." How little Mr. Gatti appreciated the taste of the general operatic public at the time was shown by the fact that the first novelties produced under his supervision were "Le Villi," a youthful and forgotten work by Puccini, and "La Wally" by Catalani, a composer unknown in America. Neither of them has been heard since. In the same season the German contingent of the institution brought forward D'Albert's "Tiefland," which was at least modern in style and had a good dramatic story, and Smetana's "The Bartered Bride," a masterpiece in the school of nationalism which held the boards during three seasons and might still be given were the constitution of the Metropolitan forces other than one which prohibits the establishment and gradual expansion of a standard repertory. In this respect opera in New York is as much an exotic now as it was three-quarters of a century ago, and nothing done within the last ten years has aimed to make it anything else.

Mr. Gatti spent the summer of 1908 in Italy and returned to New York on October 11. He repeated the lamentation over the paucity of opera singers in Italy and France, but announced the engagement of four artists for the Metropolitan company. Only one of them, Pasquale Amato, a fine baritone, got a footing in New York. The official prospectus for the approaching season had been published in the summer, there had been a generous popular subscription, and the performances began on November 16. The fruits of the season in the field of artistic achievement will be discussed in the next chapter of these memoirs; in the remainder of this I must concern myself chiefly with a controversy which resulted from the foolish experiment of making two managers representing divergent policies, each supported by powerful influences, pull together in double harness. The controversy became a public scandal. Mr. Gatti was experienced in the methods of operatic management; Mr. Dippel was a novice. Mr. Gatti was familiar with the wiles of prima donnas, the schemes of publishers, the personal aims which often actuate wealthy patrons of art, and knew when it was wise to defer or to oppose them; Mr. Dippel had an artist's knowledge of the artistic temperament, had been suddenly elevated to a conspicuous position in the eyes of the world, and knew as much about practical affairs as a few years of service as a banker's clerk could teach him. The popular opinion, fairly based on the declaration of the directors, was that he, with the help of Mr. Mahler and Mr. Herz, should have free hand in the field of German opera. Before the opera house had been thrown open it was known that the managers were at loggerheads. On November 25, 1908, the five most eminent singers in the company—Mmes. Sembrich, Eames, and Farrar, Signor Caruso, and Signor Scotti—sent a letter to the Board of Directors of the corporation now known as the Metropolitan Opera Company (it had obtained the new title by appeal to the courts after the Secretary of State of the State of New York had refused to give it that title because of its resemblance to the title of the house-owning company). In this letter, which was not made public till the controversy of which it was a feature of great interest was over, the writers said that having heard of a movement to grant Messrs. Gatti and Toscanini a contract of three years' duration they wished to express a desire "in the protection of our (their) artistic interests and the welfare of the Metropolitan Opera House, that Mr. Dippel be granted the same privileges under contract that may be acceded to the above-named gentlemen. Our confidence," the letter continued, "in the managerial and artistic capabilities of Mr. Dippel gives us sufficient reason to associate ourselves firmly with his ideas, which have been, always will be, and are for the best interests of the Metropolitan Opera House." On December 2 the Executive Committee of the Board of Directors, composed of Otto H. Kahn, William K. Vanderbilt, and Frank C. Griswold, replied to this letter and gave their reply to the public press. The committee said:

> It is not possible to administer an organization like the Metropolitan Opera under two heads, and it was never intended that it should be so administered. We do full justice to the excellent qualities of the administrative manager, Mr. Dippel, and to his intelligent and zealous labors. We desire to show him every fairness and to accord him every consideration and opportunity consistent with our conception of the paramount interests of the organization, but there can be no divided artistic authority, and while there remains a large and important field for Mr. Dippel's valuable capacities, his functions are and must be subordinate to those of the general manager, Mr. Gatti-Casazza, who is the supreme executive head of the organization.

Mr. Gatti's contract for two more years was signed with the abrogation of an optional terminating clause contained in the first contract, and Mr. Dippel was left to work out his possible salvation. It was as plain as a pikestaff that Mr. Gatti's word was law in all matters of artistic policy and would so remain for the ensuing two years even if Mr. Dippel remained in office in deference to the wishes of some of the directors and the lovers of a broad policy among the opera's patrons and the consent of Mr. Gatti. The general manager hastened to allay the apprehensions of the public by stating that the patrons of the opera should have ample opportunity to listen to French and German works, and as a sort of guarantee of good faith announced the speedy production of "Tristan und Isolde" with Mr. Mahler as conductor. The protestations of non-commercialism and high artistic ideals were redeemed by the production of "Le Villi" outside the subscription but with advanced prices of admission, though the only artists appearing in it were Mme. Alda and Signori Bonci and Amato. The five singers who had signed the communication to the directors were indignant that the answer to it should have been made public but not the letter itself. Mmes. Sembrich and Eames, having already expressed their intention to retire from the operatic stage at the end of the season, their three associates did not ask for their signatures to an explanation which was published on December 11, to the effect that Mr. Dippel had not suggested the letter and that no animosity toward Messrs. Gatti and Toscanini was intended. On December 10 at a meeting of the Executive Committee of the directors attended by both the managers, Mr. Dippel was made to realize his subordinate position and the next day he caused to be printed in the newspapers a statement asserting that "the unfortunate misunderstanding" which had arisen had been vastly exaggerated and that he was confident that the "slight differences" which existed would be adjusted. He promised in the future to devote himself to work "within the sphere" of his duties and deprecated a continuance of the public discussion. After the meeting he went to Mr. Gatti and asked an assurance that he would be retained in office in the period to come, but got a flat refusal. The Liederkranz, a German club, offered him a complimentary dinner which he wisely and discreetly declined to accept. He had met defeat horse, foot, and dragoons. On February 27, 1909, the Board of Directors announced that with the concurrence of Mr. Gatti it had been agreed with Mr. Dippel that his contract as administrative manager, which was mutually terminable on February 20, should remain in force. Mr. Gatti was to preserve his authority as general manager and assign to Mr. Dippel besides his administrative functions an important part in the artistic management. Misunderstandings and discord were to be forgotten and there was to be no line of demarcation based on the nationality of compositions or conductors. After efficient service during the rest of the season and the season which followed Mr. Dippel went to Chicago to manage the affairs of a new opera company there in which some of the directors of the Metropolitan Company were interested as a part of their scheme of universal dominion, and his subsequent activities have little or no concern with this history. As for the signers of the appeal made in his behalf Mme. Sembrich and Mme. Eames retired from the operatic stage as they had said they would, the former amid scenes of glory; Caruso, Farrar, and Scotti are still members of the company as I write, and the great tenor was presented by the directors with a diamond-studded cigarette case in appreciation of the fact that he had helped the managers out of a dilemma by singing six times in seven days—for $2,500 a time!

It is a pleasure to turn down this page of the Chronicle of Scandal in order to open one which tells of an idealistic endeavor on the part of the gentlemen to whom New York is indebted for the maintenance of that proud and great institution, the Metropolitan Opera House. Proud and great it is despite the follies committed by some of its managers. Mr. Conried, as I have noted, had drawn attention to himself before he became director of the Opera by his production of German plays at the Irving Place Theater. By encouraging the interest in the drama which had begun to show itself in the universities he became almost a national figure. He dreamed a dream of a national theater endowed by the government and what he could not realize on a country-wide scale he attempted to bring to pass with

ANDREAS DIPPEL.

THE NEW THEATER IS FOUNDED

the aid of the men of wealth and social prominence by whom he found himself surrounded. He broached the idea of an endowed theater to his associates in the Opera Company, but the directors, after seriously discussing it, decided that it was not the province of their corporation to undertake the task. As individuals, however, some of them joined a new organization which set the establishment of an ideal theater as its mission. The founders of the institution which gave New York what was first called the New and is now the Century Theater deserve gratefully to be remembered, for the playhouse played a part, not inglorious though apparently fruitless, in the history of opera during a few years following Mr. Gatti's advent. Their names were John Jacob Astor, George F. Baker, Edmund L. Baylies, August Belmont, Cortlandt Field Bishop, Paul D. Cravath, William B. Osgood Field, Henry Clay Frick, Elbert H. Gary, George J. Gould, Eliot Gregory, Archer M. Huntington, James H. Hyde, Otto H. Kahn, W. de Lancey Kauntze, Clarence H. Mackay, J. Pierpont Morgan, James Stillman, Hamilton McK. Twombly, Robert B. Van Cortlandt, Cornelius Vanderbilt, William K. Vanderbilt, Henry Walters, Harry Payne Whitney, M. Orme Wilson, and Henry Rogers Winthrop. On March 28, 1906, the founders of the New Theater Company, through a building committee composed of Charles T. Barney, Otto H. Kahn, Harry Payne Whitney, Eliot Gregory, and H. R. Winthrop, invited a number of architects who had agreed to enter a competition to submit plans for a building to be erected on a lot of land 200 feet front on Eighth Avenue and 200 feet deep on West Sixty-third Street. The jury that passed on the plans submitted was composed of Charles T. Barney, Otto H. Kahn, H. R. Winthrop, Heinrich Conried, Stanford White, Donn Barber, and Edgar V. Seeler. From the beginning of the enterprise Mr. Conried had been relied on for expert technical advice, though I have been assured that it never had been contemplated that he should be director of the theater. The purpose of the gentlemen who undertook this beautiful work was set out in the instructions to the architects in these words:

> The conception which the Founders of the New Theater Company desire to express in concrete form by means of this competition is a building suitable for the production of the classical drama and of modern plays and light opera of genuine merit in a manner worthy of the best traditions of the stage. By light opera is meant the kind of performances to which the Paris Opéra Comique is dedicated. The theater is not in any sense a commercial venture but is to be maintained for the sake of art. By the standard of its performances and the spirit of its administration it is the intention of the founders to place it in the relation toward dramatic art and literature occupied by the principal national theaters of Europe. It is designed not only to foster and stimulate art, but also to furnish a school of musical and dramatic art. All net profits will be directed to the development of such a school, accumulation of an endowment fund for the institution, the creation of a pension fund, and other like purposes.

The award for architectural plans went to Messrs. Carrere and Hastings, and the cornerstone of the beautiful building which was erected under their supervision was laid on December 15, 1908. Theodore Roosevelt, President of the United States, sent a letter to the gathering invited to the ceremony by the founders in which he said: " I am of course in cordial sympathy with your aims to give special encouragement to both playwrights and actors who are native to our own soil and I observe with especial pleasure the fact that the statutes under which your theater will be run provide that it is to be without any thought of profit, and that any pecuniary benefits which may result from its operation shall be used for the creation of an endowment and pension fund for the maintenance of a school of dramatic art and for other purposes of the same kind." The Governor of the State of New York, Charles E. Hughes, sent a message regretting his inability to be present and giving assurance of his wishes for the success of the enterprise. The Mayor of the city, Mr. McClellan, put the cornerstone in place. John H. Finley, President of the College of the City of New York, in an address on the relation of prayer and the drama, said: "If a community could make its playhouse a place where it played what it wanted to be when it wanted to be at its best the playhouse would do as much for its clean, wholesome, spiritual, and physical life as the prayerhouse." Augustus Thomas also delivered an address, Richard Watson Gilder read a poem written by him for the occasion, and "The Star-Spangled Banner" was sung. In the cornerstone was deposited a hermetically sealed box containing a summary of the exercises, a list of the participants, copies of President Roosevelt's letter, an ode by Percy Mackaye, and Mr. Gilder's poem, together with a description of the building written by the architects.

The New Theater was dedicated to the service of the drama and the citizens of New York on November 6, 1909. Mr. J. Pierpont Morgan presided, Percy Mackaye's ode was sung, Governor Hughes and Elihu Root, U. S. Senator, delivered addresses. After Senator Root had spoken Mr. Forbes-Robertson read to the theater's actors, who were grouped around a bust of Shakespeare on the stage, Hamlet's advice to the players, closing with the phrase: "Go; make you ready." The guests who had assembled at 4 o'clock P.M. were then dismissed till 8 o'clock, when they came together again to witness a dress-rehearsal of "Antony and Cleopatra," with which drama the theater was opened to the public on the evening of November 8. The rôle which the New Theater played in the operatic life of the city will be disclosed in these chronicles. For the land and building of the New Theater the founders expended approximately $3,250,000.

CHAPTER III

THE FIRST SEASON OF THE DUAL ADMINISTRATION

THE SEASON 1908-09—EMMY DESTINN—A PATRIOTIC PRIMA DONNA—CHANGES PRESAGED BY THE WAR—SIGNOR TOSCANINI; HIS QUALITIES AND TRIUMPHS—REFLECTIONS ON THE SEASON—D'ALBERT'S "TIEFLAND"—INTER-RACIALISM RAMPANT—AN AMERICAN SCHOOL OF COMPOSITION—BOHEMIANS OBJECT TO THE AUSTRIAN NATIONAL HYMN—"LE VILLI," PUCCINI'S FIRST OPERA—FIVE GENERATIONS OF PUCCINIS—CATALANI'S "LA WALLY"—THE MUSICAL REVOLUTION IN ITALY—SMETANA'S "BARTERED BRIDE"—MME. SEMBRICH'S FAREWELL TO THE OPERA STAGE—CEREMONIES AT THE OPERA HOUSE—A COMPLIMENTARY BANQUET—MR. HENDERSON'S POEM—A VERSIFIED REPERTORY—RETIREMENT OF MME. EAMES—HER RECORD AT THE METROPOLITAN —SIGNOR CARUSO TEMPORARILY INCAPACITATED

WITH the New York public disturbed by the dissensions which had broken out in the management before the doors of the opera house had been opened for the first performance, the friends of German opera fearful that the new managers would prove to be reactionary, and the rivalry of the Manhattan Opera House threatening to grow more and more formidable, the twenty-fourth regular subscription season at the Metropolitan began on November 16, 1908. During the summer sops had been plentifully thrown to the German Cerberus—by the appointment of Mr. Dippel as administrative manager, Mr. Gatti's protestations of eclecticism in taste, and Mr. Toscanini's devotion to the best types of German opera, including Wagner's dramas. That devotion, it may be said at once, was beautifully and convincingly demonstrated in the season and afterward up to the time of his departure from the Metropolitan at the close of the year 1914-15. The terms "administrative

JOINT DIRECTION OF THE METROPOLITAN 37

manager" and "joint directors" were construed by the public generally as indicating that Mr. Dippel would have powers co-extensive with those of Mr. Gatti in the determination of the artistic policies of the establishment, and that those powers would be exercised specifically in the production of old and new operas in the German repertory. The plan of the Board of Directors of the company was vague and tentative, and it was obviously necessary that there should be not only an extension of the term of engagement of the manager and conductor who had been brought from Italy but also a sharp definition of authority if the standards, commercial and artistic, of the Metropolitan Opera were to be maintained. To these ends the newcomers from abroad addressed themselves vigorously, with the consequences to Mr. Dippel that were set forth in the preceding chapter of this book. Nevertheless to Mr. Dippel was given large authority. While Mr. Gatti reinforced the Italian side of the house, Mr. Dippel reinforced the German with artists, scenery, and choristers as each thought best, under the supervision of the Executive Committee of the Board of Directors of what became The Metropolitan Opera Company as soon as that style could legally be adopted. The prospectus which had appeared in the summer promised that under the "joint direction" of Messrs. Gatti and Dippel there would be a subscription season of twenty weeks consisting of one hundred performances on Monday, Wednesday, Thursday, and Friday evenings, and Saturday afternoons, twelve performances on Saturday evenings and a special series on Tuesday and Saturday evenings "devoted to classical works of such composers as Mozart, Beethoven, and Wagner." Signor Toscanini was pronounced "the foremost conductor in Italy, the leading spirit of the Teatro alla Scala in Milan since 1899," to whom was "due the elevation of the musical taste which has manifested itself in Italy in recent years." The orchestra was to be increased to 139 by the addition of

55 players to permit alternation at the rehearsals and performances, thus saving the men from overwork. There were to be two sets of choristers, one for the Italian and French operas, one for the German. This laudable augmentation and distribution of the choral forces had already been contemplated by Mr. Conried in his first season. I recall with amusement, as characteristic of that gentleman's affectation of familiarity with operatic affairs and languages, that at an interview to which he invited me immediately after my return from my summer in the country, he remarked that the simultaneous use of two languages in a representation must cease. He could no longer listen with patience to half of the chorus hailing the advent of Lohengrin on the scene with shouts of "Ein Schwan! Ein Schwan!" while the other half shouted "Un sogno! Un sogno!" His suddenly acquired knowledge of languages, plenarily inspired, did not go far enough to enable him to distinguish between *un sogno,* a dream, and *un cygno,* a swan. But that was a venial blunder compared with his performance when at a rehearsal of "Die Walküre" he railed at the light man for disobeying the directions of the prompt-book and had himself to be set right by the information that a different act than that which he was reading was in hand.

The novelties promised for the season were Catalani's "La Wally," Puccini's "Le Villi," and Tschaikowsky's "La Dama di Picche" ("The Queen of Spades") to be sung in Italian; Laparra's "Habanera" in French; D'Albert's "Tiefland," Smetana's "Prodana novĕsta" ("Die verkaufte Braut," or "The Bartered Bride") in German. Frederick Converse's "The Pipe of Desire," and Goldmark's "The Cricket on the Hearth," or, in case it should be completed in time, Humperdinck's "Königskinder" (not "The Children of the King," as the title was translated, but "Kings' Children") were to be performed in English. The following singers, new to the stage of the Metropolitan, were to be added to the company: Ester Adaberto, Frances Alda, Emmy Destinn, Bernice James, Félice Kaschowska, Leonora Sparkes (*soprani*); Clara Boehm, Marianne Flahaut, Maria Gay, Matja von Niessen-Stone, and Mary Ranzenberg (*mezzo-soprani* and *contralti*); Angelo Bada, Rinaldo Grassi, Carl Jörn, Walter Koch, Ariodante Quarti, and Erik Schmedes (*tenori*); Pasquale Amato, Fritz Feinhals, Eduardo Missiano, Jean Noté, and Walter Soomer (*baritoni*); Paul Ananian, Enzo Bozzano, Adamo Didur, Arthur Hinckley, Coretto Paterna, Giulio Rossi, Erik Schubert, and Herbert Witherspoon (*bassi*). The conductors were Arturo Toscanini and Francesco Spetrino on the Italian side, Alfred Herz and Gustav Mahler on the German. Concerning the newcomers little need be said. Few endured. Three were not strangers to New York: Mme. Kaschowska had sung in the German season at the Metropolitan nineteen years before; Mr. Didur (who, with Signor Amato, has remained a valued member of the company ever since) had been enticed away from Mr. Hammerstein, as had Signor Bonci, the year before. Mr. Hinckley, an American, had sung with Mr. Savage's English companies and Mr. Witherspoon, also an American, had won admiration as a concert-singer. Miss Destinn deserves more extended notice. This lady, in all respects a superb artist, for ten years a member of the Royal Opera in Berlin, had been under engagement to sing at the Metropolitan Opera House for five years; but, so said the knowing gossips or the manufacturers of publicity, she had been prevented from coming to America by imperial decree. When the world war broke out in 1914 she requited the Kaiser's partiality by using her tongue and pen, the latter at least pointed, in denouncing Austria and proclaiming the right of her native Bohemia to independence. She declared her intention to become an American citizen in February, 1915, and in April, 1916, went to Europe to spend the summer vacation in a castle which she had bought near

Prague. When Miss Destinn wished to return to America she was refused a passport by the Austrian officials. She appealed to the Ambassador of the United States, and he, it is said, succeeded in obtaining the document as a courtesy, but it gave her only forty-eight hours in which to leave the country, and the lady for one reason or another failed or neglected to avail herself of the opportunity which it granted. On June 28, 1918, information came to America through the newspapers that Miss Destinn had been prohibited from singing at the opera in Prague because she had placed her services entirely at the command of the Czecho-Slovak agitation. Members of the company who remained under the new management were: Emma Eames, Geraldine Farrar, Rita Fornia, Olive Fremstad, Johanna Gadski, Marie Morena, Marie Rappold, Marcella Sembrich (*soprani*); Louise Homer, Helen Mapleson, Henrietta Wakefield, and Paula Woehning (*mezzo-soprani* and *contralti*); Julius Bayer, Alessandro Bonci, Aloys Burgstaller, Carl Burrian, Enrico Caruso, Stephen Delwary, Riccardo Martin, Albert Reiss, Giuseppe Tecchi (*tenori*); Bernard Bigué, Giuseppe Campanari, Otto Goritz, Adolph Mühlmann, Antonio Scotti (*baritoni*); Robert Blass, Herbert Waterous (*bassi*). Improvements which added to the comforts of the patrons had been made in the building. Two electric elevators were installed in the Fortieth Street lobby in addition to the two already there, for the use of the patrons of the dress and family circles; the seating-plan of the ground floor was rearranged, the ceiling and boxes were newly decorated, and to improve the acoustical conditions of the orchestral pit it had been enlarged and equipped with machinery by which its floor could be raised or lowered at will.

I have presented a greater mass of detail, much of it seemingly trivial, such as the names of the small-fry personnel of the company, than I shall in future chapters of historical chronicle. The reason ought to be given, though

Emmy Destinn
In "Die Verkaufte Braut"

Emmy Destinn

it also ought to be obvious to the reader: We are at a historical cross-ways, studying the beginning of a period in which the policies of the institution were dictated by the wishes and predilections of the gentlemen who controlled the Opera, and the whims of the ladies whose wishes controlled them, and the conclusion when those wishes and predilections were compelled to yield to a large consideration—the will of the people fixed by the events of the war in the Eastern Hemisphere. When he came to New York Mr. Gatti could consult the inclinations of the stockholders and boxholders of the Opera even to the disregard of the tastes of the general public, knowing as he probably did that those tastes were to a great extent subordinated to the desire to follow the dictates of fad and fashion. When the feelings aroused by the war—the righteous hatred of the German nation and the prejudice, natural if sometimes irrational, against all that nation's institutions, its art, science, language, commerce—became dominant they compelled a modification of the policies thitherto pursued with more or less complacency. Now arose the problem which confronted the management more inexorably at the beginning of the season of 1918-19 than it did at the close of the previous year. The solution of the problem will, probably, demand mutual surrender: the champions of the German list, and all that the term implies, will have to forego in part the principle, whose artistic righteousness is impregnable, that the language to which the music of a lyric drama was composed shall always be employed in the performance; the champions of the notion that opera is merely an elegant diversion will have to look for principles in the selection of operas and methods in their performance which shall promise to win and hold popular support. Otherwise opera will go by the board—at least for a time. Possibly the outcome will be the birth of national opera or at least the beginning of a policy which shall work to that end. Deeply deplorable will be the day when the Metropolitan

Opera shall depart from the principle of artistic integrity in performance established by Maurice Grau which gave the institution unique distinction throughout the world; but welcome the day when worthy American opera in English shall be included in the polyglot list.

The season of 1908-09 began with a representation of "Aïda"; the notable feature was the conducting of Signor Toscanini. On this I commented in *The Tribune* as follows:

> Of the new conductor it must be said that he is a boon to Italian opera as great and as welcome as anything that has come out of Italy since Verdi laid down his pen. In the best sense he is an artist, an interpreter, a re-creator. Without such men music is as lifeless to the ear as it is on the printed page. Signor Toscanini brought to the understanding and the emotions of the audience all of Verdi's score, body and soul, as it lives in him, mixing with it an abundance of affection. He used no book, but that is a matter of small importance except as it influenced the performance. It is, of course, as a brilliant German musician once said, much better that a conductor should have the score in his head than his head in the score; but unless he can convey his knowledge to the musicians under him it will avail him nothing. Evidently Signor Toscanini's head and heart are full of Verdi's music, and his transmission of what he knows and what he feels is magnetic.

Signor Toscanini never gave cause for a reversal or modification of this judgment. On the contrary, everything that he did in the conductor's chair from that first night till his departure for Italy at the end of the season 1914-15, not to return, increased the admiration of those capable of occupying the seats of judgment for his great talents. When his engagement was announced his name was known only to those who had kept themselves *au courant* of operatic affairs in foreign lands. Like Mr. Gatti he had suffered from the manner of his introduction to the American public. Much stress had been laid upon a tale which related how he had arisen out of an orchestra in which he was playing the violoncello to conduct an opera without notice, and had begun by putting the score under the seat of his trousers. This was to emphasize the fact that he had a phenomenal memory and never used a score when conducting. He gave many occasions for amazement by exhibitions of his power of memory while in New York, but great as was that faculty it was not the most admirable factor in his equipment. He was an idealist, of which fact he made lovely proof when, some years later, he gave a marvelously poetical interpretation of Weber's " Euryanthe," which he had introduced into the repertory because it provided the link between the German classics and the neo-romantic Wagner. He was, or rather he is, a native of Parma, where he was born in 1867, where he studied in the conservatory. Before coming to New York he had conducted opera in Rio de Janeiro (1886), Turin, Treviso, Genoa, and Milan. The causes which led to the severing of his relations with the Metropolitan Opera were never divulged. That there was a desire on the part of the management to meet the wishes of the public, which fully appreciated his great gifts, and the fact that his presence in the conductor's chair was always a guaranty that there would be no perfunctoriness in the performance, are evidenced by a cablegram which the chairman of the executive committee of the directors sent to him in Italy:

Am happy to hear that you are considering Gatti-Casazza's proposition, which has my fullest approval not only because it is meant as a public expression of our admiration and gratitude for what the Metropolitan owes to your unique genius, but also because it will give still greater scope and effect and force to your great personality in shaping the artistic development of the Metropolitan. I voice the sentiments of the Board and New York public and myself in expressing sincerest hope that we may continue to enjoy the inspiration of your splendid art. You may rest assured that anything in my power to make your work here sympathetic and satisfactory to you will cheerfully be done. Kindest regards.
OTTO H. KAHN.

No answer to this telegram was received by Mr. Kahn or any of the directors, but it was reported that Signor

Toscanini, who had a son in the Italian army, was patriotically giving his services to his country by directing concerts for the soldiers.

The first novelty of the season was brought forward on November 23, 1908. It was Eugen d'Albert's "Tiefland," produced under the direction of Mr. Alfred Hertz with the parts in the play distributed as follows:

Marta	Fräulein Destinn
Popa	Mme. Forina
Antonia	Mme. Mattfeld
Rosalia	Mme. Randa
Nori	Mme. l'Huillier
Pedro	Herr Schmedes
Sebastiano	Herr Feinhals
Tomasso	Mr. Hinckley
Moriccio	Herr Goritz
Nando	Herr Reiss

Mr. Dippel supervised the production, Mr. Hertz had studied the score with the composer in the summer, and Herr Schmedes had created the rôle of Pedro in the original performance of the opera in Vienna. The Spanish play, by Angel Guimera, upon which the opera is based, had been seen in New York a little more than two years before in an English version at the Manhattan Theater and also in March, 1908, when it had a revival under the title "Marta of the Lowlands." The story plays high up on the mountains of Catalonia and low down in the valleys (wherefore its operatic title) and presents a vivid picture of wickedness, misfortune, and primitive virtue such as can easily be believed to be existent amidst such surroundings as it presents. To serve his own ends a villainous lord of the manor lures a shepherd from his hills into the valley, and in the guise of a blessing for which the highland man had long been praying gives him to wife the woman whom the lord had held in vicious thraldom for years; gives her to him only in name to further his own mercenary purposes but intending to keep her nevertheless for the gratification of

A JUMBLE OF INTERNATIONAL ELEMENTS 45

his own lust. There is a period (brief, for the action is swift and all compassed within the space of a day) in which both victims remain ignorant; then an awakening which in the woman replaces disgust and hatred for her nominal husband with love and turns the obedience of the simple man of the hills into murderous rebellion. He strangles his fiendish lord and master to death and, taking his wife into his arms, carries her to his mountain home, where, in a purer air, she is to awake to a purer life.

A combination of circumstances invited to some curious speculations apropos of this production. It was a German opera, the book on a Spanish subject by an Austrian dramatist, the music by a pianist of Scottish birth whose grandfather had been a French cavalry officer, father a Franco-German by birth, an English dancing-master by profession, and mother an Englishwoman. The composer, once Eugène, now Eugen, Charles Francis d'Albert, musically a product of the National Training School of London, is the artistic "Man without a country," since so far as he has professed any allegiance at all it is to Germany, though there is less German blood in his veins than French or English. The Italian general manager of the theater at which the opera was produced had been honored on the eve of the performance by a public dinner presided over by Walter Damrosch, a patriotic American born in Breslau, at which Horace Porter, H. E. Krehbiel, George B. M. Harvey, and Count Massiglia, the last a representative of the Italian Government, had made speeches. Of late there has been much speculation touching what is to come out of the American melting-pot and such a mixture of elements as had representation at this *première* might naturally turn that speculation toward the question of the American school of music which lies in the womb of the future. Many years before I had remarked in *The Tribune* in support of a contention, steadily upheld ever since, that America must and will have a distinctively national school of composition, that the school was only awaiting that "vigorous, forward man" who, as Walter Bagehot argues in his discussion of the origin of literary schools, shall strike out that rough notion of the style which the American people will find congenial and which, for that reason, will find imitation. The characteristic mode of expression which will be stamped upon the music of the future American composer (we are still waiting for that "vigorous, forward man") will be the joint creation of the American's freedom from conventional methods and his inherited predilections and capacities. "The reflective German, the mercurial Frenchman, the stolid Englishman, the warm-hearted Irishman, the impulsive Italian, the daring Russian, will each contribute his factor to the sum of national taste. The folk-melodies of all nations will yield up their characteristic charms and disclose to the composer a hundred avenues of emotional expression which have not yet been explored. The American composer will be the truest representative of the universal art because he will be the truest type of the citizen of the world."

I have never so much wanted these words remembered as now. If ever there was an opera which came out of an interracial melting-pot it is "Tiefland." It is tragedy, but like "Carmen," which is also tragedy, it invited, if it did not cry out, for the element of local color upon which national schools are now based. That foundation is likely to be strengthened by the clash of nations which shall end in the liberation of peoples from political yokes and the establishment of the principle of self-government.

The libretto of "Tiefland" can not be said to "yearn" for music as Wagner insisted that the book of a lyric drama should, but it contains elements with which music can meet in a mutually beneficial union. There is in the symbolism of the play a large proclamation of virtue on the heights and vice in the lowlands. Verbal preachments of this kind are more likely to cause amusement than to awaken reflec-

THE MUSIC OF "TIEFLAND"   47

tion or stir the emotions; but for symbolism music has a language which the orchestra can utter potently. Very different are the moods represented by the hut of the shepherd Pedro and the mill of Sebastiano. Mr. d'Albert seems to have realized that here was the true field for the activity of his creative fancy, and what is best in his score is a reflection of the two moods. The music begins with a *ranz des vaches,* and with the early strains which are designed to depict the coming of dawn are discreetly mingled the sound of pasture bells. At the close of the prologue there comes an intermezzo to accompany the change of scene from the mountain top to the vale below which modulates in mood and melodic theme from the pastoral and peaceful element to the urban and tragic. This is, of course, instrumental music, and it is only what the orchestra utters that is likely to interest anybody from a musical point of view. The vocal part of the score is nearly all declamatory chatter floating on an orchestral current which by harmonic and instrumental eddyings and whirlings seeks to comment on or color the emotional contents of the text and dramatic situation. It is the *parlando* of the young Italians, but with less melodic flow. Much of it is delivered rapidly and in a monotone. Rapid it had to be, for the book of the play is voluminous enough to fill an evening if it were spoken instead of sung; monotonic it had to be, because there is little in the text that admits of melodic contours. Indeed, the most persistent question which the representation forced upon my mind was why music had been introduced into it at all. Save when it heightened the mood and in the climaxes at the end of the first act and beginning of the second, or published the unutterable feelings which surged in the hearts of Marta and Pedro when their lips were dumb, the music was little else than an impertinence. One thing the music of "Tiefland" may be said to do, however: to some extent it softens the horror of the play and lifts into relief its few moments of cheer. But it is a hundred times pitiful that the son of a dancing-master and composer of dances having so inviting a field before him as Spanish dances and Spanish melodies open could not get farther away from Viennese commonplace than Mr. d'Albert did in the music associated with the three women gossips of the play. Miss Destinn, who had effected her début on the American stage in "Aïda" on the opening night of the season, played the rôle of Marta. In pose, gesture, facial expression, and poignancy of utterance she recalled memories of Duse in the original form and Calvé in the operatic version of "Cavalleria Rusticana." Praise can scarcely go farther than this.

The season begun on November 16, 1908, ended on April 10, 1909, and a summary of its activities may be found in the Appendix to this volume. The plans of the management to augment the orchestra and chorus, give special performances on the Tuesday and Saturday nights, reserve "Parsifal" for holidays, and substitute benefits for a pension fund for the old personal benefits of the manager were carried out practically to the letter. Of the eight novelties announced, however, only four were given, viz. Puccini's "Le Villi," Catalani's "La Wally," Smetana's "Bartered Bride," and d'Albert's "Tiefland." A promise that three operas of first-class importance—Massenet's "Manon," Mozart's "Nozze di Figaro," and Verdi's "Falstaff"—would be revived was brilliantly redeemed. To the subscription season of twenty weeks one week was added for Wagner's Nibelung dramas and extra performances of "Aïda" and "Madama Butterfly." Verdi's Manzoni "Requiem," having been sung with fine effect at two Sunday night concerts, was repeated on the night of Good Friday instead of an opera. The performances of "Parsifal" took place on Thanksgiving Day, New Year's Day, and the birthdays of Lincoln and Washington. There were performances also for the benefit of the French Hospital, the German Press Club, the Music School Settlement, and the Pension and Endowment Fund. At the last, and also at a special performance at which Mme. Sembrich bade farewell to the operatic stage of America, the programme was made up of excerpts from various operas. After the season was over, on April 29, there was a special performance of "The Bartered Bride" at which the Legal Aid Society was the beneficiary. This occasion takes on an interest in the retrospect because of the refusal of a number of members of the Bohemian colony in New York, who at the previous performances of the work had enlivened its dances, to take part unless the project of singing the Austrian national hymn, which had been foolishly conceived by the president of the society, should be abandoned. The local Czechish community would not countenance what it righteously considered to be an affront to their love of country and an insult to a characteristically Czechish opera of which they were proud. At a late hour it was announced that "The Star-Spangled Banner" and Skroup's beautiful "Kde domov muj," a true national utterance, would be substituted for "Gott erhalte Franz den Kaiser," but the mischief had been done, the anger of the Bohemians refused to be allayed, and Smetana's opera was performed for an audience that only half filled the house. It was the first ebullition of a patriotic sentiment which nine years later compelled the banishment of the German language from the representations at the opera house. The German Press Club, which for many years had given an annual benefit performance, did not venture upon the experiment in 1917-18. It is diverting, at least, to speculate on what might have been the consequences had it done so and attempted to introduce "Deutschland, Deutschland über Alles" between the acts!

The incidents connected with the retirement of Mmes. Sembrich and Eames (from opera, not from the concert-stage) I shall reserve for description after recording some impressions made by the new operas in the season's list.

"Le Villi" was performed on December 17, 1908, for the first time in America. There are only three personages in the opera, and these were represented by Miss Frances Alda, who on April 3, 1910, was married to Mr. Gatti, (Anna), Signor Bonci (Roberto), and Signor Amato (Guglielmo Wolf). Signor Toscanini conducted. "Le Villi" is Signor Puccini's first opera and was composed while he was yet a pupil at the Milan Conservatory for a competition invited by the publisher Sonzogno. It failed to win the prize, but after revision was performed at the Teatro dal Verme, Milan, on May 31, 1884. Why it should have been thought worthy of production at the Metropolitan Opera House was a mystery in 1908 and is a mystery yet. The circumstances attending its performance, especially an increase in the prices of admission and the association with it in the list of "La Wally," both works being long dead in Europe, caused Mr. Gatti's judgment and aims to be viewed with doubt and suspicion and the ghosts of the ghastly failures have arisen to plague him in every review of his administration since. The subject of "Le Villi" is admirably adapted for a pantomimic ballet, as Adolphe Adam demonstrated seventy years ago, but not at all for an opera. A drama might have been made out of it by an ingenious infusion of contributory incident, but this was not done by Puccini's librettist. The legend has a place in European folklore. It tells of how damsels who have been betrothed and betrayed and died of a broken heart sometimes meet their miscreant lovers at midnight and indulge in a strange penchant for dancing which had been checked by their untimely death. They lure the faithless ones into a whirl which lasts until the deceivers, unable to stop, give up the ghost.

Signor Puccini has reached a pinnacle such as none of his contemporaries has attained in the United States. There is only one of his operas—the second, "Edgar," which died early and has never been resuscitated—that has

A FAMILY OF COMPOSERS

not been heard in New York. Aside from this extraordinary popularity there are historical reasons which lend a peculiar interest to his works. He is an interesting example of the transmission of hereditary gifts, being of the fifth generation of his family that has won a place in musical history. Not only he, Puccini the son, but Puccini the father, grandfather, great-grandfather, and great-great-grandfather, are known to the annals of the art in Italy. At the theatrical exhibition held in Vienna in 1892 there were performances of compositions by all the Puccinis from Giacomo, the first of the name to make a mark, who was born in 1712, down to the present Giacomo, who was born in 1858. It is a right noble succession, and though "Le Villi" is so much inferior to the other works of the last of the line that I could wish it had not been permitted to interfere with my appreciation of the operas which followed it, it would be wrong to say that it does not contain evidences of the genius which was finely disclosed in "Manon Lescaut" and went lame in "La Fanciulla del West." The best proof of the composer's innate capacity for dramatic expression lies in the music of the ghostly dance.

"La Wally" had its first American performance and (like "Le Villi," save a few other representations in the season) its last on January 6, 1909. Signor Toscanini conducted and the cast was as follows:

Wally	Miss Destinn
Afra	Miss Ranzenberg
Walter	Miss l'Huillier
Giuseppe Hagenbach	Riccardo Martin
Vincenzo Gellner	Pasquale Amato
Stromminger	Giulio Rossi
Il Padrone	Giuseppe Campanari

Had Alfredo Catalani and his librettist, Luigi Illica, taken as the keynote of their drama one of the elements to which they gave merely subordinate emphasis, "La Wally" might have gained a greater distinction than it seemed to possess when Mr. Gatti gave it place in his scheme of performances. The heroine of this story of peasant life in the early part of the nineteenth century might and ought to have been conceived dominated by a strain of romantic aloofness tinged with mystery and fraught with charm. For once in the operatic plots of modern Italy the way was open to cast a poetic glamour over the usual tragedy of love and jealousy. But the librettist was content simply to indicate his element without developing it and the composer lagged still further behind in what might have added materially to the opera's chances for life. The German source of the book is a novel by the Baroness von Hillern which was first turned into a German play and then into the Italian libretto of which the author of the novel thought so well that she made the translation for the publishers herself. The opera had its first performance at La Scala in January, 1892, about a year before the death of the composer, whose career was brief and disappointing. It has four acts, all of them short. Wally, the daughter of an old hunter in the Alps, is commanded by her father to marry Gellner, whom she does not love. Hagenbach, to whom she is deeply attached, has quarreled with her father and does not suspect Wally's feelings toward him. He unwittingly inflames her jealous rage and at the same time discovers his love for her. Thinking to win Wally, Gellner hurls his rival from a precipice, but Wally rescues him and there is a mutual declaration of love. The pair are overtaken by an avalanche high up in the Alps, and Hagenbach perishes. Faithful unto death, Wally leaps to her death into the abyss. There are hints early in the play that Wally is a maid consecrated to her own ideals and, in a sense, an incarnation of the *Edelweiss* whose loveliness is celebrated in a song sung by a mountain boy. Here is good poetic material, but this aspect of her character is lost in the girl's petty behavior with villagers in the otherwise ingeniously contrived festival scene of the second act. It is revived in the more serious moments of the girl's passive share in the attempted murder of her lover and it flowers anew, though feebly, when the avalanche sweeps down upon the pair. But the total effect of the drama is ultimately that of a small, trivial, even sordid sequence of incidents instead of the moving tragedy into which it might have been elevated.

The melodramatic novel on which this opera was built was the admiration of the German youth in the latter half of the nineteenth century, who saw in Geierwally (that is the original name of the heroine) as fascinating a creature as their elders saw in Fanchon the Cricket, a child born of the fancy of Charlotte Birchpfeiffer, who was Mme. von Hillern's mother. There is real beauty in some of the songs, especially that of Wally at the close of the first act; but less loveliness and less eloquent in the essays at dramatic music. Catalani, with undoubted talent of a high order, was a lyricist, not a dramatist. The story calls out loudly for local color, yet there is not an Alpine strain in it. Strange this and explicable only on the ground of the indifference of Italian composers before the advent of the ripe Puccini and Giordano to the teachings of the composers of other lands. From Bizet Catalani, who was his contemporary, ought to have taken a hint even if unwilling to note how effectively Auber had turned Neapolitan for the sake of " La Muette " and Weber Spanish for the sake of " Preciosa." But the orchestration of " La Wally " is delightfully refined and the prelude to the third act is a gem.

While there may not have been enough intrinsic value in " Le Villi " and " La Wally " to justify the attempt to foist them upon the people of New York, they were yet interesting in their historical aspects. It was the misfortune of " Le Villi " to have been composed at a moment when the musical taste of Italy was in a ferment. The so-called *progressisti* had cast off allegiance to Verdi and were seeking to enroll themselves under the banner of Wagner without thinking that in principle and method there was an insuperable barrier between their artistic natures and that of the German master. The revolution had been going on ever since "Lohengrin" had its first presentation in Bologna in 1868, but nothing came of it until Mascagni, piecing together shreds and patches on which he had long been at work, carried off the Sonzogno prize with "Cavalleria Rusticana." This opera set a fashion, and all who followed it found encouragement with its publishers, who at the theatrical exhibition in 1892 were able to enter no less than four new composers with operas fashioned in a general way after Mascagni's nerve-rasping little work. They were "Pagliacci" by Leoncavallo, "Il Birichino" by Leopoldo Mugnone, "Tilda" by Cilea, and "Mala Vita" by Giordano. As it had been the misfortune of "Le Villi" to appear before the new spirit had been awakened, it was the bad fate of Catalani to bring out his "La Wally" when critical Italy had just been carried off its feet by the new movement. Catalani belonged to the Verdi faction if there is any value in the evidence offered by the music of "La Wally." His previous efforts had been made in the period which I described as follows in my "Chapters of Opera" ten years ago:*

Italy had become sterile. Verdi seemed to have ceased writing. There were whisperings of an "Iago" written in collaboration with Boito, but it was awaiting ultmate criticism and final polish, while the wonderful old master was engaged in revamping some of his early works. Boito was writing essays and librettos for others with the unfinished "Nerone" lying in his desk where it is still hidden. Ponchielli had not succeeded in getting a hearing for anything since "La Gioconda." Expectations had been raised touching an opera "Dejanice" by Catalani, but I can not recall that it ever crossed the Italian border. The hot-blooded young veritists who were soon to flood Italy with their creations had not yet been heard of.

* "Chapters of Opera," page 114.

Verdi cared little for the raging of the youthful elements about him, no doubt recognizing something like chauvinism in the affected indifference of his countrymen towards " La Forza del Destino " and " Don Carlos," which had been composed for Paris, and " Aïda," written for Cairo. The true lovers of the Italian style knew the value of these works, especially " Aïda," and Verdi and the Ricordis, his publishers, held onto their following, among whom was Catalani. In the fullness of time the venerable Italian master, whose growth remains an amazing phenomenon comparable with that of his great German contemporary rival, Wagner, broke his silence with " Otello " (1887) and " Falstaff " (1893). If Verdi represented the " old school " there was no danger of its extinction after these works, which are still miles in advance of everything produced by his successors. Thus it may be said that Catalani was justified in his faith, though I can see nothing in " La Wally " that is not compassed by " Aïda " and " Otello." " Falstaff " was as plainly beyond his horizon as it was of that of his more successful rivals. As for the young composers who belonged in the Ricordi fold, their measure was taken in a general way when at the opening of the Metropolitan season of 1890-91 Franchetti's " Asrael " made its fiasco and the policy of the directors of the establishment, in trying to replace the Wagnerian drama with " Der Vassal von Szigeth " (an Italo-Hungarian opera by a Dalmatian composer) and " Diane von Solange " (an opera composed forty years before by a royal duke) made disastrous failures.

Smetana's " Prodana novésta " had its first American performance in German, as " Die verkaufte Braut," on February 19, 1909. Gustav Mahler conducted and the people of the play were these:

Mary .... Emmy Destinn
Kathinka .... Marie Mattfeld
Agnes .... Henrietta Wakefield

Esmeralda	Mlle. l'Huillier
Hans	Carl Jörn
Kruschina	Robert Blass
Kezul	Adamo Didur
Micha	Adolf Mühlmann
Wenzel	Albert Reiss
Springer	Mr. Marlow
Muff	Mr. Bayer

"Die verkaufte Braut" in story and music is Czechish to the core and there was a large infusion of Czechish blood in the performance. Mr. Mahler was a Bohemian and so is Miss Destinn. The dances are Bohemian folk-dances, and to give the true folk flavor to their performance the ballet was recruited from the Bohemian colony of New York. The spirit of the performance was rollicking and infectious. These were some of the good round dozen of reasons why the opera made an unqualified hit at its first performance and held its popularity in the rest of this and two subsequent seasons. One of the reasons lay in the charm of the opera itself, which is a masterpiece. Another in the fascination exerted by its novel local color in scene and music. Still another in the satisfaction which it brought to a long-cherished curiosity and historical interest, for its overture had for years been an admired piece of concert music and the story of its unfortunate composer was well known. Another, again, in the relief which it brought from the tragic tone which had prevailed in the repertories of both opera houses since the beginning of the season. Twenty-three operas had been brought forward at the Metropolitan, and in all but four of them the final curtain had closed on a scene of wretchedness and death; nineteen had been seen and heard at the Manhattan, and in only three of them had the audience been spared pictures of misery and dissolution, moral and physical. It was a refreshment both of body and soul to turn away from such a sup of horrors.

The opera is one in which the spirit of Bohemian peasant

life finds as vital expression as does Russian in "A Life for the Czar." Its pictures and incidents are such as may be found in any Bohemian village today, and while the style of the music is a direct offshoot of the classic Italian *opera buffa* and the ingratiating voice of Mozart speaks in many of its pages, its most pervasive idiom is come straight from the tongues of the Czechish peasantry, just as the characters, their picturesque garments and their fascinating dances, are copies from everyday life as it exists in Bohemia today. So great was the interest in the production that weeks before the date had been announced $2,000 was sent to the box-office of the theater by Bohemian citizens of New York to buy seats at the *première*.

The opera is strung on an extremely slender thread of probability. The lover of the play agrees for pay to renounce his claim upon the hand of the maiden who loves him. He barters his bride. But the written contract contains the stipulation that she shall marry no one but "the son of Micha." There is a son of Micha for whom the marriage broker wishes to procure the pretty maid and her pretty ducats, but he is a lout who stutters in his speech and is obsessed by an impediment of the mind. Though the others do not know it Hans, the hero of the story, is also a son of Micha—of the same Micha, indeed, though he is doing menial service in the house of the pretty Marie, having departed from the house of his father in the adjoining village when that father provided him with an unamiable stepmother. After his seemingly heartless conduct had made Marie tearful and then so angry and desperate that she decides to sacrifice her love and marry the "son of Micha" out of spite, Hans discloses his identity and claims his bride, leaving the booby who was an unwilling rival playing the part of a trained bear in a traveling show into which he had been lured by the wiles of a tight-rope dancer. That is all. Dances fill the gaping interstices in the first two acts of the play and a farcical episode, in which the peripatetic mountebanks appear, those of the third act. This episode is quite unworthy of the comedy, but the dances are its brightest spots. No damsels with gauze skirts these dancers, pirouetting and smirking, but lusty men and women in bodices and ample skirts of brilliant colors and stout shoes which come down upon the floor with a rhythmical clatter that sets one's blood to coursing wildly. The polka in the first act begins with a pretty pantomime and ends in a wild whirl with waving kerchiefs and flying skirts, with caps thrown into the air and maidens lifted high as the spectators break into loud huzzas at the end. In the second act a man and two women dance the *furiant,* a measure which Dvořák has introduced into the polite terminology of chamber music.

The music of "Die verkaufte Braut" roots, as I have intimated, in the style of the Italian *opera buffa* and frequently sounds like a Mozartean utterance. This reference I intend shall go to the forms employed and also to the direct tunefulness of the score. Much of the dialogue which was originally spoken is carried on in recitative, which is frankly old-fashioned though some of the singers at this performance sought to achieve greater naturalness of effect by occasionally dropping into the speaking voice. A useless proceeding. It is better to keep every element of the lyric drama in the realm of ideality which is its home. But the old forms (I mean the *buffo* songs solo and *ensemble*) of the Mozartean period and the perpetual gush of vocal melody sound strange in the work of a composer who was a devotee of Wagner and his methods. "The Bartered Bride" was written in 1866, when Smetana must have been familiar with "Tannhäuser," "Lohengrin," and "Tristan." Like Bizet he had to endure the accusation of being a Wagnerite in his opera, but it is doubtful if a score of persons of the thousands who listened with ingenuous delight to the music on this occasion could have pointed out anything in it as the fruit of Wagnerian suggestion.

What there was of such fruit lay in the flowing flood of instrumental tune which buoyed up the vocal melody and flashed and eddied, and threw its glittering spray above and around its contours most caressingly and bewitchingly. This is the kind of Wagnerism which may be found also in Verdi's "Falstaff," which despite its modernity also consorts amicably with "Le Nozze di Figaro." Mozartean also is the score in its characterization. What a delightful note of nationalism in the large rôle assigned to the clarinet, which may not ineptly be called the national instrument of the Czechs; what a delightful humorist is Smetana's bassoon in the scene between the marriage broker and Hans! What vivacity and lustiness are in the music as well as action of the national dances!

On February 6, 1909, Mme. Marcella Sembrich said farewell to the operatic stage in America at a special performance in the Metropolitan Opera House which was made the occasion of an ovation the like of which I believe has no parallel in operatic history. The lady's determination to retire from opera and devote her gifts to the concert-room was known to her friends before the season opened and announcement of the fact was made in the public prints on the day when the first performance took place. It was in no way connected with the managerial imbroglio which I have described. In the first days of January a committee which was headed by Miss Laura J. Post as chairman, a large number of music lovers representing the Metropolitan Opera and Real Estate Company, the Metropolitan Opera Company, musicians, people of social prominence, and musical critics, addressed an invitation to the public to subscribe to a fund with which to purchase a substantial gift to be presented to her in appreciation of her services during the twenty-five years in which she had, save for a few interregnums, been identified with the Metropolitan. In this invitation were the words:

As an artist Mme. Sembrich occupies an unusual position. By the gifts of voice and rare intelligence, her devotion to the highest ideals, she has rendered an invaluable service to music. As a woman she is so sincere and lovely in character that she is beloved by all. This, therefore, seems a proper occasion to present to Mme. Sembrich a gift that shall be a tribute not only of admiration but of love.

The farewell ceremony took place on the evening of the date mentioned. The programme of the entertainment was printed on white satin, the principal artists of the company appeared in a mixed bill composed of a scene from "Don Pasquale" (Mme. Sembrich and Signor Scotti), the second act of "Il Barbiere" (Mme. Sembrich, Signor Bonci, Signor Campanari, and Mr. Didur), and the first act of "La Traviata" (Mme. Sembrich, Miss Farrar, who assumed the small rôle of Flora to honor her colleague, Signor Caruso, Signor Scotti, Mr. Didur, and Signor Amato. The rest of the company graced the banquet tables in *Violetta's* house with the choristers.) The audience was the most numerous one ever gathered into the house since police regulations against crowding the aisles, to which official attention had been grievously called by the burning of the Iroquois Theater in Chicago, had come to be enforced. After the scene from "La Traviata" the curtain was closed for a short space, then reopened on the same stage-set supplemented by a canopied throne flanked by masses of ferns and flowers. All the members of the company were on the stage. Signor Gatti led Mme. Sembrich to a seat on the throne and yielded his place to Mr. Dippel, who first read a letter from the directors of the company owning the building, signed by Mr. George F. Baker. Then, speaking for the Metropolitan Opera Company, Mr. Dippel presented its gift, a massive silver punch-bowl suitably inscribed and a series of resolutions setting forth an appreciation of the singer's services and electing her an honorary member of the company. The Hon. Seth Low, once mayor of the City of New York, presented the gifts purchased by public subscription consisting of a pearl necklace and a watch and chain set in diamonds. Extremely gracious and beautiful were Mr. Low's concluding words:

> Friendships such as you have created between an artist and a community are not easily ended, and we are frankly sorry the word of farewell must be spoken. But it means you know, fare *you* well. Fare *you* well always and everywhere, fare *you* well; and let these pearls in their own beauty and in the beauty of the association through which they shine say to you now and say to you always: "Think not so much of the gift of the lovers as of the love of the givers!" Fare you well!

The orchestra, through one of its members, Adolf Rothmeyer, brought to Mme. Sembrich a silver loving-cup as a token of their admiration, esteem and gratitude, an act that was interpreted as a recognition of the singer's generosity in having distributed among them the proceeds of a concert which she had given the receipts from which went to the repair of the losses which the musicians had suffered in the San Francisco earthquake in April, 1906. There were also personal gifts from Mr. and Mrs. Dippel, Miss Farrar, Signor Caruso, and Signor Scotti, and then Mme. Sembrich took her turn at making presents, accompanying each of the mementos with a short speech. Among the recipients were four members of the orchestra who had played at the Metropolitan ever since her coming in 1883. She also addressed the audience, saying:

> My dear friends:—I have said "Thank you, Thank you, Thank you!" but these words do not help my heart. It grows fuller and fuller, so I must say something to you, else I shall cry. Now I can not sing my feelings. I am happy because you have been so good and kind to me during the many years I have sung at the Metropolitan Opera House. You have made me love you and New York has become my second home. I go away happy because I shall always remember your goodness; but I go away sad because I shall not look into your faces again over these footlights. I shall never forget the goodness and kindness of the people who have heard me at the Metropolitan Opera House, and I hope that in the

future you will always keep a place in your hearts and your memories for Marcella Sembrich. Once more I thank you and I say, not good-by, but *au revoir.*

After the function at the opera house Mme. Sembrich entertained her artistic associates and a large company of friends in the ballroom of the Hotel Savoy and on the next evening was herself entertained at a banquet arranged by a committee of musicians at the Hotel Astor. Her hosts numbered over 150. Mr. Krehbiel acted as master of ceremonies and in proposing her health said:

> It has long been a plaint that actors and reproductive musicians in dying leave only a memory behind, rising first like a cloud, roseate and fragrant, but gradually wafted away. But do the things which make for refinement die when they pass away? I should be sorry to think so. Are we not repositories of the loves that lived in our ancestors years ago? Surely, and it is because of this that we can smile as we say farewell to Mme. Sembrich—this incarnate melody, this vocal sunbeam. . . . So we be true to ourselves nothing shall take from us the reverence for lofty ideals of beauty which she has taught us. Nothing shall make us deaf to the evangel of truthfulness and loveliness and purity in art. And so Marcella Sembrich will be with us and our children and our children's children forever. She is immortal. She was not made to die.

Mr. Paderewski spoke out his pride in the fact that Mme. Sembrich was a Pole, a countrywoman of his own, and declared her to be "the most musical singer" he had ever heard. Mr. Walter Damrosch paid his tribute and Mr. W. J. Henderson, musical critic of *The Sun,* his, the latter in verse which is worthy of preservation:

> Come, all ye lovers of the lyric muse,
> Your sackcloth don nor yet your sighs refuse.
> "*Die Frist ist um;*" the iron hand of Fate
> Engraves across the years the cruel date
> When Music, locked within her silent cell,
> Weeps for the echo of her olden spell.
> The clarion trump may peal, the oboe cry,
> The sad bassoon lament, the clar'net sigh,

MR. HENDERSON'S POETICAL TRIBUTE

And all the vibrant choirs of strings and brass
Sweep dismal dissonances, dark and crass,
While Stentor voices from the trembling stage
In crackling recitation shout and rage,
And stormy passions make the theater ring
With waves of horrid sound—but who will sing?
The day goes down, the dusk draws slowly near,
For old-time art's adieu let fall a tear.
Let all the cloisters sob, the highways grieve,
For great Marcella Sembrich takes her leave!
No more shall *Gilda* hymn the dearest name
In song as lambent as her candle's flame;
No more shall "*Una voce poco fà*"
Spell R-o-s-i-n-a, *Rosina*.
That *Primavera voce* dumb shall grow
And all the theater droop in deepest woe!
No more *Norina* flouts the ancient bore,
Elvira bid *Ernani* fly no more;
No more *Marie* shall wake the martial drum,
Nor fair *Ulana* to the lakeside come!
No more shall *Marta* rustic fates dispose,
Nor praise the beauty of the virgin rose;
But we shall sing: "*Ti colgo giovin fior
Sa questo cor' cosi morrai d'amor.*"
Susanna's plots no more shall bring delight
Nor *Astrifiammante* rule the night.
Zerlina takes from Time the proffered hand
And turns her back forever from our land,
While *Violetta* comes, of all the last,
To sing *Addio* to the wondrous past.

And shall these dear ones come again no more
To glad the heart and make the tears outpour?
Must silence fall across the lyric stage
While memory feeds upon a bygone age?
Not so; for new-fledged birds will swiftly wing
Their infant flights into the budding spring,
And blithely pipe the old-time roundelays
For those who heard them not in other days.
But not for us. For she hath struck the knell,
To her creations all we bid farewell.
To younger hearts, to younger ears and eyes,
With other voices, thought and style they'll rise,
And they shall have their "bravos" and their toasts,
But ah! for us they'll evermore be ghosts
Summoned to walk, with vital essence fled,
The hollow stage, vain shadows of the dead.

> So like our salutation, we who stay
> To face the dawning of a darker day.
> Queen of the Night, Queen of the singer's art,
> Queen of the stage, Queen of the public heart,
> Hail and farewell! Your name is writ above,
> Supreme in song, still more supreme in love!

A diverting incident of the dinner which caused delighted comment for days afterwards and quite confounded the newspaper reporters was an apparently impromptu song carried on sequentially by individuals seated in various parts of the room. After Mr. Henderson had read his poem the master of ceremonies remarked: "A wonderful woman this! Not only musical herself, she is the cause of music in critics! I wouldn't wonder if there were a song even in the list of her operas." Taking up the printed menu whose title-page contained the representation of a laurel wreath bound with a ribbon on the convolutions of which appeared the names of twenty-seven operas in which Mme. Sembrich had sung, he looked it over. Mr. Isidore Luckstone, who had frequently been the singer's accompanist at her song recitals, struck a chord on a pianoforte in an anteroom and Mr. Krehbiel sang "Rigoletto" to the first *motif* of the waltz from "The Merry Widow," the most popular operetta of the day. As if catching the inspiration Mme. Homer, Emilio de Gogorza, Mrs. Krehbiel, Mr. Dippel, Mrs. Theodore J. Toedt, Signor Caruso, Miss Farrar, Signor Scotti, Frank Damrosch, and Walter Damrosch followed, each in turn carrying on the tune with opera titles as texts. The last *motif* was sung in harmony by Miss Farrar, Mrs. Homer, Mr. Dippel, and Mr. de Gogorza. As the song went on amazement and delight grew, and at the end there was an uproarious demand for more. The toastmaster began again, but with a new list, and when the round of singers had been completed the versified repertory had this form:

The Sembrich Repertory Waltz

Ri - go - let - to, Pu - ri - ta - ni, Hu - gue - nots,—
Il Bar - bie - re, La Lu - ci - a, La Bo - hème,—

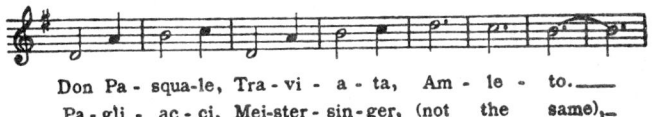
Don Pa - squa - le, Tra - vi - a - ta, Am - le - to.—
Pa - gli - ac - ci, Mei - ster - sin - ger, (not the same),—

L'E - li - sir d'A - mo' - re, La Son - nam - bu - 'la,—
Ro - bert le Di - a - ble, Lin - da di Cha - mou - nix,—

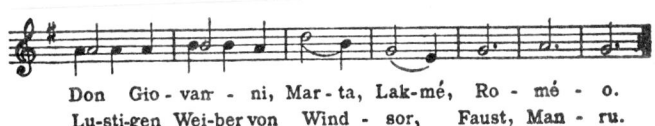
Don Gio - van - ni, Mar - ta, Lak - mé, Ro - mé - o.
Lu - sti - gen Wei - ber von Wind - sor, Faust, Man - ru.

Sung at the Sembrich banquet, February 7, 1909.
(Melody copyrighted by Chappell and Co. Used by permission of G. Schirmer)

Mme. Sembrich's repertory had not been exhausted, but the remaining titles refused the strait-jacket of versification and were not numerous enough to fill out a third stanza. Circumstances conspired to make the joke sound like an improvization, and it is almost a pity even now to divulge the fact that the singers had been coached in their parts, albeit in a great hurry, within a few minutes while the company was gathering.

Thus departed from the operatic stage of America one of the greatest stars that ever illumined it. Mme. Sembrich appeared in opera in a few European cities during the next season and continued to give song recitals in the United States until the beginning of 1917, when persistent illness compelled her retirement from the concert-field also—a circumstance which was as deeply deplored as her abandonment of the operatic stage had been.*

Though there had been no authoritative announcement of the fact till it was made by the lady herself from the stage of the Metropolitan on February 15, 1909, Mme. Emma Eames's friends knew that she would retire from opera at the end of the work in which she was then singing. The opera was "Tosca," and after the second act, in response to a hearty demonstration by the audience, she announced her purpose in a formal speech of farewell, gracefully worded and listened to with rue. Mme. Eames's connection with the Metropolitan establishment began with the restoration of the Italian régime under Abbey, Schoeffel, and Grau in the winter of 1891. She effected her début on December 14, the opening night, in Gounod's "Roméo et Juliette." It was an auspicious introduction for the young American. She was only twenty-four years old, and there was much to laud in her art and nothing to condone except its immaturity. Her endowment of beauty of person as well as voice was opulent. She appeared in the opera in which she had made her entrance on the lyric stage at the Grand Opéra, Paris, less than three years before and for which her gifts and graces admirably fitted her. She appeared, moreover, in the company of M. Jean de Reszke, who was then, and who remained until his retirement the ideal Romeo in all things except mere sensuous charm of voice. She came fresh from her first successes at Covent

* For incidents in the life of Mme. Sembrich and an account of her career, see "Chapters of Opera." New York: Henry Holt and Company. Pp. 94 *et seq.*

Garden, London, which had been made in the spring of the year and disclosed at once the lovely qualities which, when they became riper, promised the highest order of achievement in dramatic song. She had not realized all the promises of her early years, but she had written her name on the scroll of fame and been a delight to the patrons of the Metropolitan Opera House for a dozen years. She established herself so firmly in popular favor that when Mme. Melba came in 1893-94 she found it extremely difficult to win appreciation for her voice and art. The difference between the repertories of the two singers had much to do with their relative popularity. Mme. Eames's list of operas was small, but it appealed more strongly to the public which had been under German training for seven years than did the barrel-organ list of Mme. Melba. In her first season Mme. Eames sang in " Roméo et Juliette," " Faust," " Cavalleria Rusticana," and " Lohengrin." In the season 1893-94, when Melba and Calvé were first associated with her, she added " Carmen " (Micaela), Massenet's " Werther," " Die Meistersinger " (in Italian), and " Le Nozze di Figaro " (the Countess) to her list. In this year " Faust," with its " ideal cast " which she headed, was the only opera which held a candle to Calvé's " Carmen." Again a member of the company of 1894-95, she appeared as Desdemona in Verdi's " Otello " on December 3, Mistress Ford in the same composer's " Falstaff " on February 4, and Elvira in " Don Giovanni " on December 31. Absent in 1895-96 she returned in 1896-97 and disclosed further fruits of study by singing Elizabeth in " Tannhäuser," on November 22, 1896, and Elsa in " Lohengrin " (in German) on January 7, 1897. The reaction against Mr. Abbey's Italian policy had set in, and Mr. Grau had begun a restoration of the German repertory in the original tongue. It was thus that Mme. Eames was encouraged to widen her artistic horizon and in subsequent years she sang in German performances of " Tannhäuser," " Lohengrin,"

"Die Meistersinger," and "Die Walküre." Her début as Sieglinde in the last opera was made on December 14, 1898, and as Eva in the German "Meistersinger" on January 24, 1900. Other notable first performances were Ero in Mancinelli's "Ero e Leandro" on March 10, 1899; Aïda on January 3, 1900; Pamina in the Italian "Zauberflöte" on March 30, 1900; Tosca, December 12, 1902; Iris (in Mascagni's opera), December 6, 1907; Donna Anna in "Don Giovanni," January 23, 1908. During her connection with the opera house she sang in nineteen operas.

A distressing incident of the season was the vocal shipwreck suffered by Signor Caruso in the first week of March, after which he was unable to sing because of an affection of his vocal organs. At the last matinee of the subscription season and again on the following Wednesday he made ill-advised efforts to resume his duties, but the consequences were pitiful to all connoisseurs and seemed so threatening to his physicians that it was deemed advisable by the management to relieve him of his obligation to go on the Western tour undertaken by the company on the conclusion of the New York season.

CHAPTER IV

RIVALRY BETWEEN THE MANATTAN AND METROPOLITAN OPERA HOUSES

AN OPERA-MAD CITY—OVER TWO MILLIONS OF DOLLARS SPENT ON THE ENTERTAINMENT IN TEN MONTHS—MR. HAMMERSTEIN'S POLICIES—THE MASSES AGAINST THE ARISTOCRATS—THE LURE OF FRENCH OPERA—A HOUSE BUILT IN PHILADELPHIA—THE CLASH OF OPPOSITION THERE—HAMMERSTEIN CONFESSES FAILURE—PURCHASE OF HIS INTERESTS AND PROPERTIES—AGREES TO RETIRE FROM OPERA FOR TEN YEARS—REORGANIZATIONS AND AFFILIATIONS—HAMMERSTEIN TRIES LONDON—FAILURE THERE—ATTEMPTS TO ENTER THE FIELD IN NEW YORK—BUILDS A THEATER IN LEXINGTON AVENUE—OPERA IN ENGLISH—PROJECT OF THE CITY CLUB—HAMMERSTEIN ANNOUNCES HIS INTENTION TO EVADE HIS CONTRACT—IS ENJOINED BY THE COURTS—MR. STOTESBURY AND HIS LOANS—DEATH OF MR. HAMMERSTEIN.

THE two seasons which fell between the winter of 1909 and the summer of 1911 were years of operatic marvels in New York, though they were more marvelous for their plethora of incident, scandalous and otherwise, than for artistic achievement. Within three hundred days of this period the city was entertained with nearly 600 representations of opera, omitting from the count the bastard spawn of the theaters called comic opera. Within 300 days New York spent considerably over $2,000,000 for the gratification of a craze for opera stimulated by the rivalry between the Metropolitan and Manhattan Opera Houses. The end of the period was marked by the collapse of Mr. Oscar Hammerstein's career as an operatic manager, though all the wind was not taken out of his balloon until pressure was applied to it three years later by the law-courts. The mania was not confined to the managements and public; it was shared in also by the newspapers. Throughout the ferment which kept the redoubtable rival of the Metropolitan Company bobbing and whirling on the surface of the bubbling and boiling, toiling and troubling social cauldron the editors were Mr. Hammerstein's willing and active agents. He was a fecund source of "news." His audacity, intrepidity, inexhaustible energy, and good humor won their admiration. They knew him only as he appeared in the interviews, statements, pronouncements, and proclamations which the reporters brought into their offices. He was "good copy" while the fight was on, good copy during the brief space in which he troubled the operatic pools of London, and still good copy when after his return to New York he attempted to establish a new rivalry with the Metropolitan Company in defiance of a solemn covenant to keep out of the American operatic field for ten years. He became almost a political factor, for it was the period of the proletarian war on combined industries the wisdom of which is also undergoing purgation in the war crucible. His campaign of publicity was so ingeniously conducted by himself and his press agent, William A. Guard, that the editors were urgent in their invitations to the public to share their admiration and only the irresistible logic of money turned the scales against him. He fell; but even in his fall I am persuaded he triumphed over his rivals when he sold them his Philadelphia theater and all his operatic properties for a sum which enabled him to pay his obligations in America and embark upon another quixotic enterprise in London. He escaped the financial ruin which inevitably confronted him—an achievement which, though it excites no admiration in so hopelessly uncommercial a person as myself, can not be said to reflect credit on the combination of astute business men whom he fought single-handed.

The rivalry which ended in the circumstances which I have hinted at and must now relate began in December, 1906, when Mr. Hammerstein opened the Manhattan Opera House, which he had built in West Thirty-fourth Street.

The enterprise, no less chimerical at the height of its success than when it came to an end, was a flowering of the old obsession that if one operatic establishment flourishes in a community there must be room for two. Managerial flesh is Bourbonistic. It never learns. Upon it history and individual experience are wasted. The theories upon which Mr. Hammerstein based his hopes of success were chiefly two, and neither of them was in his mind when he built the Manhattan Opera House, which was originally designed as the home of spectacle and vaudeville. The first theory was based on a belief in proletarianism of a sort, a conviction or notion that he could win the masses to the support of an institution consecrated to the classes: democracy against aristocracy in art. Unlike a multitude of managers before and after him he did not confound popular opera with cheap opera. He had learned better in theaters of his own building in earlier years. He knew that the popular interest in opera of which the newspapers talked much was largely an affectation, and that aristocratic prices would help him more than they would mar him. Not "good enough" opera, but opera as good as the best was his promise. He made no pretense of scorning the help of what calls itself society; he needed it to fill the many boxes which the architect had put in his vast audience-room. He needed it to meet his payroll. So he engaged as many high-class singers as he could find and boldly challenged his rivals on social as well as artistic lines.

The second factor in his appeal, largely adventitious in origin (growing as it did out of the character of his singers), was French opera. This did not enter into his plans until his second season, though thereafter it became the dominant principle of his administration. It was a splendid weapon, and with it he dealt the blows which his adversaries could not withstand. It was a two-edged sword which cut a swath in every direction. With it he enlarged the outlook of the society-folk in respect of operatic literature. With it he humored the *poseurs* who affected to believe that an entertainment had been created for their special delectation. Among the patrons of the Metropolitan Opera House there were many who saw in it an indictment of Mr. Gatti, who had always protested that he could not find capable French singers, thereby increasing the apprehension that the Metropolitan opera was to be completely Italianized. Mr. Hammerstein adroitly fed this apprehension by proclaiming a purpose to make his repertory and performances as polyglot as Mr. Grau's had been. There can be no doubt that the success of French opera at the Manhattan was the most potent of the influences which frightened the Metropolitan people into the belief that their establishment was in danger of losing prestige, socially as well as artistically. If the society-folk enjoyed French opera more than Italian (the music being equally enjoyable and the performance good), there was a likely reason for the fact. They understood more of the words. Sometimes, it must be confessed, the enjoyment was of a most ingenuous kind. Once on a French night in the days of Grau when walking in the lobby of the Metropolitan Opera House I overheard the chatter of some young women who had just emerged from one of the boxes.

"Oh!" exclaimed one of them, "I do love French so much more than Italian! Did you hear Jean say 'jamais'?"

Had M. de Reszke said "giammai," in opera as blessed a word and mouth-filling as Mesopotamia, it would not have fallen so delightfully into the ear of the rapturous maiden who had understood an adverb from the lips of the artist whom she and her tribe were wont to speak of by his Christian name. Did we not read about the same time of a young person borne out of the Auditorium in Chicago shrieking: "I want Jeen! I want Jeen!" She had become hysterical because there had been a change in the bill, and her adored Jean was not in the cast!

PHILADELPHIA AS A MUSICAL CENTER

The repertory of Mr. Hammerstein's first season did not contain a single novelty. Moreover, Italian opera dominated it and the language used was Italian. For the next season he engaged some singers from Paris and hit upon the notion of specializing in French opera. His second prospectus announced eight novelties, all of them French but one. Of the eight promised he produced four and he gave two other French works in place of the three which he omitted. With this list he challenged popularity and support. He fomented criticism of the subscription methods of the Metropolitan management, which were said to prevent thousands from enjoying the entertainment for which their souls hungered, and his daring campaign, warmly supported by the newspapers, won a surprising success. Almost we were persuaded to believe that there really were enough people in New York to support two opera houses. But the stomach of Mr. Hammerstein's ambition had grown large by his contemplation of the vast scheme of conquest in the minds of the Metropolitan directors. They were reaching out for domination of the national field; he would do likewise. The point of departure for the new campaign, New York being invested, was Philadelphia.

Time was, before it became the national seat of government (i.e. after 1790), when Philadelphia outranked New York as a musical center. For a long time afterward it disputed for first place with New York. The first dramatic companies which came to the American shores from London played there as well as in Charleston, S. C., and Williamsburg, Va., which towns loomed as large on the dramatic map then as did the present metropolis of the nation. From the early days until the nineteenth century Philadelphia was a more influential city, musically, than New York, and there was an energetic rivalry between the dramatic companies playing in the two places. During the last decade of the eighteenth century Philadelphia laid more stress upon opera (of the type prevalent at the time,

English ballad and adaptations by English composers of a few Continental works) than New York. At the time of the advent of Italian opera, in 1825, New York had twice the population of Philadelphia, incomparably greater wealth, and a much more cosmopolitan character. Thereafter the city of Penn became largely dependent on the city of Knickerbocker for operatic entertainment. Like its predecessors the Metropolitan Company gave performances twice a week for a brief season in the Academy of Music in Philadelphia, which had long been the fashionable home of music in that city. Determined to carry the war into that city Hammerstein built an opera house there in 1908 at Broad, Carlisle, and Poplar streets, appealed for subscriptions to a season of opera, and, as if to make his challenge more emphatic, gave his opening performance one week after he had begun his New York season on the regular first night of the Metropolitan Company at the Academy of Music. Philadelphia seemed so wonderfully flattered at the prospect of having an opera all its own that its society broke down the barrier which had shut fashion within the confines of a district contiguous to Rittenhouse Square and subscribed for seats and boxes with a generosity which was remarkable if not of the dimensions trumpeted forth by Mr. Hammerstein. Scarcely had the walls of the building been reared before Mr. Hammerstein asked the moneyed men of Philadelphia to lend him $400,000 on the security of a mortgage on the opera house. A committee of citizens undertook to raise the amount, but financiers were chary, for which reason Mr. Hammerstein publicly and roundly berated them. With amazing effrontery he accused them of niggardliness and said that if he had built a drinking saloon and asked a loan on it they would readily have given him $4,000,000. With a meekness equally amazing the Philadelphians swallowed the insult to their city. The public, led as in New York by the newspapers, had as a matter of fact become enamored of their new social plaything and were in the frame of mind to be browbeaten and intimidated. The committee offered Mr. Hammerstein $250,000 on conditions which he refused and played his next card: he would close the season on January 23 or continue to give opera on a less costly scale. At the same time he gave the public to understand that Baltimore had offered to raise $1,000,000 and build an opera house for him. Baltimore had been drawn into the fighting-line and Mr. Hammerstein's hint was merely a prelude to the announcement made by the Metropolitan people on January 21 that they had acquired the Lyric Theater in that city and would give a season of two performances a week in 1909-10. Nevertheless Mr. Hammerstein got his $400,000, the loan being guaranteed or extended on his own responsibility, by Mr. E. T. Stotesbury, a member of the banking house of Drexel and Morgan.

And so the season of 1908-09 wore on to an end and the season 1909-10 began with Hammerstein striving to strengthen his intrenchments in New York and Philadelphia and the Metropolitan directors doing the same but also working on the plan, long in their minds, of gaining control of the operatic field in the entire country. Meanwhile the competition for singers caused them to raise their demands for honoraria and the cost of giving opera was growing. Mr. Hammerstein, at least, saw disaster threatening. Though he could boast that he had no board of directors to hamper his actions he was obliged to confess there was a strength which he did not possess in the wealth of the Metropolitan Company and its annual popular subscription list which was more than a royal subvention.

Before the year 1910 opened he was prepared to confess to a vision of the handwriting on the wall. On New Year's Day he gave out an interview in the newspapers in which he said that the operatic war was suicidal and offered to combine with the Metropolitan Company with a view to reducing the number of performances. Still protesting that his purpose in giving opera had no desire for money gain in it, he said: "It is at present a throat-cutting game. Operas are pitched on solely to get ahead of the rival house, and singers are engaged at exorbitant salaries to prevent them from being engaged elsewhere?" He proposed a merger into which he and the Metropolitan should go as equal partners; if the company did not accept his proposition he would go into the next season with his knowledge increased by experience. If, however, the merger were entered into he would revert to the spoken drama at the Manhattan Opera House. To this overture the directors of the Metropolitan made a curt reply: "Mr. Hammerstein is within his rights in making any suggestion he pleases. These suggestions, however, will not interfere with nor change the policy of the management of the Metropolitan Opera Company."

Through Arthur Hammerstein the story had gone out that the Metropolitan Company had proposed the merger to his father. On the day after Mr. Hammerstein had given out his interview a director of the Metropolitan Company denied emphatically that negotiations of any kind were pending between the rival institutions. He also denied that his company had offered Hammerstein compensation if he would retire from the operatic field and incidentally gave a glimpse into the Alexandrian ambitions of himself and colleagues.

The aim of the Metropolitan Opera Company and its allied interests [he said] is to give the very best opera possible not only in New York, but also in those cities where there is a demand for operatic performances of a higher order. The Metropolitan is not looking to the material side of the question, namely whether opera pays or whether it does not; and while it is true that under present conditions it is well-nigh impossible to place opera on a remunerative basis this phase of the situation does not embarrass the management in the slightest degree. The whole proposition is a very much broader one than is generally supposed. In fact it is of national scope. By this I mean that under the leadership of the Metropolitan Opera Company it will not be at all improbable that in time an operatic basis may be established in every principal city of the United States. In connection with this I have only to cite the recent formation of the Metropolitan Chicago Opera Company whereby Chicago is to have an operatic season of twenty weeks beginning the coming fall. This is the entering wedge in the great West.

Mr. Hammerstein retorted that he had never taken any stock in the negotiations, but was as full of fight as ever and thought that New York would find him giving opera for the next fifteen years. On the heels of this he announced the engagement for the season 1910-11 of Mary Garden, Lina Cavalieri, Maurice Renaud, Charles Dalmorès, and Charles Gilibert, but intimated that he would abandon opera in Philadelphia. " The enormous railroad expenses," he explained, " figuring over $30,000 a season, the steady employment of a resident orchestra, chorus, and immense working force for but four operas a week, make the present mode of giving opera without any guarantee even with large attendance unremunerative. The great edifice including the improvements made since its erection has cost nearly $1,500,000. There is a mortgage of only $400,000 on this property, leaving an investment of over $1,000,000." He added that he had been offered an annual rental of $100,000 for the Philadelphia house and threatened that unless he received a guarantee of $600,000 a year he would abandon opera in Philadelphia. Thereupon the Metropolitan Company announced that in the next season it would forego the guarantee of $7,500 each from a number of its patrons in Philadelphia and give opera at its own risk. Hammerstein reiterated his demand for a guarantee and flatly declared that in the preceding November the Metropolitan Company had offered to buy his opera house provided he would withdraw from the operatic field. He was now willing to sell the house to the company and leave the local field to the purchaser while he devoted himself henceforth to his " life's labor in the cause of art and great music in New York."

Meanwhile the Metropolitan directors were occupied in

developing their scheme of expansion and monopoly and the newspapers were busy with rumors touching the changes in the operatic world which were impending. In February, 1910, it was bruited about that Mr. Dippel would sever his connection with the Metropolitan at the end of the season and that Mr. Gatti would thereafter be sole manager. Also that Mr. Henry Russell would replace Mr. Gatti and Signor Mugnone Signor Toscanini. The executive committee gave the public to understand that action on the future administration of the Opera would not be taken until May 1. A month before that date, however, Mr. Dippel, with the consent of the directors, made it known that he had resigned as administrative director and would assume the general management of a Chicago company, the plans of which he had conceived and perfected. In this company the leading stockholders of the Metropolitan Opera Company were interested and though it was independent it would co-operate with the New York organization. His letter was dated March 30, and to it the executive committee made public answer lauding Mr. Dippel's services to the company and making a declaration plainly designed to allay any apprehensions which opera patrons might feel concerning the future of the German repertory. The declaration ran:

> Inasmuch as certain statements have been published insinuating that your resignation is due to dissatisfaction on the part of the board because of the so-called "expansion" policy, it is but just that we should give an emphatic and offical denial to such statements. The expansion policy had to be tried and tested. Whether a contrary policy would have produced materially better results is a matter of speculation and can not be a matter of certainty. We gladly bear witness to the fact that you have been a large factor in bringing about the very gratifying increase in interest and appreciation which the patrons of the Metropolitan Opera House have demonstrated in the Wagnerian performances during the last two seasons as compared with preceding years. No deterioration will be permitted of the standard which now prevails. The eclectic taste of Mr. Gatti-Casazza, who was foremost in the fight for the intro-

MR. STOTESBURY TO THE RESCUE

duction of the Wagner operas in Italy, the common devotion and enthusiasm of Messrs. Toscanini and Hertz for German art, are ample warrant for this statement quite apart from the fact that it would be nothing short of folly meeting with the instant and determined disapproval of our board no less than of the public to deviate from those traditions of internationalism in art which have made the Metropolitan opera what it is.

At this time Hammerstein was losing money on his operatic undertakings at the rate of about $25,000 a week. Three years later he testified in a court of law that the last fourteen weeks of the season in Philadelphia had cost him $80,000. There was then a strike of the employees of the street trolley lines in that city and the general attendance at the opera shrunk so greatly as to be practically negligible. On one occasion the box-office receipts were only $157. Mr. Hammerstein suspended the performances. Mr. Stotesbury had loaned him also $200,000 on the security of a mortgage on the Manhattan Opera House in New York. Mr. Stotesbury again came to his rescue in the new emergency; he agreed to advance him money to liquidate the weekly payroll of the opera house if Mr. Hammerstein would reopen it. The representations were resumed and Mr. Hammerstein made public acknowledgment of the public-spirited generosity of his patron in a curtain speech. At the end of the season it was found that Mr. Stotesbury had advanced $39,960. This Mr. Hammerstein did not repay, and when Mr. Stotesbury took legal action two or three years afterward to recover the money Mr. Hammerstein testified that it had not been a loan but a gift; and the newspapers thought this testimony, which was filled with denunciations of his patron, vastly diverting. Mr. Hammerstein was a humorist and again " good copy."

After negotiations extending over six weeks it was announced on April 28, 1910, that Mr. Stotesbury, for himself, a number of Philadelphians, and some stockholders of the Metropolitan Opera Company of New York, had bought the Philadelphia Opera House and all of Mr. Hammerstein's operatic properties in Philadelphia and New York except the Manhattan Opera House, and that Mr. Hammerstein (through his son Arthur, who held his power of attorney, he having gone to Europe) had covenanted with the purchasers not to engage in any way in the management of grand opera in New York, Philadelphia, Boston, or Chicago for a period of ten years. Mr. Stotesbury's published reasons for making the purchase were that a company supplying both New York and Philadelphia with opera could not do justice to the latter city, which was entitled to an opera company of its own and a season of ten or twelve weeks. Inasmuch as artists would not come to the city for so short a time arrangements would be made with the new Chicago company organized by Mr. Dippel and conducted by Mr. Cleofonte Campanini, who had been Mr. Hammerstein's conductor, by which there would be ten weeks of opera in Chicago and the same number of weeks in Philadelphia. There was also to be an exchange of leading singers with the New York and Boston companies. Mr. T. De Witt Cuyler, of Philadelphia, was already a member of the Metropolitan board of directors and Mr. Stotesbury was associated with him, while Otto H. Kahn, Clarence H. Mackay, and William K. Vanderbilt joined the directorate of the Philadelphia organization.

The season of 1909-10 resulted in a loss to the Metropolitan Opera Company of about $300,000. In a curtain speech on the night before his New York season was brought to a close Mr. Hammerstein said: " The past season financially has been a very unfortunate one, but there has been a deluge of musical efforts and a surfeit of grand opera. While my losses have been enormous, I am proud of knowing that those of my adversaries have been much larger. My efforts in the great cause, however, will not relax, and I am planning for next season the greatest and most sublime opera for the pleasure of my audience and the honor of myself." He owned contracts for the performing rights of a number of operas, some of which he had given and some not, and for the services of Mary Garden, Luisa Tetrazzini, Maurice Renaud, Charles Dalmorès, Charles Gilibert, John McCormack, and Mario Sammarco; these were transferred to the Chicago-Philadelphia, or Philadelphia-Chicago, Company.

Mr. Hammerstein did not long lie quiescent on the field of battle after the war with his Metropolitan rivals. Managerially he had been decapitated, but his headless trunk was like the Irishman's snake, dead but not cognizant of the fact, while his trunkless head was like that of the victim of Ko-Ko's fictitious execution:

> Now tho' you'd have said that head was dead,
> (For its owner dead was he),
> It stood on its neck, with a smile well-bred,
> And bowed three times to—

Pooh-Bah, if that aristocratic individual's circumstantial account of the incident which Mr. Gilbert's operatic people cooked up for the edification of the Mikado is to be believed. The Metropolitan's saber true having cut cleanly through the Hammersteinian cervical vertebræ, the Hammersteinian head bowed first most politely to Mr. Gilbert's home city. Its owner had been compelled to relinquish his managerial ambition for a space in four great American cities, but the rest of the world was his oyster could he but open it. Mr. Hammerstein resolved to try and inserted the point of his sword at London. He was in Europe when the contract of sale was signed by his son. Before sailing from New York he had spoken of his plans for the next season in New York and Philadelphia. These plans embraced a reform in the sale of tickets, something like that which was forced upon the Metropolitan Company three years afterwards by a disgraceful scandal, and also the employment of a Russian ballet towards which the thoughts of managers in London and New York had been turned by a Parisian success. Though barred from the field of grand opera, that of comic opera or operetta was free to him and to this form of entertainment he opened the Manhattan Opera House on September 20, 1910, with an exceedingly bright little piece called "Hans, the Flute Player" adapted from the French, which had won success at its first production at Monte Carlo in 1906 and at the Théâtre Apollo in Paris in the spring of 1910. Called before the curtain after the second act on the first night in New York Mr. Hammerstein told his audience that he intended going to London, not for the purpose of making it his permanent home but to advance the new enterprise on which he had embarked. I make no doubt but that he had already formed a resolution to set up a rival to the ancient establishment in Covent Garden and that his visit was for the purpose of finding a site for a new opera house. About a year before this time a wide thoroughfare had been opened in London in the heart of a district heavy with the clusterings of theatrical traditions. It was called The Kingsway, was about equidistant from Covent Garden and Drury Lane, and debouched into the Strand. In this spacious street Mr. Hammerstein caused a beautiful theater to be built of granite and marble at a cost of about $750,000. Of the money expended on the construction $300,000 came from the sale of the Philadelphia and New York interests, that sum being still in his hands after he had paid off the mortgages held by Mr. Stotesbury, similar encumbrances on the Manhattan Opera House, Victoria and Republic Theaters which he owned in New York, and other debts amounting to about $150,000.

With characteristic confidence and energy he began his London experiment and had seen the foundations of his new building laid when he returned to New York in January, 1911. Characteristic also was his reply to a reporter's question: "What do you intend to open the house with?"

"With debts," was the reply; "I always open a house with debts."

Oscar Hammerstein's London Opera House

There was a suggestion that the English people might not take him seriously and out came another exhibition of his character:

"I will make them. It is not a question of what they will do, but of what I shall do."

The story of the London attempt can be only a short interlude here. The opera house in The Kingsway was opened on November 13, 1911, with a performance of "Quo Vadis." Mr. Hammerstein was his own manager; he asked no English help, but called to his side two trusted, faithful, and capable servants from New York, Lyle D. Andrews and Jacques Coini, who had been respectively treasurer and stage-manager at the Manhattan Opera House. At the outset fortune seemed to smile propitiously upon the undertaking. On the opening night the receipts amounted to over $6,600, and in the first week to over $21,000. A winter season of 15 weeks was given at which 12 operas were performed, and a summer season of 12 weeks from April 22 to July 13, 1912. Among the operas performed in this second season was "Les Cloches de Corneville," which the redoubtable manager himself conducted. Then came an incident of a kind familiar enough to operatic history but concerning which the public is seldom informed. The closing days of Mr. Stanton's consulship at the Metropolitan Opera House saw such an occurrence, the closing days of Mr. Grau's another, in the first of which the reward took the shape of baubles distributed by royalty; and suspicion has touched at least one of the productions under the present administration. Doings of the kind involve no moral turpitude, yet they are always surrounded with mystery. In the present instance a wealthy and titled amateur composer wrote an opera, wanted to have it performed, and paid the piper for his dance. Lord Howard de Walden's "The Children of Don," for which Josef Holbrooke composed the music, was produced by Mr. Hammerstein a fortnight before the close of the season. It was a pretentious work and made a dismal failure, so great a failure, indeed, that although Lord Howard was the holder of a mortgage for forty thousand pounds on the opera house and had contributed a large sum for the production of the opera, Mr. Hammerstein refused to give it the third performance which the composer asked or demanded. Thereupon there came a rupture of relations which had fateful consequences.

On the last night of his season Mr. Hammerstein, following his American methods, addressed the London public in a speech from the stage in which he said that he was going to New York to look after his home interests but would be back for the next season with new singers and new operas. The business which called him back to New York grew out of entanglements at the Victoria Theater, which had been the most prolific source of supply in his earlier enterprises. Returned to America he made a contract of rental and sale of the Kingsway house through Mr. Andrews to Mr. Stanley Denton, a gentleman who was reputed to have an income of £30,000 a year. The new manager made the theater the home of a review entitled "Come Over Here," which achieved a popular success. The overhead expenses of the house, however, were so great that he became involved in financial difficulties and he defaulted in his payments to Mr. Hammerstein. Thereupon Lord Howard foreclosed the mortgage and became the owner of the house. Mr. Hammerstein lost the whole amount of his investment.

Returned to New York Mr. Hammerstein devoted the summer to an adjustment of the affairs of the Victoria Theater and to a search for new worlds to conquer, with faith in himself undimmed and courage undaunted. Up from the quagmire flew the old *ignis fatuus* of opera at popular prices. In November, 1912, he broached his new scheme to the public. He wanted to build another opera house and in it produce English opera at prices ranging from three dollars down to fifty cents, but he confessed that to do this it would be necessary for him to obtain the consent of the Metropolitan Opera Company, the contract with which, he said, prevented him from giving opera on his own account and also stood in the way of his acceptance of two offers of assistance, one from a music-publishing house, the other from a Russian impresario connected with the Royal Opera at St. Petersburg. The statement was characteristic of the time when the air was full of stories about new rivals of the Metropolitan Company and when no tale could be told so absurd that it would not find publication and credence. There was no Royal Opera in St. Petersburg with which an impresario could be connected, but only the Imperial Russian Opera administered through a court official by the Czar himself, who was not likely to concern himself with operatic projects in America. As to the other interest the statement sounded like nothing more than an echo of some talk in which Mr. Tito Ricordi had indulged two years before at a juncture when the Metropolitan people professed to be big with an ambition to foster opera in the vernacular. At a dinner which grew out of a movement inaugurated by the Metropolitan Company's offer of a prize for an opera in English by a native composer Mr. Ricordi, whose publications occupied a large part of the Metropolitan repertory, had considerable to say about the need of a greater number of opera houses in the United States. The talk was a symptom of the prevalent operatic mania, anything but philanthropic in motive, and before Mr. Ricordi returned to Italy he had given a quietus to the story that the house of Ricordi was about to engage in such an enterprise as the sanguine champions of American opera thought. Italian publishers control opera houses in Italy not for altruistic ends or always for the good of art but to promote and safeguard their publications. It was because of a fear in some circles that the system might be introduced here that the Metropolitan Company fell under suspicion in 1908-09.

In taking his preliminary steps Mr. Hammerstein was not

86 AN APPEAL TO THE METROPOLITAN COMPANY

inconsiderate of his obligations to the Metropolitan Company. He addressed a letter to the directors of the company outlining his plan and asking their consent to its execution. He also consulted Paul Cravath, Esq., one of the company's directors, who as their legal adviser had drawn up the contract of sale. Mr. Cravath was not inimical to the project, in which, like Mr. Hammerstein, he saw an educational influence which might in time result in making the popular opera a feeder to the more aristocratic establishment. It so chanced, however, that Messrs. Kahn and Vanderbilt were in Europe at the time and a consideration of the letter had to wait upon their return. After three weeks, on December 18, 1912, the directors gave their answer refusing to allow Mr. Hammerstein to proceed with his project. Their refusal, they said, was based upon their belief that New York could not or would not support two opera houses and that Mr. Hammerstein's project threatened harm to the existing institution. They gave the full text of their letter to the newspapers. They quoted Mr. Hammerstein's words (or rather those of his son Arthur, who had acted as his attorney-in-fact) in which he spoke of the enormous increase in the cost of opera by reason of the exactions of singers, the ruinous cost of the rivalry between the houses, and his conviction that one house could serve the cause of opera better than two and that the Metropolitan, because of its practical subsidy through its stockholders, could better fulfil the public need. The statement held out the prospect of opera in English at the Metropolitan " on a basis which would avoid conflict with the present season of opera in Italian, French, and German." Even " with its enormous success " of the preceding year, said the letter, the Metropolitan Company had " made practically no profit " and better results were not expected for the current year.

On the day on which the letter of the directors appeared Mr. Hammerstein, in the breezy way which made the news-

THE CITY CLUB AND "MUNICIPAL OPERA" 87

papers his willing bellmen and even champions, announced that he was willing to go ahead with his project regardless of the terms of his agreement. " If the press and the public give me sufficient evidence that they want me to give grand opera in English I will do it," were the words of his defiance. A new operatic project essentially like that of Mr. Hammerstein now began to take shape in the City Club. Whether or not it was born of the purpose of Mr. Hammerstein and the refusal of the Metropolitan directors I shall not attempt to say. It was suspected by some that the project rooted in the plan which had been outlined in the letter to the Metropolitan directors and the fact that the leading spirits of that directorate at once gave it moral and physical support lent the semblance at least of probability to the theory that the City Club's scheme of giving " municipal " opera in the New Theater, now called the Century Opera House, had been conceived for the purpose of discouraging Mr. Hammerstein from proceeding with his undertaking. Mr. Hammerstein made the charge openly at the time and met with a denial from the spokesman of the Metropolitan Company. In his latter-day communications on the subject with me he has not reiterated it, but seems to have assumed that the plan was born in the minds of some of the gentlemen of the Club before he addressed the Metropolitan directors. I am now concerned with other matters; the history of the undertaking which grew out of the public-spirited endeavor of the City Club deserves some attention which it shall receive in these chapters later. Mr. Hammerstein's acts now become more significant than his words. In March, 1913, he bought a plot of land at Lexington Avenue and Fifty-first Street and announced that he would begin within two weeks to build an opera house on it which would be opened on November 10. The style of performance should be that which he had proposed to the directors of the Metropolitan Company. The site was that formerly occupied by the Nursery and

Child's Hospital, 75 feet on Lexington Avenue by 220 feet on Fifty-first Street. The building was to cost $1,000,000. Through the newspapers he told the public that he was going to give opera in English, and if the Metropolitan directors didn't like it they might go to the courts for redress. No other man being found willing to throw himself into the breach for English opera he was going to do it. Why? He answered the question thus: "I am a child of New York. I revel in its greatness. It has about a hundred theaters, has a good society opera house, but has no opera house for the population at large. Our municipality can not and will not aid in the founding and maintaining of such an edifice and to our government such a proposition never appeals. With what I am doing I will earn the approbation of my fellow-citizens and the millions of lovers of music and adherents of musical culture. . . . The house will be known as the 'American Opera House.' I think I will open Monday, November 10, at 8 o'clock."

A merry war was thus proclaimed and right merrily was it carried on in the newspapers. On March 27 the Metropolitan directors gave out the text of the clause in the contract of sale which prohibited Mr. Hammerstein and his son Arthur from embarking in any grand opera enterprises until 1920. It seemed to be as ironbound as verbose legal phraseology could make it and deserves to be reproduced here as a matter of curiosity if for no other reason. The agreement was made on April 26, 1910, on which day $100,000 earnest money was paid on the contract price of $1,200,000. In it Oscar Hammerstein and his son Arthur as his attorney-in-fact and manager covenanted jointly and severally

that they will not, nor will either of them at any time hereafter within ten years from the date hereof be or become directly or indirectly engaged or interested or connected either alone or as a member or members of any firm or partnership or in conjunction with others, or as an officer, director, manager, stockholder, employe of any corporation that may be or become engaged in any such business, or as an employe in any other capacity whatsoever in the cities of New York, Boston, Philadelphia or Chicago in the business of producing grand opera . . . in any language, or any opera, operetta, or comic opera that has ever been produced at the Metropolitan Opera House or the Manhattan Opera House in the city of New York, or any opera or comic opera that may at any time hereafter have been first given at the Metropolitan Opera House or any opera house in the city of New York, and that no opera, operetta or comic opera of the character described will be permitted or suffered to be produced upon the premises now occupied by the Manhattan Opera House within five years from the date hereof, nor will the vendor or the party of the second part be connected in any business that interferes with or encroaches upon the field now occupied by the Metropolitan Company.

And so on at great length and equal breathlessness. When this portion of the contract of sale was made public Mr. Hammerstein, using his convenient medium of communication with the people, retorted that the overtures to purchase his opera interests had come from the Metropolitan directors, and that he had not listened to them until he had broken down so completely in mental and physical health that his physician had commanded him to cease work. Whereupon he had put the matter in the hands of his son Arthur and sailed for Europe leaving a power of attorney for his son. He denied that he had ever contemplated abandoning the giving of opera, but in his power of attorney, signed on April 15, 1910, he had expressly empowered his son to enter into an agreement in writing to the effect that he would not for the term of ten years be engaged directly or indirectly or in any way with the business of producing opera.

On April 18, 1913, Mr. Hammerstein announced to the world that he had borrowed $335,000 for his operatic enterprise and would begin building as soon as he got a title to the ground. Twelve days later he gave out a statement that if the City Club persisted in its purpose he would abandon his English opera plan and enter into competition with the Metropolitan Opera Company by giving French and Italian opera at Metropolitan prices. Later, I believe, he borrowed $450,000 from the Manhattan Life Insurance Company which he put into the Lexington Avenue property in addition to $200,000 which he had obtained from the United Booking Company for the privilege of giving vaudeville at the Palace Theater which was within the zone in which he held a monopoly for the Victoria Theater. From the profits of this playhouse he had accumulated a further sum of $100,000. He had made contracts with singers confident that his original project would not meet with opposition from the Metropolitan directors. He had taken counsel of distinguished jurists and rejected the common-sense advice of those concerned with him in the administration of his theatrical affairs. With his opera company he purposed to give performances in a large number of cities throughout the country and to sow opera houses broadcast wherever he could obtain a gift of land on which to build and a loan. He probably felt that he was justified in his effort to give opera for a supposedly famishing public no matter what interpretation the purchasers of his interests in New York and Philadelphia put upon the contract he had made with them. He was warned by them on May 15 that they would take legal steps to enjoin him if he persisted in his purpose, but the only effect of the admonition was to call out more of what the newspapers considered his humor. Thereupon, on July 2, 1913, the Metropolitan Company filed a summons and complaint in the Supreme Court of the State of New York asking that he and his son be enjoined from putting their purpose to give opera into effect. The answers of Mr. Hammerstein admitted nearly every essential allegation in the complaint, but set up a series of affirmative defenses, telling at great length how the plaintiff had forced him into the contract for the purpose of creating a monopoly, taken advantage of his wrecked body and perturbed mind, had tempted a dozen singers away from him, compelled him to pay other artists more than they were worth, and brought him to the verge of ruin. He sought refuge in the plea that the Metropolitan Opera Company was engaged in interstate trade and commerce and that its acts towards him were in restraint of trade and fell under the condemnation of the federal statute called the Sherman Act.

After the issue had been joined Mr. Hammerstein continued to publish his pronunciamentos in the newspapers. He would begin his season on November 17 and play English opera all the year around, and French and Italian part of the time. This was in October when the newspapers were showing a generous spirit toward the Century Opera, which had crystallized into a fact. If judgment went against him in the equity proceedings he would turn his contracts and properties over to a corporation which was to be organized for the purpose of giving opera in the Lexington Avenue Opera House. The Metropolitan Opera Company, having filed a demurrer to the answers of the defendants, finally decided to quit trying the case in the newspapers and filed a motion for judgment on the pleadings averring that the defendants had admitted every material allegation in the complaint and urging that the defenses set up were unsound in law and even if true were immaterial. This motion was argued before Judge Pendleton of the Supreme Court on October 18, 1913. Before judgment was rendered Mr. Hammerstein announced another change of plans. The completion of his house had been delayed by the architects, but the theater would be opened in January, 1914, and a series of operas in English would be given at popular prices. In due course Judge Pendleton pronounced judgment, granting the injunction prayed for by the Metropolitan Opera Company, holding that the giving of opera was not trade or commerce and that the Sherman anti-trust law had nothing to do with the case. This judgment was affirmed on appeal by the Appellate Division of the Supreme Court in April, 1914, but long before then work had stopped at the opera house and

Mr. Hammerstein's protestations of an unalterable determination to give operatic representations whether or no also came to an end. In view of the fact that the enterprise fostered by the City Club had made a loss of $50,000 in the season, which also came to an end for the time being about the time of the decision, Mr. Hammerstein's judicious friends and counselors were disposed to congratulate him upon his involuntary inactivity, but he was after all more an object of pity than felicitation. Within four months three of his sons died and his health was shattered that as I write he is not yet fully recovered, though some of the old spirit seems to be flaming up within him.* After some delay he completed the building of the opera house and it was used for picture shows and vaudeville performances, with a melancholy suggestion of its original purpose in the way of performances of fragments of operas. It was found to be impossible to meet the running expenses of the house

---

* Mr. Hammerstein died in New York on August 1, 1919, while this book was in process of manufacture. He was a native of Berlin, where he was born in 1847. When he was sixteen years old he left his father's home, and came to New York, where he learned, and for a time followed, the trade of cigar-making. In 1870 he established and became the editor of a journal devoted to the tobacco trade and at about the same time associated himself with Mr. Adolph Neuendorff in the management of a German theatrical enterprise which was housed at the Germania Theater in East Fourteenth Street. With his partner he was instrumental in bringing Heinrich Conried to America. A number of inventions in cigar-making machinery and speculations in real estate put him on the road to financial prosperity and a liking for theatrical management led him into the undertakings in which he accomplished many notable things but led to financial disaster at last. In October, 1891, he entered into rivalry with Rudolph Aronson for the first performance in New York of "Cavalleria Rusticana," and in the same year he built a theater in One Hundred and Twenty-fifth Street which he called the Harlem Opera House. Here he made unsuccessful efforts for a short time to give operatic performances in English and German. Two years later he built the first Manhattan Opera House in West Thirty-fourth Street, at which he made a more ambitious effort with Moszkowski's "Boabdil" and Beethoven's "Fidelio," but found himself at the end of

from the receipts, however, and Mr. Hammerstein failing to pay the interest and other charges the Manhattan Life Insurance foreclosed its mortgage and purchased the property to protect its loan. Only in the season of 1917-18, when it was hired by the Chicago Opera Company for a season of opera, did its walls give back the echoes with which Mr. Hammerstein contemplated that they should always ring.

his resources at the end of a fortnight. The opera house became first a music hall managed by Koster and Bial and finally gave way to a mercantile house. In April, 1907, he opened his second Manhattan Opera House, which became the rival for a space of the Metropolitan establishment. Of the ten or dozen theaters which he built in the course of his career only two or three were sources of financial profit to him. (See "Chapters of Opera," by H. E. Krehbiel, New York, Henry Holt and Co., pages 220 *et seq.*, and Chapters XXII, XXIV, and XXV.)

CHAPTER V

LAST SEASONS AT THE MANHATTAN OPERA HOUSE

MR. HAMMERSTEIN'S PROMISES AND PERFORMANCES—CIRCUS ADVERTISING—SPECIAL REPRESENTATIONS AND PRICES—MLLE. LABIA—REVIVAL OF "SAMSON ET DALILA"—"LE JONGLEUR DE NOTRE DAME"—ENGAGEMENT OF LINA CAVALIERI—MISS GARDEN RESENTS HER DESIRE TO APPEAR IN THAÏS—MANAGERS AND NEWSPAPER-MEN COME TO BLOWS—MISS GARDEN HOLDS THE FIELD—PRODUCTION OF "SALOME"—HISTORY OF THE OPERA IN AMERICA—OPÉRA COMIQUE AND OPÉRA BOUFFE—"PRINCESSE D'AUBERGE"—"HÉRODIADE"—"SAPHO"—JEAN DE RESZKE AND TRANSLATIONS—"TANNHÄUSER" IN FRENCH—"GRISÉLIDIS"—"ELEKTRA"

THE third season of grand opera at the Manhattan Opera House began on November 9, 1908, and ended on March 27, 1909. During this period of twenty weeks there were five regular performances a week for which subscriptions had been invited in June. Had the rule been strictly followed the season would have been compassed by one hundred representations; but advantage was taken, in accordance with New York custom, of occasions which seemed auspicious, such as popular holidays and the advent of a sensational novelty, to add four to the number of representations. In this instance there was only a quasi-novelty, Richard Strauss's "Salome," which had been flamboyantly advertised by the circumstances attending its production and withdrawal at the Metropolitan Opera House in the season of 1906-07;* but Mr. Hammerstein took occasion to prove the disinterestedness of his aims and the sincerity of his protestations by raising the price of admission on its first per-

* See "Chapters of Opera," pp. 343-357.

formance. This proceeding, in which he was but following the example of his rival, may, I suppose, be looked upon as a venial sin. The public was used to it and expected nothing else. Looked at in the light thrown on it by some of the incidents of the rivalry between the opera houses, however, it becomes worthy of comment for instruction in righteousness if not for reproof. If we could but believe the asseverations put forth by the managers of the contending opera houses there never was a period in the history of opera in which managerial altruism reached such a noble height as it did during the years of rivalry between the Metropolitan and Manhattan establishments. The dear public's consuming hunger for opera was to be gratified and its taste uplifted no matter what sacrifices of money were entailed by the devoted purveyors of the costly entertainment. Nevertheless every opportunity to exploit popular curiosity concerning a new work was seized upon as an excuse for a representation outside of the subscription and at advanced prices of admission. This proceeding, together with a system of brigandage practised by the box-offices in collusion with the ticket-speculators, made the people pay a great deal more for their luxury than a glance at the official prospectuses would lead one to conclude. In a few years it also led to some scandalous doings involving the Metropolitan Company which led up to the gates of a prison and ought to have penetrated them. Of that I shall speak later. Mr. Hammerstein's administration gave fewer instances of such exploiting of the public than did that of his rivals, but the reason might be found, probably, in the fact that he was not blessed by so large a list of subscribers that the general public looked upon the opportunity to enjoy the first night of a novelty as a gracious benison. Besides he had Philadelphia on his hands. His double-headed enterprise had reached such a stage of forwardness when he put forth his first extended announcement of the season that his new opera house was building and his companies engaged.

In June, 1908, he informed the public through the newspapers that the New York and Philadelphia houses were to be separate and distinct establishments so far as orchestra, chorus, ballet, and working personnel were concerned but would be united in "jubilee" performances in both cities "the like of which had never been attempted in any part of the world." He had retained Cleofonte Campanini as conductor for New York and engaged Signor Sturani, of Rome, as conductor for Philadelphia. His principal singers were to be Mmes. Melba, Tetrazzini, Maria Labia, Doria, Mariska Aldrich, Gerville-Reache, Garden, Agostinelli, Zepilli, Trentini, Penzano, and Severina, and Messrs. Zenatello, Dalmorès, Renaud, Sammarco, Gilibert, Dufranne, and Arimondi, the majority of them known, and some of them greatly and deservedly admired by the New York public. "Taking great pleasure in coming into conflict with traditions in grand opera," he announced with a flourish his intention to introduce a novelty which had "never before been tried anywhere," namely, "grand opera pantomime," which was to take the place of ballets when short operas were given. He had discovered the authors of such pantomimes and purposed to lift them and the art-form out of the obscurity which had thitherto surrounded them. "Salome" was to be produced in a "chaste, sublime, and impressive manner." He had purchased 35,000 yards of canvas for scenery in Glasgow and before July 1 would set three hundred costume-makers at work on his theatrical wardrobe. His weekly salary-list in the two houses was to exceed $75,000. I do not set forth these things because I think them diverting, but because they comport with my purpose to show a picture of the times. Had Mr. Hammerstein not been humored in the belief that such circus "touting" was tolerable to the public, he would not have indulged it. Had the newspapers not had an equally poor opinion of the intelligence and taste of their readers they would not have printed it without commenting on its vulgar grandiloquence. It was really for their benefit that the tone was adopted, for when Mr. Hammerstein issued his official prospectus it was found to contain nothing of this fulminant fanfaronnade; its proclamations were succinct and dignified. Decorum marked even his promises touching the ballet pantomimes; but when Mlle. Odette Valery, a dancer who was to be the wonderful interpreter of the wonderful works with which he was to amaze the town, arrived in New York the newspapers entertained their readers with an account of the two cobras and an asp which were booked to make their first appearance with the lady in "Samson et Dalila." The dancer did make a show of the snakes, I believe, in a few performances, but nothing more was heard of the pantomimes.

In his prospectus Mr. Hammerstein specifically promised to produce "Samson et Dalila" by Saint-Saëns, "Salome" by Richard Strauss, "Le Jongleur de Notre Dame" and "Grisélidis" by Massenet, and "Princesse d'Auberge" by Jan Blockx. He brought all of them out except "Grisélidis." In the list which he was less specifically bound to perform were Massenet's "Manon," Bizet's "Les Pêcheurs de Perles," Verdi's "Falstaff," Breton's "Dolores," Giordano's "Andrea Chenier" and "Siberia," Donizetti's "Linda di Chamounix," Verdi's "Un Ballo in Maschera" and "Ernani," all of which fell by the board. The chief features of interest were the novelties and the singing of Mme. Melba in "La Bohème," "Otello," and "Rigoletto" between December 14 and January 11, which was the period of her engagement. In Mr. Hammerstein's preceding seasons the chief deficiency in his forces was in the women's contingent. This was measurably made good by the presence in the new company of Mlle. Labia, who effected her American début on the opening night in "Tosca." The lady had not only youthfulness and loveliness of form and feature to commend her, but also youthfulness and loveliness of voice and a fine complement of dramatic talent. Her facial expressions, movements, gestures, and poses all published a vitality which made one harmony with her vibrant vocal expression. There was fine metal in her voice and much emotional color. In quality it reminded me frequently of Calvé's voice when it was in its prime, especially in the higher register, and it was given out with greater spontaneity. A production of historical interest was that of "Samson et Dalila" on November 13. The music of this opera was familiar to the New York public from frequent performances in concert style since its first production sixteen years before by the Oratorio Society. Once within this period an attempt had been made to give it dramatic representation. This was on February 8, 1895, when it was brought forward at the Metropolitan Opera House for the purpose of displaying the physical and vocal strenuousness of Signor Tamagno. There were hopes then that the opera might be added to the repertory of the lyric playhouse in Broadway, but they went down with the ruins of Dagon's temple in the last act. Mr. Hammerstein's performance showed that, despite the predominantly oratorio character of much of its music, the work has considerable dramatic vitality, and since its revival at the Metropolitan Opera House in the season 1915-16 it has remained in the effective repertory of that establishment, though largely through the agency of Signor Caruso.

The first real novelty of the season was "Le Jongleur de Notre Dame," which had its first performance in America on November 27, 1908, with the following distribution of parts:

```
Jean, the Juggler .............................. Mary Garden
Boniface, the Cook ........................... Maurice Renaud
The Prior .................................... Hector Dufranne
The Poet ......................................... Louis Vallez
The Painter ............................... Andrea de Segurola
The Sculptor ........................................ M. Vieulle
The Musician ................................. Armand Crabbe
```

The old tradition of the monk who in his youth had been a juggler and who, while his artistic companions were practising their arts within the walls of the monastery, sought to do honor to the Virgin Mother by performing his mountebank tricks in secret before her altar, was put into shape for M. Massenet by Maurice Lena. It is a quaint and lovable tale. The mixture of devotion and the arts characteristic of the monastic life of the Middle Ages provided an unusual but nevertheless inviting background for an opera. Its obvious drawback lay in the fact that it afforded no opportunity for the introduction of the female voice, for there was no way in which the element of love between man and woman, which has been the most pervasive motive for dramatic writing since the art began, could be introduced into it without spoiling the tale. For Miss Garden's sake, we were told (though I am still skeptical on the point), M. Massenet rewrote the part of Jean. The device might have added a desirable variety to the music had it been entrusted for execution to a better singer than Miss Garden, or an actress more imbued with a sense of the ingenuous pathos of the story. Under the circumstances of the performances I could but regret the change. The affecting note of sincerity which provides a potent charm in the mediæval tale was turned into a dissonant note by the lady's silly by-play during M. Renaud's touching recital of the legend of the sage-bush, which is one of the gems of the score. The first impression created in me by the music was that it was more ingenious than inspired. It suggested an exaggerated eclecticism ranging from the modern French to the ancient ecclesiastical styles, with somewhat abrupt transitions from one style to the other.

On January 19, 1909, Mr. Hammerstein informed the public through the newspapers that he had engaged Lina Cavalieri for his company. The lady, better endowed with physical charms than artistic, had been a member of the Metropolitan company in the previous season and was now conducting a "beauty shop" in Fifth Avenue. "Salome" was in preparation at the Manhattan and its production was expected within ten days. Mr. Hammerstein said that he could not expect more from Miss Garden than the performances of "Salome" and "Pelléas et Mélisande" for several weeks, and that he had enlisted Miss Cavalieri's services especially for "Thaïs," an opera which had become popular and which he wanted to keep in his list. Thereby he opened another chapter in New York's Operatic Book of Scandal. Miss Garden at once made a vigorous protest against the assignment to Miss Cavalieri of a part which she had created in America. Both singers had appeared in the opera in Paris, Miss Cavalieri having been the heroine at its most recent revival there; but Miss Garden, who was born in Scotland and brought up in the United States, was of the opinion that an Italian lady brought up in Europe could not properly represent a courtesan of ancient Alexandria as conceived by a group of French authors. Miss Garden therefore promptly hired a lawyer to protect her monopoly of the privilege of displaying her physical charms with the scantiest garments allowable to the public gaze. Mr. Hammerstein had covenanted with Miss Cavalieri (and the public by announcement) that the inestimable privilege should be Miss Cavalieri's also; but the contract proved to be in a double sense *nudum pactum.* Miss Garden had her lawyer; Mr. Hammerstein a press agent. The case was taken to that public forum, the newspapers. Miss Garden served notice on her manager that she had summarily severed her connection with his company. The manager capitulated without more ado. Miss Cavalieri asked that the opera be stricken from her list in a letter which was printed on the morning of the day when the opera was repeated with Miss Garden in the character of the Alexandrian woman who had lived a life of harlotry and died the death of a saint. She renewed her contract with Mr. Hammerstein, who agreed that thenceforth as long as she was engaged by him no one but she should appear at his performances in any new character which she had created except with her consent in writing. Both ladies were engaged for the next season, when Miss Cavalieri had an opportunity to enact the part of Massenet's Salomé in "Hérodiade," a woman of a different type than that conceived by Richard Strauss and begotten by Oscar Wilde. The season was less than a month old, however, when another aspirant for the mingled roses and penitential weeds of Anatole France's heroine appeared on the scene. This was Miss Carmen Melis (whose name should have justified her art), who said that she wanted to show what she could do with Thaïs and could not see why the part should be held in trust by any singer. Miss Garden disposed of the presumptuous newcomer in short order by informing Mr. Hammerstein (of course, through that favorite medium of communication between artists and managers, the newspapers) that the moment any singer other than she sang the part she would walk out of the theater. The opera was sung six times in 1909-10, but Miss Garden remained the only Thaïs known to New York until April 25, 1912, when Mme. Lavarenne appeared in the part in the Lyric Theater at a performance by the New Orleans Opera Company. Miss Farrar threw her garments into the ring at the Metropolitan Opera House on February 16, 1917. Once again in this season Mr. Hammerstein tempted the fates as embodied in the redoubtable Scottish woman. He asked her permission to perform "Le Jongleur de Notre Dame" in its original form—that is, with a man-singer in the part of Jean. She gave her consent and even said that she would buy a box and witness the performance; but when Mr. Devries made a success in the part Miss Garden exacted and obtained an apology from her manager.

In the moment of Miss Garden's triumph in the "Thaïs" affair members of the journalistic areopagus became involved in the quarrel. The story had gone out among the gossips of the press that Mr. Hammerstein had been paid to offer the delectable privilege in controversy to Miss Cavalieri. The *New York Press* newspaper sent two reporters to the manager, who asked if the story was true. Mr. Hammerstein ejected them from his office and held language in a letter to the managing editor of the paper which was highly reprehensible in him and highly derogatory to the reporters. Thereupon the two reporters, accompanied by their managing editor, sought Mr. Hammerstein in upper Broadway, and, coming upon him as he was leaving the Knickerbocker Hotel, demanded an apology. He refused to make it, and they fell upon him, smote him with their fists, *vi et armis* landing several blows upon his body. For this Mr. Hammerstein caused their arrest on a criminal charge. The next day there were two physical collisions between the newspaper-men and Mr. Arthur Hammerstein, who had been challenged to a trial at fisticuffs by the manager editor and had accepted the gage as the champion of his father. The first violent meeting took place outside the police court at which the criminal charge was to be tried; the second within its walls. The laws of the State of New York and the dignity of the tribunal had been shockingly violated, but no punishment was meted out. The criminal causes and an action for damages begun by the musical critic of the newspaper dribbled along until they were lost in the sands of time. And Miss Garden and Miss Cavalieri both signed contracts with Mr. Hammerstein for the next season.

On January 28, 1909, in the midst of the painful perturbations which I have recorded, "Salome" was produced in a French version at the Manhattan Opera House and Miss Garden had an opportunity to divest herself of her clothing piecemeal in the presence of a public with a well-whetted curiosity. The story of the first production of the opera at the Metropolitan Opera House and its suppression at the command of the directors of the owners of that institution in the season of 1906-07 is fully told in my book " Chapters of Opera." Had the original production been spared the interference of the Metropolitan directors, the question of the attitude of New York's music lovers toward the work would soon have been settled and the public been spared Mr. Hammerstein's revamping of the unsavory mess. It was no secret in January, 1907, among those familiar with operatic affairs that a failure of the drama was presaged by the small sale of seats for the representations projected by Mr. Conried and diligently kept before the public while the controversy between Mr. Conried and the Metropolitan Opera and Real Estate Company was raging. It is very likely that the astute Mr. Hammerstein saw the handwriting on the wall at the time, for three or four days after the work had been performed, and while the question of its withdrawal was still pending, he told me that he had declined to purchase the performing rights in the preceding summer, partly on the advice of Mme. Lilli Lehmann, and that he was glad he had done so; adding that he would not produce "Salome" even if Mr. Conried surrendered the performing rights. The reason of his subsequent change of mind is not far to seek, nor need we attach any more importance to his broken purpose than Jove is said to do to lovers' perjuries. Mr. Hammerstein would not have thought of producing "Salome" if it had not been for the opportunity which it gave for that association to which most that made appeal to his public was due. The curiosity which was potent enough to fill his theater at doubled prices of admission was directed not to the play of Wilde, not to the musical investiture of that play by Richard Strauss, but to Mary Garden, and to her chiefly because of the lascivious dance. Mr. Conried had felt the public pulse and renounced his project with but little show of unwillingness. There was talk by him and the directors of his company of transferring the performance to another theater; but it dribbled away. So did the proclaimed purpose to give it "on the road." So did the announced intention to give a long series of representations before the subscription season of 1907-08. Mr. Conried surrendered his rights in the drama at what must have been a large pecuniary sacrifice; and within a year or so Mr. Hammerstein acquired them.

Why? After his own utterances on the subject I can not believe that he had become convinced that the withdrawal of the work from the repertory of the Metropolitan Opera House had left the public hungering with so consuming a hunger that to satisfy it was either an artistic duty or a promising financial enterprise. No. A new factor had entered into the proposition. Miss Garden wanted to be seen in the titular rôle, convinced that by her acting, dancing, and disrobing she could achieve the success which had not looked with propitious eye upon the first production. Moreover, Miss Garden's vision was not directed upon New York alone. Paris had welcomed Miss Fremstad's moving dramatic impersonation and hailed her interpretation of the music with delight. Even if Miss Garden could not hope to cope with Miss Fremstad's singing, she could outdo her acting if she were to do the dance of the seven veils herself and not by proxy, as Miss Fremstad had done it, and thus throw a shamelessly generous exhibition of her body into the balance. Miss Garden could not sing in German, however, nor could any of her associates at the Manhattan Opera House. So the project was evolved of performing the drama in French, a proceeding which did not seem very revolutionary, since Oscar Wilde had originally written " Salome " in that language, and the English version, which had failed to gain a foothold in Great Britain and America, and the German, which had ravaged Germany, were both translations. Paris heard " Salome " in German; New York was the first city in the world to hear it in French.

This sounds somewhat paradoxical and perverse; but perversion is the theme of " Salome " in all its elements and to discuss it anew because of one added aspect would scarcely be worth while. Nor is there much need of discussion of the effect of a French text upon the music. By the composer's own confession, words and the human voice were tolerated by him only as necessary evils. Against his will was he compelled to consort with the earth-born babblers of articulate speech. Naturally there was one viewpoint from which the association of such music as this with the French language seemed anomalous. Elegance of expression is inherent in all forms of French art; dramatic truthfulness and vigor, sometimes to the verge of uncouthness, of German. The nervous chatter of Burrian's German Herod was much more characteristic of the neurasthenic created by Strauss than was the better cadenced and more or less tuneful singing of Dalmorès's Tetrarch. But this was largely a matter of interpretation. The French artist would not miss an opportunity to sing a phrase if it offered itself; the German was willing to sacrifice everything to an illumination of the pathological nature of Herod's pitiful case. As for the preachments and denunciations of Joachanan, in which is contained the bulk of the sustained music of the score except the final beatification of the necrophilism of the unspeakable Salome, they did not seem to be either helped or hindered by the change of tongue. The stage-set was beautiful, though the picture was marred by incongruities and anachronisms such as the introduction of the familiar winged bull of Assyria into Herod's palace. The light effects were of great beauty and the people of the play magnificently caparisoned. The color scheme was more garish than in Mr. Conried's production and there was more than a suggestion of barbarism in the habiliments of Herod, but these high lights only served to accentuate the beauty of Miss Garden's person and raiment. Of the latter, however, there was very little, and in the climax of the dance the utmost limit of disrobing ever reached by a lyric artist or actress within a long memory was attained. To have thrown off any more in emulation of Istar she would have been all but obliged to doff her cuticle.

For the sake of history the story of the opera's career outside of New York may be briefly rehearsed. Mr. Hammerstein announced it in his prospectuses for Philadelphia and Boston. In the former city the Methodist and Baptist clergymen made an energetic protest. The Presbyterians followed on the eve of the opening of the opera house, adopting a preamble and resolutions which described the work as "a realistic portrayal of the immoral motives that resulted in the bloody tragedy of John the Baptist" and "inconsistent with that sacred reverence which all Christians cherish for that godly man." Committees of the Christian League and the State and County Federation of Catholic Societies sent a letter to the mayor of the city on the day before that set for the performance. The mayor not only declined to interfere, but was chairman of a committee of citizens who gave a complimentary dinner to Mr. Hammerstein on the evening of the day. The manager announced that he would produce "Salome," and his purpose was applauded. A week later he announced that the last performance would be on March 1. He did not dare longer withstand the undercurrent of dissent among his subscribers. In Boston the presentation of the opera was opposed by Eben S. Draper, Governor of Massachusetts; George A. Hibbard, mayor of the city; Bishop Lawrence of the Protestant Episcopal Church, Vicar-General George J. Patterson of the Roman Catholic Church, George A. Gordon of the Trinitarian body, ex-Governor Curtis Guild, and other prominent citizens. The representatives of the churches were especially indignant because the date of the projected performance had been set in Holy Week. Hammerstein withdrew the opera.

The last novelty heard in New York in the season 1908-09 was "La Princesse d'Auberge," which Mr. Hammerstein brought forward on March 10, 1909, with the parts distributed among his singers as follows:

Rita, a tavern-keeper's daughter	Mlle. Labia
Katelyne, a widow and shopkeeper	Gerville-Réache
Reinilde, her adopted daughter	Mlle. Zepilli
Merlyn, a young composer of music	M. Valles
Marcus, a fellow-musician	M. Crabbe
Bluta, father of Rita and a tavern-keeper	M. Gilibert
Raino, a blacksmith	M. Dufranne
Rita's sisters	Miss Koelling Miss Tancredi Miss Severina
A student	Sig. Venturini
An old peasant	Sig. Reschiligian
A young peasant	Sig. Daddi
An old servant	Miss Hume
A citizen	Sig. Fosetta

Conductor, Sig. Campanini

The opera, which was sung in French, was originally written in Flemish, and its authors, Nestor de Tiére and Jan Blockx (who died in 1912), were enthusiastic Flamands who strove to keep alive a native expression among their countrymen in the Netherlands. They did not find it an easy task, for, besides Flemish, the inhabitants of what once was Flanders, speak French, Walloon, and Dutch. French art has long pervaded the culture of the country, but the Teutonism of the Flamands is strong and continues to be in rebellion, though peacefully, with Southern ideals—peacefully yet puissantly enough to preserve many idioms as well as customs and manners. It is possible for a student of folk-music, who is keen on the scent of racial and popular idioms, to find Flemish traces in the opera, though it is necessary that his curiosity be piqued and his perceptions sharpened in advance by the discovery that the music does not sound French. Some ten years before this American production the opera had been performed at the Flemish Theater in Antwerp, in a few cities of Holland, and afterward (in French) in Brussels; but its success was local and no greater than that of scores of contemporaneous French, German, and Italian operas which promptly found their way into the limbo of forgotten things. In the search for attributes which promise to bring success works which contain national traits are now receiving unusual attention from managers, and to this tendency the great world war will doubtless give a new impetus. Picturesqueness of scene and attractiveness of musical color frequently atone for lack of depth and beauty of musical thought or melodic invention. New York has been privileged to enjoy much opera of this character in recent years: witness the Japanese pictures and music of "Iris" and "Madama Butterfly"; the Russian of "Siberia," "Boris Godounow," and "Prince Igor"; the mixed Polish and gypsy of Mr. Paderewski's "Manru"; the Spanish of "Carmen" and "La Navarraise"; the Italian of "Pagliacci," "Cavalleria Rusticana," and "A Basso Porto." "Princesse d'Auberge," following the dramatic lines of the three operas last mentioned, deals with a story of Belgian low life. It tells of the moral and physical ruin wrought in a man of fine intellectual fiber by association with vicious and vulgar companions and surrender to debasing appetites. Retribution comes through crime instigated by jealous passion. The cause of the moral devastation and the physical suffering which overwhelm the sweet and innocent with the base and guilty is a wanton who traffics with her charms to promote the business of a dissolute innkeeper. Incidental to the exposition of the story there is an opulent procession of scenes from the life of a city famous for its roystering gaiety whenever occasion invites its populace into its beautiful public places and streets. The city is Brussels, the time the middle of the eighteenth century. The tragic hero of the vulgar tragedy is Merlyn, poet and musician. The woman who wrecks his soul and body is Rita, whose beauty and popularity among the students and gay roysterers of the city have given her the name by which the opera is designated. The fateful agent of the hero's destruction is Rabo, a blacksmith, who had once enjoyed the embraces of Rita but had been cast off in favor of the artist. The innocent sufferers are Kateline, the mother of Merlyn, and Reinilde, a pure maiden who loves him and seeks in vain to win him from his dissolute companionship so that he may be true in service to his art. Secondary to Rabo as a vehicle of fate is Marcus, also a musician, and friend of Merlyn, who is enamored of Reinilde and who to win her for himself contrives to throw his friend into the toils of the wanton. There are other characters in the play who serve purposes not essential to the story, but externally useful—the dissolute father of the siren, who provides the comedy found in the antics of a drunkard, and his three other daughters who, with inferior charms but equal looseness, help Rita carry on the trade of the inn. The posture of the people of the play being thus set forth, the incidents present themselves to the imagination almost involuntarily. In spite of the promptings of his good genius, the prayers of his mother and sweetheart, the artist fails to tear himself away from his Circe. Then comes retribution in the shape of his jealous rival, who provokes a quarrel by denouncing her who had been his bawd, and in the duel which ensues stabs him to death. As he breathes his last, mother and sweetheart enter to proclaim the news that success had crowned the musician's effort to win the national laurel. Maddened by grief and rage, the pure maiden is about to plunge a knife into the profligate woman's heart, but lets it fall and leaves her to the tortures of her conscience.

And now for the Flemish elements of the work. Of what do they consist? The story might be located anywhere in civilized Christendom and its people found there. Not so the scenes. An excellent and characteristic environment for the play had been provided. There are four stage-settings and every one of them was sumptuous and historically and technically correct. These pictures might, of course, be introduced in an opera with French, German, or Italian investiture; but they become doubly effective when viewed through the atmosphere created by Flemish music. This music is recognizable first of all, perhaps, in the large admixture of bell chimes in all the concerted pieces which inspire the popular scenes. When Dr. Burney in his memorable tour through Europe reached Antwerp he descanted first of all on the passion for carillons prevalent in the Netherlands. When he got to Amsterdam he lamented the lack of all music except " the jingling of bells and ducats." The audience on this occasion was entertained by similar sounds. It was only in the dialogue and the dramatic songs that the ear was not saluted by the imitation of bell chimes from the orchestra. In the last act national idioms again had expression in the direct and literal quotation of a Flemish song (written by Prudens van Duyse), which must have amused the hunters of melodic parallels. It is a splendid specimen of tune written in the simple folksong manner, but in its first period there is a strong resemblance to the famous political song of the Netherlanders, " Wilhelmus von Nassauen," and in the second to an American Sunday-school hymn (" I'm a Pilgrim "), a parody of which has long afforded amusement to college students in this country. Musical nationalism was discernible to the more sophisticated minds also in most of the choruses, in which the opera is singularly rich. Though they moved in dance rhythms, there was a sturdiness in their melody which published a Teutonic rather than the Gallic spirit. Also a soundness coupled with elaborateness of structure not ordinarily found in French operas. The composer makes use of Wagner's system of typical phrases and the orchestration is frequently brilliant.

When Mr. Hammerstein issued his prospectus for 1909-10, which proved to be his last season as an operatic impresario, his plans were not fully or accurately formulated. Even the date of the opening was changed afterward from November 15 to November 8; but this was for the purpose of taking advantage of the annual fashionable gathering for the horse show. He, however, promised twenty weeks, and, though ruin was staring him in the face long before the expiration of the term, he kept his promise to the letter. He published no official list of singers, but laid stress upon his list of operas, putting forth the boast that "in the matter of exclusive rights of operas" he stood "unique among impresarios and directors of opera houses in the world." So far as French operas and the United States were concerned, the claim was no doubt justified. The Metropolitan Company had been permitted to become impotent in this department, and, though in its prospectus for the same season it proclaimed the exclusive ownership of nine French operas, only two of them have seen the stage lights at the Metropolitan. Three of the nine were said to be operas by Claude Debussy, and though they have been permitted to figure in the announcements of Mr. Gatti down to the end of the period with which I am particularly concerned, they were little more than flocculent dreams when the composer died on March 26, 1918. Of the operas for which he claimed the sole right of representation in America, Mr. Hammerstein said they were "the masterpieces of living composers," though Offenbach, who composed "Les Contes d'Hoffmann," had long been dead. But that is unessential. "The novelties claimed by another institution," he said, were operas which he had rejected. Obviously he was in a bellicose mood. He had acquired his novelties not by excessive expenditures, but by reason of "the confidence possessed by authors and composers in the abilities of Mr. Hammerstein to properly present their works." These novelties were Richard Strauss's "Elektra" and "Feuersnoth"; Massenet's "Hérodiade," "Grisélidis," "Sapho," and "Cendrillon"; Leoncavallo's "Zaza"; Victor Herbert's "Natoma" and "The Violin Maker of Cremona." The performing rights of "Elektra" he had procured in Berlin three months before the first performance of the opera in Dresden on January 25, 1909. A cabled report concerning that *première* stated that he had secured the American rights for $5,000 cash and a guaranteed royalty of $18,000 for thirty performances in addition to $6,000 for the right of reproducing the music—a phrase which I can not interpret. Nearly $1,000 a night may not have appeared to be an excessive fee to Herr Strauss when he looked upon the world as his oyster, but to enable Mr. Hammerstein to pay it New York would have had to be a worse operatic Bedlam than it was; and that it was bedlamite enough I have tried to show. Deferring the announcement of the full list of singers engaged, he reported the re-engagement of Mary Garden, Luisa Tetrazzini, Mme. Gerville-Réache, Augusta Doria, Emma Trentini, Lina Cavalieri, Charles Dalmorès, Maurice Renaud, Hector Dufranne, Charles Gilibert, Giovanni Zenatello, Mario Sammarco, Florencio Constantino, Armand Crabbe, and Giovanni Polesi. The engagement of John McCormack had been announced on January 4. His former musical director, Cleofonte Campanini, having departed from him, Mr. Hammerstein informed the public that he had relegated "the one-man conductor" system to the past and engaged six conductors, De la Fuente, Anselmi, Sturani, Cartier, Charlier, and Scognamiglio.

Before beginning his regular subscription performances Mr. Hammerstein opened the Manhattan Opera House for a season of "educational opera," as he called it at first, which began on August 30 and endured until October 30. In this preliminary season he not only made trial of a considerable number of singers, some of whom remained with him throughout the regular season, but also experimented with operas some of which went over into the subscription repertory without any material change either in casts or stage-settings, while others, notably "Le Prophète" and "La Juive," might well have done so. In them some singers of notable excellence were heard, such as William Beck, Marguerite Sylva and Zerola, the last a tenor whom he had recruited from an Italian company which began a summer season at the Academy of Music and made the customary shipwreck. After the season got under way, however, these singers were heard from chiefly in the newspapers in connection with the disaffections and disagreements between them and the rival managers, Mr. Hammerstein and Signor Ferrara. There was downright value in the experiment not only as a test of the inextinguishable notion that the public is clamorous for opera at low prices, but also as a means of giving singers with operatic aspirations the routine which is denied them at large houses in fashionable seasons. The operas performed in this preliminary season were "Le Prophète," "Carmen," "Lucia," "Traviata," "Aïda," "La Juive," "Rigoletto," "Tosca," "Pagliacci," "Louise," "Faust," "Les Contes d'Hoffmann," "Cavalleria Rusticana," "Trovatore," and "The Bohemian Girl," the last sung in the original English.

In the season proper Mr. Hammerstein tried to give *opéra comique* (as he politely termed it, though it was largely *opéra bouffe*) on Saturday evenings; but the experiment proving a failure he admitted the fact like a brave man and abandoned it, substituting for it grand opera at popular prices. He came creditably near to keeping his promises in respect of novelties. He had said that "Hérodiade," "Elektra," "Grisélidis," and "Sapho" would be among his new productions, and they were; he also said that "Cendrillon," "Feuersnoth," "Natoma," and "The Violin Maker of Cremona" would be given, and they were not. Of old works the only ones promised in the list of operas and not given were "Crispino e la Comare," "Siberia," "Lohengrin," "I Puritani," "Die Meistersinger," and "Le Prophète." After disclosing in a performance of "Tannhäuser" how slight was the grasp of French singers upon the spirit of Wagner's dramas, the other operas by that master were gladly spared. The sensational feature of the season was the production of "Elektra," which had seven performances, the first on a special night with prices raised to $10.00 for the best stalls and $2.50 for the poorest. The receipts at the *première* amounted to $19,117.50 according to Mr. Hammerstein's figures, and the excitement was intense. There was another extra performance on the afternoon of Washington's Birthday and five representations in the subscription. Between the first performance on February 1 and its last on March 5 the opera served its purpose and lived out its welcome. The season ended on March 26. Had it laster any longer I fancy that " Salome," which was at once revived, would have proved the more popular work of the two although its novelty was worn off. Of the French operas " Thaïs " and " Les Contes d'Hoffmann " disclosed the most enduring qualities. " Sapho " was distinctly a failure (receiving only three performances) and so was " Grisélidis," though Miss Garden appeared in both of them.

If one Salome could move the pool so pleasantly for an operatic manager, what was more natural than that another should follow? Despite the agitation against the drama by Richard Strauss, which may have had some influence in the rapid collapse of interest in " Elektra " at a little later day, the composer's star was not in the descendant; nevertheless Mr. Hammerstein seemed determined that that of Massenet should be kept in the ascendant. On November 8, 1909, he brought out " Hérodiade," distributing the parts among his singers as follows:

Salome	Luisa Cavalieri
Herodias	Mme. Gerville-Reache
A Slave	Miss Carew
John the Baptist	Charles Dalmorès
Herod	Maurice Renaud
Vitellius	Armand Crabbe
Phanuel	M. Vallier
High Priest	M. Nicolay
A Voice	M. Venturini

Conductor, M. de la Fuente.

There are Salomes and Salomes, as poets, romancers, and painters have amply demonstrated, though they are at one in skill in dancing and the purpose to which they apply it. The woman created for the music of Massenet by one Italian and two French opera-book makers has nothing else in common with the perverted creature of Wilde and Strauss. She is a lovesick damsel, sentimental and silly as a schoolgirl, and at the last a penitent Magdalen. For a study of her and Massenet's work I must refer the reader to my "Second Book of Operas";* I can not consume time and space with the subject here. It is entertaining but not significant. Ten days after its production another opera by the same conductor was heard at the Manhattan Opera House for the first time in America. This was "Sapho." The date was November 18, 1909, and the cast as follows:

Fanny le Grand	Mary Garden
Jean Gaussin	M. Dalmorès
Divonne	Mlle. d'Alvarez
Irene	Mme. Walter-Villa
Caoudal	M. Dufranne
Césaire Gaussin	M. Huberdeau
La Borderie	M. Leroux
Innkeeper	M. Villa

The rapidity with which Mr. Hammerstein was bringing his novelties forward threatened danger to some of the operas in his list, especially to those of M. Massenet. French music, as a rule, but especially that of M. Massenet, depends for its effectiveness on refinement in presentation above all else. It might have been better for "Sapho" if more time and greater care had been bestowed upon its preparation. Not that any less violence would have been done to it by the performer for whose sake it was put into Mr. Hammerstein's repertory even if weeks and months instead of days had been devoted to study. Miss Garden never was an exponent of the principles for which M. Massenet stands, despite the fact that he has given musical

---

* "A Second Book of Operas; Their Histories, Their Plots, and Their Music," p. 89. New York: The Macmillan Company.

investiture to several dramatic women whom she felt called upon to impersonate. Her appeals were rudely, vulgarly physical, whereas his are graceful, subtle, and psychological. The best illustration of the divergence between the methods of the creator and interpreter was made in the second act of the opera. A courtesan wishes to stir up tender and amiable emotions in the heart of a young law-student who has seen the whirl of Parisian gay life but has not yet been engulfed in it. He is a native of Provence and the woman sings to him some of the song of the Magali—a melody which Mistral immortalized in the poem, which Gounod introduced into his opera on the subject and which, in some unexplained manner, got into the truly great dramatic ballet of Berlioz's "Les Troyens en Carthage." The dramatic motive is ingenious and Massenet's use of the song to color the amiable moments of his opera admirable and ingratiating. An artist with the slightest modicum of understanding of the situation would have made the incident insinuating and alluring. Miss Garden sang the song as if it were the veriest gutter ballad and ended it with physical postures and wriggles which destroyed all the illusions that ought to have remained hers during the rest of the drama. No dolt ever came out of Provence who could have been surprised by the disclosures which were made concerning Fanny le Grand's character in the next act.

We had been invited to form a kind and good opinion of Massenet's talent by the operas from his pen which we had heard in recent years. Without storming our senses and imaginations like the younger Italian composers, he had won his way to at least statistical representation alongside of Puccini, the most popular of modern composers. He had written much and we had heard at least half of his operas— "Hérodiade," "Manon," "Le Cid," "Thaïs," "Werther," "Le Portrait de Manon," "La Navarraise," and "Le Jongleur de Notre Dame." Plainly we ought to have ac-

A SENSATIONAL PRODUCTION

quired a taste for his music unless we were willing to confess a readiness to be bored for the sake of things for which he was not responsible. It ought not be hard to acquire a liking for "Sapho." Even those who feel disposed to be moralists when they sit in the theater have accustomed themselves to hear "Carmen," "Traviata," "La Bohème," and "Manon" without moral retchings. "Sapho" is little else than a compages from these operas. Like all of Massenet's operas it has moments of lyrical beauty and holds the interest of the knowing by its unfailing technical deftness. There are moments of banality in the score, but some of them seem to be intentional. Nothing but realism would fit into some of the scenes, and the conversation in the first act which depicts a masquerade in the studio of a Paris sculptor would be operatically unnatural if it did not float upon the tonal undulations of a vulgar waltz. There is genuine humor, though of a low order, in the restaurant music made by a band consisting of a clarinet, cornet, and tuba—the little German bands of our back yards. But there is also much flowing melody in the score, melody which affects the emotions even if they are not inspired by them, which is not deep but yet appealing; and in the play there are pictures full of movement and effective to the eye.

"Elektra" was performed for the first time in America on February 1, 1910. In the mood then prevailing in the popular mind the incident was stupendously momentous, not a historical trifle like the battles of Leipsic, Waterloo, and Bunker Hill or the meeting of the barons at Runnymede. The lyric tragedy, indeed, was one of the sensations of the hour throughout the Occidental world (Great is *Reklame* and Strauss is its prophet!), and this book would be a vain thing if it did not tell when it was first produced in the United States, where it was produced, how it was produced, by whom it was performed, and what effect it made upon its hearers. As incidentally contributory to the chronicle, a study of the work by a writer compelled by his duty to a newspaper to write down his impressions may be tolerated. The time, then, was February 1, 1910; the place the Manhattan Opera House in New York; the language French; the conductor Henriques de la Fuente; the stage-manager Jacques Coini; the impresario Oscar Hammerstein; the actors these:

Elektra	Marietta Mazarin
Chrysosthemis	Alice Baron
Klytemnestra	Mme. Gerville-Réache
Orestes	M. Huberdeau
Ægisthus	M. Duffault
Foster-father of Orestes	M. Nicolay
A Young Servant	Sig. Venturini
An Old Servant	Mr. Scott
The Confidante	Miss Desmond
Overseer of the Servants	Mlle. Taty-Lango
Train-bearer	Miss Johnstone
First Servingwoman	Alice Gentle
Second Servingwoman	Mlle. Severina
Third Servingwoman	Miss Milda
Fourth Servingwoman	Mme. Walter-Villa
Fifth Servingwoman	Mme. Duchène

I have already made record of the first performance of the work in Europe and the facts touching Mr. Hammerstein's acquisition of the right of performance in America. It was written as a spoken play by Hugo von Hofmannsthal, a Viennese dramatist. After Strauss had provided it with music a French translation was made by M. Gauthier-Villar. There was just such an audience in attendance on the first American performance as a sensational incident of the first magnitude might have been expected to summon. It could not have been larger, it could not have been more attentive, it could only amaze the observer who saw it sit for two hours while a tale of horror was unrolled before it and music dinned into its ears which lacked nearly every one of the elements supposed to be at-

Mme. Mazarin

Mme. Gerville-Réache

In "Elektra"

tractive to the ordinary lovers of the old opera or the modern lyric drama. The audience and the critical observer recognized one thing in common, which was that the man of operatic miracles, oppressed by difficulties greater than he had ever confronted before, fulfilled a promise which seemed beyond the possibility of fulfilment. A German work which has affrighted the souls of managers and singers of the majority of German opera houses was performed by a company predominantly French, in a style which compelled the admission that its spirit in general had been grasped, that there were few deficiencies in details to deplore, and that in respect of the principal actor there had been a performance nothing short of marvelous. Little was the surprise of the knowing· that Mme. Mazarin had suffered a physical collapse after she had accomplished an almost superhuman labor and was made to realize that she had been successful. The measure of that success can not be described even at this date. For two hours she was on the stage shrieking in the Straussian manner the emotions of Hofmannsthal's maniacal Electra; yet when a kind dispensation of the composer permitted her to sing, she sang; and always she freighted the imagination of the audience with the image of a tragic character unfathomably pathetic because of its offense against all that is good in art. Compared with her all the rest of the performers were marionettes, not excepting the representative of Klytemnestra, who ought to have seemed dominant with her regal pose and attire.

It is not correct to say, as a majority of commentators have said, that Hofmannsthal's tragedy is a paraphrase of the " Elektra " of Sophocles. It is based on the classic in some of its elements; it recalls it in some of its pictures; it roots in it in some of its moods; it follows it in some of its phases; but it is as un-Hellenic as Bernard Shaw's Cleopatra is unantique. Perhaps it will be urged that the modern dramatist was not called upon to treat his subject in an Hellenic manner. Then he might have created a modern story of revengeful matricide. The whole *raison d'être* of the story of Electra lies in its antique elements. A dramatist has no more right to modernize them than he would have to take a vulgar murder of today on the East Side of New York and trick out its representation with thymele and choral ode. Motives and manners ought to be synchronous in art; they always will be in the minds of true artists. In Æschylus the solemnity of a religious rite rests upon the deed of Orestes; and Electra is not thrust into the foreground. In Sophocles the physical horror in which Electra compels us to participate is ameliorated by the thought continually forced upon us that it is a sacrificial act which we must witness, or have witnessed. In the version of Euripides, where there are suggestions of greater realism and greater religious skepticism, we are yet kept in a mood of awe which is saved from mere horror by the poet's art— his appreciation of beauty. Hofmannsthal is not content to lead us into the shambles and the charnel house; we must also go with him into the presence of the mentally diseased, into the madhouse. There was no healthy person in Wilde's "Salome" except the Baptist and a few other inconsequential people, inactives. There is no healthy person in this "Elektra" except a few inactives. Willy-nilly we must witness the deeds and hear the words of pathological subjects. Sexual perversity is the keynote of everything. Electra's mind is not so much filled by the awfulness of the murder of her father as by rage at the carnal lust of her mother which led her to do the awful deed. She has no sympathy with the natural instincts of womanhood which her sister pleads as her reason for not wishing to commit the crime of parricide; but when she hears of the death of Ægisthus she plays like a wanton upon the sexual and sensual chords which Chrysosthemis had sounded. Then she fondles the body of her sister and seeks by all manner of device to turn her exaggerated sense of sexuality into a motive for the crime which she herself can not commit.

DECADENCE IN THE MUSIC 121

Not a feature of this degeneracy are we spared. This is as little Hellenic as is the substitution of a maniacal thirst for the blood of her mother for the solemn religious duty with its premonition of the fateful consequences which Æschylus continually kept before the mind of his public. Timotheus of Miletus is popularly supposed to have been banished from his country because of his musical innovations, which it was believed would tend toward the effemination of the Spartan youths. But if the decree of banishment by the Spartan Senate be read it will be found that it was not alone because Timotheus added to the number of the strings of the kithara that he was condemned, but because in a poem sung at one of the Olympian festivals he made light of the birth-pains of Semele. That was Hellenic. Things which were once too sacred to be treated lightly are the piquancies of the decadent poets and dramatists of today.

It is mournful to contemplate this tendency in the drama; it is no less mournful to contemplate a parallel tendency in Strauss's music. With all its brilliancy, with all its capacity to stir the emotions and fire the imagination, it is decadent. It is shown to be decadent by the very elements which arouse astonishment and admiration. In "Elektra" it fills the same place and serves the same purpose as in "Salome." It creates atmosphere for the score. It is decorative. It heightens the mood of the text. It illuminates the psychological and physiological bestiality of the people of the play. It does not, as music in its best estate in the compositions of Wagner does, act the part of the Greek chorus in commenting on and reflecting the horror (and when it may, the cheer) of the drama, but revels in it and glorifies it. This is best observed in the maniacal dance which at the last exhausts the vital force of Electra. Its counterpart in the earlier drama is not the dance of Salome, but the apotheosis of her unnamable lust with which the play ends. The music of "Elektra" is virtuoso music of the highest order. Never before has dissonance been so freely used and never before has dissonance been so robbed of its terrors by the magic of instrumentation. Never before have musical thoughts (for which the conception of melody has long stood and will stand again when Strauss and "Elektra" are forgotten) of such paltriness and banality been made to sound so impressive by application of characteristic and brilliant instrumental color. Electra's cry of "Agamemnon!" has an agonizing sound, but it consists of nothing more than the tones of the common chord, now minor, now major. Musical symbols like these, however, float on a flood of music which surges onward as resistlessly as a stream of lava. In supreme moments like that at the meeting of Electra and Orestes the orchestral song becomes a hymn against whose eloquence our judgment and emotions are as powerless as were the forces of nature when the Finnish Orpheus chanted his runes. But with all our admiration we recognize the great model—Richard Wagner. Had there been no "Tristan und Isolde" there would have been no such song as Strauss has given us between Electra and her brother. In spite of the potency of the modern music, what a difference in the potential melos! Marvel as we may at the music of this lyric drama in its newest phase, there can be no other conclusion than that its brilliancy is the strongest proof of its decadence. The age of greatest technical skill—virtuosity, as it is called—is the age of greatest decay in really creative energy.

The noise of the explosion of "Elektra" is over. How long will the reverberations last? Until public curiosity is satisfied. Not a moment longer. That has been the story of Richard Strauss's operas from the beginning. Each is looked forward to with the expectation that it will provide a sensation, a new thrill. The sensation having been felt, the thrill experienced, there is an end of the matter. Such art-works are not like jealousy, " which doth make the meat it feeds on." Interest burns itself out speedily because it finds no healthy nourishment in them; nothing to warm the emotions, exalt the mind, permanently to charm the senses, awaken the desire for frequent companionship, or foster a taste like that created by a contemplation of the true, the beautiful, and the good. Pathological subjects belong to the field of scientific knowledge—not to that of art. A visit to a madhouse or infirmary may be undertaken once to gratify curiosity; æsthetic pleasure can never come from frequent contemplation of mental and moral abnormalities or physical monstrosities. No pleasure can accrue to lovers of beauty from the fact that there is harmony between such dramas as "Salome" and "Elektra" and the musical investiture which Richard Strauss has given to them. Taste for the play is likely to be paired with taste for the music; and the reason is that the taste, like the things that it approves, is unhealthy. Curiosity is easily satisfied; the taste for truly beautiful things grows with its gratification, and, though it changes its ideals, it changes them slowly and never departs wholly from its fundamental principles. Even with the deplorable tendency of today toward nervous degeneracy, with all its sorrowful consequences, there is no need to fear that neurasthenia will overwhelm all forms of art or even dramatic music speedily. Mozart and Beethoven have not yet been dethroned and the banishment of their music to the limbo of forgotten things is not imminent.

In discussing "Elektra" in this place I have departed from the chronological order of Mr. Hammerstein's production of novelties for no reason except to humor a notion that a less grewsome topic would make a fitter, or at least a more amiable, conclusion to this chapter. There remains for consideration one more novelty, Massenet's "Grisélidis," the third work by that composer contained in the season's list. It was performed for the first time on January 19, 1910, M. de la Fuente conducting and the characters of the play distributed among the artists as follows:

Grisélidis .... Mary Garden
Fiamina .... Mme. Walter-Villa

Bertrade .... Mme. Duchène
The Marquis .... M. Dufranne
Alain .... M. Dalmorès
The Devil .... M. Huberdeau
The Friar .... M. Villa
Goudebaud .... Mr. Scott

This opera, like "Le Jongleur," is in sharp contrast with the somewhat lurid "Thaïs" and the romantic "Manon" and "Werther," in which there is more or less portrayal of domestic passion. So many operas by a single composer ought to speak well for the versatility of the composer, as it surely does of his industry and fecundity. M. Massenet's individuality is incontestable, but it leans heavily on sameness. The French wits who thought it clever to dub him "Mademoiselle Wagner" twenty-five or thirty years ago never had the opportunity to greet him as "Madame." The features of his art which were the most charming then remained the most charming to the end of his career. He did not grow older in thought or riper in creative ability, but only more facile and finished in expression. "Grisélidis" was the first product of an amiable pose which was continued in "Le Jongleur." It was once common gossip in Paris that Massenet composed "Le Jongleur" to answer the flings of the boulevardiers that his inspiration required the spur of Sibyl Sanderson's charms. "Grisélidis" had already disclosed the absurdity of the accusation. It preceded "Le Jongleur" and was as little adapted to the type which he had associated with Miss Sanderson as "Le Jongleur" was adapted to Miss Garden—or any other woman for that matter. Both operas are, in fact, easily explained by the essentially sentimental spirit of French art when religion is concerned in it. Gounod's attempt to write an oratorio on so sublime a subject as the fall and redemption of man and Massenet's picture of the touching piety of an honest mountebank—it is all one; the music is bound to run out into a gentle strain of religious balladry. Except for César Franck's "Beatitudes," the basic type for French religious music is "There Is a Green Hill Far Away."

French music is still ingenuous in its pursuit of beauty. It has not accepted inspiration from Ibsen. Oscar Wilde, to whom modern Germans point as the highest development of dramatic genius outside of their own country, has not yet appealed to the people for whom he wrote what his German admirers think a transcendent masterpiece. They will have none of Wilde's poem. Electra's bestial ferocity as pictured by Hofmannsthal found no more favor among the French than Salome's perverse passion did. Let thus much be said in favor of the artistic tendency of a people who were willing to hark back to a miracle tale like of "The Juggler of Our Lady" and to a legend like that of "Grisélidis." Who, indeed, but a Frenchman would have thought of calling "the patient Grizel" back to life? That marvelous model of patience, humility, fidelity, and wifely obedience! We thought that the lachrymal floodgates which the perusal of her sufferings kept open for three centuries or more had long ago been closed. And to present her with truly mediæval simplicity, without philosophic gloss inspired by modern thought in these days of female assertiveness—what daring!

It is difficult to tell where the image of Grizel, or Griselda, or Grisélidis came from. The popular comedians were playing "La Mystère de Grisélidis" in Paris in 1793, when there were already at least twenty French versions of the old story. Boccaccio had told it in his "Decameron"; Petrarch had made a Latin romance of it ("De Obedientia et Fide Uxoria Mythologia"), and Chaucer had put it into the mouth of his clerk in "The Canterbury Pilgrims." The Italian poet Zeno made an opera-book of it, which was composed by more than a dozen composers between 1701 and 1796. Of all of these operas I can recall only a single relic. In her song recitals Mme. Sembrich used to sing occasionally an aria beginning "Per la gloria d' adorarvi," from the

"Griselda" which Bononcini brought forward in London in 1723, and which was so successful that it filled Handel with pangs of jealousy and provoked John Byrom's famous epigram about the little difference between tweedledum and tweedledee. Other incidents of historical interest are associated with this predecessor of Massenet's opera. Anastasia Robinson enacted the part of Griselda, and if Dr. Burney is to be believed it was her conduct and song as the saintly sufferer that completed the conquest of Lord Peterborough, who married the prima donna after he had caned Senesino for having been rude to her behind the scenes. That the story of the opera could provoke levity as well as tears nearly two hundred years ago is also proved by some lines which appeared in *The Freeholder's Journal* on March 14, 1722, apropos of the wretchedness of the libretto written by Signor Rolli, a friend of Bononcini's and a hearty hater of Handel:

> Cast from her kingdom, from her lord exiled,
> Griselda still was lamblike, mute, and mild.
> But Rolli's verse provoked the saint to roar,
> She rav'd, she madd'ned and her pinners tore.
> Till Bononcini smooth'd the ragged strains
> And sanctified the miserable scenes.

Massenet's opera was a mystery before it was an opera. Its authors, Armand Sylvestre and Eugène Morand, produced the play at the Comédie Français on May 15, 1891. To make an opera out of it required little else than the prefixing of a prologue and the investiture of the lines with music. Thus changed, Massenet brought it out at the Opéra Comique on November 20, 1901. In the cast were two artists known to New York. M. Huberdeau, who appeared in the Devil's part in Hammerstein's production, was the original operatic Gondebeau, and Mlle. Bréval, one of Mr. Grau's prima donnas at the Metropolitan Opera House in 1900-01, was the Grisélidis. The opera differs in some particulars from the mediæval legend, but the story may first be told in its old form. It is all about a charcoal burner's daughter who becomes the wife of the Marquis of Saluzzo. He, to test her obedience, robs her of her infant daughter, whom he sends to the Queen of Pavia to be brought up. Her son, who was born four years later, is also sent away, and, as in the case of the daughter, the mother is told that he has been murdered. Finally, a decade or so thereafter, the Marquis tells his wife that he intends to divorce her and marry another woman. He strips her of all her rich apparel and sends her in rags back to the dingy hut from which he had taken her. Thence, after a space, she is summoned again to the palace, but this time to receive her rival and deck her out for the wedding ceremony. To all these things this most amazing of all loving and dutiful wives submits without a murmur and is rewarded at the last by the restoration to her of her children and her husband's love and confidence.

The changes which the modern dramatizers of the Griselda story have made seem to have had for their chief purpose the rehabilitation of the character of the Marquis, who for centuries has suffered denunciation as a cruel, tyrannical, and abnormally suspicious husband. In the opera he is as uxorious a knight of the slipper as any window-storming suffragette could wish. It is not he who fears to trust his wife, but his friar, who is supposedly Grisélidis's father-confessor. It is not he who subjects her to trials and temptations, but the Devil, who, being a henpecked husband, has as sorry an opinion of womanhood as has the Friar for reasons which he does not divulge. In introducing this devil M. Massenet and his collaborators have been more naïvely mediæval than the creator of the familiar of Dr. Faustus. He is not Goethe's devil, who was so much of a gentleman that the only observable abnormality about him was his limping gait. He is not even the rather too gaudily dressed cavalier of Barbière, Carré, and Gounod. He is a devil from the roof of Notre Dame Cathedral called into life. His ostensible purpose in the opera is to accomplish the destruction of the innocent Grisélidis; the real object of his introduction is to bring a comic element into the play. And surely a Devil who has a wife shrewish enough to keep him in hot water is comical enough. He would have served his purpose without so much *opéra bouffe* as M. Massenet burdened him with. He has horns and possibly hoofs, though he is lighter on his feet than Mephistopheles. He has a fur cloak with tails of which he makes picturesque use. He lays a wager with the Marquis that Grisélidis will play him false just as Mephistopheles does with the Ancient that he will lead Faust astray and Satan does with God that Job will not withstand his wiles. The Marquis is guilty of no wrong, but only of the weakness which afflicted Posthumus Leonatus in Shakespeare's " Cymbeline " and Adolar in Weber's " Euryanthe." The Devil, having made a bet, tries to win it. He prevails upon his wife Fiamina to play the part of a slave to the Marquis, who has gone off to the Holy Wars, and introduces her as mistress into the castle over which Grisélidis imagines that she reigned. Grisélidis remains mute and uncomplaining. He brings back her shepherd lover Alain, who had poured out his passion in an exquisite song in the prologue and had been most unaccountably thrown over in favor of the Marquis at first sight; and, though she wavered slightly then, she is held to a sense of her wifely duty by the sight of her child. In a rage at being cheated by maternal love, the Devil steals the child and hides him away. Then the Devil in the disguise of a corsair attempts to persuade Grisélidis to go down to the ship whose pirate captain, he says, is enamored of her, on the promise that there she shall find her son. But the Marquis returns from the Crusades, and when the Devil brings forth false witness against Grisélidis the good Marquis refuses to believe him, and if he had suspicions they vanish when he sees his lovely wife. At the last the Devil (who has been aping Gounod's melodious fiend in other things) hides himself in a column and thence proclaims that the lost boy Loys is his. Then the loving parents kneel down before the shrine of St. Agnes, and as they pray the tryptich opens and there is their child unharmed. Happy parents! Asinine and discomfited Devil!

Mr. Hammerstein's plans for the season contained an anomalous feature growing out of his desire to make his scheme as comprehensive artistically as that of the rival establishment. As the international character of the operas performed at the Metropolitan Opera House had long been the boast of its operating company and much of its success had been due to its German contingent, Mr. Hammerstein determined to include operas from the Wagnerian list in his repertory. He announced " Tannhäuser," " Lohengrin," and " Die Meistersinger," but, having no German singers in his company, he was compelled to resort to French translations. A like exigency had forced the Metropolitan Company to give " The Bartered Bride," a Bohemian opera, in German in the preceding season, and the same expedient was afterwards followed with " Boris Godounoff," " Prince Igor," and " Pique Dame," Russian operas which were sung in Italian, and " Iphigénie en Aulide," a French opera, which was sung in German, a proceeding exactly paralleled, so far as the effect upon the work was concerned, by Mr. Hammerstein's French " Tannhäuser." Mr. Hammerstein was not only audacious in all his undertakings, he was also courageous in confessing his mistakes. Finding light French opera ineffective for his purposes he abandoned it; after three performances of " Tannhäuser " he became convinced that the work was too German in spirit to prove acceptable in French, and he put it upon the shelf and made no effort to produce its companions. It was a manly act, for with manifold shortcomings the performances were yet indicative of a sincere striving for artistic good. So far as the general public was concerned I shall not undertake to estimate the extent to which the use of the French language militated against the success of the opera. No doubt many more of Mr. Hammerstein's patrons understood German than understood French; no doubt those who understood German preferred operas which are German in subject and spirit sung in the German tongue; but it is much to be feared that the majority of opera-goers in New York today are as blithely indifferent to the language used by the stage people as were the English people of Addison's day, when opera was half English and half Italian, or the Hamburg people of Handel's early day, when German recitatives and Italian arias alternated with each other in the same scene. Our population is composed of many elements, and the enjoyment of each element is unquestionably greater at a performance given in the language native to it than in any other tongue. But, on the whole, it has been made plain a thousand times that the general attitude is one of indifference to everything except the personality of the singers, their singing, and the pictures by which they are surrounded. In fact, it is not unlike that of Boileau when he went to the Académie and asked the box-keeper to put him in a place where he could hear Lully's music but not Quinault's words. Mme. de Staël condemned the German composers of her day because they followed the sense of the text too closely, whereas the Italians, she said, made the melody and the words conform to each other in a general way. Long after Mme. de Staël, George Hogarth, an English writer and the author of a charming and instructive book on the history of opera, put it down as his conviction that the words of an operatic air were of small importance to the comprehension of the business of a piece. They merely express a sentiment, he said—a reflection, a feeling. It is quite enough if their general import be known, and this may most frequently be gathered from the situation aided by the character and expression of the music.

However, Mr. Hogarth wrote before Wagner had accomplished his reform and before such things as a people's characteristic ideals and a people's characteristic manner of expression had received wide recognition. The French were the first people after the Italians had invented the form to develop a style of operatic music based upon the genius of their language, though two of the composers who took part in the development were foreigners—Lully, an Italian, and Gluck, an Austrian. But the French have been quite as careless about preserving the spirit of foreign works in the translations which they have made for their own delectation as any other people. In this respect, indeed, all the nations meet on common ground. A case in point comes to mind: The lovers of Wagner's dramas are not likely soon to forget what Jean de Reszke did to restore them in their native tongue to the repertory of the Metropolitan Opera House. At the time when the public was crowding the house to enjoy his impersonation of Tristan I remarked to him that I would pay a handsome sum could I be present to witness the enthusiasm of the impressionable French people when he should sing the rôle at the Grand Opéra in Paris.

"I have already been asked by the director to sing it," said M. de Reszke, "and have said that I would do so, provided he would give me a new text made under my supervision."

"You surprise me," I replied; "did not Catulle Mendès make a translation? Surely he knows French and German thoroughly."

"He did indeed, but"—turning to his valet—"bring me 'Tristan und Isolde' from the piano." He opened the book and, turning to the page, sang "Tristan's Ehre, höchste Treu'" in German and then 'La gloire de Tristan" with the notes of "Ehre" on the last syllable of "Tristan." "What do you think of that? No; I'll not sing such stuff. I must make a literal translation note for note, and then a poet may put it into lines."

CHAPTER VI

NEW YORK'S ANNUS MIRABILIS

OPERA IN NEW YORK AND EUROPEAN CAPITALS—A STUDY IN CONTRASTS—THE COST OF OPERA AT THE METROPOLITAN—ARTISTIC DOINGS IN THE SEASON OF 1909-10—A SEASON AT THE NEW THEATER—THE RUSSIAN DANCERS PAVLOVA AND MORDKIN—A LARGE ROSTER OF SINGERS—UNFULFILLED PROMISES—THE SEASON'S NOVELTIES—LORTZING'S "CZAR UND ZIMMERMANN"—PAËR'S "LE MAÎTRE DE CHAPELLE"—VICISSITUDES OF GLUCK'S "ORFEO"—MILITARY OPERAS—FRANCHETTI'S "GERMANIA"—BRUNEAU'S "L'ATTAQUE DU MOULIN"—RUSSIAN OPERAS IN AMERICA—"PIQUE DAME"—TSCHAIKOWSKY AND MOZART

I HAVE already told the story, in all save its artistic phases, of the contest between the Metropolitan Opera Company and Mr. Hammerstein which ended with the retirement at the end of the season 1909-10 of the latter from the operatic field, and, for a reason which must have been obvious, have completed it with an account of Mr. Hammerstein's discomfiture when he attempted to return to operatic management later. I have also given some critical attention to the artistic activities of the Metropolitan Company during the first year of its reorganization and to the by no means inglorious achievements of Mr. Hammerstein during the last two years of the Manhattan Opera House. To keep the account of the disastrous rivalry intact I was obliged to depart from a strictly chronological procedure in the historical narrative, and shall be constrained to do so again in the review of the artistic doings of the Metropolitan establishment within the period covering the incidents which I have narrated, which is the business of the present chapter. I shall do this in order to avoid, so far as is possible, monotony and dryness in the recital, but more particularly to lift into deserved prominence a few things which loom larger in retrospect than they did in contemporaneous contemplation. Some of these things have relation to efforts made to habilitate English opera in its two aspects of performances of foreign works in the language of the country and of the production of the works of American composers. Others were factors in a lofty, even an idealistic, striving to establish an alliance between the Metropolitan Opera House and the New Theater like that existing in Paris between the Académie Royale, popularly called the Grand Opera, and the Opéra Comique. So far as they fell within the scope of these memoirs both of these proved abortive; but both remain as ideals toward which, haply, a wider vision opened by the universal physical and cultural struggle which is now pending will eventually be directed. To opera in the vernacular I feel that a special chapter is due, though it will be necessary to refer to the outcroppings of the movement as they enter chronologically into the historical narrative.

There remains something to be said about the external features of the season in which the rivalry between the Metropolitan and Manhattan opera houses came to an end. The situation which it presented was one that was artificially stimulated, though the forces which lay at its root have existed and have had periodical eruptions in the world's capitals as long as opera itself has existed. New York offers historical precedents as well as London and Paris. But neither of the foreign cities ever produced its parallel. It is a long time since London tried the experiment of maintaining two fashionable operatic establishments at the same time; yet London has a large population, great wealth, a hereditary society to which opera has belonged as a sort of privileged entertainment. It is nearer to New York (or New York is nearer to it) in these particulars, as well as in language and social and artistic life, than any other city of the world. Nevertheless its operatic season is, as a rule, two months shorter than the normal season in

New York, and in the corresponding season of 1909-10 there were only 89 representations devoted to 21 operas in the British capital, whereas New York heard 176 performances of 43 operas. Comparison with Paris, Berlin, Vienna and St. Petersburg, as I pointed out in an article published in *Collier's Weekly* at the time, is made difficult by reason of the different conditions which prevail at their lyric theater—those of them which approach those of New York in magnitude of apparatus and seriousness of aim being government institutions. In the case of some the management is an affair of state absolutely, and deficiencies are covered year after year from the privy purses of the monarchs; in others, notably the two significant institutions in Paris, the lessees receive a subvention from the public exchequer, in return for which they are obliged to submit to a considerable regulation from the state. In all these cities, however, there is no limitation of the season to five months, as is the case in New York, but the performances go on practically all the year round. There is, moreover, greater variety in the character of the representations. Counting operas and ballets, there was a greater number of performances at the two official lyric theaters of Paris in 1908, the last year whose official figures are available, than in the New York season of 1909-10; but here is a significant fact: the combined receipts of the Grand Opéra and Opéra Comique did not equal those of the Metropolitan Opera House during the five months which made up the year in New York. The Grand Opéra, to be explicit, took in $626,000 in the twelve months of 1908, the Opéra Comique $498,800, making a total of $1,124,800. If the receipts of the Metropolitan Opera House from November, 1909, to April, 1910, did not reach this sum little reliance can be placed on the statements which were made from time to time during the period by its officials.

This is a large amount of money to draw from the people of one city for a single institution of amusement—using that term in its most dignified sense. But to it must be added the sum taken in by Mr. Hammerstein's Manhattan Opera House during a similar period of twenty weeks, and to make the comparison complete also the money contributed by the public for a preliminary season of two months of opera to which Mr. Hammerstein applied the epithet "educational," and some weeks of a vain effort to re-establish the Italian form in its old home at the Academy of Music. Both seasons failed, but the mere fact that they were undertaken with the regular seasons in sight proved that the managers were obsessed with the idea that New York was harboring such a passion for the lyric drama as to be willing to put into the exchequers of the managers nearly twice as much money as had ever been asked of any city in the world, regardless of its size, and support over one hundred concerts of magnitude and first-class importance, and some sixty theaters, little and big, besides.

Since the Metropolitan Opera House opened its doors to the public in 1883 the cost of giving opera there has more than quadrupled, the larger part of the increase having grown up since Mr. Grau laid down the reins of management. In 1909 the directors of the lessee company cheerfully announced a willingness to face a loss of at least $300,000, whereas it was an open secret that the closing years of the administration of Maurice Grau and the opening years of Mr. Conried's had yielded revenues which enabled those gentlemen to retire from their professional labors with fortunes in their pockets. The largest dividend which the stockholders of an opera company ever received, in all probability, was paid in the last year of the Grau régime, when 32 operas were brought forward in the subscription season. In the season which we have in mind, whose losses were probably greater than the large sum which the directors faced with equanimity a year before, nine more novelties or quasi-novelties were brought forward, including the French works at the New Theater; but there was what should have been an extra source of income—namely, the New Theater itself. It is therefore not to be wondered at that critics of knowledge and experience have continued to look back with regret as well as admiration to the time when great works, new to the repertory, were brought forward with devotion and beauty at the Metropolitan Opera House, and old works were performed with a vocal splendor never equaled since.

There were many explanations offered when both an artistic and financial credit were changed into a debit; but there has never been a doubt in the minds of experienced observers but that too small knowledge and appreciation of artistic needs, too little understanding of artistic methods, and too mean an appreciation of the wishes of the judicious public combined with too willing a deference to the whims of a few fashionables and amateurs, too great a disregard of the rights of some of the stockholders of the operating company, too large a complacency on the part of the owners of the opera house, too much disregard of the things which make for public respect and permanency of interest, and—finally and chiefly—too eager a desire to destroy the opposition of Mr. Hammerstein, were the principal contributory causes to so much of the Metropolitan's season as must be voted an artistic failure.

It seemed difficult at the time, it is difficult still, to make the claim of the enormous losses suffered by the managers due to increase in the cost of giving opera agree with certain well-known facts. Least of all does it seem wise or righteous to charge this increase to the rapacity of singers. Mr. Grau made money enough in the last three or four years of his administration to retire with a fortune, though Jean de Reszke at the last cost him as much as Caruso has ever cost the Metropolitan management—at least, as far as remuneration went—and Grau paid artists like Sembrich, Eames, Calvé, Plançon, and Edouard de Reszke besides. Mr. Conried's first seasons were also notoriously profitable. Of

THE METROPOLITAN SEASON 1909-10

course the doubling of the chorus and orchestra added greatly to the cost of the establishment, but it was this doubling which made it possible to give opera in other places which were a source of profit, not of loss to the institution. There was a report that the Metropolitan Opera Company lost $135,000 on the venture in the New Theater, but a deficit of an average of nearly $3,400 a performance is scarcely conceivable. In Brooklyn the season was profitable to both the Metropolitan Company and the stockholders of the Academy of Music, who played in partnership; in Philadelphia and Baltimore there were guarantees which saved the company from loss and probably yielded a profit. In New York it was said at the outset of the season that the subscription had been the largest ever known in the history of the house. It would seem to be obvious, therefore, that the increase of cost was in the administration and the artists ought to be held guiltless. But I feel little inclined to concern myself with financial matters more than I must in trying to set down the history of this extraordinary operatic year.

The season of the Metropolitan Company which has called forth this long, but I hope not purposeless excursion, began on November 15, 1909, and ended on April 2, 1910, and comprised twenty weeks. But these twenty weeks of the local subscription period, with its five performances a week, did not by any means sum up the activities of the company; there was also a subscription series of twenty representations in the Borough of Brooklyn, a subscription season of two representations a week for twenty weeks at the New Theater in Central Park West, many special performances (for which, as for a summary, reference is made to the Appendix) and subscription seasons in Philadelphia, Baltimore, and Boston, which, though they do not belong to the local record, belong to local history because of their connection with the story of the rivalry of the company with Mr. Hammerstein and the influence which they had on the home performances. The first representation of the company took place in Brooklyn on November 8, and before the season opened at the Metropolitan Opera House performances had already been given in Philadelphia and Baltimore, which cities eventually heard twenty performances each. The Boston performances were eleven in number, five in January and six in the last week of March. After this labor there remained before the company a Western tour and a visit to Atlanta, Ga., which had become the home of an annual opera festival. The season began with a proclamation of harmonious co-operation between the Managing Director Mr. Gatti-Casazza, with the Administrative Director, Mr. Dippel, and ended with the departure of the latter for a new field of operations which had been opened for him by the organization of the Chicago-Philadelphia Opera Company. There he remained for a year, after which he embarked upon the sea of theatrical speculation as manager of an operetta company. The performances at the New Theater were given on alternate Tuesday and Fridays evenings and Wednesday and Thursday afternoons, and were in pursuance of a high and beautiful purpose which had actuated the founders of the institution, viz. to provide a home for a high type of comic opera as well as the best type of spoken drama. The operas given were lighter in character than those which made up the list of the parent house, embracing specimens of *opéra bouffe* as well as German *Singspiel* and some of them received representations also at the Metropolitan. The season at the new and beautiful playhouse offered much that was valuable and interesting and had the experiment been undertaken under any other than the conditions prevailing at the time which compelled competition not only with the Metropolitan but also with the Manhattan Opera House, it might have proven a success and done much toward a stabilization of the art-form in the American metropolis; as it was it turned out to be a disastrous failure from a popular and financial point of view. The causes scarcely need inquiry; they are too obvious.

Toward the end of the season there was an unusual number of double and even triple bills at both houses, the reason being that the Russian dancers Pavlova and Mordkin, who had been engaged for the month of March, proved to be so popular and exerted so much greater an attractive power than any opera or combination of singers that the management learned that it could throw artistic integrity and promises to the winds even in the department on which it had laid considerable stress in the prospectus. The ballet programme went largely by the board. "Vienna Waltzes," which had figured in the preliminary announcement, was performed but once, and then only because the German Press Club, which had bargained for it for its annual benefit, insisted upon having it. "Die Puppenfee," "Sylvia," "Les Sylphides," and "Chopin," though on the list, were not given, short divertissements after long operas taking their place. Operatic novelties promised but not performed were Leo Blech's "Versiegelt," Goetzl's "Les Précieuses ridicules," Goldmark's "Cricket on the Hearth," Humperdinck's "Königskinder," Laparra's "Habanera," Lehar's "Zigeunerliebe" ("Amour des Tziganes"), Leroux's "Chemineau," Maillart's "Les Dragons de Villars," Offenbach's "Contes d'Hoffmann," Rossini's "Signor Bruschino," Suppé's "Schöne Galathea," and Wolf-Ferrari's "Le Donne curiose." The operas which had a first production in New York, either at the Metropolitan Opera House or the New Theater, were Franchetti's "Germania," Tschaikowsky's "Pique Dame," Mr. Converse's "Pipe of Desire," Bruneau's "L'Attaque du Moulin" and Paër's "Il Maestro di Capella," the last in an abbreviated form. To these works I shall recur presently. In familiar operas the public was permitted to see new impersonations of Elsa, Floria Tosca, and Santuzza by Mme. Fremstad and Floria Tosca by Miss Farrar.

Notable achievements from an artistic point of view were representations of "Tristan und Isolde" and "Die Meistersinger" under the direction of Signor Toscanini and "Pique Dame" under that of Herr Mahler, who had been engaged for a limited number of performances only and who after the season was over devoted himself wholly to the direction of the concerts of the Philharmonic Society.

The roster of singers was a formidable one for a reason explained in the prospectus: the inclusion in the company's plan of performances in Brooklyn, Philadelphia, Baltimore, and Boston as well as at the New Theater and on the customary spring tour "so widened the scope of the operations of the Metropolitan Opera Company as to require an extraordinary number of artists." As compared with the season of 1898-99, when Mr. Grau first attempted to give opera in the original version in three languages, said the prospectus, the personnel had been increased from 36 soloists to nearly 100, the orchestra from 65 to more than 150, the chorus from 75 to 180. The company now possessed facilities to give two performances a day and also had a working agreement with the Boston Opera Company for an interchange of singers. In the old and approved list were found the names of Frances Alda, Emmy Destinn, Geraldine Farrar, Olive Fremstad, Johanna Gadski, Louise Homer, Lillian Nordica, Alessandro Bonci, Enrico Caruso, Riccardo Martin, Albert Reiss, Pasquale Amato, Otto Goritz, Antonio Scotti, Adamo Didur, Robert Blass, Allan Hinckley, and Herbert Witherspoon. To these were added a large number of newcomers, many of them Americans, engaged, no doubt, with an eye to the requirements of the New Theater, like most of the new operas. Every prospectus before and since has contained names which loom much larger in that document than they loomed in the house-bills subsequently, and the readers can well be spared an enumeration of all the strangers who figured

CLARENCE WHITEHILL
As Escamillo in "Carmen"

in this season's list, contenting themselves with Anna Case, Ima Gluck, Alice Neilsen, Jane Osborn-Hannah, Mariska Aldrich, Marie Delna, Jeanne Maubourg, Edouard Clément (who, like Mme. Delna, had been an ornament of the Paris stage), Hermann Jadlowker, Leo Slezak, Dinh Gilly, and Clarence Whitehill. The conductors were Arturo Toscanini, Alfred Hertz, and Gustave Mahler, the assistant conductors Vittorio Podesti, Egisto Tango, and Max Bendix. An announcement which became a stereotyped formula in the Metropolitan prospectus, and has been found to have no value or significance so far as the public is concerned, told that the company had bought the "sole and exclusive producing rights for America of three operas by Debussy, viz. 'La Chute de la Maison Usher,' 'Le Diable dans le Beffroi,' and 'La Légende de Tristan.'" The composer is dead and we have not yet heard anything of these scores beyond this seemingly idle announcement and the intimation that not one of them was written. Another statement deserves quotation: "As heretofore the operas will be sung in French, German, and Italian, and the long-expressed desire to produce grand opera in the ENGLISH LANGUAGE with an *all-star* cast will positively see its fulfilment during the season." Back of this utterance were two facts: the promise to produce Mr. Frederick S. Converse's opera "The Pipe of Desire," which had been made and left unfulfilled in the preceding season, was to be redeemed and attention was invited to the competition then in progress among American authors and composers for an original opera in the English language for which a prize of $10,000 had been offered by the Metropolitan Company in December, 1908. The story of that competition and the award I purpose to relate in a subsequent chapter where it can be brought into perspective with other incidents in the campaign for vernacular opera, which is as old in New York as opera itself —a fact to which managers and composers obstinately keep their eyes shut.

The season had been in progress for a fortnight when the first quasi-novelty was brought forward at the New Theater, which gave a rich and beautiful setting to the audience and the piece, but was found to be defective acoustically, a fault which was partially remedied the next season. The work was Lortzing's "Czar und Zimmermann," which was performed in the original German. Here was a case in which a foreign work might have made a deeper impression on an American audience than it did had it been given in English; but to do that it would have had to be provided with a better translation than is usually bestowed upon foreign operas and the spirit of the comedy and music been more faithfully preserved than it was by some of the performers. Lortzing's *Singspiel* is a classic— bewitchingly Mozartian in its music and altogether delightful in its comedy. Its subject—the familiar episode in the life of Peter the Great which tells of how he learned to appreciate the feelings of the "plain people," as Lincoln called them, by working in a Dutch shipyard as a common carpenter—has appealed to many composers, but has never been treated so successfully by any lyric dramatist as by Lortzing. The opera had been brought forward at long intervals in New York in its original form as well as in English dress but never quite adequately, which was one reason why it appealed to the New Theater audience as a new and beautiful thing. It received four performances in the season. The New Theater was also first in the field with the first real novelty of the year, albeit a rather trifling one. This was an abbreviation, done into Italian, of Fernando Paër's little masterpiece entitled "Le Maitre de Chapelle" (in Italian "Il Maestro di Capella"). The piece was written for the Théâtre Feydeau a century ago. Paër was an Italian, but his principal work was done outside of his native land—in Vienna, where he brought forth his "Camilla," in which Rossini played a child's part when he was only seven years old; in Dresden, where he pro-

"IL MAESTRO DI CAPELLA"

duced "Leonora, ossia l'amore conjugale," the book of which a year later Beethoven and his collaborators turned into "Fidelio"; in Paris, where as Napoleon's chapelmaster, conductor of the Italian Opera, and Rossini's associate he did good work but nothing comparable with the sparkling opéra comique which in a transmogrified form the people in the New Theater heard on this occasion. A puissant personality in his day the present generation would probably never have heard of him if Signor Pini-Corsi, the basso-buffo of the Metropolitan company, had not revived an abbreviated Italian version of it in order to display his amiable musical buffooneries. The little comedy (what was left of it) was musically as sparkling as champagne but with as sound and sweet a body as the best vintage of Johannisberg. The play is all about a music-master of the old type who has written a lyric piece on the subject of Antony and Cleopatra and teaches his cook how to sing it, telling the audience meanwhile of the musical devices, vocal and instrumental, which he has employed in its score. Pini-Corsi played the composer and Miss Alma Gluck the cook, and it was difficult to say whether the veteran buffo or the fresh young novice deserved the greater admiration. It was practically Miss Gluck's début in opera, and while the buffo kept the sides of all who understood him aching with laughter by his song and action Miss Gluck delighted both sight and hearing by her piquant play, her lovely voice, and her thrice admirable singing. But if "Le Maître de Chapelle" was to be presented in translation, why did we not have it in English? What a lesson for the composers of operetta in the vernacular! As for the music Rossini himself would have been proud of it, which, I make no doubt, excited his envy. The fragment was consorted in the performance with Mascagni's ferocious "Cavalleria Rusticana" and a set of dances in character by Rita Sacchetto.

There was nothing in the performances at the Metropolitan Opera House to invite special comment until December 23, when Gluck's "Orfeo ed Euridice" was produced under the direction of Signor Toscanini with new stage-settings and the parts in the hands of Louise Homer (Orfeo), Johanna Gadski (Euridice), Bella Alten (Amore), and Alma Gluck (Un Ombra felice). So far as America is concerned "Orfeo" is the oldest opera in the current list —the oldest opera and one bearing a much-needed lesson which, it is greatly to be feared, is not yet appreciated at its full value because of the perverted taste of the operatic public for music so highly spiced with dissonance and mongrel tone that the original mission of the art has been forgotten and its potency dissipated because of the prevalence of a taste for pruriency, lust, and the shambles. There was nothing of all this in this revival, but much loveliness of scenic spectacle and much beautiful music grateful to the ear, warming to the emotions, and powerfully appealing to the imagination. It is no extravagance of speech to say that for the first time the present generation of opera-goers in New York were privileged to enjoy a performance of the opera with which the operatic reforms culminating in Wagner's works began, which was worthy of the poet, the composer, the institution at which it was presented, and also of the beautiful old legend—in short, an adequate performance. Old opera-goers in New York whose memories go back sixty years might be able to recall not only all the representations which "Orfeo" has had in New York, but also the very first performance of an opera by Gluck in America, for "Orfeo" was the only one of the composer's works that up to then had been seen in the theater on this side of the Atlantic. Time and again, especially in the old days of German opera at the Metropolitan Opera House, there was talk of producing "Armide" or one of the "Iphigenias," but talk was all that came of it. Excerpts from "Alceste" had been sung at the music festivals in Cincinnati, but "Orfeo" had provided the only opportunities which Americans had had to learn of the dramatic quality of the artist who cleared the path down which Wagner walked to glory. The first performance of "Orfeo" in New York was in English and took place at the Winter Garden on May 25, 1863. Mlle. Felicita Vestvali was the repsentative of the mythical bard, and Carl Anschütz conducted the performance. For the details of that performance the reader must be referred to other sources; they are outside my ken. My knowledge, however, easily goes back to a revival which, while it can not be recalled without a smile at some of its features, must yet be remembered with gratitude. On January 8, 1886, the American Opera Company produced the opera in English at the Academy of Music, and between that date and the end of March performed it ten times in New York and three times in Brooklyn. Mme. Helene Hastreiter was the Orpheus of these performances, and Miss Emma Juch the Eurydice; Theodore Thomas conducted. The opera was tastefully staged and a fine intelligence marked all the scenes and tableaus up to the final ballet, the culminating feature of which was a Bacchic procession seemingly conjured up by Orpheus for the diversion of the denizens of Elysium. This incongruity was forgotten, however, in the absurdities which marked the productions of the opera at the Metropolitan Opera House previous to the one under discussion. The first of them took place on December 30, 1891, when "Orfeo" was given in Italian as a companion piece to "Cavalleria Rusticana." Here was contrast with a vengeance! But that was not all. "Orfeo's" stage-furniture was the most absurd jumble of ancient pagan and mediæval Christian notions ever conceived. The underworld of the Greeks was represented by the hell of "Asrael" which had come over to Mr. Abbey from the German régime. At the Academy of Music we had seen Ixion, Tantalus, and the other fabled heroes of Hades suspending their labors while the song of Orpheus enriched the atmosphere of their prison house;

but now we saw only the flames of the hell of mediæval theologians, the ascending smoke of torment, and scores of capering red devils. The Elysian Fields were the magic gardens of Merlin (borrowed from Goldmark's opera of that name), with their tropical forest vegetation of the carboniferous era, a sea in the background and golden-winged cherubim and seraphim to keep company with Eurydice and her associates of terpsichorean proclivities, who expressed the whole gamut of their emotions by standing on their toes. The sisters Giulia and Sophia Ravogli, who in some inexplicable way had won praise for their performance in London, were the inspiring cause of this revival. It endured for four representations, largely because it was associated with Mascagni's opera, which had been introduced to the stage of the Metropolitan Opera House with it. In the season of 1893-94, "Orfeo" returned to the stage of the Metropolitan in the company of another hot-blooded little drama which since then has formed a lasting companionship with Mascagni's. On December 11, 1893, it was given as a curtain-raiser for "Pagliacci." Neither stage-manager nor ballet-master disclosed a glimmer of intelligence touching the opera. Now the underworld was a sort of modified wolf's-glen abounding with grinning skulls lighted up from within like the illuminated pumpkin of the Headless Horseman. The Elysian Fields were in cloudland, the blessed shades were a mixed company of Sunday-school angels, Amazons from Niblo's Garden, and short-skirted, bespangled dancers, all of whose emotions were also in their toes. Though Mme. Scalchi sang the music of Orpheus, there was but one performance; and that was quite enough, as every one agreed. Once more Gluck's opera suffered the degradation of being drafted to kill time before the introduction of a novelty—this time Massenet's "Navarraise," on December 11, 1895. Mme. Brema appeared in the titular rôle, and Mme. Calvé introduced the gunpowder opera, which had been written for her by MM. Cain and Massenet.

A NEW AND BEAUTIFUL OUTFIT

"Navarraise" lived through five performances, but "Orfeo" died on the first night. Died and slept the sleep of death until its lovely resurrection under circumstances now to be detailed. For this resurrection the thanks of every sincere lover of dramatic music is due to the management and Signor Toscanini. There was much in the representation to call out laudatory comment. The scenic outfit was beautiful and appropriate. It scarcely needed the affecting music of the first scene to attune susceptible persons to the melting mood; the picture seized upon the imagination and emotions at once. This picture, like that of the third scene representing the Elysian Fields, was an artistic triumph. Both had models in the beautiful revival which Gluck's opera had had in recent years in Paris. Puvis de Chavannes might have painted the models. The serenity of Greek loveliness rested upon the glade in which Eurydice was laid to rest and upon the mead over which the blessed shades wandered through an atmosphere burdened with the song of the mythical minstrel. Strong in contrast, but not less appealing to the fancy, were the pictures at the entrance and exit of Hades. More might have been expected of the choreographic scenes than was offered, in view of the fact that so much attention had recently been given to the so-called revival of classic dancing; but it was a refreshment to see something else than the conventional pirouetting of former times. Mr. Toscanini's treatment of the music was reverential; more than reverential—it was loving; and his spirit had its counterpart in that of Mme. Homer. Hers was a lovely impersonation—lovely to the eye, in figure, pose, movement, gesture, and equally lovely in voice and song. She had an admirable companion in Miss Gluck, who sang "In quest' asilo" with exquisite taste. To close the first act Mme. Homer sang an Italian version of "Divinités du Styx" from Gluck's "Alceste," following, at Signor Toscanini's suggestion, a plan adopted at the revival of the work at the Théâtre de la

Monnaie in Brussels in 1893. It required only the change of a word to make the interpolation appear apposite to the occasion, for the situations in the two operas are very much alike. But there are objections of considerable cogency to be urged against the device. For one thing, Orpheus had only a moment before given utterance to an invocation of the deities of the underworld in a dramatic recitative and announced his intention to conquer them with the sight of his grief and tears. Alkestis addresses her invocation to the Stygian ministers to whom she is about to offer herself as a sacrifice for a husband not yet dead. Here was a dramatic point which should have been considered. There was also an objection pertinent from a musical point of view. The orchestration of "Orfeo" is extremely continent throughout, the impressive trombones being used sparingly and only to emphasize great effects, like the "No!" which the Furies hurl at Orpheus when first he appeals to their pity; but in the air from "Alceste" trombones and trumpet are much in the foreground. The introduction of this air recalls a singular incident in musical history. Originally the first act of the opera ended with a recitative. When Gluck carried it to Paris he recognized that, however dramatic propriety might be served by such an ending, it was musically a lame and impotent conclusion. So he introduced the air beginning "Addio, addio, O miei sospiri," which Berlioz retained in the version made for the Théâtre Lyrique in 1859, although he felt, as every discriminating critic has felt from the beginning, that the style of the air was too archaic to fit into the rest of the score. Though it was known that Gluck had himself introduced the air, suspicion was aroused touching its authenticity, and this was turned into conviction by Berlioz's statement that the music was unquestionably that of an air composed by an Italian named Bertoni for his opera "Tancredo," which Berlioz said he had seen in the Italian's score and which the Italian averred to be his in a letter which Berlioz printed. And this remained the conviction of the world until some fifteen years or so ago, when M. Tiersot established the fact that the air was not Bertoni's but Gluck's and had been taken from the latter's opera "Aristeo," produced at Parma in 1769. This does not meet the objection raised by the old-fashioned, undramatic character of the air, for "Aristeo" was written seven years after "Orfeo" and the opera is an obvious reversion to the old manner which critical historians would have us believe Gluck forever put aside when he wrote "Orfeo." When Mr. Thomas produced the opera with the American Opera Company he omitted the air, though Mr. Chorley and Mr. Hallé had included it in their English paraphrase which Mr. Thomas used. On January 29, 1910, the opera was given at the Metropolitan with the admirable Marie Delna in the part of "Orfeo." Though Signor Toscanini had introduced the air from "Alceste" for Mme. Homer, he permitted Mme. Delna to interpolate in its place an air from Gluck's "Echo et Narcisse." Its sentiment is one of those noncommittal expressions which serve in any moment of tragic perplexity in the old-fashioned lyric; but it was shorter and made an effective ending.

On January 22, 1910, "Germania," an opera by Luigi Illica and Alberto Franchetti, was performed for the first time in America with this distribution of parts:

Giovanni Filip Palm	Giulio Rossi
Frederico Loewe	Enrico Caruso
Carlo Worms	Pasquale Amato
Crisogono	Antonio Pini-Corsi
Ricke	Emmy Destinn
Jane	Christine Heliane
Lena Armuth	Marie Mattfeld
Jebbel	Leonora Sparkes
Stapps	Adamo Didur
Luigi Adolfo Guglielmo Lützow	Paolo Wulman
Carlo Teodoro Körner	Ludovico Nepoti
Hedwig	Marie Mattfeld
Peters	Aristide Baracchi
Captain of the German Police	Eduardo Missiano
A Lady	Florence Wickham
A Youth	Rita Barillo

There are good reasons for thinking that Signor Franchetti had more to do than is ordinarily the case with the composition of the book of "Germania." Illica is librettist-in-ordinary to the composers of Italy. He can turn his hand to any subject and produce a serviceable book with or without local color at a moment's notice; but he must have had some special inducement to produce a libretto like that of this opera, which was obviously written as much for consumption in the study as for hasty consultation in the opera house—the book, I mean. The stage-directions read like those of literary plays never intended for public performance. They tell of things which could never be divined from the performance alone. For instance: one of the stage-folk opens a scroll and examines it. "A caricature of Haugwitz!" he exclaims, laughs, and shows it to his companions. Now read the stage-directions: "Students approach, curious to see; all laugh at the caricature, which represents the minister as a pig grubbing up mushrooms, which Napoleon, represented as Pluto, seizes and devours. Each mushroom bears the name of a German state, province, or city." Plainly, whoever was responsible for bookmaking of this type had something more than the ordinary operatic performance in view, and this must have been the composer of "Germania." Baron Franchetti, although listed as an Italian and born in Turin, is a scion of the house of Rothschild, whose founder hailed from the Judengasse in Frankfort. His higher musical education was acquired at the Hochschule in Munich and at Dresden under the tutelage of Draeseke, an arch-Wagnerite in the days when such men were notable for their rarity. Before he had made his name widely known he composed a symphony, like a good German, and it was as a symphonist that New York first heard of him as long ago as 1887. Mr. Theodore Thomas gave the composition a hearing at a concert of the Philharmonic Society. He also played a piece of between-acts music from an opera entitled "Asrael," by the same composer, and thus helped to create curiosity touching the personality of the author of the opera when it was chosen by Mr. Edmund C. Stanton to open the season of the Metropolitan Opera House on November 26, 1890. The occasion was for several reasons an interesting one. For one thing it introduced Mr. Andreas Dippel to New York, then a young tenor and at the time of this production one of the managers of the institution which lifted him out of the obscurity of the Bremen municipal theater. It was also the beginning of an amusing and futile experiment to effect a compromise between the German régime which prevailed at the opera house at the time and the desire of the boxholders to hear Italian opera instead of German. Franchetti was a composer with a name which had an Italian sound; Smareglia was another; and from them New Yorkers received the two most astonishing operas that they had ever heard—"Asrael" and "Der Vassal von Szigeth." In "Asrael" there was noticeable a tendency on the part of the composer to veer from the Italian style of its day to the German. Had Wagner lived to hear it he would probably have explained the phenomenon on racial grounds, saying that Franchetti's music was like the language spoken by his people, the Jews, without national idiom because it was an acquired, not a native, tongue. There is more than a hint of that peculiarity in the music of "Germania," which I am strongly inclined to believe was written with an eye on the theaters of Germany rather than those of Italy. It has for a background a series of incidents calculated to put German patriotism in a ferment. It pictures the uprising of the German people under the leadership of their poets, philosophers, university students—the Tugendbund and Louisenbund—against the Napoleonic oppression. The martyrdom of Palm, the Nuremberg bookseller, is the chief incident of the prologue. A gathering of the patriots and the resolution of a private quarrel into a patriotic outburst by the opportune appearance of Queen Louise and the young prince who came down into our own day as William I of Prussia, German Emperor, is another. A symphonic delineation of the Battle of Leipsic, followed by a picture of the battle-field, with the Little Corporal and his guard moving past the background in the retreat from Germany, is still another. These things, which are treated as accompaniments to a story of love and intrigue which, while commonplace enough in its elements, is yet handled with a fine command of pathos by both librettist and composer, are animated by many appealing touches of detail introduced to heighten the local color. The first music heard is that of one of the most familiar folksongs of Germany, " So viel Stern' am Himmel stehen," which a poor old woman is overheard teaching to her nephew. At a gathering of patriots we are introduced to the counterfeit presentments (mostly mute) of such historic personalities as Palm, Loewe, Fichte, Humboldt, the Schlegels, Theodor Körner, Lützow, and Carl Maria von Weber. When the last three appear, in the company of their patriotic brethren, there is a spontaneous outburst of the chorus in the stirring song, " Lützow's wilde Jagd," which the veritable Körner wrote and the veritable von Weber composed, and which was a sort of German " Marseillaise " during the last year of Bonaparte's European domination. It was a pretty impulse which prompted the introduction of these elements, but in introducing them the librettist and composer played havoc with the verities of history. The period covered by the drama is from the capture of Palm to the Battle of Leipsic—1806 to October, 1813. At that time, though the melody of the love song " So viel Stern' " was known, it had not been printed to the words which are used in translated form in the libretto, but was sung to words which would have served the librettist better had he known them, for they began: " O, du Deutschland, ich muss marschiren." There is no error in the use of the old student song " Gaudeamus igitur " (which, by the way, N. P. Willis is credited with having introduced

ANACHRONISMS IN THE SCORE

in America), but there is a dreadful anachronism in everything in the opera appertaining to Körner, Weber, and their song "Lützow's wilde Jagd." The prologue in which it is sung is supposed to play in 1808; the song was written by Körner on April 24, 1813, and composed by Weber in the summer of 1814. "Voices blend in snatches of Weber's 'Wilde Jagd' already popular," says the librettist in one of the glosses which serve as stage-directions. Popular eight years before its creation! If this was to be accepted as a poetic license the librettist should have omitted his note. But this is only one of many blunders in excuse of which it may be said that, though they may cause a smile, they do not affect the effectiveness of the opera.

The opera is effective. Its pictures are beautiful. Its political element is ingeniously used to emphasize the pathos of the love story. A soldier-student returns from his country's service to his love. In his absence her ruin has been accomplished by one of his friends. He does not learn the fact until after he has made the woman his wife. Scarcely have the marriage vows been exchanged when the friend, who was thought to have been killed in battle, staggers into the home of the wedded pair. The woman had promised to hold her peace because she wanted no murder. The seducer can not face the ordeal with which he has been confronted. In spite of his friend's protest he insists on going on his way. The husband accompanies him in the capacity of guide. The wife, no longer able to control her emotions, writes a word of farewell and rushes off through darkness and storm. Her husband learns the truth from the innocent prattle of a child. He seeks him, of whom he is now a deadly enemy, at a meeting of the patriots in Königsberg, denounces him, insults him, and compels the man, who is overwhelmed with contrition, to accept his challenge to a battle with swords; but even as the blades are crossed there appears Queen Louise with her child and asks that the blades be used in the service of Germany. The husband forgets his private wrong and the two meet death on the battlefield of Leipsic, where the wife finds her husband dying and her seducer dead.

The story is well handled by the librettist, though much that is inconsequential has been introduced into the book and its commentary, the stage-directions. It has been treated with skill, which frequently rises to admirable heights, by the composer. Signor Franchetti's style is empirical. He oscillates from Wagner to his modern colleagues, makes attempts at being German in style, but falls back upon the early Verdi when he becomes most fluent. He uses Weber's thrilling song with fine skill. The delineation of battle in the symphonic interlude and the way in which the mood of the final scene—the epilogue—is preserved are both masterly.

When "Germania," in which an Italian sought to glorify the patriotism of Germany, was produced in New York profound peace prevailed throughout Christendom except in the chronically disturbed Central American republics. If Mars had been wading through blood in Europe as he is while I write these words, and America had been at peace with the warring peoples, what a riot and revel of patriotic demonstration might we not have seen with the Germans driving Bonaparte out of their country on the stage of the Metropolitan Opera House, the Carlists and Spanish Republicans trouncing each other on the stage of the Manhattan, and the Frenchmen putting the Prussians to flight at the New Theater as they did a fortnight after the production of Franchetti's opera! True, Mme. Calvé was not in New York at this particular juncture, but "La Navarraise" would not have long remained on the shelf with our brethren of Teutonic origin mingling their voices (in spirit if not in fact) with "Lützow's wild' verwegene Jagd" in "Germania" and our Gallic contingent shouting "Victoire!" in Bruneau's "L'Attaque du Moulin," which had its first American performance at the New Theater on February 8, 1910. There was, of course, no special significance in the production of two military operas within a fortnight by the forces of the Metropolitan Opera House. There might have been such a seeming if Mr. Dippel and his German cohorts had charged themselves with the production of "Germania" and the French contingent of Signor Gatti had brought forward "L'Attaque du Moulin" without his help. But both of the productions were under the care of the General Manager, who occupied a neutral attitude at the time as between France and Germany. Moreover, no one who had gone even a small distance into the conditions prevailing at the Metropolitan Opera House needed to be told why the two operas chanced to be produced in this season. The demands of a firm of Italian music publishers read in effect: If no novelty from our press, no Puccini. Hence "Germania." Mr. Hammerstein had threatened the prestige of the house in upper Broadway by his successful production of French operas. Hence "L'Attaque du Moulin." None of Massenet's operas being available (Hammerstein practically had them all), search had to be made elsewhere; and the choice fell on Bruneau's "L'Attaque."

On the whole, it was not a bad choice. There are older and better French composers than M. Bruneau, but few who had been more talked about and few more entitled to respect. Saint-Saëns, whom we know even now but slightly on the operatic stage, does not belong to the school of younger men who write criticisms as well as music in France and are so deft at passing the candied stick of mutual compliment from mouth to mouth that they make for each other pages of history. So nothing of his was to be expected. There was talk of the things by Debussy which have figured in the Metropolitan prospectuses for years, but preliminary talk is always in inverse ratio to performance at our opera houses. Therefore Bruneau was reasonably natural. Berlioz was left out of consideration, of course (he is still left out!), for the world seems to share France's fear of the most gifted composer that she has produced since the Romantic period set in. Yet it would have been interesting then (it would be interesting now) to witness an experiment with "Benvenuto Cellini" or "Les Troyens à Carthage." But all this is idle retrospection and speculation. "L'Attaque du Moulin" was added to our repertory, and the fact ought to cause no regret. No time more propitious for its revival than the present could be conceived. It is worth a revival. The opera has a most moving and pathetic story at its base. Zola conceived it, which means much in favor of its dramatic strength. Louis Gallet threw it into dramatic verse and Alfred Bruneau gave it musical investiture. It is, perhaps, unfortunate for our knowledge of French music that Bruneau's works are so little performed. Like many another young Frenchman, he started out with fine achievements (of which "L'Attaque du Moulin" is one) and finer protestations. At the beginning of his career he fell under the spell of Wagner, but soon realized that the Wagnerian method, as understood by his compatriots, was not wholly compatible with French artistic principles. He did not turn on his model and try to rend him, like Debussy, but made an effort to unite the new German style of dramatic expression with the old French conceptions of elegance and clarity. He himself said "conciseness" also, but after hearing this opera it is not possible to say that he successfully pursued this ideal. He wanted, he said, to follow the great German in his symphonic treatment of themes; but he did not believe it necessary to shuffle off all the old formulas; and so he gave the world an opera in which there is some orchestral play with typical phrases, which are typical only from the most arbitrary point of view (except the military signals borrowed from the French and the German military codes), and as much of the familiar sentimental melody style as Gounod or his master Massenet ever indulged. Nothing in the dramatic situations of the opera—which has a story calculated to keep nerves and emotion on a tension and the mind on a *qui vive* from beginning to end—is permitted to interfere with the composer's desire to write a set piece of music whenever he feels like it. Even a sentinel on guard over a man condemned to death sings yards of tune about home, mother, and sweetheart with the nonchalance of the Tommy Atkins who steps out of the sentry-box in Gilbert & Sullivan's operetta; though this one gets a slit in his windpipe for his pains, which he never would have invited had he behaved like a real soldier instead of an operatic marionette.

What is most admirable in Bruneau's opera is the effectiveness of its musical declamation. This is in the best sense French, and the composer did not need to explain it, as he did some years ago in London, by telling how he had hit upon the device by speaking his text loudly and noting the natural inflections of his voice prompted by his emotions. Such inflections were the beginning of all emotionalized speech, and one of the inventors of the operatic form, Caccini, told his generation how he had studied and utilized them more than three centuries ago. The opera, as has been said, has a fine story, which was well put together by the librettist but is made too diffuse for good dramatic effect by the composer's willingness to be a sentimental musician. The plot deals with a short tale by Zola, a fantasy based on the Franco-Prussian War of 1870. Flamand, who is betrothed to the daughter of a French mill-owner, helps to defend the mill against an attack of the Prussians. He is a non-combatant and therefore is sentenced to death by the Prussian captain; but is offered a chance to save his life in return for a service to the enemy. He refuses. His fiancée suggests his escape by the murder of the sentinel who was set to guard him, and puts the murderous knife into his hands. He uses it successfully, but meanwhile his prospective father-in-law, the mill-owner, is made a victim in his stead. He is a willing victim, having the happiness of his daughter and her lover in mind, and to save them he is guilty of falsehood. At the last the young man returns at the head of some French soldiers and drives the Prussians away from the mill, but they carry the miller with them, and a shot tells of the voluntary sacrifice of his life for the sake of his loved ones. All the characters, down to the least significant, are drawn with strongly individual lines, and the largest of them, the miller, the lover, the captain of the Prussian soldiers—who are spoken of euphemistically as " the enemy " for diplomatic reasons, as was explained at the original production of the opera in 1893, when the time of the action was set back to 1792—the miller's housekeeper, Marcelline, and Françoise, the miller's daughter, were effectively impersonated at the performance in the cast of which there were two artists who took part when the opera was originally performed—Mme. Delna and M. Clément. The former filled her original part, but the latter was the hero-lover in New York, whereas he had been the sentinel in Paris. The cast was as follows:

Dominique .... Edmond Clément
Merlier .... Dinh Gilly
Le Capitaine ennemi .... Andrea Segurola
La Sentinelle .... Georges Régis
Le Tambour .... Paul Annanian
Françoise .... Jane Noria
Marcelline .... Marie Delna
Geneviève .... Christine Helaine
Le Capitaine français .... Leo Devaux
Le Sergeant .... Bernard Bégué

A report, which in my mind is as vague as a mere tradition, has it that many years ago, fifty at least, a troupe of Russian singers visiting the United States gave performances of Verstowsky's opera " Askold's Tomb." I recall finding the libretto in a library, and the fact impressed itself upon my mind that it bore an American imprint. So far as my knowledge goes, however, until Tschaikowsky's " Pique Dame " was produced at the Metropolitan Opera House on March 5, 1910, no distinctively Russia opera had been heard

A FAITHFUL NATIONAL SCHOOL

in New York. True, the National Opera Company gave Rubinstein's " Nero " some thirty-odd years ago at the Metropolitan, but not even the composer would have dared to assert that " Nero " was in any sense a national opera. Rubinstein was not identified with the Russian school of composition which has so profoundly stirred the musical pool in recent years, and, indeed, was only slightly tinctured with Slavism musically. In this he was, unfortunately for him I think, a man without a country. He himself made confession to that fact when he humorously but yet pathetically set down the fact that he seemed to be neither fish, flesh nor fowl, inasmuch as the Russians said he was a German, the Germans that he was a Russian, the Jews that he was a Christian, the Christians that he was a Jew, the Classicists that he was a Romanticist, the Romanticists that he was a Classicist. In this he reminds me of Dudley Buck's description of himself in Biblical terms as " Issachar, a strong ass crouching down between two burdens," after I had deplored his lack of dramatic talent in a piece ostensibly dramatic and a Boston critic had spoken of the dramatic quality of his church music. " Nero " has a Roman subject, was composed to German words and without a tinge of either Latinism or Slavism. Now, no composers have been more faithful to their literary and musical idioms than the Russians since they have risen to the dignity of a school. Glinka was but slightly idiomatic in his operas, but he went to Pouschkin for the subject of " Rousslan and Ludmilla," and the same author furnished forth the material for Dargomischki's " Russalka " and Moussorgsky's " Boris Godounow," which provided one of the points of high light in the Metropolitan season of 1912-13. Lermontow and Gogol are other names which come to mind as men whose writings have found their way into operas. In view of the fact that no composer of our day has enjoyed a popularity like that of Tschaikowsky, it was a little strange that we had to wait so long before hearing one of his operas. " Pique Dame " had been promised in the season before in an Italian version under the title "La Dama di Picchi"; it was heard on this occasion in German, and, if the circumstances had urgently demanded, might have been sung for the greater part in Russian, since there were so many Slavs concerned in its performance—Anna Meitschik, Leo Slezak, Adamo Didur, and Adolph Mühlmann—all the principal characters but one. There was also Gustav Mahler, specially brought back to the opera house to conduct the work. The cast was as follows:

Hermann	Leo Slezak
Count Tomsky	Adamo Didur
Prince Jaletzky	John Forsell
Czekalinsky	Wilhelm Otto
Tsurin	Adolph Mühlmann
Tschaplitzky	Glenn Hall
Narumoff	Anton Ludwig
The Countess	Anna Meitschik
Liza	Emmy Destinn
Pauline	Florence Wickham
The Governess	Marie Mattfeld
Mascha	Leonora Sparkes
Chloe (in the interlude)	Alma Gluck

Let it be said at once that the occasion was one of extraordinary interest, one that made the "Villis" and "Wallys" of the Italian list sink into insignificance. Pouschkin's story is much more sententious than that of the opera-book. The composer's brother in adapting it was obliged to expand it, not only for the sake of the stage-spectacle which St. Petersburg and Moscow demand, but also to create sympathy for its principal characters. In the original story a young lieutenant, obsessed by the gaming mania, frightens an old woman to death in an effort to extract from her the secret of her success at cards—a success which has given her the sobriquet of "The Queen of Spades." He gets it from her ghost, plays the three cards enjoined, wins on two, ventures his all on the third, but at the moment which should be his final triumph the ace of hearts in his hands changes into the

THE COMPOSER'S CONFESSIONS 161

Queen of Spades, the specter of the woman whose death he had accomplished confronts him, and with his last penny there goes with him also his last glimmer of reason. He is sent to a madhouse, but the young woman in the story remains as decorous in her behavior as Goethe's Charlotte and marries a man of her choice. Modest Tschaikowsky added characters and situations to this story, created a betrothal between the heroine and a royal personage whom she did not love, made the motive of the hero's mania a desire to obtain money enough to enable him to marry, and sent the heroine to self-destruction because love of money had supplanted love of her in his insane mind. So, too, he sends the lover to self-inflicted death and gives the spectators a moment, but only a moment, of commiserating sympathy for the ill-starred pair. Unfortunately, this part of the story is imperfectly brought out, too much time is occupied with inconsequentials, and the ultimate impression left upon the mind is scarcely one of interest in the fate of the hero, to say nothing of the sympathy which the composer labored hard to create.

Tschaikowsky was given to laying bare his heart to his friends, and he has told how he wept when he composed the last pages. Then, curiously analyzing his feelings, he discovered that he had come to associate the character of Hermann with a friend who was destined to sing the part when his work was brought out at the Imperial Opera at St. Petersburg in 1890. "Pique Dame" brought curiously to mind the eclectic character of the music of the Russian school. The individual note in it is undeniable. It is amazing that so modern a composer as Tschaikowsky could find such varied and eloquent dramatic accents without once poaching on Wagner's preserves. He makes the frankest kind of excursions into Mozartian fields in the intermezzo which interrupts the action of the second act yet provides delightful recreation and refreshment. There were many enigmatic things about Tschaikowsky. Many of his self-accusations are not to be taken seriously, and no doubt much of his life was hidden even from his intimate friends. In one of his letters written from Florence, where he composed "Pique Dame," he said that he had stolen the beginning of its music from Naprawnik; yet that composer was unable to find out what and where the alleged pilferings were. Tschaikowsky never seems to have mentioned that the pastoral interlude is almost pure Mozart. No doubt he thought it unnecessary. It was too obvious to call for deprecatory comment, and for it there was sufficient confession in his well-known love for the composer. To Mozart he paid tribute in the Serenade for Strings, the Suite "Mozartiana," and in one of the letters to his patroness, Mme. von Meck. This letter is all eulogy. "Why do you not like Mozart?" he asks his friend; "I not only like him, I idolize him. For me the most beautiful opera ever composed is 'Don Juan.'" Two years later, writing about Glinka to the same lady, he contrasts the latter's character with that of Mozart very much to the disadvantage of the former. In September, 1880, he tells his friend that, seeking recreation from his own music-making, he has taken up the study of Mozart's "Magic Flute." "Never before," says he, "has so nonsensical and stupid a text been set to such glorious music. How grateful I am to Fate that Mozart's music has not lost for me a single hair's-breadth of its natural, unaffected fascination. You have no idea, my dear friend, what strange emotions pour through me when I sink myself in it. It is something wholly different from the passionate ecstasy which a Beethoven, Schumann, or Chopin awaken in me."

There are other archaic touches which come with a pleasurable shock to the knowing in this music. Thus, after Pauline has sung a beautiful romance in the second act for the delectation of her friends, she deplores its melancholy mood and proposes a song from the steppes, in which they join. It is "Maschenka," a folksong, which is reproduced with a fine preservation of its native manner and spirit.

Again, when the old Countess, returning from the ball, rails at the decadence of social manners since the days of her youth, when counts and dukes were at her feet in Paris, she recalls that once, in the palace of the Prince de Condé, she sang a romance for the King of France; and she sings it, repeating it again in a murmur as she falls asleep. It is the air from Grétry's " Richard Cœur de Lion " beginning " Je crains de lui parler la nuit." But all these ingenious and gracious devices are of small account compared with the dramatic music in the voice of Tschaikowsky when the issue has been joined and he tells of the emotions of Hermann and the luckless Lisa. Not only in his orchestration, which is admirable throughout, but in his themes and their development he discloses a genius for dramatic expression which is remarkable and for which not even his symphonies and symphonic poems had prepared us. The opera was splendidly sung and beautifully staged under the direction of Herr Mahler, who had brought it forward at the Court Opera in Vienna in December, 1902, when Mr. Slezak also took part in the performance.

CHAPTER VII

POPULAR OPERA AT THE CENTURY THEATER

PRODUCTION OF AN ENGLISH OPERA—"THE PIPE OF DESIRE"—
A VERSATILE PREDECESSOR OF THIS AUTHOR—IMPORTANCE
OF OPERATIC TEXTS—A FANTASTIC OPERA—JUMBLING OF
MYTHOLOGICAL AND FOLKLORE ELEMENTS—ENGLISH
OPERA AT THE METROPOLITAN—A PRIZE COMPETITION—
"MONA"—EARLY HISTORY OF "NATOMA"—AGITATION
FOLLOWING THE CONTEST—ACTION BY THE CITY CLUB—
PLANS FOR POPULAR OPERA AT THE CENTURY THEATER—A
DISASTROUS EXPERIMENT—A STUDY OF FINANCIAL RESULTS
—THE SYSTEMS OF THE METROPOLITAN AND CENTURY COM-
PANIES COMPARED—OPERATIC TRANSLATIONS—THE TRAIN-
ING NEEDED BY SINGERS AND COMPOSERS—NATIONAL
SCHOOLS OF MUSIC—MUSICAL IDIOMS—NEED OF A FORWARD
MAN AS AN EXEMPLAR—EARLY AMERICAN OPERAS

ANOTHER promise made in the previous year, but left unfulfilled, was made good in the dying hours of the season 1909-10 by the production at the Metropolitan Opera House on March 18 (it was afterwards played also at the New Theater) of Frederick S. Converse's opera, "The Pipe of Desire." It was given with the following cast, which was changed at the New Theater by the substitution of Mme. Mariska Aldrich for Mme. Homer:

Iolan	Riccardo Martin
Naoia	Louise Homer
The Old One	Clarence Whitehill
First Sylph	Leonora Sparkes
First Undine	Lillia Snelling
First Salamander	Glenn Hall
First Gnome	Herbert Witherspoon

The words of this opera, or "operatic fantasy" as it was called, are English, and the composer is an American of old New England stock. Moreover, all the singers in the cast

PRODUCTION OF AN AMERICAN OPERA

were native Americans. Much was made of these facts in the announcements, but their significance lies in the application of them. Once the *New York Tribune,* in whose chair of musical criticism I have sat for nearly forty years, had a musical reviewer who composed two operas. He wrote also the words, which were English, and the operas, or one of them at least, had performances in New York and Philadelphia. By precept and example, Mr. W. H. Fry, the critic in question, championed the cause of opera in the vernacular with a great deal of zeal. His arguments were sound sixty years ago and are sound today, but neither his arguments nor his operas affected the status of opera in the United States—a fact which hurts my professional pride somewhat. Much later, when German opera supplanted for a space the Italian form at the Metropolitan Opera House, writing for the newspaper which had enjoyed the rather unique distinction of having on its staff an editor who was as good a composer as he was a critic and as good a political writer as he was a composer, I hailed the fact with gladness because I thought and said that it was a step toward the nationalization of opera, a consummation devoutly to be wished, but impossible of realization so long as the Italian system was dominant. A memory of the illtempered criticism which my attitude called forth thirty years ago came to mind on the evening when Mr. Converse's opera was brought forward and I observed that every one of the artists concerned in it was associated with the German representations at the Metropolitan except Mr. Martin, a Kentuckian. But there were features of the performance which were calculated to give pause to the enthusiasm of those in the audience who were thoughtful as well as patriotic. Of what good is the use of the vernacular in an opera if the words which are sung can not be understood? What is the use of an English text if it is even less intelligible to the hearer than German, French, or Italian? If nationalization was in any degree the aim of this production, that aim was completely destroyed in the performance. It is an old story that there are two ways of looking at an operatic libretto. That which used to prevail in France (and still prevails), and which was given to Germany by Richard Wagner, is that the text is largely the determining factor in the work and that the province of music is to give the words a greater beauty and a heightened potency. That is the lesson which Lully and Gluck taught the French and which their successors made the foundation of the French school. It is also the lesson which Wagner taught his people when he achieved the regeneration of the lyric drama, not only in Germany but throughout the world. But these men, while they gave practical instruction to their singers, made their great reforms possible by studying the genius of the language which they used and making expressive use of its idioms. They did not leave the matter of verbal utterance wholly to the singer; they made it a part of their system of musical declamation. Every would-be representative of nationalism in art ought to follow their example, provided he accepts the theory that the lyric drama is a rational form of art. There is another point of view—and it had able champions in the past—which reduces the question of language to a matter of indifference. Mme. de Staël condemned the German composers because in their music they followed too closely the sense of the words, and lauded the Italians because they made the "air and the words conform to each other only in a general way." This notion of the relationship between the words and music of an opera is the general one even today—there is no use denying that fact—and so long as it remains so it will be a difficult task for anybody to demonstrate that we ought to hear German, French, and Italian operas in English translations. Many of the old pieces would sound absurd in English because they were written without consideration for the dramatic proprieties; they retain their charm because of their music, which the audience recognizes as conforming to the drama "in a gen-

THE PLOT OF "THE PIPE OF DESIRE" 167

eral way." In the case of the performance which I am considering, except for a few short phrases distributed among all the performers and the lines which Mr. Whitehill sang, nobody understood what was being uttered.

Was it the fault of the composer? In a small degree, yes. Of the singers? In a large degree, yes. But chiefly it was the fault of the librettist. Mr. George Edward Barton's book is an extremely amateurish performance. If it has any value it is purely literary. It is a fairy-fantasy woefully weighted with what the author no doubt thought was profound symbolism. But in its execution there is a most amusing jumble of operatic shreds and patches. The story runs something like this: The king of the fairy-folk (elves, gnomes, sylphs, and salamanders) has a musical instrument, the pipe, the sound of which provokes unrest among all who hear it. He plays upon it at the request of his subjects, and they find in the music only inspiration to a merry dance. A mortal wrests it from him, and though "it is forbidden," he plays upon it. Its voice summons his love from a sick-bed and makes her struggle over rocks and through streams to reach his side. She is stricken with a fever, her mind is turned awry, and she dies in his arms. Had he put restraint upon his impatient desire for a day he would have enjoyed a full measure of marital happiness. Then he curses God and lives out his span of life in a few moments and dies by the side of her who was to have been his wife. The king of the fairy-folk proclaims the moral of the piece, which is that disobedience to divine law is always punished.

This is the poetical conceit proclaimed in words which are anything but poetical and which have about as much dramatic potentiality as a proposition in Euclid. On the stage, however, there flit about shadows of familiar operatic personages and elements. The "Old One," as the king is called, is a mixture of Wagner's Wotan and Ambroise Thomas's Harper; the first salamander is an absurd caricature of Loge, the first gnome of Mime; Naoia, the mortal woman, goes mad like Lucia and Marguerite and dies stricken like Mireille. The pipe is Oberon's horn, Tamino's flute, and Papageno's bells, though it fails to discourse music of the kind that its nature and magic power would seem to invite. The elves dance about Iolan, the shepherd, like the Flower Maidens around Parsifal. The gnomes and salamanders burst through the ranks of the dancers like the satyrs in the Bacchanalian scene in " Tannhäuser." But the imitations are all absurdly infantile and only evoke a pitying smile because of their futility and incongruity.

Mr. Converse has given a musical setting to this singular phantasmagoria in the Wagnerian manner. Once on the entrance of Naoia, near the close of the opera, he drops into something which might be described as real song, but the rest of the opera is formless declamation more or less melodic, over a stream of instrumental music which flows on with moments of placid beauty at times and foams in passionate surges in the climaxes. There is the usual application of the device of typical phrases which we were told were symbols of the magical pipe, law, the shepherd, fate, and so on. The themes are deftly woven into a fabric which is frequently of exquisite sheen and iridescent beauty, but it is difficult to associate them, except in an arbitrary way, with the dramatic elements and agencies for which they are supposed to stand. They have none of the onomatopoetic character or the delineative force of Wagner's *motivi*. The romantic nature of the subject and the scene of merrymaking which the painter, costumer, stage-manager, and ballet-master made one of real beauty and charm would seem to call for a deal of melody, but as Grétry cried out " Six francs for an E-string! " after listening to an opera by Méhul in which the violins were replaced by violas, so one might have been tempted after an hour of Mr. Converse's opera to offer dollars for a frank, old-fashioned, unaffected tune. It is predominantly music which betrays the processes of reflection, but much of it is beautiful and

Mr. Converse's subtle mastery of harmonic and instrumental devices is most admirable.

I have been precipitated by the consideration of Mr. Converse's opera and some of the circumstances attending its production into a chapter of history and discussion relating to a subject which must occupy my attention frequently and seriously during the remainder of this critical chronicle. The history will stand by itself as complete as I think necessary to my purpose and as accurate as I can make it. The question now confronting me is that of national opera in its two phases of original composition and the performance of foreign works in translated form. It was but a natural consequence of the polyglot policy established by Mr. Grau that the minds of the directors of the Metropolitan Opera Company should be directed towards the obvious propriety of extending the same hospitality to English opera that had been accorded to Italian, German, and French—to English opera, not necessarily to English translations, for that would be to violate the principle upon which the boasted policy of the establishment rested. As early as February, 1908, Mr. Otto H. Kahn, chairman of the executive committee, telling of things which were to follow the reorganization of the company, said: "It has been the idea of a number of the directors for a long time now that the Metropolitan Opera House would be more truly a national institution if English opera were given there. Mr. Dippel, Mr. Mahler, and I have discussed this recently, and we believe that such a course would be an improvement. One of the results would be the encouragement of native singers." On November 29 of the same year Signor Gatti proposed to the directors that a prize be offered by the company for an opera in English. Action was at once taken on the proposition, which, the General Manager said, had been prompted by a number of commendatory letters which had followed the announcement of his purpose to produce " The Pipe of Desire." Publicity of the action of the company at once brought out from Mr. Hammerstein the statement that six weeks before he had signed a contract with Mr. Victor Herbert for an English opera to be produced at the Manhattan Opera House. As a matter of fact the purpose of Mr. Hammerstein to bring forward such an opera had been proclaimed by him in his prospectus for 1907-08, but not fulfilled. " Natoma," the opera in question, was offered to Mr. Gatti after the purchase of Mr. Hammerstein's interests, and one act of it had a trial on the stage with orchestra at the Metropolitan, but Mr. Gatti rejected it. It finally reached the Metropolitan's boards through the Philadelphia-Chicago Company under Mr. Dippel's management. I mention these facts here as forming an incident of the rivalry between the opera houses, not as a reflection on the judgment of Mr. Gatti, which I think was sound and in no wise impeached by the subsequent performance of the work. Formal announcement of the Metropolitan contest was made on December 15, 1908. The prize was to be $10,000. The conditions in brief were these: The composer must be a native citizen of the United States, though the place of his residence was immaterial; the opera must be original and never have been performed or published in whole or part prior to the making of the award; it must be what is commonly known as " grand opera " and not require more than three and one-quarter hours in performance; the libretto must be in English and might be based upon any drama, novel, or other literary composition, but, if so, must be a new adaptation; the contest was to close on September 15, 1910, after which date no manuscripts were to be received; if book and score were productions of different persons, both names were to be submitted with means for identifying the respective labor of the authors and an agreement between them as to the division of the prize if awarded; the jury was to be appointed by the directors of the Metropolitan Company and an agreement of two-thirds of the members was to be necessary to an award. The usual methods for preserving anonymity were prescribed and the jury empowered, should it deem it expedient, to reopen the contest and receive additional scores "for a period of eighteen months after the contest shall have been reopened." The Metropolitan Opera Company pledged itself to produce the opera during the season following the award, and reserved for itself and its affiliated theaters exclusive performing rights in the United States, Canada, Cuba, and Mexico for a period of five years without payment of royalties or other compensation to the authors, and the same rights for five succeeding years on the payment of royalties of $75 for each act, but not more than $150 for the entire opera. The company also reserved to itself and its affiliations performing rights on fixed terms of royalty payments on the operas which might be submitted other than that winning the prize. The other conditions of the contest were immaterial.

About three months before the expiration of the two years' term the report became current that the directors intended to extend the period of competition for a year, and there was a decided flurry of protest and indignation among the composers who had submitted scores and their friends. Mr. Kahn, questioned by newspaper reporters, admitted that such action had been taken. This was plainly outside the province of the company and was denied by an official statement put forth on September 12, 1910, which characterized the report as an erroneous impression which "seemed to prevail," and stated that the contest would be closed on September 15. The jury selected by the directors in December was composed of Alfred Hertz, one of the conductors of the Metropolitan Company; Walter Damrosch, George W. Chadwick, and Charles Martin Loeffler. They set about the examination of the scores submitted in competition to the number of thirty, and on May 2, 1911, announced the award of the prize to an opera entitled "Mona," the composer of the music of which was Horatio W. Parker and the author of the libretto Brian Hooker. The former, then and still Professor of Music at Yale University, had long been known as a composer in the United States as well as England, where performances of his oratorio " Hora Novissima " in 1899 at the Three Choirs Festival in Worcester and later at the Chester Festival, and of " A Wanderer's Psalm " at the Hereford Festival, won him such repute that in 1902 he was honored by Cambridge University with the degree of Doctor of Music. Mr. Hooker, a Yale graduate in 1904, was instructor of rhetoric in the university from 1906 to 1909. A consideration of the merits and demerits of " Mona " may be deferred until the story of the season in which it was performed is told.

Interest in English opera grew apace after the award of the Metropolitan Company's prize. Straightway there was a great ado in the newspapers about English opera and operas in English. And a certain man named Tito Ricordi, speaking down Boston way, where baleful prophecies were rife touching the future of the Boston Company, proclaimed that the burden resting on the country was a paucity of opera, not the surfeit that seemed to be indicated by the disastrous season through which New York had but recently passed. So Mr. Ricordi was invited to sit down at dinner in New York with managers, composers, singers, and critics and further expound. Being a man with a heart in the cause, albeit a foreigner, he talked right eloquently about the excellence of the English language in song, the prodigious talent of American singers, and the folly of sending them abroad to learn how to pronounce foreign words badly. There should be a great national institution in the United States, he said, where they might learn to sing English; and, chiefly, there should be English opera companies permanently housed in forty or fifty American cities. Very disinterested was this advice of Mr. Ricordi, of course, for he was drawing royalties from only one-third of all the performances giving at the Metropolitan at the time, and

AN AGITATION FOR NATIONAL OPERA 173

he did no more than hope that he might supply the forty or fifty theaters of his dream (which was like that of Mr. Hammerstein and the Metropolitan Company) with more Butterflies, Toscas, Bohemians, and Girls of the Golden West. But before he returned to his native Italy the operatic muse had changed her complexion, and Mr. Ricordi said that he didn't mean opera at popular prices, but costly and aristocratic opera like that at the Metropolitan. And so he spoiled his pretty evangel.

Another effect of the competition was the organization of a "Society for the Promotion of Opera in English," which aimed, as its proclamation put it, "to advocate and maintain the principle that American opera-goers should be enabled to understand and more fully enjoy opera by hearing it sung clearly to them as frequently as possible in their own language." Foreign operas were not to be cast into utter and outer darkness; all that could reasonably be expected was that "side by side with German, French, and Italian the language of this country shall be given equal dignity and importance in those opera houses by the performance of standard and new works in English and the gradual organization of companies properly fitted to interpret opera in the tongue of the great mass of opera-goers." This document was signed by David Bispham, Reginald de Koven, Walter Damrosch, Horatio Parker, Charles Henry Meltzer, and Albert Mildenberg. If the organization still exists it is only on paper or in the minds of its self-constituted officers. My impression is that it talked itself to death in a single meeting.

Still another product of the agitation was a movement inaugurated by a substantial civic institution which resulted in a serious and resolute effort to put into concrete form what had thitherto been merely floating, fleeting, futile, flocculent effusion of speech. At a luncheon of the City Club in the spring of 1912 the subject of opera was the order of the day. Again, in the words of the double who undid Dr.

Hale, everything that had been said was again said and so well said by composers, singers, managers, and patriotic promoters of opera that further speech on the topic became an impertinence unless followed by action of some sort. At the end the president of the club appointed a committee charged to investigate the question and ascertain whether or not it was feasible to produce first-class opera in New York at popular prices—meaning the prices prevalent at the theaters in general. The committee consisted of Edward Kellogg Baird (chairman), William C. Cornwell, Edward R. Finch, Otto H. Kahn, Roland Holt, Norman Hapgood, Isaac N. Seligman, and Arthur E. Stahlschmidt. Its inquiries made during the ensuing twelvemonth we were assured went with particularity into the circumstances surrounding operatic production at the municipal theaters of Italy, Germany, and France; their cost, management, subsidies, and deficits. As a result it drew up a report which laid down a plan for "the production of Municipal Opera in the city of New York." The title was a misnomer; but that does not matter much. Municipal opera on the European continent is opera under the supervision of municipal government and enjoying its financial support. As a rule, so far as my knowledge goes, the theater is owned by the city, and, though its management may be placed in the hands of lessees, the economic as well as the artistic administration is under the care of an officer of the city government. In this sense a municipal opera is as inconceivable in the United States as a municipal playhouse. The proposition of the committee embraced these features: a fund of $450,000 was to be raised for the purpose of producing opera at popular prices for three years, subscriptions to this fund being payable in instalments covering the period; for the first year $52,761.00 was required for the purchase of scenery, costumes, etc.; the cost of producing opera was estimated at $14,500 per week, or $232,000 for two seasons of eight weeks which were contemplated at the time—four weeks

OUTLINE OF THE CITY CLUB'S PROJECT 175

before the Metropolitan season and four weeks after; estimating the receipts at two-thirds of the capacity of the house, they would amount to $199,547, leaving a deficit of $32,453; this deficit would be diminished from year to year and at the end of the fourth wear be wiped out; the management of the enterprise was to be placed in the hands of a director, American or foreign, who was to be given freedom of action in the selection of repertory and artists, but was to carry out the policy of the Board of Directors " as outlined from time to time " and be responsible to it; the repertory was to be cosmopolitan—English, French, German, and Italian—but no experiments were to be made with novelties; the Metropolitan Opera Company was to furnish properties, costumes, scenery, etc., at a nominal rental, the use of these by both companies being feasible because the popular season was to begin about the 1st of September, 1913, and there would thus be no conflict with the Metropolitan season, at the beginning of which members of the company, including chorus and ballet, were to be free to accept engagements elsewhere; at the conclusion of the Metropolitan season 1913-14 the popular season was to be resumed for another period of eight weeks. In this last feature the plan was little else than a parallel with the experiment made in October, 1900, when Mr. Henry W. Savage and Mr. Grau formed a partnership for a season of English opera at the Metropolitan. This experiment, moreover, had the additional merit of being a really intelligent and dignified effort to habilitate not only opera sung in the vernacular, but opera composed in English. The company was an excellent one, Mr. Savage an experienced and enterprising manager, and the repertory of the season given under his joint management with Mr. Grau from October to December, 1900, under the title of the Metropolitan English Grand Opera Company, while it contained operettas (among them some of Gilbert & Sullivan's) and some specifically English works (Goring Thomas's " Esmeralda "

176 INCORPORATION OF THE CENTURY OPERA CO.

being one), was otherwise quite as pretentious as the repertory of the regular company which followed it save that it omitted the later dramas of Wagner. Its list of singers was made up to a considerable extent of artists who had gained routine in the Carl Rosa Company in London and elsewhere in Europe. Yet the season was less successful than the seasons which Mr. Savage had been accustomed to give at the theaters, probably, as I suggested in my " Chapters of Opera," because of the air of aristocracy which it wore without being able to assume the social importance which belonged only to the foreign exotic. The Century Theater was nominated as the home of the ambitious new undertaking because it had been built with a view to co-operation between it and the Metropolitan Opera House, which made an interchange of scenery practicable. Sops were thrown to subscribers by the offer of titles; by subscribing for $1,000 or more one became a " Founder of Opera for the People "; or one might become a " stockholder " for from $100 to $1,000, or a " subscribing member " for $100 or less. The plan was to become operative on the receipt of subscriptions amounting to $300,000, a board of directors was to be elected by the founders and stockholders on the basis of the amount subscribed, and the City Club, through its board of trustees, was to appoint three directors each year.

On May 4, 1913, the City Club announced that subscriptions amounting to one-third of the $300,000 had been secured. Mr. Kahn subscribed $30,000, William K. Vanderbilt and Clarence H. Mackay $15,000 each, Harry Payne Whitney $5,000, and members of the City Club $25,000. The Century Opera Company was incorporated on May 9, 1913, with a capital stock of $300,000 and organized by the election of Edward Kellogg Baird, president; Otto H. Kahn, vice-president; Alvin W. Krech, treasurer; Edward R. Finch, secretary, and the following Board of Directors: Otto H. Kahn, chairman; Edward Kellogg Baird, Edmund L. Baylies, William C. Cornwell, Andreas Dippel, Edward

OTTO H. KAHN
Managing Director of the Metropolitan Opera Company

R. Finch, Alvin W. Krech, Thomas W. Lamont, Philip M. Lydig, Clarence H. Mackay, George McAneny, Paul M. Warburg, Harry Payne Whitney, Henry Rogers Winthrop, and Frank A. Vanderlip. These gentlemen made a fair representation of three public institutions: the Metropolitan Opera House, the Century Theater, and the City Club. They chose Milton and Sargent Aborn as General Managers of the company and intrusted them with the administration of the first season of opera, which began at the Century Theater on September 15, 1913, with a performance in English of "Aïda." The Messrs. Aborn had had experience in giving opera of the crude and cheap English variety, their peripatetic companies being generally made up of singers who had gained some stage experience in operetta or native and foreign companies, and novices ambitious to enter the operatic field. There were many companies like theirs devastating the musical territory of the Middle West, but, backed by the dignity and money which the new institution afforded them, the managers organized a creditable and capable troupe, which contained such singers as Lois Ewell, Elisabeth Amsden, Kathleen Howard, Mary Jordan, Morgan Kingston, Alfred Kauffman, Thomas Chalmers, Gustav Bergman, Morton Adkins, and Louis Kreidler—a company comparable with the organizations which Mr. Savage had long been maintaining "on the road." The original plan to give a season of eight weeks, four before and four after the Metropolitan season, was abandoned in favor of one which contemplated thirty-five continuous weeks, with six evening and two afternoon performances each week, one performance of the opera on the list in its original tongue, the other performances in English. The egregious absurdity of such a scheme was apparent to all who had made even a cursory observation of theatrical and operatic affairs, but it was still further emphasized by the announcement that the repertory would be made up of thirty-three operas and that the last three weeks would be devoted to three representations of Wagner's Nibelung tetralogy and eight of "Parsifal."

I have neither time nor desire to enter upon a discussion of the performances of the company, which came to an end on April 18, 1914, after thirty-one weeks of activity. The season, originally planned for eight weeks, extended by the management to thirty-five, was curtailed four weeks ostensibly to allow time for alterations in the house prior to the second season. About the middle of the season Mr. Baird tendered his resignation to the Board of Directors of the company following financial difficulties in which the *Century Opera Magazine* (a publication of which he was the chief promoter) became involved. His resignation was not accepted and he remained a member of the directorate in the second season (1914-15), which terminated in the dissolution of the enterprise. During the thirty-one weeks of the first season twenty-six operas were produced. No new works were attempted, and those announced but not given were "Mignon," "King's Children," "Tannhäuser," "Traviata," "Salome," "Tristan und Isolde," the four dramas of "The Ring of the Nibelung," and "The Huguenots." The failure of the grandiose Wagnerian list was not at all deplorable, though its performance in English might have made a significant contribution to the discussion of the practicability and value of translations. Six operas were sung in their original tongue, viz.: "Aïda," "La Gioconda," "The Jewels of the Madonna," "Madame Butterfly," "Tosca," and "Lohengrin." In the third week "The Tales of Hoffmann" received eight performances (in English). A second week was vouchsafed to this opera as well as to "Madame Butterfly," "Louise," "Hänsel and Gretel," "Aïda," and "Thaïs." Humperdinck's fairy opera was associated with performances by the International Ballet. It received 29 performances in all, "Aïda" and "The Tales of Hoffmann" 17, "Madame Butterfly" and "Thaïs" 16, and "Louise" 15. The operas not mentioned in this enumeration were: "Lucia," "Samson and Dalilah," "Faust," "The Bohemian Girl," "Carmen," "Bohème," "Romeo and Juliet," "Rigoletto," "Cavalleria Rusticana," "Manon," "The Secret of Suzanne," "Pagliacci," "Tiefland," "Martha," and "Natoma." There were signs of disaffection in March, 1914, when Alfred Szendrei, conductor of the company, in a letter to the newspapers declared that the orchestra and chorus were incompetent, the rehearsals insufficient in number, and that he had been ashamed of many of the performances which he had conducted. To this the General Managers retorted that Mr. Szendrei was disaffected because he had not been re-engaged for the next season. A week later the Messrs. Aborn announced that, despite rumors to the contrary, English operas would be given at the Century Theater in 1914-15, but for only 29 weeks instead of 35. In May they proclaimed that the exclusive use of English, which had become the rule after the early weeks, would be abandoned and all operas be sung in the original languages. The policy of devoting an entire week to a single opera was also abandoned. A few weeks of the season 1914-15 sufficed to disclose that financial losses much greater than those made in the first season confronted the company. The receipts at the box-office showed a falling off of forty per cent. The General Managers advised that the company be transferred to Chicago, where they thought financial and social conditions had been less affected by the war than in New York. This was done, but the change resulted in no betterment of the company's affairs. Mr. Kahn withdrew from the directorate, though he still offered generous financial support to the undertaking on conditions looking to a more permanent foundation; but after six weeks in the Northwestern metropolis the season was summarily closed and the company disbanded.

Through the courtesy of Mr. Baird I am able to present some figures from the report of certified accountants touching the first season which may be of value to future experimenters in the field of popular opera. The average weekly receipts were $11,961.19, the average weekly expenditures $13,695.60, making a net loss for the season of $53,766.71. In the first 16 weeks there was an actual profit of $9,202.90; in the last 15 weeks a loss of $79,712.28. This would seem to me to indicate a total loss of $70,910.18 instead of $53,-766.71 as based on the difference between the average weekly receipts and expenditures. The company, says Mr. Baird, " suffered its first big loss in the fourteenth week with the production of ' The Bohemian Girl.' The directors were strongly opposed to producing that opera, but the management urged that it was a ' sure fire ' opera on the road, and they took full responsibility for including it in the repertoire." The next large loss occurred in the seventeenth week, when " Louise " was the repeated bill. At the first eight performances of the opera the company made a profit of $134.38; at the second the company incurred a loss of $4,560.78. " In every instance of a repetition," says Mr. Baird, " the company suffered a big loss. The repetition of several operas that had already been produced at eight performances earlier in the season lost the company over $25,000 in the latter half of the season. The reason for this is perfectly plain. The public had been absorbed. There were not enough people who had not seen the opera that season and who wanted to see it to justify its repetition. Hence to repeat meant a sure loss. Here again the policy of the management must be brought into question. The directors did not favor the numerous repetitions. It is against all the traditions of opera production. Several members of the board were also members of the Metropolitan board. That company in all its history had never given sixteen performances of the same opera in one season. In fact, it is the policy of that company never to give a repetition of an opera in the same week. They even go further than that— they never announce the repetition of an opera the week it is on the boards, for the reason, as Mr. Gatti says, ' to pre-

NEGATIVE RESULTS OF THE EXPERIMENT

vent its drawing against itself.'" There is validity in Mr. Baird's contention, but his comparison of the first half of the season with the second half, as well as his reference to the policy of the Metropolitan Opera House, needs amplification. In the second half of the season the Century Company was in competition with the Metropolitan season; the Century Company gave eight performances a week for 31 weeks, the Metropolitan Company six performances a week for 23 weeks; the Century Company produced 26 operas, none of them unfamiliar to the public, the Metropolitan 36 operas, of which five were novelties; to satisfy the subscribers of the Metropolitan every novelty must be given at least five times, but it is impossible to give that number of performances to every opera in the list; boxholders or subscribers to all the evenings and afternoons of the season would not tolerate five performances in succession of any work—a changing audience might, as we see from the fact that a dozen new plays may run an entire season in as many theaters in New York without exhausting the theatrical public of the city, including the visitors within its gates; opera is in a different case.

The extraordinary auspices under which the experiment was made and the fact that it combined the two elements, generally disassociated, of popular opera in different languages and popular opera wholly in the vernacular, differentiated the performances of the Century Opera Company from those of the hundreds of its predecessors made during a longer period than any living memory can compass. The questions raised found no solution, for the season proved disastrous and the performances in themselves, though sometimes highly creditable, offered nothing with which the public was not familiar. The controversy as to the relative popularity of what may for the sake of discussion be called the foreign and the native forms of the lyric drama had been carried on in New York for eighty years with success in the earlier days leaning now toward one side, now toward the other, but in latter days going steadily toward the exotic. Even in connection with the Century season I find the memorandum in my records that the nights on which the operas were given in their original tongues were the best patronized—a circumstance explained largely, if not wholly, by the greater fondness for opera of the city's citizens of foreign birth than that of the native. In respect of this, then, the best that can be said for the experiment in its first phase is that it was inconclusive. Nor was anything contributed by the performances to the solution of the question concerning the advisability of substituting English for the original languages in our operatic representations generally, in "nationalizing" the art-form, as the champions of the exclusive use of the vernacular are fond of saying. On this point let me speak now, and if possible let it be understood that I do so as a staunch and devout well-wisher of English or American opera. Considerations which ought to be obvious to every cultivated mind determined the question of what language can most righteously be employed in an operatic performance on the day when the art-form was born. The proper language in which to sing operatic music from an ideal point of view is the language for which the music was composed, the only language to which the musical idiom is native.

It is as destructive of the spirit of Italian or German or French music to sing it in English as it would be to sing English opera in Italian, German, or French. No paraphrase can be fitted to music without some loss to the beauty and potency of the original text as well as the music. The beauty, like an exhalation, vanishes. No people can feel the power of the phrase, "For the Lord God omnipotent reigneth," in Handel's "Hallelujah" chorus like the English, unless it be sung in the original and understood. There is no English, French, or German equivalent for "O, patria mia, mai piu ti rivedrò," as it is made to sound by Verdi, nor in any language but German for that exhalation of

ESSENTIALS OF A GOOD TRANSLATION

Isolde's spirit, " Mild und leise wie er lächelt." The essence of French melody departs when another vessel is substituted for French verse in French lyrics. These are facts, incontrovertible, enduring because they rest upon the genius of national art. Assuming that it is essential that the words of an opera be understood—a fact that I am entirely willing to admit, so far at least as operas of the most modern type are concerned—what is to be done to make opera in the vernacular palatable? Shall we educate the public down to the level of the mass of translated texts or reform the repertory *ab initio*? If the latter, what shall be done for the people who have acquired a liking for operas whose texts, reasonable in the original tongues, become prosaic and absurd in translation? " Carmen " is an admired opera, deservedly so; yet how many of us would preserve a serious frame of mind if we were to hear Zuniga ask of Don José in melodious recitative: " Is yon building the factory at which young girls are employed at cigarette-making? " Who that has heard " Lohengrin " in English has not smiled broadly at the climax of the scene before the cathedral when the knight of the swan turns at the foot of the steps and rings out the question: " Elsa, with whom conversest thou? " Perhaps the truthful relation of an incident of the Century Company's season will help elucidate this point. On November 4, 1913, at 4 o'clock in the afternoon, I sat in my chair at the theater and saw Bide-the-Bent enter a hall in the castle of Sir Henry Ashton, where a lot of wedding-guests were making a jubilation, and informed them that Lucy Ashton (or rather, Lucia, for Lucy doesn't fit the music) had killed her husband immediately after the ceremony of marriage. It was startling news, though no one would have thought it from the conduct of the merry company, nor even from the words of the messenger, which, though they look somewhat disjointed, ungrammatical, and repetitious in print, flowed quite placidly on a stream of tune nicely punctuated with reiterations by the chorus. This was how Bide-the-Bent conveyed the tidings:

> Cease ye, O, cease these sounds of gladness,
> Grief I bring ye, a dire misfortune.
> From the chamber where, sad and silent,
> To her Lord I Lucy guided;
> Cries of anguish broke loud upon us,
> 'Twixt suspicion and fear sore divided,
> Terror seized me; I burst upon them;
> Sight of dread appalled my senses.
> By her husband the bride was kneeling;
> In her hand she held the dagger,
> And her anguish recommences.
> Wretched maid! She'd slain her husband!
> Gazing near, and from her lips a smile broke forth.
> Ah! Her spirit most unhappy,
> Reason's bonds had cast away;
> Her spirit unhappy,
> Her spirit most unhappy,
> Reason's bonds, yes, reason's bonds had cast away.
> Ah! Heaven in mercy the crime forgive her!
> Sad was her fate, cruel hatred's prey,
> Sad was her fate, cruel hatred's prey.
> Gazing forth with eyes all vacant,
> In her hand she held a dagger.
> Ah! May heaven the crime forgive her!
> Sad was her fate, cruel hatred's prey,
> Sad was her fate, cruel hatred's prey,
> Sad was her fate! Ah, yes! Sad was her fate;
> Ah, yes! sad was her fate.

Mr. Alfred Kauffman sang these words and enunciated them with a distinctness which was painful and which made some of his hearers realize what was meant by him who said that words which were too foolish to be spoken might be sung. But it really did not seem to signify much, so far as the people who heard them on this occasion were concerned. It was opera; it was opera in English; it was opera at popular prices; that sufficed the audience. To proceed with the argument: In the opera of today it is peculiarly essential that a fine regard for the music be had in translating operatic texts into English. Addison thought so as long as two hundred years ago. He not only pleaded in his way for English opera and wrote the book of one, but he assailed Italian opera, whether in the original or translated form (or, as was the habit in his day, in both tongues), with his prettiest wit. In one case he tells of an Italian line which read, literally, "And turns my rage into pity," but for the sake of rhyme was translated, " And into pity turns my rage." By this means, he says, the soft notes which were attached to pity in the Italian fell upon the word rage in the English, and the angry sounds which were tuned to rage in the original were made to express pity in the translation. Are there English versions of foreign scores which could stand such a test today? Would it not be necessary first to appoint a commission of literary musicians, or musical literary men, to retranslate all of the operas for the English repertory? I open some of the scores most conveniently at hand. In the English " Parsifal " in a passage of Kundry's recital to Parsifal, " Thy father's love and death " is given as " Thy father's death and love," whereby a sweet consonant harmony falls upon the word death and a poignant dissonance on love.

There are other phases of the question which invite consideration. It involves not only a knowledge of the art of singing, pure and simple, i. e. the art of vocalization, but also a knowledge of the art of diction, and this on the part of the composer and maker of the book as well as the singer. From the composer it exacts this knowledge plus the capacity to give the drama musical expression in the spirit of the people for whom he writes and whose language he employs. Our singers have not been trained in English song in the sense that the students of French song have been trained since the establishment of the French school of music, or the Germans since Wagner gave them a distinctively national art. There was a brief blossoming of English art under Purcell, but all that has survived (the ballad operas which rejoiced the souls of Englishmen and Americans in the eighteenth century and the mongrel works of Balfe and Wallace) is found in the operettas of Gilbert & Sullivan—works worthy of study by the creative as well as interpretative artists of today, from this point of view as well as others. It is significant, but humiliating, that the singers of English at the Century Theater and Metropolitan Opera House who have been most intelligible have been foreigners, and this despite the handicap of their foreign accent. Moreover, it is the affectation and conceit of so-called "grand opera" singers and composers which has helped to make them unintelligible in English. Singers and composers in the field of musical comedies and operettas have little difficulty in making them understood. There is an analogy here with the notoriously poor acting of opera singers. "I am not here to act, but to sing," said an indignant comic opera tenor to Mr. Barker, the English stage-manager, when he was employed at the Casino in New York. "God forbid that I should ever undertake to tell a tenor how to act!" was the fervid reply; "I am only trying to tell you how to get on the stage." And then he told me that the everlasting torment which he expected for his misdeeds on earth was to have to train opera tenors in heaven—or hell—I have forgotten to which place he had consigned himself.

We need, then, a national school of composition as well as of singing. How shall it be created? Not by prize competitions; not by subventions, private or public; not by the piling up of costly buildings and dubbing them "national" opera houses; nor yet by the establishment and maintenance of gigantic educational institutions. If these things could beget a national art, England ought long ago to have had it. These things are helpful, but they are not determinative. The determinative factor, if an answer to the question may be ventured upon, is the coming of a creative genius who shall by concrete example point the way to the goal and compel a following. He may be a product of earlier strivings (as Wagner was the continuator of Gluck,

Beethoven, Weber, and Marschner), but he must be strong enough to hew out an individual path, which shall be alluring to his people and along which his contemporaries and successors shall gladly follow him, so that they, too, may reap of his success and his glory. Two factors are here set down as essential: the genius who shall strike out the national notion and the geniuses who shall adopt the notion and present it again in their manner. The imitation need not, indeed it must not, be slavish. Only one German composer since Wagner has successfully applied that great musical dramatist's system, and he, Humperdinck, knew how to modify it so that it might become subservient to the individualism of his style and his subjects. All others—I might make an exception in the case of Richard Strauss—have failed because they could not mix original inspiration with reflection. They copied the body only; they could not copy the spirit. Purcell had no successors in England because before a capable man arose the Italian exotic had struck root in the soil of English fashion and was nurtured, as it has been ever since, by the aristocracy.

The foundations of all national schools of music in Europe, with the exception of the French and Italian, rest on folksong idioms; but the foundations were laid by such forward men as the Scandinavian Gade and Grieg, the Pole Chopin, the Russian Glinka, and the Bohemian Smetana. In each of these cases there was an element of national character which was imitated from the folksong of the various peoples, but the force which impressed this element upon the artistic music of the world, which introduced the characteristic flavor into the art-works written in classic forms, or modified those forms so that the vessel might the better hold the contents, was the individual genius of the men who struck out the new paths.

The risibles of every veteran observer of the opera, especially of every veteran reviewer for the press, are excited whenever there is a discussion of the question of English opera by the calm assumption of youthful enthusiasts or their old exploiters that the subject is novel. " English opera has never had a fair trial," say they, yet English opera is nearly if not quite two hundred years old in America; " American composers have never had an opportunity," yet native operas are as old in America as native plays; " our singers have never had a chance to show what they can do," yet American sopranos, contraltos, tenors, and basses have graced the boards of Europe and America for three-quarters of a century and one of the tuneful tribe, the daughter of a Boston shoemaker, sang her way to the titular throne of Portugal. That our singers have not been as numerous in our fashionable opera houses as the foreign contingent is true, but the reason lies in the attitude of the public toward opera which has compelled managers to employ the best talent to be found the world over. Great talent has never gone begging for recognition because it was American. Opera in America, as I have had many occasions to remind discontented, impatient, and uninformed enthusiasts, is much older than they think. Traces of it are found in the theatrical records of the early decades of the eighteenth century, and the English type of opera as it flourished in its native habitat was industriously cultivated in the Colonies and States of America from 1749 to 1825, in which latter year Italian opera came to compete with it; and it has been industriously cultivated ever since from coast to coast. It would profit those who wish to speak intelligently on the subject to consult what Mr. O. G. Sonneck and other historians have written about it, as well as to scan the pages of the " Catalogue of Opera Librettos Printed Before 1800," compiled by Mr. Sonneck for the Library of Congress. A great deal could be written about the use of American subjects by native and foreign librettists and composers as set forth in that confessedly incomplete list. Native operas do not of necessity require native or national subjects, but if they are wanted it will be found that our woods are literally as well as metaphorically full of them. There was abundance of romance in our early social and political history, as anybody may learn by a perusal of the books written about us by our European visitors in the period immediately before and after the war of the revolution. Let me glance at a few titles taken from Mr. Sonneck's catalogue, which indicate the character of the musical plays: " The American Adventurers "; " The American Indian "; " L'Americana in Europa," an Italian ballet; " L'Americano," set to music by Piccinni; " The Cherokee," set by Stephen Storace; " Columbus; or, A World Discovered "; " The Fair American," for which Thomas Carter wrote the music and which was produced at Drury Lane, London, on May 18, 1782; " La Familie Americaine," words by " Citoyen " Bouilly, who wrote the libretto on which " Fidelio " is based, music by " Citoyen " Dalayrac; " Le Huron "; " Gli Inglesi in America," a ballet. None of these titles piques curiosity so much as a German play with music entitled " Pocahontas," printed in Jamestown in 1784 and the same year in Ansbach, Germany. A Johann Wilhelm Rose is named as the author of the words, but the name of the author of the music is unknown. Mr. Sonneck quotes the following remarks, in German, from the preface: " This play has lain longer than Horace demanded in the desk of the author, who wrote it thirteen years ago to please a friend. That the savage maiden speaks wittily will surprise no one who knows, from Captain Smith's Travels, that wit was a prominent trait in the character of the women of Virginia." I have read enough about Pocahontas to know that she was capable of affection, pathos, and melancholy, but as a representative of the witty women of Virginia she strikes me as a novelty.

Here are some notes on operas the librettos of which were reprinted in America on the occasion of their performances here:

" ' The Dead Alive, or The Double Funeral.' A comic opera in two acts, with additions and alterations, as performed by the old American Company in New York, with universal applause. By John O'Keefe. . . . With an account of the author. New York, printed by Dodge, Allen & Campbell, 1789." This is a reprint of the libretto of an opera for which Samuel Arnold wrote the music, which was originally produced at the Haymarket, London, on September 24, 1789. The performance in the United States before the end of the year shows how close were the ties between the London and American theaters at the time.

"'The Deserter,' a comic opera in two acts at the Theatre, New York, with universal applause. By Mr. C. Dibdin. New York, Samuel Campbell, 1787." This was an English version of Monsigny's "Le Déserteur," which had its first American representation on June 8, 1787. In London Monsigny's authorship of the music was recorded and it was noted that there was additional music by Philidor and Dibdin. New Yorkers were left to imagine that all the music came from Dibdin's brain.

"'The Lord of the Manor,' a comic opera in three acts, as performed with universal applause by the American Company. Philadelphia, H. Taylor, 1791." The date of the first American performance of this opera has not been discovered.

"'Love in a Village,' a comic opera written by Mr. Bickerstaff, as performed at the New Theatre in Philadelphia." This opera, a great favorite in its day, was a *pasticcio,* the music being drawn from a dozen composers, among them Arne, Boyce, Carey, Galuppi, Geminiani, Giardini, Handel, and Larry Grogan. "Who in the name of St. Patrick was Larry Grogan?" asks Mr. Sonneck.

A taboo rested on the drama and opera, then more closely connected than they are now, in Boston for a long time after these forms of entertainment were popular in New York, Philadelphia, Charlestown, Baltimore, and other places, but even Boston is represented among these reprints of foreign librettos, as we note from "The Spoil'd Child.

THE FIRST AMERICAN OPERA

A farce in two acts, as performed at the Theatre in Boston. First American edition. Boston, Thomas Hall, 1796." Bickerstaff was the author of this book, and the play had been performed in Baltimore.

The most interesting records in Mr. Sonneck's catalogue for the students of American opera are those giving information about the works which were written and composed in America prior to the nineteenth century. The list is not long and might be extended by appeal to private collections; but I am confined to the Congressional catalogue. Here is the title of what Mr. Sonneck assures us was the first American opera, " The Disappointment; or, The Force of Credulity." A new American comic opera, of two acts. By Andrew Barton, Esq. New York, printed in the year 1767." Concerning this opera Mr. Sonneck says: " This first American ballad opera with eighteen airs indicated by title (Air IV, ' Yankee Doodle '), was to have been first performed by the American Company at Philadelphia on April 20, 1767, but it was withdrawn, ' personal reflections ' rendering it ' unfit for the stage.' " Another opera with a text written by an American was " The Reconciliation; or, The Triumph of Nature," a comic opera in two acts by Peter Markoe, published in Philadelphia in 1790. This was a ballad opera based on a German piece entitled " Erastus." The dedication reads: " To His Excellency, Thomas Miflin, Esq., President of the State of Pennsylvania; and to the Honorable Thomas M'Kean, Chief Justice of the said State; this comic opera approved by them in their official capacity according to law; but withdrawn from the managers of the theatre after it had remained in their hands more than four months, is . . . inscribed. Evidently authors and managers had the same troubles 135 years ago as now. A woman also shows up among these pioneer American librettists, one who, if she were alive today, would probably be found parading in front of the White House in Washington in an effort to bring feminine pressure to bear on the

President in one of the few ways distasteful to man. Her opera has a political theme: "'Slaves in Algiers; or, A Struggle for Freedom.' A play interspersed with songs, in three acts, by Mrs. Rowson. As performed at the New Theatres in Philadelphia and Baltimore. Printed for the author, 1794." Mrs. Rowson was the wife of the leader of a regimental band in England, say the annotators of John Bernard's "Retrospections of America," 1797-1811: "He and his wife came to America with Wignell in 1793. He was eclipsed by Mrs. Rowson, the author of 'Charlotte Temple, A Tale of Truth,' of a comedy called 'Americans in England,' and other works, and an actress of average ability." The lady's musical play was first performed at the New Theater in Philadelphia on December 29, 1794. The music was composed by Alexander Reinagle, one of a number of English musicians who were extremely influential in New York and Philadelphia in the last years of the eighteenth and first years of the nineteenth century, before the German invasion had set in. He came of a family of musicians, and his nephew, Alexander Robert Reinagle, composed the psalm-tune known in the hymnals as "St. Peter's." Finally I reach "'Darby's Return.' A comic sketch, as performed at the Theatre in this City (New York) with universal applause." This opera was written by William Dunlap in 1789 and produced in November of that year.

CHAPTER VIII

THE FIRST SEASON UNDER MR. GATTI-CASAZZA ALONE

OPERA AT THE METROPOLITAN IN 1910-11—REDUCTION OF FORCES—FAILURE OF AN AFFILIATION WITH CHICAGO AND BOSTON—ILLNESS OF SIGNOR CARUSO—DEATH OF M. GILIBERT—GLUCK'S "ARMIDE"—THE BALLETS OF LULLY AND GLUCK—ROUSSEAU'S SARCASM—VISITS OF PUCCINI AND HUMPERDINCK—PRODUCTION OF THEIR NEW OPERAS—"LA FANCIULLA DEL WEST"—HOW MR. BELASCO TRAINED SINGERS TO ACT—A FAILURE AND ITS CAUSE—"KÖNIGSKINDER"—A "SUFFRAGETTE" OPERA—"ARIANE ET BARBE-BLEUE"—HOW A SATIRE WAS CONSTRUED AS A PLEA FOR WOMAN'S SUFFRAGE

THE twenty-sixth season of opera at the Metropolitan Opera House, which began on November 14, 1910, and ended on April 15, 1911, was the first in which Signor Gatti was sole manager *de jure* as well as *de facto,* and also the first in which he was untrammeled by the rivalry of Mr. Hammerstein and unvexed by unseemly scandal. The fever of expansion had been allayed and a becoming modesty characterized the announcements in the prospectus. The performances at the New Theater and the Baltimore enterprise were abandoned and the Philadelphia representations limited to eight, the needs of that city in the latter half of the season being supplied by the company with an invertible title (Chicago-Philadelphia in the West and Philadelphia-Chicago in the East). The forces were therefore reduced fully one-half. A few singers were added to the local roster and a promise of significant help held out by affiliation with the Chicago and Boston organizations. The newcomers in the Metropolitan list whose names proved worthy of record were four men: Dimitri Smirnoff, tenor; Leon Rothier,

William Hinshaw, and Basil Ruysdael, basses. It was said that of the Chicago company Nellie Melba, John McCormack, and Maurice Renaud would occasionally be drawn into the performances of the Metropolitan company, and of the Boston organization Lydia Lipkowska, Carmen Melis, Alice Nielsen, sopranos; Florencio Constantino, tenor, and George Baklanoff, barytone. The value of the affiliation proved to be negligible. Mme. Melba sang once in " Traviata " at a special performance, and once in " Rigoletto " in the subscription; then she was announced as ill and betook herself to England. Mlle. or Mme. Lipkowska sang a few times, as did also Signor Constantino, but the public seemed indifferent to the performances, which were devoted to old operas by Verdi. Mme. Melis, who had made an agreeable impression at the Manhattan Opera House in the previous season Miss Nielsen, and M. Baklanoff (a fine artist) were not heard, and M. Renaud, "the most finished and versatile of French artists whom the foresight of Maurice Grau had retained for the Metropolitan, but whose contract Mr. Conried canceled at the cost of a penalty,"* and who had been one of Mr. Hammerstein's strongest props during the years of rivalry with the Metropolitan, was heard only in one performance with Mme. Melba and in a few of those of the Chicago company.

The season was financially profitable, though Signor Gatti had to contend with a deal of ill-luck. Signor Caruso was seized with an affection of the throat and sang for the last time in the season on February 6, 1911. The fact was woeful to the subscribers, grievously disappointing to the public, and seemed full of evil portent for the future of the institution; but nature's law of compensation remained operative, and the public was taught a better appreciation of operas which were not in Signor Caruso's repertory than it would have received had the popular idol remained more persistently in the public eye and ear. German opera, which

* "Chapters of Opera," p. 365.

seemed to be threatened by the enforced retirement of Mr. Dippel in the preceding season, came into particular prominence because of the enforced retirement of Signor Caruso in this. By a peculiarly happy dispensation Miss Farrar, the most popular of the company's singers after Signor Caruso, was dowered with an opera ("Königskinder") which made a strong appeal to the most enthusiastic and faithful element among the city's music-lovers, and what happened after February 6 may be set down as a sort of educational campaign, the effects of which were garnered in later years when it was found that operas could succeed without the great singer's participation and fail in spite of his help. The most striking instance of the latter sort is connected with the opera which Signor Gatti had selected to be the culmination of the season's glory—Puccini's "Fanciulla del West." More about this in due time.

It has been my custom in making a retrospect of a season to take a glance at the promises held out in the prospectus. This, of course, is merely a matter of habit. Since opera became the greatest of all social fads there has been no real need of managerial promises beyond the one that a season of opera will be given. The subscriptions for the new year begin to come in before the end of the old. No questions are asked about the repertory, few about the singers. The comparison between promise and fulfilment, however, is interesting and becomes valuable when, as in the present instance, it discloses a nicer balance than it had been possible for a reviewer to record for a long term of years. When the public was invited to subscribe for the season in the summer, performances were promised in French, German, Italian, and English. The principle that all works should be sung in the language to which they were native was to be upheld. There had been talk of performances in the vernacular of two operas which seemed amenable to translation: Goldmark's "Heimchen am Heerd" (which is German, and pretty German, for "The Cricket on the Hearth") and Humperdinck's " Königskinder "; but the director put a quietus on it immediately after his return from Europe. The plan was impracticable in the case of the latter opera at least because there would be no time to prepare an English version before a date which had to be considered in order to enable him to insure the privilege of a "world première." Nevertheless he announced an opera, "Twilight," by Arthur Nevin, American in subject, language and authorship, in mid-season, and withdrew it about the time when the public had been told to expect its performance. It was plain to all close observers that Signor Gatti had not been permitted to exercise the discretion which ought to have been vested solely in him in announcing that the new opera would be performed, and also that he felt no heart-burnings when he proclaimed later that its manuscript material was of a kind that made the promised production impossible.

Meanwhile a singular combination of circumstances led to a fulfilment of the prospectus in regard to a vernacular performance. Mr. Dippel, who had undertaken the management of the Chicago Opera Company, the activities of which were chiefly given to French opera, had carried with him from New York a desire to give some representations in English. He was encouraged in this desire by Mr. Clarence Mackay and Mr. Otto H. Kahn; but the Chicago season was not long enough to enable him to bring it to fruition. As Mr. Hammerstein's quasi-successor, Mr. Dippel, had come into possession of the score of an American opera, " Natoma," of which the authors were Joseph Redding and Victor Herbert. The opera had been offered to Signor Gatti and the music of the second act given a practical trial on the stage of the Metropolitan Opera House. The director did not think it worth producing, and with his judgment I find myself in full accord. .Mr. Dippel, however, had begun to talk about opera in the vernacular in Chicago; Mr. Ricordi had joined in the widespread chorus, and with

CHARLES GILIBERT

a display of energy quite without example in our history, Mr. Dippel, when he brought the Chicago company to Philadelphia, produced Mr. Herbert's work first there and afterward in New York. Next, to give emphasis to his patriotic enterprise, he changed his plans for a series of performances in New York, and devoted three out of ten representations to the new opera, though he found it necessary at the last performance to associate a foreign curtain-raiser with it.

Interesting incidents, though they were made to assume a commercial rather than an artistic character, were the visits of two composers who came to supervise or witness the first production of their latest compositions, which were among the novelties of the season. Signor Puccini, who had visited New York in 1907, when his old opera, "Manon Lescaut," had its first performance at the Metropolitan Opera House, came to attend the *première* of "La Fanciulla del West," and Herr Humperdinck to give *éclat* to that of "Königskinder," two operas which opened their eyes on the lamps of the stage at the Metropolitan. For the Italian composer the management arranged a reception in the foyer of the opera house and for his opera two special performances at double prices. The German opera was produced in regular course. Despite all attempts to make a new opera by the most popular operatic writer alive a sensational occurrence, Puccini's opera was an artistic failure, while the German opera turned out to be the most popular production of the season. "Königskinder" also helped its predecessor, "Hänsel und Gretel," to achieve wider recognition, and it was admitted to the aristocratic company of the operas in the subscription list after having been reserved for extra holiday and popular Saturday night performances ever since it had gotten into the Metropolitan list in 1905, when the composer had been a guest of Mr. Conried and his company. The presence of the Russian dancers was a fortunate incident at the waning of the season, when Signor Caruso's illness seemed to threaten disaster. Mme. Pavlova and her companion, M. Mordkin, had disclosed themselves to their admirers before the season opened, and, though they were supported by a very mediocre company of dancers, they were enthusiastically greeted at the performances in which they took part until the first week of January. Then they departed, but came back very opportunely for the second fortnight of March. A distressing occurrence was the death of Charles Gilibert on October 11, 1910, three days after his arrival from London to join Signor Gatti's forces. M. Gilibert had been a member of Mr. Hammerstein's company during the four years of that impresario's consulate, but before that time had been associated with the Metropolitan company, having been brought to America by Mr. Grau. He made his New York début on December 18, 1900, in Gounod's "Roméo et Juliette." He was born in Paris in 1866; studied at the Conservatoire, where he carried off prizes in singing; appeared for the first time in opera at the Théâtre de la Monnaie in Brussels; was a member of the company at that theater for ten years before being engaged by Mr. Grau. He died of an abscess of the brain. Not only a most admirable dramatic artist, he was one of the most finished concert singers of his time, perfect in vocalization and diction and in all things sympathetic and engaging. So great was the esteem in which he was held that his fellow-artists at the Metropolitan gave a concert on January 25, 1911, as a memorial to him and for the benefit of his family, which yielded the sum of $16,400, of which sum $1,000 was donated to the widow of Galetti-Gianoli, a buffo-basso of the company who had died in London in the preceding summer. Among M. Gilibert's finest impersonations were those of Masetto in "Don Giovanni," Dancairo in "Carmen," Dr. Bartolo in "Il Barbiere," the Father in "Louise," the Sergeant in "La Fille du Régiment," the Sacristan in "Tosca," and Schaunard in "La Bohème."

AN ANCIENT NOVELTY BROUGHT FORWARD

The season was opened with a novelty—an extraordinary proceeding which was made more extraordinary by the fact that the novelty was an opera of which the music was 133 years old and the book 90 years older. The opera was Gluck's "Armide," which was composed in 1777, but whose book was written by Quinault for Lully in 1686. The revival of interest in "Orfeo" by the performances of the preceding season, coupled with the choice of "Armide" as the first opera of the present, invited to curious speculations. Until "Orfeo" was resurrected the oldest opera in the local list was Mozart's "Nozze di Figaro," which had then reached the ripe age of 125 years. "Orfeo" was nearly a quarter of a century older. Why had Signor Gatti's choice fallen on "Armide"? Was it in obedience to a longing which the works of modern composers had left unsatisfied? Were inherited tastes of which we had long been unconscious, and which were still undefined, making themselves felt in obedience to a law of progress which we had never troubled ourselves to understand? Orchestral composers were storming the citadel of heaven with serried ranks of pipers, blowers and drummers, making pompous proclamation of small thoughts, yet archaic instruments were coming to the fore and archaic composers coming again into their rights. Affectation was everywhere visible in musical culture, yet we were turning more and more to simplicity and finding it satisfying and lovable. There was something gratifying in the contemplation of these facts, but were they also an affectation? Were we again playing at shepherds and shepherdesses? An answer was not at hand. So far as the phenomenon which we were observing was concerned, it was easier to conceive it as the outcome of a number and variety of other motives and purposes.

For one thing, "Armide" invites an opulent investiture. The history of opera differs greatly from that of the spoken drama. As an art-form it has appealed to the senses rather than to the intellect and emotions from the beginning. The farther one goes back into the records the more amazing are the stories of the scenic splendors. French opera had its beginning in an entertainment which mingled spectacle, dance, pantomime, and music. Henri III produced " Circe, ou le Ballet Comique de la Reine," by the Piedmontese fiddler Baltazarini, at the Palais du Petit Bourbon in October, 1581, in honor of the marriage of the queen's sister. The performance, which began at 10 o'clock in the evening, lasted till 3:30 the next morning, and cost 1,200,000 écus—whether gold or silver is not stated in the accounts. If they were écus of silver, the sum was the equivalent of $720,000; if of gold, of $1,200,000. Even in Mannheim it was nothing unusual to spend $20,000 on the mounting of a single opera at about the period which saw the original production of " Armide " in Paris. There was evidence in Signor Toscanini's reverential attitude toward the music of Gluck's opera that a large impulse in his case was admiration and love for the old work. Perhaps this was paired in Signor Gatti's mind with a hope that a brilliant show would add to the luster of his administration. I can easily imagine that the scenery, costumes, and other paraphernalia which the manager provided for " Armide " cost the modern equivalent of the Mannheim operas which Dr. Burney tells about, and it may have excelled them all in beauty and even surpassed the original production in Paris. It had an excellent modern model, and while engaged in this fanciful speculation I might go further and say, too, that in some particulars I imagine that it was sung better than when Gluck superintended its production and told Marie Antoinette how supremely admirable his opera was going to be. The French singers were not remarkable at the Académie in Gluck's day, and, indeed, have never been remarkable for beauty of voice, except in the periods of Italian domination. In some respects, however, it is to be imagined that the eighteenth-century representations surpassed that of the twentieth. It can safely be assumed that there was greater consistency

THE BALLET IN FRENCH OPERA 201

and unity of style in the performance—as there still is at the Grand Opéra in spite of its decadence—a larger effectiveness in the dramatic declamation—that is, a better diction—and much more meaning and charm in the ballet. No doubt the prevalent exhibition of interest in dancing had something to do with the production of Gluck's opera, which is as full of dancing as were the operas which excited the ridicule of Rousseau. Rousseau loved Quinault, had a sincere admiration for Gluck, and despised French singing. He looked with forgiving eyes on the dancing diversions in Quinault's operas, but thought the ballet of his successors absurd. "In every act the action is generally interrupted at the most interesting moment by a dance given to the actors, who are seated, while the public stands up to look on. It thus happens that the *dramatis personæ* are absolutely forgotten. The way in which these *fêtes* are brought about is very simple. Is the prince joyous? His courtiers participate in his joy and dance. Is he sad? He must be cheered up, and they dance again. . . . Priests dance, soldiers dance, gods dance, devils dance; there is dancing even at interments—dancing *apropos* of everything." In the preceding season the patrons of the Metropolitan Opera House had waxed so enthusiastic over the dancing of Mme. Pavlova and Mr. Mordkin, whose dancing was wholly extraneous to the play, that it would not be surprising if Mr. Gatti had concluded that the time was ripe for a revival of some of the old operas in which the ballet took part in the action, even though the part was as little essential as Rousseau's description implies. But I fancy that there was even a greater difference between the terpsichorean compositions of the Vestris family, as well as their performance, and those of the Metropolitan ballet-master and his corps than there was between the French of the singers.

So far, then, as it was the hope of creating an interest in the old opera by its dancing diversion which led to the tardy performance of "Armide," it is to be feared that Mr. Gatti was disappointed. Such aimless caperings as were indulged in by the ballet-contingent could charm no cultured person; and before we can have a classic ballet of the kind which in Gluck's day had so much potency that the will of Vestris was paramount to that of Gluck, we must have balletmasters educated in the classic traditions and a corps of dancers trained in graceful and significant pantomime. A larger justification for the opera was found in its opportunities for scenic attire, and here the introduction of elements which had become familiar through more modern works helped in the establishment of a sympathetic attitude between the old opera and the modern spectators. "Armide" is a romantic opera. Chivalry and supernaturalism play a large part in it, and it was no doubt agreeable to find how devices in modern stage-mechanism could be employed to make it delectable to modern taste. The enchanted gardens of the Damascan sorceress recalled memories of Klingsor's magic realms; the naiads who moved gracefully about in the placid waters of the brook recalled memories of Wagner's Rhine-nixies; the zephyrs which carried off Rinaldo and his charmer on their couch of roses would never have been had not M. Gounsbourg made an opera out of Berlioz's "Damnation de Faust" so that the sylphs might float through the dreams of Faust sleeping on the banks of the Elbe. That Armide should suggest Venus and Kundry was inevitable, for they are of a tribe, and though there came a temptation to smile at the ingenuousness of poet and composer in having an exorcism of one Kundry follow hard on the heels of another in the fourth act, these things were not made a bit incongruous by the archaism of the music. On the contrary, a greater charm went out from the music of the scenes of enchantment than from the accents which ought to have stirred the emotions and imaginations of the audience in the scenes of tragic import—the alternating tempests of love and hate which tore the heart of the play's heroine. Here it must be confessed that the music of the opera sounded less moving than that of "Orfeo" or "Alceste." There is a superb chorus at the close of the first act of "Armide," but it pales its fires in the presence of the two lyric dramas in which Gluck celebrated the passion of married lovers. So there is strong and dramatic utterance in the scene beginning "Enfin il est dans ma puissance," in which Armide empties her heart of hatred in the presence of the sleeping crusader, but it scarcely reaches the height of Alcest's invocation of the Stygian divinities. As for the rest, there is far too much song and spectacle in proportion to its dramatic action.

If "Armide" was incorporated in the local list to widen the opportunities of Signor Caruso, the purpose was accomplished to the extent of one-half. Its music proved to be a splendid vehicle for the singer's matchless voice, and he paid it honor due by singing it in a noble and dignified manner to the complete forgetting of the exaggerated pathos which he had so long affected in the operas which had brought him his greatest popularity and worked the greatest harm to his voice. But the hero of Tasso's "Gerusalemme liberta" was a sorry figure as Signor Caruso embodied him to the eye. The tenor had grown stout in figure and almost ludicrously awkward in movement. When he disposed himself to sleep in the enchanted garden it was impossible not to feel an apprehension that the smile innumerous spread over the audience might become audible. It was really a painful moment, and that the desire to laugh was suppressed was a higher tribute to the singer than an outburst of applause at the end of his entrancing song would have been. Mme. Fremstad was happier than her companion in every respect. She looked, sang, and acted her part convincingly and triumphantly. It was she who dominated the work so far as the too loquacious Quinault, who had to spread a paucity of dramatic action over five acts in order to conform to the laws of the Académie, would permit her to do so. She was much hampered by her female companions who would be singing and her gorgeous retinue who danced in and out of season; yet some of those companions were able coadjutors and deserved well at the hands of the audience. Especially was this true of Alma Gluck, who, as she had done in "Orfeo," proved herself the best stylist in the company. The opera was produced with the following cast:

Armide	Olive Fremstad
Renaud	Enrico Caruso
Hidrauot	Pasquale Amato
La Haine	Louise Homer
Sidonie	Leonora Sparkes
Phenice	Jeanne Maubourg
Lucinde	Alma Gluck
Ubalde	Dinh Gilly
Le Chevalier Danois	Angelo Bada
Artemidore	Alfred Reiss
Aronte	Andrea Segurola
Une Naiade	Marie Rappold
Un Plaisir	Alma Gluck

Conductor, Arturo Toscanini

On December 10, 1910, there was a first performance on any stage of a new Italian opera by Puccini. This was "La Fanciulla del West," the libretto of which had been fabricated by G. Zangarini and C. Civinni out of Mr. David Belasco's melodrama, "The Girl of the Golden West." The management had put its finest talent at the service of the composer, who had come to America to direct the production; Mr. Belasco had taken upon himself the task of training a company of foreigners, who knew as little about the 'Forty-niners as they did about the antediluvians, how to look and act like the argonauts of California and their parasites; Signor Toscanini threw himself devotedly into the interpretation of the music, and all that could possibly be done to make the affair a brilliant and momentous one in operatic history was done. It was momentous, but not in the sense expected by Signor Gatti. The time was a Sat-

GIACOMO PUCCINI

urday night, but instead of the popular prices which ordinarily prevailed at the last performance of each week, the prices were doubled. There was a fine attendance, but not an extraordinary one. The performance was fine also, such an one as there is no risk in saying the opera would not have received at any other opera house in the world, for nowhere else would the factors essential to a presentation of the characteristically American play been brought together. The play was familiar to the public, and Mr. Belasco's association with Signor Puccini in the most popular of the latter's operas whetted the natural curiosity in a work which was not only national in plot, but was also to have its first representation in an American theater. The excellent merits of the performance had recognition, and between the curtains the singers, the composer, Mr. Belasco, and Signor Toscanini were repeatedly called out and vigorously applauded. After the opera there was a reception for Signor Puccini, at which there was much mutual congratulation over an achievement which it was assumed was a great thing for American art. While I am writing this down, however, I am also recording an artistic failure. The best evidence of this failure was in the opera itself, though the management refused to acknowledge the fact until three years later, when, without there having been any diminution of the favor in which the composer's other operas were held, and Signor Caruso, Mme. Destinn, and other popular members of the company were still in his service, Signor Gatti dropped "La Fanciulla del West" from the active list of operas. Meanwhile operas in which only lesser lights shone became the permanent admirations of the public. This was in a way a rebuke to the artistic policy of the administration. A rebuke to its business policy followed hard on the heels of its first performance. Signor Gatti announced another representation for the following Saturday evening, also at advanced prices of admission. He could not fill the house a second time, whereupon the opera took its place in the regular subscription repertory and there remained until the end of the season 1913-14, after which it was heard no more. For the next novelty, which was Humperdinck's "Königskinder," also an opera which New York was to see and hear before the rest of the world, and to which the composer's presence was to give *éclat*, there had been less tumult of preparation, less clanging of the cymbals of *réclame*, but a different public, and the opera was placed in the subscription list at normal prices at the outset. Nevertheless, it had 11 performances in its first season to 9 of "La Fanciulla," and before it fell out of the list in 1913-14 had 30, as against 22 of its more favored Italian rival.

The history of "La Fanciulla del West" has a prelude in that of "Madama Butterfly," which I have related with considerable detail in my "Second Book of Operas."* In the spring of the year 1900, at the Herald Square Theater in New York, Mr. Belasco produced what proved to be a futile farce entitled "Naughty Anthony," in which Miss Blanche Bates played the principal part. Threatened with failure, he took up Mr. John Luther Long's story, "Madame Butterfly" (whose theme the American author had borrowed from Pierre Loti's "Madame Chrysanthème"), and in a desperate hurry constructed a play out of it. With its pictures and pathos, especially its scene of all-night vigil, Miss Bates took so strong a hold on the playgoers of the town that Mr. Belasco's season was saved. The play was carried to London, and there Mr. Francis Nielson, stage-manager at Covent Garden at the time, recognized its operatic possibilities and sent word of his discovery to Signor Puccini, who was looking for the subject of a successor to "Tosca." Signor Puccini came to London, the Japanese drama found favor in his eyes, and he bought the privilege of turning it into an opera. "Madama Butterfly" was pro-

* Second Book of Operas; Their Histories, Their Plots, and Their Music." By H. E. Krehbiel. New York: The Macmillan Company, 1917. P. 109.

BELASCO'S "GIRL OF THE GOLDEN WEST"

duced at La Scala on February 17, 1904, and, though it made so great a fiasco that the composer withdrew it from the stage and subjected it to a revision, in its new form—which destroyed the feature which had been most effective in the play, the vigil—the opera was successfully brought forward at Brescia on May 28, 1904. An English version, after a trial performance at Washington, was produced at the Garden Theater in New York on November 12, 1906, by the Savage Opera Company. It had a run of nearly three months before it reached the stage of the Metropolitan Opera House on February 11, 1907. There it has remained one of the most popular of Italian operas in the list ever since.

As a result of the success of "Madama Butterfly," Mr. Puccini arranged to have Mr. Belasco send him every play which he might produce which he thought adaptable to operatic use, and in pursuance of this, when he wrote "The Girl of the Golden West," he sent it to the composer in Italy. The play, which has its scenes in and near a mining camp in California, tells the story of the reclamation of an outlaw by a barmaid who loves him. There are scenes of drinking, dancing, and gambling, the climax of which is reached when a rascally sheriff of the county, a gambler and himself in love with the girl, discovers from a drop of blood which drips upon his hand from the ceiling of her room that the man for whom he is hunting, wounded by a bullet, is in hiding in the attic. He is about to seize him when the girl offers to play him a game of poker—the stakes herself against the life and liberty of her lover. They play, and the girl wins by the cheating device of producing a card which she had concealed in her stocking. Depraved as the sheriff is, he is, in the popular phrase, a "game sport"; he leaves the girl to the enjoyment of her dishonest victory, and the play ends with a picture of the lovers riding over the mountain trail towards a new life in the East. Several incidents of the play were fashioned on stories of life in

California in the days of the mining mania told to Mr. Belasco by his father, one of the pioneers. The betrayal of a wounded man by a drop of blood has history behind it, and Jake Wallace, a wandering banjoist and ex-negro minstrel, was a veritable character, name and all. To heighten the local color of the play Mr. Belasco not only used dropcurtains with artistically illuminated pictures of Rocky Mountain scenery, but banished the orchestra with its conventional between-acts music, and for it substituted a band of men-singers and players on the concertina, banjo and bones, giving them music such as was familiar to the men of 'forty-nine—for instance, songs like "Coal Oil Tommy," "Pop Goes the Weasel," "Rosalie, the Prairie Flower," and "The Camptown Races." Here, along with the rude bardic touch lent by Jake Wallace, should have been food for the imagination of Signor Puccini as well as his librettists. To the latter it proved to be so much Choctaw, which need cause no special wonder; to the former, little better. This was less excusable, for Signor Puccini had had occasion to study the play and talk about it with Mr. Belasco. When he came to New York to attend the Italian production of "Madama Butterfly" the melodrama was playing at the Academy of Music. He was invited to witness it, but could not fix a date, and when he presented himself at the Academy one evening there was no seat to be had. So he stood throughout the performance. After the second act he went behind stage to see Mr. Belasco, whom he embraced, saying: "I want the play; I have already the minstrel song in my head." With Puccini was Mr. George Maxwell, representative in America of the Ricordis, Puccini's publishers, a canny Scotsman who tried in vain to check the composer's enthusiasm lest it should interfere with the business negotiations which were bound to follow—an unnecessary concern, for Mr. Belasco had sold the opera privilege of "Madame Butterfly" to Signor Puccini for $1,500 and was so delighted with his operatic association that he was willing to give up his new work for a similar bagatelle.

And so " La Fanciulla del West " was passed through the transmogrifying imaginations of Signor Puccini and his literary collaborators and the product brought to New York. Quite naturally the newspapers were full of the composer and his opera. Signor Puccini confided the fact to a reporter of the *Tribune* that he thought the music was the most dramatic he had ever written and that he had dedicated the score to Queen Alexandra of England because of her admiration for " Madame Butterfly." He also said that he had striven for American atmosphere and had introduced a few measures of Indian music and some " ragtime," but had made no attempt "to assimilate essentially American themes." Mr. Belasco hastened to put his knowledge, skill, and experience at the service of the management. He undertook not only to make actors out of opera-singers notoriously indifferent to dramatic truth in action and wholly slaves of convention, but also to make likenesses of American miners, Indians, and outlaws out of a crowd of foreigners who knew nothing of the ways and habits of the persons they were expected to represent. He used all the " business " of the original prompt-book, and, though his labors were arduous and long, he succeeded remarkably well in making the opera look like his play. He could not make it sound like it, but that was the fault of the art-form and Signor Puccini. Commenting on the result to a reporter for the *Tribune* after the first performance, Mr. Belasco said : " What I consider most remarkable is the repose that the people learned in their actions. American frontiersmen are outwardly a phlegmatic lot, and the Latins who were on the stage were naturally anything but this. For them to gesticulate was as natural as to talk and eat. In addition, they had been appearing constantly in opera in which gesticulation and constant movement were especially taught. Under these conditions it might be expected that it would be exceedingly hard to get them to act otherwise; yet any one who saw them at the first performance could scarcely believe that they were anything but Americans." This was true, but it was amusing to note that in subsequent performances the influence of Mr. Belasco's teachings rapidly wore off, and that in the next season only the costumes remained to distinguish California miners from brigands of the Abruzzi. The device which Mr. Belasco adopted to secure the repose which he was proud of was to make the actors put their hands in their pockets as soon as they began to gesticulate. Caruso, Amato, Dinh Gilly, and Destinn were apt pupils, though it was not without effort and much persuasion that the first could be induced to sing with his back to the audience when the situation demanded that attitude, and the last to wear cotton stockings, she having, as she very well knew, two excellent reasons for thinking that her nether limbs should be enclosed in silk. The parts in the opera were distributed as follows:

Minnie	Emmy Destinn
Dick Johnson (Ramerrez, the Road-agent)	Enrico Caruso
Jack Rance (Gambler and Sheriff)	Pasquale Amato
Nick, Bartender at "The Polka"	Albert Reiss
Ashby, Wells-Fargo agent	Adamo Didur
Sonora	Dinh Gilly
Trin	Angelo Bada
Sid	Giulio Rossi
Bello	Vincenzo Reschiglian
Harry	Pietro Audisio
Joe	Glenn Hall
Happy	Antonio Pini-Corsi
Larkins	Bernard Bégué
Billy, an Indian	Georges Bourgeois
Wowkle, his Squaw	Marie Mattfeld
Jake Wallace, a Minstrel	Andrea de Segurola
José Castro, with Ramerrez's band	Edoardo Missiano
The Pony Express Rider	Lamberto Belleki

Conductor, Arturo Toscanini

Signor Puccini was recreant in "La Fanciulla del West" to the trust which he had invited in "Madama Butterfly."

The latter opera, it may be admitted, in spite of all the praise that I have at various times bestowed upon it, proclaims very little that well-read (to say nothing of well-traveled) people did not know to be wholly fictitious about the costumes, fashions, habits, and ethics of Japan. What makes the charm of the opera is its music and to a great extent that part of the music which is based on the use of folk-melody. If Signor Puccini could make so much of the square-toed, unemotional tunes of the Japanese and blend it so ingeniously as he did with the music of his native land, why was it that he did not put at least one little splash of American pigment on the musical canvas of "La Fanciulla"? He planned the work for America, its story was thoroughly American, he had had an opportunity to observe the effect of popular American tunes upon the play. He did not plan "Madama Butterfly" for Japan, but for the world. The absence of anything in the score savoring of American music was a disappointment. There had been music in the old melodrama which cried out in spirit at least for admission to the opera. It was not necessary that we should have had "Pop Goes the Weasel," or "Camptown Races," or "Old Dog Tray," but if we were denied the flavor of them, why should we have references to them in the text and at least one musical quotation which it might be said· became intelligible only if one stood on his head? Why give us Stephen C. Foster's "Dooda, dooda da," upside down? What strange conception filled the minds of the librettists when they wrote the bewildering reference to "Old Dog Tray" which the miners sang while pounding rhythmically on the tables with their fists? "Il mio cano, dopo tanto mi ravisera" ("My dog, will he recognize me after so long a time?")—that is what Jake Wallace sang when he made Jim Larkins homesick! This tune was the bit of Indian melody which we were told Signor Puccini had incorporated in its score. If so, the Indian who contributed it was familiar with Denza's "Funiculi, funicula." When Puccini reached London after the American *première* of "The Girl" he answered the criticism of a want of American color in the opera by saying that the slave songs of our South were barbarous noises. Was that the reason why he permitted a negro minstrel to wander around miners' camps singing an Indian tune? An Indian tune like that given to " Che ferrano i vecchi miei " might have tickled the ears of 'Forty-niners or tried their tempers; it couldn't give a mammy-sick schoolboy nostalgia.

The musical structure of the opera is erected on the modern German notion (against which Signor Puccini has often protested, though never so effectively as in " La Bohème ") that the words are to float on the instrumental flood and that vocal melody is therefore of secondary importance. Nine-tenths of the time his vocal melody is nothing and his instrumental nothing better when it is striving to be " national." Instead of upholding melody as the first essential of opera, he no sooner reaches a dramatic moment than he drops it altogether and resorts to harmonic and instrumental effects to keep up the emotional excitement which in the first instance was created by the play. He uses music as mere color—as a creator of atmosphere—as frankly as Richard Strauss in " Salome," but much less ingeniously. He could not compose music for the scene of the card game, so he makes noises in the bass voices of his orchestra while the game progresses; but Strauss froze the blood of his listeners with uncanny sounds while murder was doing in the cistern. Puccini only piques curiosity. When will the basses stop their iteration? Signor Puccini and his librettists followed Mr. Belasco up to the last act. Then they introduced a lynching scene amid the redwood trees and gave the tenor another chance to sing a song and the soprano a chance to make another appeal for the tenor's life; more song, Italian song like all that which both soprano and tenor had been singing from the beginning of the opera. But by this time the manner has become so familiar that the listeners can care little for it and there is interest only in the excited dramatic scene which Mr. Belasco had succeeded in creating by his training of the Italian chorus and the galloping back and forth of horses. There were many horses in " La Fanciulla " because the resources of the Metropolitan Opera House are not small. They have never been small, and in the matter of horses they had long before discounted the present production. When Spontini's " Hernando Cortez " was produced on the same stage in the long-agone German period I figured out that there were more horses on the stage than Cortez ever brought into Mexico. But horses do not make up for a want of music with the tang which is native of the soil and which must go with this play if ever it is to be made into a popular opera.

On December 28, 1910, Humperdinck's " Königskinder " had its first performance on any stage at the Metropolitan Opera House under the direction of Alfred Hertz and the supervision of the composer. The cast was as follows:

The King's Son	Hermann Jadlowker
The Goose-Girl	Geraldine Farrar
The Fiddler	Otto Goritz
The Witch	Louise Homer
The Woodcutter	Adamo Didur
The Broommaker	Albert Reiss
Two Children	{ Edna Walter { Lottie Engel
The Senior Councilor	Marcel Reiner
The Innkeeper	Antonio Pini-Corsi
The Inkeeper's Daughter	Florence Wickham
The Tailor	Julius Bayer
The Stable Maid	Marie Mattfeld
First Gate-Keeper	Ernst Maran
Second Gate-Keeper	William Hinshaw

Though the performance was what the Germans would have called an *Uraufführung*, there were few elements of novelty in this opera. New Yorkers had known it, or known of it, for twelve years as a spoken play, and its overture and two orchestral interludes had figured in their concert-rooms for about the same length of time. The drama was brought to New York in 1898 by Mr. Conried and produced at the German Theater in Irving Place with incidental music and songs, and two years or so later it was produced in English at the Herald Square Theater. As I have explained in my "Second Book of Operas,"* the work was originally a new experiment with a very ancient form— melodrama in the antique and only proper sense of the term. "The second and third acts have their prelude, and the songs of the minstrel have their melodies and accompaniments, and all the principal scenes have been provided with illustrative music in the Wagnerian manner, with this difference, that the dialogue has been 'pointed,' as a church musician would say, *i.e.* the rhythm was indicated with exactness and even the variations of pitch, though it was said that the purpose was not to achieve song, but an intensified utterance halfway between speech and song." Herr Humperdinck's experiment, familiar enough in small forms, proved to be abortive when applied to an extended drama, and was abandoned, so that "Königskinder" as given at the German Theater was merely a play with music specially composed for it. It was so near an opera in spirit and the musical investiture which Humperdinck had given it, however, that its complete translation was inevitable, and after Herr Humperdinck had visited New York to witness the triumph of "Hänsel und Gretel" he gladly accepted a commission to make the operatic version and give the right of first performance to the Metropolitan Company. It was Mr. Dippel's plan that the opera should first be performed in an English version, but, as I have explained elsewhere, the need of hurry in order to save the privilege of a world *première* led to a retention of the original language, and to the best of my memory it has had no English performance as yet, though it was scheduled in the Century Company's list for 1913-14. To the fact of a first performance I fancy

*Op. cit., p. 201.

THE DUBIOUS VALUE OF FIRST PERFORMANCES 215

a great deal more importance was attached than such an occasion warranted, except from a business point of view, and this was minimized when the management put the German work at once in the subscription repertory after withholding " La Fanciulla del West " for two special performances at double prices. The proceeding disclosed a policy of the management which was promptly rebuked by the public, and it would have worked no harm to art, nor lessened the prestige of the company, to have permitted both operas to be presented in Europe before bringing them out in New York. It will be understood that I am speaking purely from an artistic point of view, having no desire to raise a discussion of the validity of the commercial traditions of the theater. There would have been a truer standard of judgment in respect of Puccini's opera had it been compelled at the beginning of its career to forego the fictitious advantages of the local popularity of its subject, its original author, and its singers; and of " Königskinder " it may be truthfully said that it would have benefited had it been delayed till an equally sympathetic representation, even if it had not been so good in Berlin, had demonstrated that, for the sake of the play as well as the music, the opera needed the pruning which it subsequently received.

There is allegory, too much allegory, in the story of " Königskinder," but in its simple externals it is beautiful and touching. It is all about a goose-herd, held in thrall by a witch, who, through love for a wandering prince, breaks the bonds of enchantment, is called by the prescience of a minstrel and some children to royal estate by the side of her lover, fails of recognition because of the boorishness of those who should have been her proud subjects, and dies by the side of her lover in the loneliness of a forest, where their bodies are covered by a pall of snow, to which the citizens of Hellabrunn are led too late by a group of children directed by a bird. With what exquisite charm Miss Farrar was likely to invest so romantic a heroine the artist's admirers might easily have guessed; but it is doubtful if any imagination ever reached the figure which she bodied forth. She was a vision of tender loveliness, as perfect in poetical conception as in execution. Memories of the picture which she presented walking through the massive towngates followed and surrounded by her white flock will die only with the generation that witnessed it.

The last of the three novelties produced by the Metropolitan Company in the season of 1910-11 was "Ariane et Barbe-Bleue," an opera in three acts, libretto by Maurice Maeterlinck, music by Paul Dukas. The date was March 29, 1911; the language French. Signor Toscanini conducted, and the cast was as follows:

Ariane	Geraldine Farrar
Barbe-Bleue	Leon Rothier
The Nurse	Florence Wickham
Selysette	Jeanne Maubourg
Ygraine	Leonora Sparkes
Mélisande	Rosina Van Dyck
Bellangère	Henrietta Wakefield
Alladine	Lucia Fornaroli
An old Peasant	Georges Bourgeois
Second Peasant	Bernard Bégué
Third Peasant	Basil Ruysdael

The names of the authors of this opera compel respect and therefore the work invites interest; but if one were to wish to be serious in an analysis of it, the result, I fear, would not bring honor either to the original authors or those who were concerned in its representation. The title of the opera piques curiosity because of the singular juxtaposition of the names composing it. We have a school of Maeterlinckian expositors who seem to be as serious as the members of Browning clubs in their interpretation of all that the Belgian poet has written. So, too, we have a school of musical critics who hail with gladness everything which differs so much from the old ideas and canons of beauty that they are able to show their peculiar prescience and their extraordinarily exquisite sensibilities only by indulging in long compages of words equally vague and grandiloquent which normal minds, though ever so willing, can not assimilate. Of course assimilation, which implies a sort of understanding at least, is not necessary in these enlightened days. If you want to be reckoned among the inner brotherhood it is only necessary to affect to admire what is new and what you do not understand. To make a case out of the new opera: The French Ariane is the old Ariadne. She was an operatic heroine when opera began. A famous poet made a dramatic creation of her and a more famous musician set her to music early in the seventeenth century. She was the daughter of Minos, King of Crete, who, becoming enamored of Theseus, gave him the clue which helped him out of the famous maze and enabled him to kill the monster who had exacted a sacrifice of Athenian maidens for years. Theseus did not treat her well, according to tradition, and for that reason we have one arioso which has been sung to the music of Monteverde since the early part of the seventeenth century and which is a finer piece than anything of a like character written since—certainly much more moving and convincing than anything in the opera heard on this occasion for the first time in America. By a strange coincidence M. Maeterlinck's opera followed by about a year in Paris M. Massenet's setting of the antique story as put into dramatic form by Catulle Mendès; but M. Massenet, it seems, does not appear to have been as appealing to us as M. Dukas, who is a representative of the new French school that has no affiliation with the men who have maintained the principles and the glory of the old French school. M. Maeterlinck's heroine is called Ariane, we imagine, because in his opera-book she attempts to show how one may escape from a labyrinth. She sees the light, or knows the thread, and points it out to the slaves of her sex. She does not follow the light herself, however, and the moral of the drama, if there is any, is lost at the end of the play when she—if Miss Farrar interpreted her correctly—sorrowfully and hesitatingly takes herself out of the embraces of the monster man.

Here is the story of the opera; Blue-Beard has had five wives who have disappeared so mysteriously as to cause suspicion and anger among the peasantry who live about his castle. He is now bringing home a sixth wife. We hear the angry mutterings of the country-folk warning her of her threatened fate. Ariane enters, undaunted, self-reliant, radiant. She has faith in her beauty and the love of her husband. She will learn the secret of the ominous disappearance of her predecessors with the help of the seven keys, six of silver and one of gold, which had been entrusted to her. If her predecessors were lost, she argues, it was because of their hesitant timidity. She will not hesitate; she will be brave, resist the tyrant, and thus overcome him. She throws aside the six silver keys, but her nurse picks them up and with them unlocks in succession six of the seven doors which open into Blue-Beard's hall. What do the secret chambers disclose? Only heaps of glittering jewels of many hues. They have no interest for Ariane. With the seventh key she opens the seventh door. A dark passageway, out of which issues the sound of singing, remote, muffled, melancholy, confronts her. She is about to move into the gloom when Blue-Beard arrests her steps.

"You, too? It was a mere trifle that I asked of you."

"You asked more of these than I ever gave."

"And you have sacrificed the happiness which I had purposed to give you."

"The happiness which I desire does not dwell in darkness. When I know all it will be my privilege to pardon."

Blue-Beard seizes his victim to take her away by force, but she raises an alarm and the peasants break into the hall. The monster draws his weapon, but Ariane coolly addresses the mob:

THE STORY CONTINUED

"What would you? He has done me no harm."

The peasantry withdraw from the hall, Ariane closes the door and calmly faces Blue-Beard, who, with humble mien and downcast eyes, glances irresolutely at the edge of his scimitar.

Guided by the light of a flickering lamp in the hands of her nurse, Ariane gropes her way through the gloomy passage and at length comes into a subterranean chamber, where she finds the missing wives of the monster, huddled together, listless, inactive. She arouses them from their semi-stupor. The lamp goes out, but through the blackness there shines a tiny ray of light. The imprisoned women had often seen it, but to them it meant nothing. It is an inspiration to Ariane. She traces it to its source in a bit of clear glass in a grimy pane. She breaks the pane and by the light thus released discovers a huge window besmeared with pitch. Her companions catch the infection of her example and merrily smash the frail barrier which had shut them out from sunlight. She leads them singing triumphantly into the glory of day.

They come again into Blue-Beard's hall. Liberated from the dungeon, they are happy in the companionship of Ariane, though they see no escape from the castle. She discloses to them the secret of power which lies in their physical charms.

"I do not marvel more that he did not love you as he should have loved you, nor that he coveted a hundred women while he possessed not one."

Blue-Beard is heard returning to his castle, and there is tumult without. Terror falls upon all the women except Ariane. The peasants attempt to bar his entrance and attack the retainers, who at length run away and leave him to the enraged country-folk, who bind him and deliver him up to the vengeance of his victims. The old wives are frightened more by the angry mob than at the coming of their tyrant; but Ariane calmly unbars the door. When

Blue-Beard is brought into the hall the five women fall on their knees, but Ariane advances to him and tenderly dresses his wounds. Strange sight! The women gather around, curiosity growing into sympathy and sympathy into horror when Ariane calls for a dagger. She is about to kill him, of course. No; she cuts the cords that bind his hands. He gazes in silence at the liberated women and while he so looks at them Ariane kisses him on the forehead and says: "Farewell!" Now he seeks to detain her, but she will not have it so. "I am going far away," she says, "down yonder where they are still waiting for me!" To one after the other of the wives she offers her hand to lead them with her, but they turn away from her help and gather around Blue-Beard, whose look of longing is all that she carries away with her from the scene.

A pretty story, which might have been more prettily told by a better and more leisurely pen than mine, and obviously an allegory. Miss Farrar expounded it to the world through an interview in the *Tribune:* " Blue-Beard is the old-fashioned man who regards women as his slaves, and the five wives are the old-fashioned woman who is happy in being regarded as such. Ariane is the emancipated woman, the woman who has learned to think for herself, who has come to respect herself. The golden key is the key of her knowledge, the knowledge that is to admit woman into her kingdom of the future." In the presence of Miss Farrar, M. Maeterlinck's statement that he had no philosophical teaching in mind when he wrote his play and the evidence furnished by the play itself fall to the ground. We are living in a happy day when a prima donna may tell us what a poet means even if she disagrees with him. Nevertheless, it may be that M. Maeterlinck knew what he was talking about when he made light of his " Ariane et Barbe-Bleue " and said it was intended only for a comic opera and had no moral lesson attached to it. I am willing to go a step farther and say that, while indulging his love for symbolism to the extent of giving the name of Ariane to his heroine, he did not hesitate to take his dramatic motive from Offenbach's "Barbe-Bleue," for which Meilhac and Halévy wrote the words. In this delightful old *opéra bouffe*, as in Maeterlinck's drama, Blue-Beard's wives are not killed, but live in a subterranean chamber of his palace until the chemist, who was supposed to have poisoned them, becomes troubled by qualms of conscience and brings them forth to confront the monster, who now is less disturbed by the thought of murder than by the conviction that he is a polygamist. The conviction is more than he can bear, and he readily consents to a pairing-off of all his supposedly dead wives to an equal number of gentlemen who had been condemned to death but had been kept (like Maeterlinck's wives) imprisoned in a dungeon under Blue-Beard's palace. To his sixth wife Offenbach's monster promises fidelity and obedience, a much more complete victory for woman than Ariane obtains. Critics who are fond of diving so deeply into the subject of their studies that they frequently bring up mud on their heads ought to compare the books of Dukas's opera and Offenbach's farce. For them there was edification in the symbolism of Maeterlinck. Symbolism is a fine thing with which to occupy one's mind when the dialogue and incidents of a play are no longer interesting. When Golaud maunders about his broken head it is instructive to reflect on the symbolism of the fact that he ran against a tree at precisely twelve o'clock; but somehow this does not promote the dramatic action which ought to be the business of "Pelléas et Mélisande." M. Maeterlinck had told us that he did not attempt to teach any deep lesson in "Ariane et Barbe-Bleue," but M. Dukas and Miss Farrar knew better. Therefore M. Dukas wrote music which is profoundly serious and of great interest to musicians, as well as very beautiful at times. There are also many things in it which are futile. What value has a chorus if all the words are unintelligible? All the tale of Ariane's apprehended doom and the determination of the peasants to save her is told in detached fragments of song which can only be called words out of courtesy to the libretto. The bits of strophic song by women's voices which arise from the depths when the forbidden door is opened help the orchestra to disseminate a strangely fascinating atmosphere over the scene, but if it was not intended that they should be intelligible why were they written? Dukas had as little use for them as his model Debussy had for articulate speech in his "Sirens." Vocal tone is used only for color. There is little attempt at melody, but only at declamation over the instrumental part. The people act and speak; the orchestra interprets the drama. The music is not as subservient to conventional forms as that of the Symphony in C, which had been heard a few weeks before at a concert of the Symphony Society, but for the greater part it is more vertebrate than that of Debussy, after which it was modeled. Perhaps Maeterlinck is a wag, and M. Dukas did not know it. The story goes that the poet sent his book to Debussy, who returned it, saying that it was impracticable. If so, Debussy's judgment was sound. Such a book was not for him nor is it dramatically good. For one thing, it is designed for one singer, which is a serious defect. Moreover, it is an opera in which the actress who is expected to carry the burden of the work is compelled two-thirds of the time to sing and act in semi-darkness. I fear that M. Dukas took M. Maeterlinck's book much too seriously. Had he looked at Offenbach's "Barbe-Bleue," as I feel sure M. Maeterlinck did, he would have realized that the conclusion of the play is farcical and called for a light touch in the score. In Offenbach's book the sixth wife brings Blue-Beard into an attitude of submission and keeps him for herself. In Maeterlinck's book the sixth wife delivers her companions back into slavery and leaves them there. The tender attitudinizing of Miss Farrar and M. Rothier at the last were as little part of the poet's purpose as the melodramatic action in which Miss Farrar indulged when she cut the tyrant's bonds. All the instruction which Ariane gives her liberated sisters tends only to fit them better to be the playthings of man which at the end they show themselves determined to remain. Mélisande must disclose the wonder of her hair; Ygraine the lovely contour of her arms; Bellangère of her shoulders; Alladine is made to discard her veils and wrappings, wherefore she throws herself upon a couch and kicks up her heels in sheer enjoyment of her semi-nudity. Not a suggestion of the need of intellectual or moral qualities. Whence, then, came the talk about an allegory of woman's emancipation? That consummation is better set forth in Offenbach's farce. M. Maeterlinck wrote a satire, not a plea for woman's suffrage.

CHAPTER IX

A VISIT FROM THE CHICAGO-PHILADELPHIA COMPANY

INFLUENCES OF HAMMERSTEIN AT THE METROPOLITAN—THE DECAY OF FRENCH OPERA—HAMMERSTEIN'S CHICAGO SCHEME—PHILADELPHIA BRINGS NOVELTIES TO NEW YORK —" NATOMA "—SOME OF ITS PREDECESSORS—A CENTURY OF AMERICAN OPERA—THE LIBRETTIST'S POETRY—" IL SEGRETO DI SUSANNA "—A GERMAN OPERA SUNG IN ITALIAN—" QUO VADIS? "—NERO THE SINGER IN OPERA AND HISTORY—STORY OF THE OPERA, AND COMMENTS

IN his four tempestuous years at the Manhattan Opera House Mr. Hammerstein spun Ariadne threads which the historian of the future will probably find running through the maze of opera in New York for many years, and he will be credited with clear prescience as well as the qualities which my story of his career plainly discloses. The Metropolitan Opera Company apparently picked up one of these threads when it resolved to meet Mr. Hammerstein's challenge contained in his promise to incorporate original English opera in his repertory when it established its great prize contest. It followed another somewhat deviously when it entered into an agreement to co-operate with the gentlemen who wished to give opera a local habitation and a name in Chicago and Philadelphia, and still another when it recognized the need of satisfying the demand for French opera which Mr. Hammerstein had created, though the policy which had been pursued by Mr. Conried and Mr. Gatti made it necessary to call in the help of the Chicago-Philadelphia–Philadelphia-Chicago Company. Under the direction of Mr. Conried and his successor French opera, which had provided the high lights of Mr. Grau's concluding seasons, was permitted to languish. In the five years of the Conried régime there were only 57 representations in French and of the six French operas performed only one was new to the public. This was Berlioz's "Damnation de Faust," which had its first American representation at the Metropolitan on December 7, 1906. In Signor Gatti's first year the only French operas in the list were "Carmen," "Faust," and "Manon," which, combined, had 19 representations; in the second the operas were "Manon," "Faust," "Fra Diavolo," and "Werther," and the representations were 14 in number; in the third there were only 13 representations, though two novelties, "Armide" and "Ariane et Barbe-Bleue," were consorted with old favorites, "Faust" and "Roméo et Juliette." To supply the demand which Mr. Hammerstein had ingeniously fostered resort was had in this year to periodical visits from the Philadelphia-Chicago combination organized out of the singers which had been Mr. Hammerstein's. I am not quite certain but that the Chicago enterprise had its inception—or, if not its inception, at least its determinative impetus—in one of Mr. Hammerstein's projects of universal conquest, the spirit of which also animated the Metropolitan Company in the period of great rivalry. After the season 1908-09, which Mr. Hammerstein looked upon as a season of prosperity, he decided to build an opera house in Chicago. Mr. Rabinoff took a hand in the enterprise, which was conducted with the utmost possible secrecy. He bought an option on a site for the building in North Clark Street for $5,000, employed a lawyer to look after his legal interests and a firm of architects to make the designs. The Auditorium Theater was under lease at the time to Messrs. Klaw & Erlanger, who were giving cheap vaudeville performances at such a loss that they offered to transfer the lease, which had eight years to run, to Hammerstein for nothing; but he refused it, bent upon carrying out his North Clark Street project. Meanwhile the Chicago project of Mr. Dippel, warmly espoused by Mr. Clarence Mackay, took form and Klaw & Erlanger disposed of their lease to the Chicago Grand Opera Company, getting, it is said, $100,000 for what, Mr. Hammerstein told me, had been offered to him as a gift. Official announcement of the organization of the Chicago Grand Opera Company was made on December 9, 1909. It had the financial backing of fourteen wealthy men, three of them—Mr. Vanderbilt, Mr. Kahn, and Mr. Mackay—from New York. They were not in the directorate, but were represented by Mr. Dippel. After completing a season of ten weeks in Chicago in 1910 the company went to Philadelphia, its name undergoing a change in transit, and gave the projected season there, then coming to New York and playing at the Metropolitan on eleven successive Tuesday nights and one Saturday night, beginning on January 24, 1911. Out of twelve performances eight were devoted to French operas, two wholly to English, one to a double bill of English and an Italian paraphrase of a German opera, and one to a combination of the last with a French work. The English opera was "Natoma," by Joseph Redding and Victor Herbert; the German work was Wolf-Ferrari's "Susannen's Geheimniss," which, first announced in French as "Le Secret de Susanne," was given in Italian as "Il Segreto di Susanna." The French operas in the list were "Thaïs," "Louise," "Pelléas et Mélisande," "Les Contes d'Hoffmann," "Carmen," "Le Jongleur de Notre Dame," and "Quo Vadis," the last a novelty in New York. "Thaïs" and "Louise" received two performances each. Cleofonte Campanini conducted all the representations. The reception given to the company was little short of stupendous. The great audience-room was filled on the first night from floor to ceiling, and the audience as brilliant in appearance as imagination could paint it and as keenly alive to artistic impressions as if it had been starving for opera for years. It was a splendid tribute to the singers, the operas, and (justice demands that it be said) to Mr. Hammerstein. The singers and the operas were all fresh from the Manhattan Opera House and the impression was that of a Manhattan season somewhat delayed and interrupted. There were a few newcomers in the list of singers; Edmond Warnery replaced M. Périer and Dalmorès as Pelléas, and Marguerite Sylva Mme. Bressler-Gianoli and others as Carmen.

"Natoma," a "Grand Opera in Three Acts," whose early history has been told in these memoirs, had its first appearance on any stage in Philadelphia on February 25, 1911. I was present at the performance, which was obviously looked upon as a momentous event upon which hung everlasting things. Philadelphia had till then been lukewarm toward the child whose parentage it shared with Chicago, but on this night it donned its gayest garments, crowded the vast theater (renamed the Metropolitan Opera House), and at times during the performance it fairly seethed with excitement. It was plain enough to the initiated that the climax of enthusiasm was expected by those who were prepared to acknowledge it to follow the close of the curtain on the second act, which marks the climax of the play. The public's impatience, however, would not brook delay and the audience burned its powder after the first curtain, thus necessitating the employment of considerable effort and artifice to rekindle a sufficient demonstration to bring the authors, conductor, manager, stage-manager, and singers before the curtain according to schedule. But it was done, and, judging by the number of recalls, the success of the opera was overwhelming. If there were any persons in the house who were not in a transcendental state of joy it must have been those who are accustomed to sit in solemn silence in the dull, dark dock of judgment and who had not been convinced that Messrs. Redding and Herbert had solved a great problem, or that a monumental work of art had been sent down the ways into the ocean of lasting popularity.

I am, perhaps, attaching more importance to the production of "Natoma" than it deserves; but a discussion of it under the circumstances forms a proper part of a picture of the times. The composer had confided to a reporter of the *Tribune* that the fate of English opera was concerned in an appreciation of it. In Philadelphia its production seemed an achievement of national significance. In New York it was an episode in the movement to which much attention had been directed by the Metropolitan prize competition, the production of " The Pipe of Desire," the promised performance of Mr. Arthur Nevin's " Twilight," and the agitation of the musical patriots who in their eagerness to promote opera in the vernacular seemed to be behaving like children who on the dawn of every first of January look out of their windows with the expectancy of seeing a new world. A society for the promotion of national opera had been talked to death at a single sitting, yet I can not recall a speech or newspaper article of the time (except my own) which betrayed knowledge of some of the most obvious facts of operatic history. Neither composers nor singers, neither managers nor critics who took part in the excited discussion of the day seemed aware that more than half a century before William H. Fry had written English operas, both words and music, one of which at least had been performed in New York and also in Philadelphia, the scene of the latest *accouchement;* that George F. Bristow's " Rip Van Winkle " had also been performed at the Academy of Music in New York fifty-six years before, and that the then manager of the now venerable institution had anticipated the Metropolitan Opera Company by offering a prize for the best original grand opera by an American composer. Signor Arditi, too, of amiable memory, had written " La Spia," based on Cooper's novel, an American subject like that of Mr. Bristow's opera and Mr. Walter Damrosch's " Scarlet Letter," which latter had scarcely had time to become a matter of history, having been produced only fifteen years before. Kidlings all these operas, however, compared with two operas which may be added to the

American list published in a preceding chapter of this book. Pelissier, a Franco-American, aided and abetted by a Connecticut Yankee named Elihu Hubbard Smith, produced "Edwin and Angelina" in 1796, and Benjamin Carr and William Dunlap achieved a run with their opera, "The Archers," in New York in the same year. As for performances of foreign works in the vernacular, the first opera house built in New York on the social lines of the Metropolitan was practically put out of business by the rivalry of companies who sang in English, but (a fact worth considering) in the early days of rivalry between English and Italian companies, when success went now to the one form, now to the other, it was the singers who triumphed, not the language.

"Natoma" came to New York on February 28, 1911, three days after its production in Philadelphia, and was sung by the same people, the cast being:

Natoma .... Mary Garden
Barbara .... Lillian Grenville
Lieut. Paul Merrill .... John McCormack
Don Francisco .... Gustav Huberdeau
Father Peralta .... Hector Dufranne
Juan Bautista Alvarado .... Mario Sammarco
Pico .... Armand Crabbe
Kagama .... Constantin Nicolay
José Castro .... Frank Preisch
Chiquita .... Gabrielle Klink
A Voice .... Minnie Egener
Sergeant .... Désiré Defrère

The libretto of "Natoma" was written by an American (I wish it had not been) and its music by a man of Irish extraction and German training. They are a popular pair, and they deserve to be, but that has nothing to do with the case brought before the judgment seat by their opera. Neither has the fact that the story of "Natoma" is American. Some carping critics had objected that it is not American, because its scene is laid in Southern California at a time when that part of the country was still under Spanish domination. But perhaps this is made all right by the circumstance that the heroine is an Indian and the so-called red people (though they are not red) are better entitled to be called Americans than any other race, despite the fact that they may not be autochthones but immigrants from Asia. Where Mr. Redding's heroine came from I am at a loss to tell. Speaking in the meter of the epic poem of the Finns, which Mr. Longfellow has fastened upon our Indians, she would fain make us believe that she is queen of a tribe indigenous to the lower part of California. But when she invokes her people's god it is Manitou to whom she prays—a proceeding about as natural as if Mr. Herbert were to ask us to believe that his great-grandfather was wont to kneel and cry: "O me taw Boodh!" in his devotions. However, I do not want to go deeply into the ethnology of Mr. Redding's book; it is enough that I believe the abelone to be edible in spite of the legend which Natoma tells about in a sort of runic rhyme. I accept his Spanish dances, though not sure that the Spanish aristocracy danced the minuet in public squares, and pretty positive that they did not dance it as Mary Garden and Mr. Sammarco danced it. I am also somewhat disturbed by other incidents designed to illustrate the social life of the Spanish residents of California a century ago. I do not believe that a fond father who had watched long and lovingly for his daughter would permit her to rush out into the moonlight at the first tinkling of a guitar and to stay there long enough to send one wooer about his business and throw herself into the arms of another whom she had met for the first time an hour or so before. This does not seem at all Spanish, certainly not aristocratic; in fact, not altogether proper.

The heroine of " Natoma " is an Indian girl who shows her love for an American naval officer by killing a man who is seeking to abduct her mistress in order that that mistress

THE STORY OF THE OPERA

may, I suppose, marry the man whom the Indian girl also loves. How it all comes about might be a little plainer if the opera were written in a language which would compel studious application for an hour to the libretto. As it is we only see a case of love at first sight, because of which an Indian girl who is ten times as interesting as her rival is jilted and who is so far from being swayed by ordinary human feelings that she stabs a man to death for attempting to do what he could not possibly have done under the circumstances surrounding him. He seeks to abduct a lady seated between her father and lover in a public place at a popular festival, with a squad of American sailors with drawn cutlasses in the background and the plaza crowded with soldiers and other persons who had evidently gathered together to do the things which opera writers expect of them under such conditions—offer wares for sale, sing, dance, and make merry. In this case, however, the scene is particularly interesting because of its exposition of the genius of the librettist in particular. We know it from many operas, but in its gay Spanish garb it recalls most vividly the second and last acts of "Carmen." It is thus in Bizet's opera that the people assemble to see the show and greet the notables as they arrive in pairs or groups. All is ready for the entrance of the toreador, and he comes; but he is not Escamillo but Pico. If he were Escamillo of the last act he would sing of his love for Carmen; if he were the bullfighter of the second he would sing a resounding, albeit somewhat vulgar, stave about one of his feats of arms; being Pico, he sings a song which as illustrative of the librettist's taste and skill in versification cries for preservation. Here it is:

> Who dares the bronco wild defy
> Who looks the mustang in the eye?
> Fearless and bold,
> Their master behold!
> Aie!

> With a leap from the ground
> To the saddle in a bound,
> And away! Aie!
> See where the bull upon his knees
> Snorts when his neck we tighter squeeze!
> Wild are his eyes!
> Fiercely he dies!
> Aie!

Perhaps a drama with such a lyric for the climax of its most animated scene deserves to be analyzed; if so, it must be done by a braver and more patient writer than I. Let me hasten to say something about the music. There are many differences between "Natoma" and the Wild West drama with which an Italian composer had recently endowed our lyric stage. "La Fanciulla del West" was more effective without Puccini's music; "Natoma" would be utterly impossible without the musical integument which Mr. Herbert gave it. The people would move about like marionettes without motive, uttering words which would be intolerable to people of sensibilities because they would probably be understood. Smothered by the instrumental voices of Mr. Herbert's score, their inaninity was only obvious at intervals, and the play achieved the semblance of a lyric drama. Mr. Herbert succeeded better than I could have wished at times in divorcing himself from himself. He is in "Natoma" not the carefree, happy, conventional melodist that he is in his best operettas, but an opera-maker of the modern type who relies upon his orchestra, upon themes harmonized and orchestrated to give color, life, and meaning to persons and situations not deserving of such painstaking skill and so much clever craftsmanship. He applies local color when he thinks it will be effective. He uses Indian themes to give vitality to his heroine, and he does it so well that he makes Natoma (who, I neglected to state, goes to a nunnery at the end) a figure of considerable interest. He indulges in exotic and esoteric harmonies when the need of something unusual seizes upon him, and shows that here, too, his is anything but a prentice hand. He tries, and generally with success, to avoid the frivolities of the manner which he has employed in his popular stage-pieces, but he does not once swing himself up to a sustained and passionate cantilena. Hence the last pages of his first act, to which a situation is violently created calling for a love-duet, like that in the same place in "Madama Butterfly," fail of their purpose; but he achieves results of dignity and value in the solemnities of the final scene.

Most voluble and voluminous of all the managers in his advocacy of opera in English both before and after the production of "Natoma" was Mr. Dippel; yet the first translation of which he made use was not one into English, but into Italian. There was some justification for taking "Boris Godounoff" out of its original tongue, as was done at a later date by the Metropolitan Company, for even the polyglot members of Mr. Gatti's organization could scarcely be expected to use the Russian language, but there was no excuse for a French performance of "Tannhäuser" by Mr. Hammerstein except the predominant Gallicism of his forces, and none at all for the performance of "Susannen's Geheimniss" in Italian. There are only three characters in the arch little comedy, and one of them (played by Francesco Daddi) is a mute; a second (Countess Gil) was sung by Miss Caroline White, an American, and the third (Count Gil) by Signor Sammarco, who had mastered enough English to carry a part in "Natoma." Moreover, the play is one which would have worn an English dress right jauntily. Originally it was a French farce. Max Kalbeck, an Austrian musical writer, turned it into German, and the German book was set to music by Ermanno Wolf-Ferrari. Three races are suggested in the name of the composer, but I can not stop to inquire how much the German, how much the Italian, or how much the Jewish element in the composer's physical and mental constitution have to do with the music of "Il Segreto di Susanna," as it was called on the bills when it was produced at the Metropolitan on March 14, 1911, for the first time in America. It sounded delightful in Italian; it would, no doubt, have sounded a little more natural in German, since it was composed to German words; and a clever translator might have reconciled the public to an English version unless Signor Sammarco had offended its ears by his pronunciation. The secret which Susanna harbored, keeping it from her husband, was that she smoked cigarettes. The Count did not smoke; the servant, as he makes violent assurance by dumbshow, does not smoke; the Countess was not known to smoke, yet the Count smells smoke in her drawing-room and even clinging to her hair and clothing. Sharply catechized, the Countess admits that she has a secret and that it relates to something with which she whiles away the lonely hours which the Count spends at his club. A lover, of course, concludes the Count. He flies into a rage, smashes the furniture, and, dashing out of the house, leaves the Countess in despair. She finds consolation in a cigarette after locking the door. But the Count returns unexpectedly, his fury still upon him, and, finding the door locked, breaks down the barrier. Susanna, caught *flagrante delicto*, hides her cigarette behind her back. He seizes her roughly and burns his hand. The secret is out— confession, mutual forgiveness, and the Count, enrolling himself among the devotees of Dame Nicotine, takes a light from his wife's cigarette. The dumb servant, who has been in Susanna's secret, fires his tobacco as the curtain closes. From the beginning the intermezzo is highly enjoyable, largely because of its sprightly comedy, but chiefly because of the exquisite music, full of Mozartian melodiousness and also Mozartian characterization supplemented by modern ingenuity in delineation. Quite marvelous is the skill with which the composer turns smoke into music or music into smoke as one chooses to look at it. With this work Wolf-Ferrari won as righteous a place in the American

Ermanno Wolf-Ferrari

"QUO VADIS?" MADE INTO AN OPERA

lyric theater as he did in its concert-rooms with "La Vita Nuova."

It was rather singular that the removal of Mr. Dippel's organization from the bustling metropolis of the Middle West to the Eastern city popularly supposed to be extremely deliberate of action seemed to bring to it an access of energy. Most of the operas in its Chicago repertory were not new, but needed only to be revamped; but in Philadelphia two works new to the country were called into active being, "Natoma" and "Quo Vadis?" The latter, an opera in five acts, book by Henri Cain, after the historical novel by Sienkiewicz, music by Jean Nouguès, first performed in the City of Brotherly Love on March 25, was brought forward at the Metropolitan on April 4, 1911, with no significant change in its cast except the substitution of Signor Guardabassi for M. Charles Dalmorès, a substitution which weakened the performance materially. Among the actors were two brothers, Walter and Arthur Wheeler, herculean young Philadelphians, who assumed the characters of the gladiators, Ursus and Croton, to humor themselves and the social set to which they belonged. The cast at the Metropolitan was as follows:

Lygie	Alice Zepilli
Eunice	Lillian Grenville
Poppe	Eleanore Cisneros
Petrone	Maurice Renaud
Neron	Vittorio Arimondi
Vinicius	Mario Guardabassi
Chilon	Hector Dufranne
Pierre	Gustav Huberdeau
Sporus	Armand Crabbé
Demas	Constantin Nicolay
The Young Nerva	Emilio Venturini
Iras	Marie Cavan
Myriam	Clotilde Bressler-Gianoli

Conductor, Cleofonte Campanini

Sienkiewicz's historical novel was tremendously popular when it was first published, and it still holds the imagination of multitudes in thrall. It stirred the devotion of religious devotees, captured the fancy of lovers of the picturesque, and exacted an interest by no means ignoble of the students of classic literature and history. What the pseudo-historical novel did in its way M. Henri Cain's dramatization repeats by means of ingenious use of theatrical and lyrical devices. The romance covers too large a territory to be embraced in a single play, even if the play were not made sluggish by music, and M. Cain has presented a series of incidents rather than a closely knit and logically developed tragedy. But he has done his work with great skill, a large element of which is exhibited by the manner in which, while making the persecution of the Christians under Nero the main theme of the opera, he has blended with it the charm of the scenes in which Petronius and Vinicius are disclosed as heroes of romantic love. He has not been a mere transcriber or paraphrast, but has disclosed himself as a poet and also a scholar in his use of classical and Biblical material. Unfortunately, the desire for a vast and varied spectacle has persuaded, perhaps compelled, him to introduce a multitude of personages and incidents worthy of better treatment as inconsequential stalking-horses, and thus marred the play in the eyes of historical students. In this he has been helped obviously against his own will, as any reader of the book in the original or the translation can see by the uncouth treatment to which much of it was subjected by the stage-manager.

For instance, how came the elephantine basso Arimondi to be cast for the part of Nero? The composer wrote his music for a tenor and it had to be altered to bring it within the range of Arimondi's dracontine voice. Had M. Nouguès desired to be strictly within historical lines he would have given the part to a baritone, for that in greatest likelihood was the character of voice which the tyrant possessed. It was naturally weak and of a rude quality. *Quamquam exiquæ vocis et fuscæ,* says Suetonius of him. I have always fancied that the historians have not treated Nero fairly either as poet or singer. He certainly studied faithfully and industriously under Terpnos, the finest kitharist of his day, and it is while describing his virtues, not his vices, that Suetonius says that his musical performances gave such joy to the people that public prayers were appointed to be put up to the gods on that account and "the verses which had been publicly read were, after being written in gold letters, consecrated to Jupiter Capitolinus." It is true that there were some persons who, rather than hear him sing, slipped privately over the walls when the gates were shut or counterfeiting themselves dead were carried out as to their funerals. But these may have been either poor judges or prejudiced and satiated individuals like Petronius Arbiter himself, who in "Quo Vadis?" sends the Cæsar a letter counseling him to sing no more and then dispatches himself before Nero can send the Prætorian Guards to lay hands upon him. This is not quite so much license as Barbier took when in his libretto for Rubinstein's "Nero" he had Thraseas interrupt the imperial singer while he is singing "Of the Grief and Love of Iphigeneia," the disturber preferring to suffer death rather than hear more of the song, which, like all that Nero sang, had at least a noble theme. M. Cain utilizes the same dramatic motive, but brings it into a little greater consonance with history, for the sarcastic letter of which we hear the conclusion, in the last act of the opera, is plainly intended to represent the famous Satyricon which the veritable Petronius wrote for Nero's chastisement.

But we must not lose ourselves in these historical excursions, pleasant as they may be and helpful to an understanding of the opera. However, if it was in bad taste and worse judgment in Mr. Dippel and Signor Campanini to turn a rough baritone into a rougher bass, it was inexcusable to present Nero in the Falstaffian dimensions of Arimondi. Those who remember Sienkiewicz's romance will easily be able to reconstruct the story of the opera from a few hints which I shall give with interpolated remarks on the music. There are five acts, one of them (the fourth) being divided into two scenes for the sake of dramatic contrast. The first and fifth acts are in effect prologue and epilogue to the drama which is developed in the second, third, and fourth acts. This idea is more than hinted at in the titles given to the opening and closing scenes. The first is " Eunice's Kiss." Its chief disclosure is the love of the Grecian slave, Eunice, for her master, Petronius, who, when the play opens, is still *arbiter elegantiorum* and the director of Nero's pleasures exactly as he figures in history. Incidentally, it introduces Vinicius, who tells of his passion for Lygia and refuses to be comforted with the gift of Eunice which Petronius attempts to force upon him, all ignorant of her love for him. That love is poetically disclosed at the end of the act when, being left alone, she embraces the statue of her master and presses passionate kisses upon its marble lips. We are also introduced to the personage who is most active in promoting the progress of the drama—Chilo, a busybody and gossip-monger, dealer in amulets, spy and mischief-maker generally. There is much hymning of Venus by the two female slaves, Iras and Eunice, and exchange of confidences between Vinicius and Petronius, at the conclusion of which the latter presages the outcome of the drama so far as he is concerned. Some day, the Arbiter confesses, he will grow weary of life. Then will he tell Nero the truth about his artistic performances which now he is lauding, and die amid scenes of evening loveliness. Incidentally, Chilo is retained by Vinicius to discover the meaning of a symbol which Lygia had drawn in the sand—the figure of a fish. The symbol is one with which all students of classical antiquity are familiar.* What Chilo's inquiries into the

* Among the primitive Christians the fish was a symbol of Christ, the letters of its name in Greek, ICHTHYS, forming the initials of the words in the brief but comprehensive creed: *Iseos CHristos, THeou Yios Soter*—Jesus Christ, God's Son, Saviour.

meaning of this symbol leads to is disclosed in the second, third, and fourth acts. The fifth deals again with the loves of Eunice for Petronius and Vinicius for Lygia, and their different outcomes—the suicide of the first pair and the escape to happiness of the second. In both acts poet and composer have put forth their finest efforts, M. Cain by creating an exquisite atmosphere with the aid of a poem by Catullus, and M. Nouguès by creating music which, though imitative of Massenet, languid and sensuous, is still appropriate, redolent of the scenes, and inoffensive to good taste and judgment. In other parts of the opera he is just as eclectic while striving for greater individuality, but does not escape triviality and commonplace; while in striving to characterize by typical themes, especially in the case of Chilo, he is nothing short of vulgar. Nero's orgies are accompanied, moreover, by the cheapest kind of circus music. These orgies fill up nearly all of the second act, the climax of which is found in the burning of Rome. The scene is an impressive one, but the conflagration is nothing more than a lurid illumination of the background. The song which Nero wishes to sing is interrupted by a mob that demands the death of the tyrant. Nero asks two of his sycophants to sacrifice themselves for his sake, but they refuse. Then Petronius leads out the Prætorian Guards and silences the revolt, while dancers fill the stage and wriggle and writhe in a futile effort to represent one of the corybantic scenes with which the era of Rome's profligacy is associated.

The third act shows a bustling picture on the banks of the Tiber. Amid many incidents Chilo pursues his effort to learn the meaning of the mystic symbol and at length succeeds. Vinicius attempts to carry off Lygia with the help of a gladiator, but Ursus, Lygia's gigantic slave, hurls the gladiator into the river. In this scene the Apostle Peter appears to the Christian congregation and relates the incident which lives in the tradition which gave title to book and opera—the meeting between Peter and Christ on the

Appian Way, the Apostle's question, "Whither goest Thou, Lord?" and the answer which sent the Apostle back to his persecuted flock. The fourth act brings to a culmination the religious element in the play. It is divided into two scenes, obviously for the sake of dramatic contrast, though, since the composer felt it incumbent upon him to connect the scenes with an orchestral interlude which continues the mood of the Christian canticles of which by this time every ear must have long been weary, the effect is most monotonous and deplorable.

> Pious orgies, pious airs,
> Decent sorrows, decent pray'rs,

are always welcome for a change even in an opera, but when the dramatic interest is centered on rapid alternation of exciting incidents and variety of scene they become tedious if not vexatious. It is true that the librettist seems to have been as desirous as the novelist to keep the motive in view which finds expression in the title of the work, but a theatrical audience expecting a series of pictures of life in Rome when the empire was sunk to its lowest level of wicked debauchery can well get along without so much hymning as MM. Cain and Nouguès indulge in. In the first of the two scenes the Christians, whose hiding-place has been discovered and betrayed by Chilo, are herded in the bellunarium of the Coliseum and subjected to indignities of many kinds. The second shows a portion of the arena in the circus and the imperial box. A gladiator is slain and dragged out. Ursus is brought forward to do battle with the aurochs and goes behind the scenes to do the deed which forms the most exciting incident in the novel, while in the opera the spectators tell of the progress and outcome of the battle—a fatuous dramatic device always, but here peculiarly so, though I must confess its necessity. The giant presents himself before Nero's box with the maiden whom he has rescued from the horns of the wild animal in his arms and asks her liberation as a reward for the deed. Vinicius rushes into the arena and claims her as his wife. Nero, in a rage, commands the massacre of all the Christians who have been driven into the arena. Chilo, conscience-stricken at the awful result of his deed, denounces Nero as the author of Rome's destruction. There is a popular revolt and a battle between the people and the Prætorian Guard. Petronius fulfils his destiny as he had foreseen and predicted it. With Eunice at his side, surrounded by voluptuous pleasures, he permits a physician to open his veins and hers, and together they sink softly into death.

CHAPTER X

NOVELTIES OF A SEASON AND A PRIZE OPERA

THE INTERESTING FEATURES OF 1911-12—SOME EXCELLENT ADDITIONS TO THE METROPOLITAN FORCES—THUILLE'S "LOBETANZ"—CHARACTERISTICS OF MATINEE AUDIENCES—USE OF WAGNERIAN MATERIALS—THUILLE AND HIS MUSIC—OUT-OF-DOORS OPERATIC FESTIVALS—WOLF-FERRARI'S "LE DONNE CURIOSE"—A VISIT FROM THE COMPOSER—DIVIDED ALLEGIANCES, RACIALLY AND MUSICALLY—"I GIOJELLI DELLA MADONNA"—VISIT FROM THE PHILADELPHIA COMPANY—MASSENET'S "CENDRILLON"—CINDERELLA AS AN OPERATIC HEROINE—BLECH'S "VERSIEGELT"—A DIVERTING COMEDY WITH BRASS ORNAMENTS—PRODUCTION OF THE PRIZE OPERA "MONA"—WANT OF OPERATIC SUITABILITY IN A STRONG AND BEAUTIFUL DRAMATIC POEM—THE PROVINCE OF MUSIC IN A DRAMA—OBSTACLES PLACED BY THE POET TO SYMPATHY FOR HIS HEROINE—PROFESSOR PARKER'S MUSIC—EARLIER ACHIEVEMENTS OF THE COMPOSER—CHARACTERIZATION BY MEANS OF TONALITY—THEMES AS MUSICAL SYMBOLS—MONTEVERDE'S "ORFEO"

THE story of Mr. Gatti's fourth season as manager of the Metropolitan Opera Company would have little interest were it not for the new operas produced in the course of its twenty-two weeks from November 13, 1911, to April 13, 1912, and the significance, never fully realized because never pursued to its legitimate conclusion, of the experiment to habilitate opera in the vernacular by native authors. It is but right that a generous portion of this chapter should be devoted to the production of the opera which was the outcome of the competition described in Chapter VII of this book. If management, critics, and public had been gifted with prophetic knowledge at the time, the production of "Mona" should have loomed up as an incident of national and enduring importance. But there was no premo-

SOME NOTEWORTHY DÉBUTS

nition in 1911 of the throes and agonies which were impending for the world, and what should have been a nascent day for America's lyric drama was permitted to pass as a mere episode of the season, interesting, indeed, but of no particular influence upon the mind or conscience of the Metropolitan management. The novelty excited more curiosity than any of its five companions, but it endured no longer. Two of these five other novelties were brought to New York by the Philadelphia-Chicago Company, which gave representations at the Metropolitan Opera House on Tuesday evenings from February 13, 1912, to March 19, inclusive. There were a few notable additions to the company's forces in the season. Margaret Matzenauer, a contralto with a voice of great beauty and opulence, effected her début at the opening performance as Amneris in " Aïda "; Hermann Weil, baritone, his as Kurwenal in " Tristan und Isolde " on November 17; Putnam Griswold, basso, his as Hagen in " Götterdämmerung " on November 23, and Heinrich Hensel, tenor, his as Lohengrin on December 22. It is noteworthy that all of these artists were recruited to strengthen the German ranks of the company, though Mr. Griswold, who had won distinction at the Court Opera in Berlin, was an American. Three representations in the season's list were given up wholly to the Russian Ballet, which also filled the second part of several evenings at which short operas were performed. An incident which deserves record was the performance in concert style of Monteverde's " Orfeo " on the last Sunday night of the season. All the rest which is essential to the season's history may be read in the page devoted to it in the Appendix, and we may therefore now direct our attention to a study of the new operas. The first of these was " Lobetanz," in three acts, book by Otto Julius Bierbaum, music by Ludwig Thuille, brought forward on the first Saturday afternoon of the season, November 17, 1911.

Lobetanz, a strolling minstrel, comes upon a bevy of maidens who are making preparations for a festival of song commanded by the king in the hope of restoring to health a daughter who is gone into a melancholy decline. The maidens urge the singing fiddler to enter the lists of contestants, but he is meanly clad and tries to escape, whereupon they tell him of the sad plight of the princess and twine garlands of roses about him to hide his rags. In the contest the minstrels fall to quarreling like those in "Tannhäuser." Into the midst of the discord fall the tones of Lobetanz's fiddle coming from an arbor in which he had concealed himself. The princess commands his presence and a song, but when he sings she is so deeply moved that she swoons. A tumult follows, Lobetanz is accused of having practised the black art upon the fair lady, but he eludes those who would seize him. The princess, who has lost her heart to the unknown singer, wanders through the forest and finds him near the hut of a forester. There he had taken refuge and fallen asleep in a favorite seat of the princess's in the boughs of a gigantic linden tree. He tells the forester of a dream that a raven had stolen his cap, and the forester informs him that it was more than a dream, for he had seen the bird flying with the cap towards the gloomy machine on gallows-hill. Lobetanz resumes his musings and is dreaming of his mother when the princess comes to him. While they are exchanging professions of love the king enters with his train of huntsmen and Lobetanz is taken. Now he is tried for witchcraft and condemned to death. Again the princess falls ill, and he sits in prison among weird and lewd companions who jeer at him for his presumption in wooing a king's daughter, and make mock of death in a grim pantomime. Comes the headsman to lead him to the gibbet on the hillside. Curious folk gather around to see him die, believing that his blood will release the princess from the wicked charm which binds her. Her moribund body is brought before him and a last permission to speak is vouchsafed him. He asks for his violin, and as he plays upon it a ruddy glow suffuses the cheeks of the supposedly dead woman. Now the king speaks: not only shall his life be given to the minstrel if he restore the princess to life, but even her hand in marriage. Lobetanz plays a dance-tune, and king, princess, headsman, and common folk fall to capering. In the midst of the mad dance the raven flies into the assembly and drops the minstrel's cap upon the gallows-arm. It is not an omen of death, but a symbol of marriage and connubial bliss. Curtain.

A new opera, and that a German one, produced at a Saturday matinee, the first of the season. It seemed as if there must be a peculiar significance in such a circumstance; but the purpose of the management was too deep to be easily divined. The proceeding was quite as revolutionary as that of Mr. Grau many years before when he opened a season with " Tristan und Isolde," though custom seemed to have set apart " Faust " or " Roméo et Juliette " for that function. Maybe it was a tribute to the German contingent among the opera's patrons; it was gracious to think so. But it is an old story that the Saturday afternoon audiences at the Metropolitan Opera House have for decades accepted any and every thing offered to them with grateful and indiscriminate gladness. They are not to be frightened into non-attendance by an opera that has grown musty with age and threadbare with repetition so long as the gods and goddesses of their idolatry take part in the performance, and they can with equal certainty be relied on to welcome a new work if for no other reason than that it is presented on a Saturday afternoon. The audience that heard " Lobetanz " was more than kind in its acceptance of the work, but after it had been subjected to the rule of giving every novelty a representation on each subscription night in a week and was never heard of more I am at a loss to know what the public thought of it. No doubt the box-office spoke the sentence which has been pronounced on the majority of novelties produced in the course of the period with which these memoirs are concerned. Certain it is that the final closing of the curtain on the afternoon must have left many minds in a state of bewilderment. The opera began as if it were going to appeal to the tastes and emotions habituated to romantic plays. The fact that it was reminiscent of many things which opera-lovers knew well and liked well worked no harm to it. What if Klingsor's Flower Maidens and the interloper Parisfal appeared in the first act and after them a dozen or fifteen Beckmessers sang in grotesque mimicry of the Wartburg minstrels? Even matinee-folk take kindly to "Parisfal," "Tannhäuser," and "Die Meistersinger." With such echoes the opera began only to mount the cothurnus of grewsome, grisly, ghastly tragedy in its later scenes; still it was possible to enjoy the skill with which the poet and composer used the materials of Wagner. But when, after its most effective musical scene, it ran out into the banal mood of the waltzing operettas of the Vienna type those who were most desirous to like the work were most confounded.

Thuille's music was an unknown quantity in America when "Lobetanz" came to run its brief career. Before then I can recall seeing only one of his compositions in the larger forms listed on an American programme. It was an overture entitled "Romantic," which was originally designed as an introduction for the composer's first opera, "Theuerdank," and the only portion of that work which found its way into print. Yet Thuille had filled a considerable place in German music when, still a comparatively young man, he died in 1907. He was a Tyrolean by birth who finished the music studies begun under the care of his father, an enthusiastic amateur, and other teachers in Upper Austria, at the Hochschule in Munich. He concluded his course at that institution in the year in which Horatio Parker, whose name is linked with his in the record of the season, began his. After a short absence from the Bavarian capital he returned to it, and teaching, composing, and conducting a singing society he remained there till his death. There, too, he formed a friendship with Richard Strauss, who produced some of his early orchestral music at Mannheim. Alexander Ritter, who had a hand in the working out of Strauss's destiny, persuaded him to undertake operatic composition and wrote for him the libretto of "Theuerdank," which had a performance in Munich, but made a failure. Then Bierbaum wrote "Lobetanz" for him in 1896 and "Gugelino" in 1900. The former opera reached Berlin in 1898 and took a firm hold on the German stage. In August, 1911, three months before its American *première,* it was performed in an open-air theater at Zoppot, an idyllic spot in the midst of a forest. Here a clearing intended for the production of children's plays had been turned into a large theater in which for three years, under the trees, with the forest providing most of the scenery, operas were given very much in the style of the High Jinks conducted by the Bohemian Club of San Francisco. There were then in Germany many idealists who dreamed that out of such idyllic representations there might grow a new form of lyric drama. Such a consummation is not impossible under the redwood trees of California.

On January 3, 1912, the Metropolitan Company brought out the second novelty of the season, Ermanno Wolf-Ferrari's "Le Donne Curiose," an opera in three acts, which had its first performance in America. Like its composer, the opera is half German, half Italian in its history, though it is all Italian in its subject and style. The libretto was adapted from the comedy of the same name by Goldoni; was composed to the German translated text, no doubt with the Italian words in view; was published in Germany and there had its first performance—a hybrid, but not a mongrel. Signor Toscanini conducted the performance, and the parts were distributed as follows:

"LE DONNE CURIOSE"

Ottavio	Adamo Didur
Beatrice	Jeanne Maubourg
Rosaura	Geraldine Farrar
Florindo	Hermann Jadlowker
Pantalone	Antonio Pini-Corsi
Lelio	Antonio Scotti
Leandro	Angelo Bada
Colombine	Bella Alten
Eleanora	Rita Fornia
Arlecchino	Andrea de Segurola
Asdrubale	Pietro Audisio
Almoro	Lembert Murphy
Alvise	Charles Hargreaves
Lunardo	Vincenzo Reschiglian
Momolo	Paolo Ananian
Menego	Giulio Rossi
Un Cervitore	Stefen Buckreus

I have discussed "Le Donne Curiose" in my "Second Book of Opera"* and do not wish to waste words either in a description of its contents or an estimate of its merits, which to me seem great. Quite as interesting as the work itself, and perhaps as significant from a historical point of view, was the fact of its admission to the repertory of the Metropolitan Company, which, for reasons which I shall not attempt to explain, lest I do wrong to the management, had seemed since the accession of the new management under the domination of a single Italian publisher. I need not hesitate to say that much nor apologize for the intimations I have already thrown out concerning the reasons why such operas as "Le Villi," "La Wally," and "Germania," which were foredoomed to failure here, were brought forward by Mr. Gatti. Three days after the first performance of his opera at the Metropolitan, Wolf-Ferrari arrived in New York. On the day after his arrival he attended the first repetition of it and, as he said, for the first time in his life heard one of his Italian operas sung in Italian. The explanation of this somewhat anomalous circumstance was that his works had not been published in Italy, but in Ger-

* "A Second Book of Opera" by H. E. Krehbiel. New York: The Macmillan Company, 1917. P. 234.

many, a fact which after the declaration of war against Germany by the United States brought them under the laws of this government touching the property of enemy-aliens. Why his works had been published in Germany the composer himself explained: the Casa Ricordi maintained a monopoly of opera in Italy and he had found it impossible to contract with it on its terms, notwithstanding its advances after the failure of Puccini's "Fanciulla del West." The performing rights of "Il Segreto di Susanna" had been sold to a rival firm in Italy, and those for his new opera, "I Giojelli della Madonna," had been withheld from Italy until it had had representations in Germany and the United States. The opening wedge for his operas in this country had been driven by Mr. Dippel when he produced "Il Segreto di Susanna" in March, 1911, with the Philadelphia Company. Wolf-Ferrari was not so completely a stranger to Americans as Thuille, however, for, besides his delicious little one-act comedy, which had won instantaneous admiration, his setting of Dante's "Vita Nuova," performed for the first time in America by the New York Oratorio Society under the direction of Dr. Frank Damrosch on December 4, 1907, had been heard in other cities and had made a profound impression. In the style of his music there is a mixture of national and racial characteristics corresponding with the mixture of blood in his physical constitution. He was born in Venice on January 12, 1876, his mother being an Italian, his father a German Jew and a painter. His musical studies from 1893 to 1895 were made in Munich, and in 1902 he became director of the Liceo Benedetto Marcello in his native city. This post he resigned in 1909 to make his home in Germany, probably because he had become convinced that appreciation would come to him quicker in Germany than in Italy. Like Rubinstein, he suffered from disagreement touching his national and racial status.

Wolf-Ferrari had already written his first opera, "La

"I GIOJELLI DELLA MADONNA"

Sulamita," when he went to Munich to continue his studies. His operatic version of the story of Cinderella, "Cenerentola," was performed in Venice in 1900, and "Le Donne Curiose" in German as "Die neugirigen Frauen," in Munich. The book is a paraphrase of Goldoni's comedy of the same name deftly made for the composer by Count Luigi Sugana. "It turns on the curiosity of a group of women concerning the doings of their husbands and sweethearts at a club from which they are excluded. The action is merely a series of incidents in which the women (the wives by rifling the pockets of their husbands, the maidens by wheedling, cajoling, and playing upon the feelings of their sweethearts) obtain the keys of the clubroom and effect an entrance, only to find that instead of gambling, harboring mistresses, seeking the philosopher's stone or digging for treasure, as is variously suspected, the men are enjoying an innocent supper. In their eagerness to see all that is going on the women betray their presence. Then there follow scoldings, contrition, forgiveness, a graceful minuet, and the merriment runs out in a wild furlana."

"I Giojelli della Madonna," which had received its first performance in Berlin in December, 1911, and been heard for the first time in America in Chicago on January 16, 1912, was performed at the Metropolitan Opera House on March 5, 1912, by the Philadelphia-Chicago Company, Cleofonte Campanini conducting, with the following cast:

Gennaro	Amadepo Bassi
Carmela	Louise Bérat
Maliella	Carolina White
Rafaele	Mario Sammarco
Biaso	Francesco Daddi
Ciccillo	Emilio Venturini
Stella	Jenny Dufau
Concetta	Mabel Riegelman
Serena	Marta Wittkowski
Grazia	Rosina Galli
Totonno	Edmond Warnery
Rocco	Nicolo Fosetta

MASSENET'S "CENDRILLON" 251

In this opera the composer followed the spirit of young Italy into the slums of Naples and to it sacrificed the beauty and distinction of style which had won for him sincere and almost universal admiration. His music is as mixed in manner and spirit as the population of Naples, and despite its occasional beauty quite as disreputable as part of that population. For the reflections which it provoked in my mind I must, being unwilling to repeat or paraphrase what I wrote at the time, refer to the criticism printed in my " Second Book of Operas."*

"I Giojelli" was one of the operas produced by the Philadelphia-Chicago company during its visits to the Metropolitan Opera House. Its only other novelty was Massenet's "Cendrillon," which was performed on February 26 with the following distribution of *dramatis personæ:*

Cendrillon	Maggie Teyte
Mme. de la Haltière	Louise Bérat
The Prince	Mary Garden
The Fairy	Jennie Dufau
Noemie	Mabel Reigelmann
Dorothée	Marie Cavan
Pandolfe	Hector Dufranne
The King	Gustave Huberdeau
Dean of the Faculty	Francesco Daddi
Master of Ceremonies	Désire Defrère
The Prime Minister	Constantin Nicolay
Voix du Héraut	Charles Meyer

Signor Campanini conducted the performance. The story of "Cendrillon" is more or less the story of Cinderella. Massenet having produced his opera some six years after Humperdinck had set the operatic stage afire, figuratively speaking, with "Hänsel und Gretel," a very familiar nursery tale, it is not much to be wondered at that Henri Cain, who wrote Massenet's libretto, should have become a little fearful lest the world should think that the authors had been influenced in their choice of a subject by the success of the

*Op. cit., p. 239.

German work. So M. Cain took the trouble to write a letter to M. Jullien in which he said that he and his collaborator had been dallying with the tale of Cinderella and had even sketched their opera before Herr Humperdinck had launched his delightful opera. He might have spared himself the exertion. In the first place " Hänsel und Gretel " existed as a little play written for performance by the children of the composer's sister, who made the book, some time before it became an opera. In the next place there had been operas based on nursery tales, even on that of Cinderella, long before MM. Cain and Massenet were born. There was a French " Cendrillon " as early as 1759. Steibelt, a very considerable fellow in the musical world, who carried pretty much everything before him until he tried some mountebank tricks against Beethoven in Vienna, won a large reputation with an opera on the subject which came out in St. Petersburg in 1809; Isouard produced a Cinderella opera in 1910, and it is possible even yet to hear in the concert-rooms an air from Rossini's " Cenerentola," which had its first representation in 1817 and in which Alboni made a triumph. The public may easily be pardoned for forgetting such things, but it is not so pardonable when historians like Clément and Larousse and the German Riemann falsify the record, as they do when they state that Manuel Popolo Garcia, who introduced Italian opera in New York in 1825, performed a Cinderella opera of his own composition in that first season. As a matter of fact he performed two operas for which he had composed the music, but the Cinderella opera which he brought out was Rossini's.

After all it did not much matter. If Massenet's " Cendrillon " had preceded " Hänsel und Gretel " by as many years as it was preceded by other operas on the subject, it would not be better in the eyes of contemporary criticism than it is. Somewhere in " Jean-Christophe " there is an intimation that no matter what contemporary French composers try to do and be, there is a little Massenet at the bot-

LEO BLECH'S "VERSIEGELT"

tom of their hearts. The remark, I take it, was not intended to be wholly complimentary either to the French composers of today or to their most prolific representative, M. Massenet. With "Cendrillon" and "Hänsel und Gretel" in mind, it must be said that there is nothing which makes Humperdinck's setting of a nursery tale appealing, charming, compelling to the intellect as well as the emotions which finds a parallel in Massenet's setting of the story of Cinderella. The story is as much the property of the French as any other people. Humperdinck did wonders by treating his fairy tale in the manner employed by Wagner in treating the Teutonic myths, using the system of typical phrases with excellent effect, but taking his musical themes, as he took his literary, out of the mouths of the little denizens of the nursery. M. Massenet did nothing of the sort. He took a children's story and made an opera in his style out of it, with all the familiar grace and elegance, but without once admitting the atmosphere of the nursery. A pretty opera, but conventional, and in this performance robbed of much of its musical and dramatic grace by Miss Garden's representation of Prince Charming.

"Versiegelt," a German comic opera, the book by Richard Batka, a musical litterateur; the music by Leo Blech, at the time one of the conductors at the Court Opera in Berlin, was performed for the first time in America on January 20, 1912, under the direction of Alfred Hertz, with the following distribution of parts:

Braun, burgomaster .... Hermann Weil
Elsie, his daughter .... Bella Alten
Frau Gertrud, a young widow .... Johanna Gadski
Frau Willmers .... Marie Mattfeld
Bertel, her son .... Hermann Jadlowker
Lampe, constable .... Otto Goritz
Neighbor Knote .... Marcel Reiner
Champion Marksman .... Basil Ruysdael

The little work, which shared the afternoon with "Pagliacci," would have been more diverting as a spoken drama than it proved as an opera. If we were bound to have it in a lyric form, we should have chosen for it the musical manner of Wolf-Ferrari rather than that too plainly characterized by the name of the composer. As a spoken drama, indeed, "Versiegelt" had existed on the German stage for some three-quarters of a century. All of its elements and all of its characters were familiar, but their new combination was ingeniously made by the librettist. The story is this: An old widow is attached by affection to a wardrobe, an heirloom in her family. Unable on a sudden call to pay her taxes, she appeals to a friend, a younger and more fascinating widow, to harbor it for her so that it may not be sold by the taxgatherer. She wins the consent of her friend by representing that the burgomaster has fallen a victim to her charms. Now the second gossip is more eager to become *Frau Bürgermeisterin* than anything else in this world, so she not only makes a place for the wardrobe among her household goods, but also undertakes to promote a love affair between the older widow's son and the burgomaster's daughter. The wardrobe is transferred to her apartment, where it is discovered by the too vigilant chief of police. While he is gone to make sure that there is no double of the piece of furniture which has become his legal prey, the burgomaster comes to make love to the charming young widow. He is about to embrace her when the chief of police enters, and the burgomaster hastily conceals himself in the wardrobe. Suspecting a fraud against the tax laws, the police official affixes his seal on the piece of furniture and goes out to investigate. There enter the burgomaster's daughter and her lover, against whose union the burgomaster had set his adamantine face. Seeing an opportunity to promote her ambition, the merry widow tells the young people that the mayor is under seal in the wardrobe and goes out to summon the neighbors, most of whom are attending a shooting match. The lovers now play a bit of comedy for the benefit of the unwilling prisoner. The maiden makes violent love to her sweetheart and he as violently rejects her unmaidenly advances, protesting that respect for her father will not permit him to receive them. All this, of course, in front of the wardrobe so that the conversation may be overheard by its occupant. At last the burgomaster calls out to be released from imprisonment, but the artful daughter makes the delivery conditional upon his signing an agreement that she shall marry the man of her choice and give her a handsome dowry to boot. He signs the document through an aperture in the wardrobe door and secures his liberty, but insists upon the young folks taking his place, hoping thus for both amusement and revenge. Nothing could be more to their liking.

Meanwhile the villagers, headed by the *Schützenkönig,* are brought in by the scheming widow to be witnesses of the compromising attitude of the burgomaster. The crowd make merry at the expense of the official, but are amazed when, the door being opened, the lovers are found within. In the midst of the consternation back comes the chief of police with a tale that the burgomaster and the lovers have indubitably been murdered, since he had sought in vain for a trace of them throughout the village. The burgomaster confronts him, orders him to enter the wardrobe, which is carried back to the home of its owner, leaving two pairs of lovers, old and young, kissing each other as the curtain falls. An old conceit, ingeniously exploited and cleverly set to music by a youthful and not too adept disciple of Wagner—not too adept, I say, because had he been more a dabster he would not have been so monotonous in his use of the *blech* in his orchestra. For the rest the music rests on " Die Meistersinger " when the action is in progress, and on Millöcker when a halt is made for lyric song.

On March 4, 1912, " Mona," the opera for which the Metropolitan Opera Company had offered a prize of $10,000 three years before, received its first performance under circumstances of unusual interest. Mr. Gatti redeemed the promises of the directors of the company in a magnificent manner, so far as the representation was concerned, and essayed the most significant experiment in the field of native or national opera that the country had witnessed up to that time and the most instructive one that the country has ever seen. The fact that the work did not achieve success in a sufficient degree to lead to its retention in the repertory in the succeeding season or its restoration in any season since was and is deplorable. The fault, beyond question, lay largely in the work itself; but had the attitude of the company in 1912 been like that which it was compelled to assume by the untoward circumstances of the world-war five years later it is likely that the opera would have received a revision at the hands of its authors which might have saved it from the not wholly deserved fate which befel it. I am not quite sure but that a more ardent desire or a greater zeal in behalf of national opera ought not to have moved the directors to a more determined effort to habilitate a work which in every respect disclosed a lofty striving. It was the firstling of inexperienced men, but they were men of fine capacities and high ideals. The history of opera is full of instances in which the failures of masters were redeemed by a revision of works whose weaknesses had been disclosed in the original productions, and the ailing spots in "Mona" to which a remedial hand might have been applied were obvious, while the merits of the poem and score were so great that an attempt ought to have been made to save it as an example of national art and for the encouragement of American authors. But of this no thought seems to have entered the minds of the opera company's directors or the newspaper critics—perhaps not even the minds of Mr. Hooker and Dr. Parker. A few years later operas of much smaller artistic significance were given much more generous treatment by the management, public and press, simply because of the posture of circumstances—a posture which ought not to become too dominantly influential if the inter-

HORATIO W. PARKER
Composer of "Mona"

ests of art are to be subserved rather than the financial prosperity of the institution. The phase which the problem of national opera has now assumed did not seem imminent in 1912, when its solution might have been undertaken in a sane and orderly manner. It is now become a condition the resolution of which is quite as likely to work disaster to good taste and sound judgment as to bring valuable results, or at least to lead through a darkness of disappointment and failure before emerging into the light of success.

There must presently be a discussion of the questions which have precipitated these reflections; now the business in hand is the new opera. The story of "Mona" can not be told better than Mr. Hooker tells it in the argument with which he prefaced the poem when he printed it in literary form,* and which I reproduce as preliminary to my discussion:

> In the days of Roman rule in Britain Quintus, the son of a Roman governor by a British captive, has grown up as one of his mother's people known to them as Gwynn; has won place and power among them as a bard making their peace with Rome; and is to wed Mona, the foster-child of Enya and Arth and last of the blood of Boadicea. But a great rebellion has brewed in Britain under Caradoc, their chief bard, and Gloom, the Druid foster-brother of Mona. She by birthright and by old signs and prophecies is foretold their leader; and thereto she has been bred up hating Rome and dreaming of great deeds. This Gywnn withstands in vain; and lest he lose Mona and all his power, is driven to swear fellowship in their conspiracy. Even so for urging peace he is disowned and cast off by them and by her.
> Nevertheless he follows her as she journeys about the land arousing revolt; holding back the Roman garrisons from seizing her and secretly saving her life and the life of the rebellion many times. For this he is blamed by the Governor, his father; but answers that through Mona he will yet keep the tribes from war. The Governor lays all upon him, promising to spare the Britons if they bide harmless, but if they strike, to crush them without mercy. Gwynn therefore, meeting Mona, upon the eve of the battle, so moves her love for him that she is from then utterly his own.

* " Mona; an Opera in Three Acts." New York: Dodd, Mead and Co., 1911.

And in that triumph he begins to tell her of his plans for peace. But she, not hearing him out, and barely understanding that he is a Roman, cries for help and calls in the Britons upon him. Yet even so she will not betray him and lies to save his life. They make him prisoner and, led by Mona and the guards, rush forth against the Roman town.

The fight is crushed. Arth falls and Gloom is hurt to death, saving Mona against her will. Gwynn, escaping in the turmoil of defeat, comes upon them and tries to stay further harm, telling Mona of his heritage and beseeching her aid. But she, having taken him for a traitor, takes him now for a liar; and deeming all their woe his doing and her fault for having saved his life, she slays him with her own hand. Then presently come the Governor and his soldiers; and Mona, before she is led away captive, learns how Gwynn spoke the truth and how by yielding up her high deeds, womanly for love's sake, she might have compassed all her endeavor.

This is a tale with an old foundation, as old as humanity probably, but one which, in one phase or another, is perpetually new. A woman, carried away by an emotional frenzy, unsexes herself, and in trying to accomplish what she conceives to be a great mission sacrifices the life and happiness of herself and those who love and appreciate her best as well as the cause to which she feels herself consecrated. She sees the love-light in the eyes of a brave, unselfish man who, unknown to her, is accomplishing what she had set to be her aim. She dreams of love, she feels the hands of little children in the dark, unborn and crying to them to mother them, but puts all aside because she thinks she

> could not be
> A woman, loved and loving, nor endure
> Motherhood and the wise ordinary joys
> Of day by day.

And so she leads her people in a hopeless cause and kills her lover only to learn at the last that had she listened to God's voice and yielded to weakness, the strange fear of her lover's glad eyes, the "warm pain" in her blood answering him, the "little foolish whisper" in her heart, drunk of the joy that was proffered, been only a woman instead of following dreams, she "would have won" all that she strove for in vain by putting woman's nature aside. It is a preachment, of course, and a wise one, though there be many now who will say that it is become an impertinence and a foolishness. Mr. Hooker made no hesitation in confessing the purpose which he had in mind when he wrote his really strong and poetical book. This book, however, is not suitable for operatic purposes. It is defective even with a spoken representation, though it visualizes well and its lines are full of picturesqueness and frequently of strong beauty. But the inexperience of the authors was exemplified in their indifference to some of the prime requirements of a lyric drama. When music enters the play in its highest estate it is for the purpose of proclaiming and celebrating an emotional state up to which the dialogue has led. The dialogue itself in an opera is a necessary evil and an intrusion. There is a paucity of action in "Mona," but that is not a fatal defect in an opera, speaking of action as movement and the doing of things on the stage, the changing picture, outward incident. It is not the highest province of music to accompany these things even in the modern drama in which music has surrendered much of its nature and purpose. Music can prepare for movement and incident and situation, but its highest potency is in proclaiming and hymning after their arrival the emotional states which they produce. Therefore excess of dialogue and neglect of melody are fatal to lyric drama. If there is to be proper celebration of emotional states, then dramatic conversation must yield to lyricism, lyricism in the musical score no less than in the verbal text. Only once did Mr. Hooker break away from the Tennysonian verse-form which he chose for his dialogue, and only once did Dr. Parker write the kind of music which the public, whether rating it good or faulting it as bad, justly considered the kind of music that was called for. It was in the chorus of Britons near the close of the second act of the opera. There should have been many such straightforward musical episodes even at the sacrifice of the constructive method which the composer had chosen to adopt.

The play is a fine one, but the poetry too full of artistic elements to win recognition in a mixed art-form like the opera. That to some may seem an anomaly, and to them it will appear more anomalous still if not directly paradoxical that in the defects of the composition there lay the most interesting phase of the experiment made by the authors. There are elements in the work so ingenuous as almost to invite a smile; but they were presented with a sincerity and strength which almost confounded the knowing. It is doubtful if either of the authors had ever seen or looked into "Norma," which, like theirs, is a Roman-Druidic opera, or "Le Pardon de Ploërmel," in which Dinorah dances with her shadow and prattles with it, just as a half-witted character, Nial, does in "Mona." I doubt if either Mr. Hooker or Professor Parker had even a bowing acquaintance with Meyerbeer's "Les Huguenots," in which there occurs a benediction of poignards like, yet very unlike, a scene in which the Druidic swords receive a consecration in this opera; yet the presentation of the old features in the new work was so fresh, honest, and ingenuous that it carried conviction to the minds of the audience. Something of the same nature may be said of every character drawn by the poet and clothed in music by the composer. They were not only remarkable as first creations, but so strikingly effective that old observers were compelled to sit back and marvel at what had been accomplished by novices and wonder more what they might accomplish at a second trial. It was felt to be a pity that in creating the character of the heroine every element which might have drawn the spectator in pity toward her was omitted. The parallelism with Boadicea was obvious; but Boadicea asks sympathy of him who contemplates her story if for no other reason than its obvious conclusion. When Mr. Hooker brings Mona to the pass where there can be no other outcome than the historic

AN UNSYMPATHETIC PRINCIPAL CHARACTER

he shrinks from making it, because suicide would, forsooth, be a commonplace ending. So he makes no ending at all. The woman addresses a speech to her dead lover, confessing her failure, and the drama flickers out like a candle in the wind, leaving the audience in doubt as to whether they shall go home or wait to learn the end of the "strange, eventful history." The poet, seeking to proclaim the womanly mission of woman, permits the womanly instincts in Mona only a few widely scattered utterances and interrupts each one so rudely that it is impossible to think of her otherwise than as the Judith which she proclaims herself to be in the first act. The witling Nial * has told her that she is beautiful:

> Beautiful! Will my beauty break the chain?
> If I might make thereof a charm to snare
> The leader of our enemies—and then
> While he leaned down and loved me strike one stroke
> Into his wolf-heart, and leave Britain free . . .
> I dream this; who shall make it more than dream?
> —Give me the sword.

A Judith? Nay, a worse than she; for Judith killed the enemy of her people to save them, while Mona assassinates

---

* It is a pity that Mr. Hooker saw fit to call Nial a "changeling." The word has only two possible meanings in ancient British folklore. A changeling is a weak and starveling elf, generally of great age, who has been substituted by the fairies for a human babe before christening. In Shakespeare's mind a changeling was also a human child thus stolen, for Titania has in her train

> "A lovely boy, stolen from an Indian king,
> She never had so sweet a changeling"—

so sweet, indeed, was this boy as to excite Oberon's jealousy. But Nial is merely a simpleton, a witling, a weak-minded lad, a soulless physical husk, as he thinks, who not only propounds all the sound philosophy of his people but sees the aural envelope of all the people of the play. All his talk about shadows and souls was venturesome dramatic material—but here the musician came to the help of the poet and incidents which were perilously near the border line between the pathetic and the ludicrous were saved by Professor Parker's exquisite music.

her lover after her cause is lost and for mere revenge. There can be no other motive for her act except the fatalism of which she is the victim, and the manner in which she gives Gwynn the deathblow robs her of the last vestige of sympathy such as is called forth by the tragic heroines in even the most awful of Attic tragedies. Only once before she realizes the failure of her imagined mission does she yield to her gentler nature. It is in the love scene of the second act when the woman in her, like Tennyson's equally mistaken but gentler princess, answered to the voice of love and

> All
> Her falser self slipt from her like a robe,
> And left her woman, lovelier in her mood
> Than in her mould that other when she came
> From barren deeps to conquer all with love.

But even here it requires but a word to loose the fanatical demon within her. Gwynn had pleaded his love and won her to a confession of tenderness. He is glad and wishes her to know that she has fashioned her country's happiness with her own:

> *Gwynn:*
> This night
> Thou hast saved Britain!
>
> *Mona:*
> Britain. . . . Let me go!

It was only as an opera composer that Professor Parker was a novice, and since the production of "Mona" he has written another opera which had a production before a gathering of musical clubs in Los Angeles, California. Of its music I shall not speak, for, though it marked a material departure from that of "Mona," I have but seen it on the printed page, and only hearing is believing in the art of sounds. Before he essayed the dramatic field, however, he had written much and well in nearly all the forms, large

Louise Homer
In "Mona"

PROFESSOR PARKER'S METHODS

and small, except the symphony, his only essay in this department, I believe, having been made in his student days at Munich nearly a generation ago. In all this music, whether vocal or instrumental, he had been a frank and graceful melodist, a respecter of form, and a masterly contrapuntist. It surprised his friends not a little, therefore, that in his first adventure in the operatic field he was willing to forego to a large extent his characteristic lyricism and in its place to substitute dramatic declamation over an orchestral part restless in ever-shifting tonality. At times this orchestral part achieved symphonic consistency and fluency and rose to eloquence in the climacteric moments, as in the love duet, the final speech of Mona, and when propelled by the rhythmic pulses of the Roman march it brought agreeable and much-needed energy into the score, which had suffered from long stretches of monotony imposed by the interminable dialogue and its heavy-footed delivery. It was not to be expected of Professor Parker that, having a strong, vital, and tragical drama to clothe with music, he should revert to the archaic methods to which Wagner gave the deathblow. He frankly uses the system of typical phrases, or musical symbols (which has become the easy makeshift of many composers lacking in melodic invention), though he did not see fit to give them labels or expound their significances (neither did Wagner, for that matter), nor adhere to them with the logical consistency of the creator of the system. In addition, quite unconsciously, as I am willing to believe, he employed a system of characterization by means of keys. I would not have too much significance attached to this statement or to have it accepted too literally. There are, indeed, two prevailing keys (E-flat major and E minor) for the heroine; the dominant key of Nial's music is D major and of Enya's G minor. The feature has an interesting side, but I lay no stress upon it; may interest some musicians, but not all; it cannot interest the public at all unless it affects them emotionally and in a sense unconsciously. Not even musicians are agreed in holding belief in the emotional characteristics of keys. Some do; many more do not. The whole matter, like the supposed relationship between keys, colors, and perfumes, is more or less (more rather than less) fanciful and at the best a thing in which personal equation plays too large a part to admit of discussion on general lines; also, I fear, a thing of affectation. There are musicians, many of them, including composers, who can not recognize absolute pitch, and a capacity which is so rare among musicians ought not to be expected of the ordinary operatic public. If not pitch, then certainly not key. A Beethoven might have been privileged to feel and say that Klopstock's poetry is too much in D-flat *maestoso,* but we can not think the fact justifies a similar basis of criticism for an occupant of box-seat or orchestra-stall at the Metropolitan Opera House unless the occupant be another Beethoven or one like him. The device of Wagner in using instrumental color or combinations as he does in " Lohengrin," where he gives voice to the dreamy ecstasy of Elsa not only by her words but also in the *timbre* of the wood-wind choir, and the chivalric character of the Knight of the Swan in the brilliant, militant tone of the trumpet is much more to the purpose because much more obvious. But that is an entirely different matter.

And so is the employment of typical phrases, *Leitmotive* as they are called in German. They make an intellectual appeal even when their invention and application are baldly arbitrary; they may make an emotional appeal also when they become in a sense onomatopoetic or where their relationship to the thing — emotion, passion, character, or agency—is recognizable, as is the case frequently in Wagner's dramas. Where the symbols in no wise suggest their objects they are an impertinence and nothing better than a crutch for a composer's creative fancy. I confess that I found many admirable elements in Professor Parker's themes and his employment of them. They were invited

PAUCITY OF FRANK LYRICISM

by the drama, but they should not have stood in the way of a freer, wider, more generous use of lyricism in the old and accepted sense. It would be easy to hold the poet responsible for the paucity of let us say desirable even if conventional tune, but poet and composer were here working hand in hand from the conception of their work till its completion, and Mr. Hooker was no more to blame than Dr. Parker for the paucity of varied lyric forms which the play would not only have tolerated but which it even invited. There was also too little concerted music. There was no thrill in the first act till several voices were united in harmony, and then it was over in a moment. In the second act the listeners grew weary waiting for the love scene, which, when it came, was scarcely a duet, and refreshment did not come till it was brought with the Druidic chorus, for which, without compromising himself or his artistic nature, Professor Parker might have found a capital model in Mendelssohn's " Walpurgis Night." In the last act there was again only monologue and dialogue (save for a few muttered words by the Roman soldiers) until the end. How much more wisely did Wagner, the founder of the constructive system used by Professor Parker, build! Even in "Götterdämmerung" when the occasion warranted it he let Gunther's men sing like a veritable *Liedertafel!* This was the cast for "Mona," for which Mr. Hertz did a noble service in the conductor's chair:

Mona, Princess of Britain .... Louise Homer
Enya, her foster-mother .... Rita Fornia
Arth, husband of Enya .... Herbert Witherspoon
Gloom, their son, a Druid .... William Hinshaw
Nial, a changeling .... Albert Reiss
Caradoc, chief bard of Britain .... Lambert Murphy
Roman Governor of Britain .... Putnam Griswold
Quintus, his son .... Riccardo Martin
An old man .... Basil Ruysdael

Monteverde's "Orfeo," the performance of which in concert form took place on Sunday evening, April 14, 1912, had its first representation on the occasion of the marriage of the son of the Duke of Mantua to Margherita of Savoy, A. D. 1607. Its score had been arranged for modern orchestra by Professor Orefice for the Associazione Italiana di Amice della Musica, under whose auspices the revised score was published and the opera performed at an International Exhibition in Rome in 1911. At the Metropolitan performance it was sung in an English version made by Mr. Charles Henry Meltzer, and the parts were distributed as follows:

Eurydice .... Rita Fornia
Musica ⎫
Sylvia ⎬,................................... Maria Duchène
Proserpina ⎭
A Nymph .... Anna Case
Orpheus .... Hermann Weil
Pluto .... Herbert Witherspoon
Charon .... Basil Ruysdael
A Shepherd .... Anna Case
Another Shepherd .... Henrietta Wakefield

The archaic novelty was heard with little interest. Its historical significance made little appeal to the vast majority of the audience, composed of the ordinary type of Sunday night concert-goers, who were much more interested in getting as much as possible out of the stars who sang airs of the modern kind before Monteverde's work was taken in hand. These stars were Mme. Destinn and Signor Amato, whose admirers kept up such a hubbub after each of their airs in their desire for more that the evening was largely worn away before the old opera could be begun. By that time a weariness had set in which interfered with appreciation of the beauty, not to mention the significance, of the old music.

CHAPTER XI

AN INCREASE IN TICKET PRICES AND A SCANDAL

THE COST OF SEATS AT THE METROPOLITAN OPERA HOUSE ADVANCED—REASON GIVEN IN EXPLANATION—SPECULATION IN THEATER TICKETS IN NEW YORK—RELATION BETWEEN MANAGERS AND SPECULATORS—ATTITUDE OF THE METROPOLITAN MANAGEMENT—AGENTS HYPOTHECATE TICKETS BELONGING TO SUBSCRIBERS — CRIMINAL PROCEEDINGS AGAINST AN AGENT—WHY THEY WERE NOT PROSECUTED—COST OF GIVING OPERA IN NEW YORK—SOME COMPARATIVE TABLES

AN increase in the prices of admission to all parts of the house except the dress-circle, balcony, and family-circle was the incident of greatest public interest in the Metropolitan season of 1911-12 outside the artistic doings of the establishment. The advance in price was from $5 to $6 on the seats which for convenience' sake I may call fashionable, and was sought to be justified by the management on the ground of necessity because of the growing cost of the performances. It was cheerfully accepted by the public, and I do not know that it falls within the province of that criticism which I have held to be an essential element in history, though it invites an inquiry into the changes which have taken place within recent years in the business of opera-giving which I shall attempt presently to make. One of the consequences of the change, however, which came before the beginning of the season 1913-14 is in a different case, and deserves not only criticism but reprobation. I have already alluded to it as a scandal which led up to prison gates which would have opened had justice received its due. By this I did not mean to imply that the Metropolitan Company was guilty of an offense against the penal laws of the State of New York, but that by its employment and countenance of a system in connection with the sale of subscription tickets which was and is vicious and contrary to the good of the public it made possible a procedure which grievously wronged many of its most generous patrons, compelled an appeal to a court of equity, and led to a criminal inquiry. The procedure was not only illegal, it was distinctly criminal, and the fact that the only sufferers from it were patrons of the opera, who should have been protected by the company at all hazards, will remain a "blot in the 'scutcheon" of the company as long as the incident is remembered, or at least until reparation is made by a reform in the methods which made a gross imposition on the public possible. There is no extenuation in the fact that the sufferings of the victims were not due to monetary losses (except in the case of the few who appealed for protection to the courts), but only to vexation, anxiety, and unnecessary embarrassment and labor.

The two incidents were closely related and may be combined in the narrative. For many years the theater-going people of New York had been (still are as I write) victims of a system of brigandage at which theatrical managers and the speculators in theater tickets have connived. In the case of theaters of the ordinary type the imposition by the ticket agents of large premiums upon the price has followed only in the case of plays which have become established in popularity. In such cases the speculators frequently purchase practically all the desirable seats in the house for weeks in advance, thus compelling the public to buy of them and pay whatever premium the popularity of the play enables them to exact. For the thousands of transient visitors at the city's hotels the system works an accommodation when not forced to the degree of an intolerable exaction. For many regular habitués of the playhouse it offers a convenience, since many of them, especially persons of wealth, are in the habit of maintaining accounts with the ticket agents and make periodical settlements with them as they do with ordinary tradesmen. These are the advantages which dealings with ticket agencies instead of the box-offices offer to that fraction of the public, a small one, able and willing to pay for a favored location or to avoid an advance visit to the theater. To the public in general it works nothing but hardship, against which they should be protected by the laws which license playhouses and are supposed to regulate the reciprocal duties and privileges of manager and patron. To managers the system offers the advantages of an advance sale which sometimes capitalizes a new venture or guarantees a season. In the degree that it does these things the ordinary manager encourages the ticket speculator frequently to the extent of conniving with him in defrauding the public. Ordinarily the ticket agent acts as a broker, buying for his customer and charging a commission. In that capacity he is an unexceptionable servant to society and may be regarded even as a boon or a benefactor; the legitimacy of his vocation is unquestionable. It is only when without the assistance of the manager he becomes an extortioner that he also becomes a nuisance and an evil; with the assistance of the manager he sinks to the status of a brigand, the manager with him, and the two become proper objects of the penal code. It is of interest in these chapters of reminiscence that amidst the throes of his operatic dissolution Mr. Hammerstein made an effort to secure a reformation of the evil. It is not necessary to credit him with altruistic motives, but the fact is that he made an appeal to District Attorney (afterward Governor) Whitman and that at his instigation a statute was drafted in the District Attorney's office (by Mr. Arthur C. Train, I believe) designed to regulate the business of ticket speculation, like the ordinance which became a law under the administration of District Attorney Swann early in 1919. A bill embodying the law was introduced in the General Assembly of the State, but influences of which I know nothing prevailed in the minds of the State's legislators and the bill failed of passage. The utmost that was done thereafter by the guardians of the public was to enforce, more or less laxly, a municipal ordinance under which it was found to be possible to prohibit the traffic in tickets on the sidewalks in front of the theater doors.

The reform vainly undertaken by District Attorney Whitman to suppress the evil was resumed by District Attorney Swann, who gathered evidence touching the dealings between the theater managers and ticket agents which disclosed to what an amazing extent the patrons of the playhouse had been made the victims of managers and middlemen. Practically eighty per cent. of the tickets to theaters in New York City, it was said, were sold at the time by the managers to ticket speculators. The Tyson Company in the case of one production made a contract to buy 400 tickets every night for 24 weeks, the nominal value of these tickets being $120,000 and the price paid twenty-five per cent. less. These tickets were sold, of course, at as large a premium as the public demand made possible. Further testimony before the District Attorney was to the effect that the Tyson Company sold 1,200,000 tickets a year; Tyson and Company (a different concern), approximately 200,000; John McBride, 500,000; Bascom, Inc., 120,000; The Broadway Ticket Agency, 100,000; The United Theatre Ticket Corporation, 110,000, and The Times Building Ticket Agency, 30,000. At what discount these tickets were bought and at what advance over box-office prices they were sold need not detain me in this history.

What was business comparatively in the little at the ordinary theaters a decade or two ago had for a long time been a wholesale business at the Metropolitan Opera House. There it grew up under the influence of close personal and business relations existing between Maurice Grau and Frederick Rullman. An old-time friendship existed between the

SPECULATION AT THE METROPOLITAN

two men, and the privilege of buying large blocks of opera tickets, which in time developed into a highly advantageous one, was largely the reward which Mr. Grau bestowed on his friend for financial aid in times of distress and threatened disaster. Mr. Rullman became a stockholder in the opera company organized by Mr. Grau in 1897 and remained such until the retirement of Mr. Grau and the subsequent organization of the Conried company. Mr. Rullman's purchases of opera tickets no doubt varied in amount from time to time, and as to the full volume of his business I am not informed. His estate, or the business organization which has succeeded him, was in 1918 a subscriber to the extent of $73,000 or more a season. The subscription was next in magnitude to that of Tyson and Company, prior to 1911. In the theaters it is the popularity of a particular play which gives stimulus to sporadic speculation. At the Opera the bills are varied, but the command of fashion, consorted with the popular adoration of a few singers and the whims and fads of the moment, have made the speculative traffic in seats a safe and profitable venture for years. In consequence the ticket agencies became large purchasers of season tickets. In 1911 Tyson and Company and Rullman were said to have subscribed for about one-half of all the fashionable seats in the house. They also bought tickets admitting to the cheaper portions of the auditorium. The terms of payment were matters of private adjustment between the management and the agents, but the price was understood to be those of the box-office less a rebate, or discount, of 15 per cent. Other subscribers for the season were allowed the same discount, but of these there were comparatively few outside of the stockholders of the company which owns the building who have the use of their boxes as an equivalent for the rental of the theater. Tyson and Company and Rullman were practically the only subscribers to all the subscription evenings and matinees of the seasons. They in turn had lists of subscribers for different days of the week, these subscribers finding their advantage in such a subscription in the fact that they had accounts with the agents for other tickets as well and were sometimes accommodated in the disposal of their seats on occasions which offered no attraction for them or when they could not attend the opera. Other subscribing agencies were Tyson and Brother, John McBride, J. W. Miller and Tyson and Company.

In March, 1911, the directors abolished the rebate on tickets to subscribers, and Tyson and Company and Ruliman announced to the public on the 25th of that month that in consequence in the next season their price for the orchestra chairs would be $6 instead of $5, which was the box-office price. Simultaneously the management of the opera announced that it intended to devise a plan which would save the public from the increased charge. This announcement was followed on March 31 by a statement from the opera company that the hotel ticket agencies would not be permitted to charge more than ten per cent. over the box-office prices. Naturally this left the public under the impression that purchasers from the ticket agents in the coming season would be able to buy an orchestra seat for $5.50. In less than a fortnight, however (on April 11, to be exact), the Board of Directors of the opera company issued an official announcement that in the next season, that of 1911-12, the price of stalls in the orchestra and orchestra-circle would be advanced to $6, but that there would be no increase in the cost of admission to chairs in the dress-circle, balcony, and family-circle. At the same time the ticket agents were informed that their purchases could be made but with a reduction from the old rebate. The information was given to the subscribers in a circular letter in which the reason for the advance was set forth. The public, it was said, had become more exacting than formerly, demanding the best performances from every point of view, whereas they had been wont to be satisfied with performances if they

REASONS GIVEN FOR THE INCREASE

had only included "some leading stars." In those earlier days, so ran the argument, "the production of opera involved consequently little expense aside from the outlay for soloists"; now it was become necessary to engage "the most eminent orchestra conductors, the training of a well-equipped cast composed of high-class artists, a thoroughly drilled chorus of the best obtainable material, *mise-en-scène,* stage management, and general accessories which will satisfy the most fastidious demands and the employment of a large and highly trained corps of assistants in all branches of stage work—all of which with the added factor of the general rise in the cost of labor and material has caused an enormous increase in the expense of the production of opera as now given at the Metropolitan Opera House." The letter explained further that there had been a very heavy loss recurring each year by reason of the things enumerated and that this loss had been borne entirely by the few stockholders of the Metropolitan Opera Company. To eliminate this loss entirely would require a material raising of prices throughout the house, but as this might mean a "real hardship" to the holders of lower-priced seats the advance was confined to the orchestra and orchestra-circle.

The Metropolitan Opera Company being a business corporation not subject to an accounting financially to the public I am neither able nor disposed to traverse its statements concerning its losses during the period of competition with the Manhattan Opera House. It is enough for present purposes to direct attention to the facts, for which I go to its own prospectuses. There was no increase of prices in 1909-10 when the management made proclamation of a great augmentation of artistic forces to enable it to give seasons of opera in Brooklyn, Philadelphia, Baltimore, and Boston, as well as at the New Theater and the Metropolitan in this city. Then Toscanini and Hertz were the principal conductors, the chorus numbered 180, the orchestra

150, and among the leading singers were Destinn, Farrar, Alda, Fremstad, Gadski, Homer, Nordica, Bonci, Caruso, Martin, Scotti, Didur, Blass, Hinckley, and Witherspoon. In 1911-12 a few singers, Bonci, Nordica, and Blass among them, had been dropped from the roster and as many, including Slezak, Matzenauer, Gilly, Rothier, and Griswold, added; Toscanini and Hertz were still the conductors, the artistic administration remained practically unchanged, but the chorus had been reduced to 120 and the orchestra to 100. Mme. Tetrazzini, who had been announced among the prima donnas, sang five times in the course of the season. The reduction of the chorus and orchestra was a natural consequence, of course, of the abandonment of the scheme for giving opera in Baltimore, Washington, Boston, and other cities which had required practically a double organization in these departments.

This, then, was the posture of affairs when in the summer of 1913 Tyson and Company purchased tickets to the value of $157,000 for the approaching season of opera. Of these tickets 200 or more were bought for regular patrons of the opera who had been accustomed to make their subscriptions through the agents. The remainder were bought for the usual purposes of speculation. Tyson and Company and Rullman were said at the time (and the statement went unchallenged) to be purchasers of about one-half of the fashionable seats in the house and practically the only purchasers of seats for all of the subscription performances. A short time before the control of Tyson and Company had passed into the hands of Richard J. Hartman, a promoter of speculative enterprises of various kinds, who fell under suspicion at the opera house to such an extent that credit which had formerly been extended to the firm was refused him. In the early days of September, having collected $61,000 from their subscribers, Tyson and Company opened formally a special deposit account at the Metropolitan Trust Company. Wishing to raise money to pur-

TICKETS PLEDGED AS COLLATERAL

chase more theater and opera tickets Hartman negotiated a loan with the Trust Company and pledged the tickets purchased from the Metropolitan Opera Company as collateral. With $100,000 thus obtained he liquidated the debt due to the opera company. In time the special deposit account reached the sum of $220,000, but the Trust Company permitted Tyson and Company to draw against it and only two-thirds of the tickets had been redeemed for Tyson and Company's subscribers when they were confronted by the fact that the opera season was about to open and that they were unable to meet their obligations to their patrons. Subscribers who went to Tyson and Company with their receipts and demands for their tickets were informed that they could not deliver them, as they were in the hands of the Trust Company, which held a lien on them.

The dilemma in which the subscribers to the opera were placed by the action of Tyson and Company and the opera and trust companies was a peculiar one and not without its diverting side, though few of those concerned were in a mood to see anything humorous in it. For years there had been much complaint on the part of persons who had found it impossible to secure seats at the opera house because of the fact that practically all the desirable stalls were subscribed for, especially on the nights, made popular by fad, fashion, and a singer or two, which were always announced as sold out as soon as the weekly sale opened. At these poor souls the customers of the ticket agents were in a position to smile commiseratingly or derisively as their dispositions prompted. Suddenly it appeared that these fortunate and much-envied beings had been living in a fools' paradise. They had imagined that they were subscribers to the opera, but found that they were only customers of brokers against whom they were powerless to enforce the most ordinary kind of business contract—to compel delivery of goods bought and paid for. Consternation seized them at the prospect of not being able to take part in the social function which marks the opening of the operatic season. That opening was only a day or two distant. Some subscribers evolved the theory that the custom of many years and the acts of the opera company had made Tyson and Company agents of the opera company. Had not Lord Chief Justice Coke laid down the maxim, *Qui facit per alium facit per se,* and was there not evidence that Tyson and Company were agents of the opera company in the fact that the letters which had been sent out to subscribers with the Metropolitan Opera House heading telling them of the reason of the increase in prices in 1910, also told of the reallotment to the agencies of the seats thitherto held by them, and another dated April, 1912, offering to renew the subscription of patrons and concluding with the suggestion that all communications be sent to Tyson and Company? The opera company said that it was not responsible for the use which Tyson and Company had made of its circular letter, but the inference seemed clear and some of the persons who held the not unnatural view proposed to test the validity of the proposition by presenting their receipts to the opera officials and demanding admission to their seats. But they were forestalled by an official announcement of the opera company which was curt and to the point: "The Metropolitan Opera Company begs to announce that it will honor only the regular tickets issued by the Opera Company."

Meanwhile the opera opening was approaching. The trust company opened an office at the Manhattan Hotel, where it offered an opportunity to subscribers who could produce evidence that they had paid for their tickets to rebuy the same tickets at a small discount (50 cents on $6), adding the threat that tickets not "taken up" would be put on sale to the public on noon of November 17, the first night of the season. Loud and indignant protests followed this action, but to all complaints the assistant treasurer of the trust company replied that all the subscribers owned was a

TICKETS WITHHELD FROM SUBSCRIBERS 277

contract with Tyson and Company, that the latter would deliver tickets, while the trust company, having taken the tickets as collateral for a loan, would protect itself by realizing on them. Mr. Edmund L. Baylies, of counsel for the trust company, but also a member of the Board of Directors of the opera company, stated the attitude of his client to be that Tyson and Company never had a clear title to the tickets, which he said had been delivered in person by an employee of the opera company to the trust company in the presence of Hartman. The ticket agents never having a clear title but only one subject to lien, the subscribers had never acquired a title of any kind, clear or clouded. In short they had bought a right of action against Tyson and Company and nothing more. With this statement Mr. T. De Witt Cuyler, a member of the directorates of both the opera and trust companies, took issue. He denied that he had knowledge of the intended hypothecation and said that on September 14 Hartman went to the opera house in a taxicab and gave the management a check for $100,000, whereupon Earl Lewis, an employee of the controller's office, "under instructions" accompanied Hartman to the office of the trust company to have the check certified before releasing the tickets. Mr. Beverly Chew, an assistant vice-president of the trust company, met this statement with a flat denial. " The tickets were delivered to me in my office by an official of the opera company and the check was passed in the same place." He would not say that the opera company knew that the tickets were to be hypothecated, but Mr. Cuyler was present at the meeting of the executive committee of the trust company when the loan was approved.

Tyson and Company, the center of the storm area, were bestirring themselves to get the tickets released at least for the first night. They offered to redeem the tickets for the opening performance, but the trust company rejected the offer as unfair to the other subscribers. An indignation meeting was held on the forenoon of November 17, opening day, and a committee of subscribers appointed to lay the case before the prosecuting attorney of the county. Then one hundred indignant victims of the swindle descended on the office of the trust company to demand their tickets. There they learned that Tyson and Company had raised $2,800 with which to secure the release of the tickets for the first week. Twenty-six subscribers who had paid a second time received a refund of their money. Two energetic individuals had secured their tickets by action in replevin and the sky became overcast with threats of legal proceedings of various kinds. The District Attorney now took a hand in the matter, and on November 19 Hartman, as the head of Tyson and Company, was haled before a police magistrate on a charge of grand larceny. Mr. Lewis testified to facts like those recited by Mr. Cuyler, with the modification that he had made delivery of the tickets at the opera house on receiving the check and had accompanied Hartman in the taxicab called by the latter on his invitation to ride along since they were going to the same place. There was no evidence in contradiction and the magistrate held Tyson and Company for the grand jury. Then the representative of the District Attorney announced that on the evidence the status of the trust company was that of a receiver of stolen goods,—an obvious deduction and a determinative. The case was not pressed to an indictment. Why? If I were to venture an explanation which is something more than a shrewd guess it would be this: before the end of the week the patrons of Tyson and Company received their tickets without more ado; their rights had been secured; the prosecuting officer did not think himself justified in sending a man to jail on evidence concerning which he was himself skeptical; and the scandal came to an end. At a later day Hartman's rascality came out in a new charge of misappropriation of a client's funds, and on that he was convicted and sentenced to state prison for a term of seven years. On January 3, 1914, the Metropolitan Opera Company, whose only concern in the matter seemed to be to keep its skirts clean of everything except the bona fide sale of tickets and the delivery of the goods to Tyson and Company, announced that thenceforth persons subscribing through the various ticket agencies might transfer their subscriptions to the Company or continue them through the agencies. Only 10 per cent. of the subscribers availed themselves of the invitation, and the old system was restored, though the opera company prohibited a charge larger than that of the box-office for subscription tickets; over sales other than subscriptions it did not attempt to assume control.

As a sequel to the chapter of history concerned with the increase in prices of admission in 1911 I purpose now to conduct an inquiry, limited in scope (not because of any unwillingness on my part but because the avenues of information are few and narrow), into the cost of opera-giving in New York which was alleged to be the reason for the advance. This increase was effected by means of the devious device of first abolishing the rebate allowed to subscribers, thus leading the speculators to announce an advance in prices of from $5 to $6, then proclaiming the latter sum to be the standard and restoring a rebate to the agents but not to patrons who made their subscriptions through the box-office unless they were season subscriptions. Whether or not this led to the fortification of the system of speculation which became an almost intolerable evil I leave to the judgment of the readers of the history who are willing to read in the light of the facts disclosed by the scandals which followed hard on the heels of the advance as I have related them.

In order that there may be no misconception of the motives underlying the inquiry let me add that during the last decade and longer there had been a persistent proclamation of altruistic purposes as distinguished from selfish commercialism on the part of the directors of the Metropolitan Opera Company. It was the burden of the song chanted in the newspaper interviews by both parties in the course of the struggle between the Metropolitan Company and Mr. Hammerstein when the rivalry between the Metropolitan and Manhattan houses was at its height. When Mr. Hammerstein attempted to re-establish this rivalry in defiance of an agreement to remain out of the operatic field for ten years, it became a note in the legal proceedings successfully prosecuted to enjoin him from carrying out his purpose. Public sympathy and judicial decree were asked on the ground that the public good, not private gain, was the aim of the generous gentlemen who are maintaining an institution which is unquestionably an elegant and lordly ornament of our civic and social life. To review some of the details of the administration of the institution which has thus been proclaimed as a beautiful and beneficial public trust can therefore be looked upon as a proper privilege and laudable purpose to which even an altruistic aim might be attributed if I were to choose to claim it.

During the last two generations the price of admission to the opera has been increased from 400 to 600 per centum. In some of its features, I make no doubt, the increase in the cost of opera-giving has grown in proportion with the charge for its enjoyment. It would be interesting to inquire into the causes of the increase in cost and also to attempt to determine whether or not the advance in artistic achievement bears any reasonable ratio to the increase in cost to the givers of opera and its patrons; but this would be a more formidable task than I am ready to undertake and one which the policy of reticence pursued by the Metropolitan Opera Company concerning their financial affairs (a policy which is their unqualified right) makes impossible to one not concerned in it. The only basis which we have for such a comparative study is provided by the reports which were placed at my disposal for public use during several years when the owners of the Metropolitan Opera House were also the purveyors of the entertainment, and a report concerning two seasons which, for a purpose still incomprehensible to me, Mr. Conried made in the spring of 1906. These, and these only, are open to me for analysis.

There was a period, not an ignoble one either, when the public paid much less to attend the opera in its fashionable home than they do now to enjoy the most modest theatrical entertainments—barring the moving-picture shows. When the Academy of Music was new, in 1854, Max Maretzek rented the house for a space to Mr. Hackett, then manager of an opera company headed by Mme. Grisi and Signor Mario, two of the most refulgent stars that ever blazed in the operatic firmament. Counting on their power of attraction coupled with that of the new house, Mr. Hackett charged $3 for the parquet (orchestra) stalls and from $12 to $40 for the boxes. These prices the public thought exorbitant and showed its resentment by staying away from the performance on the first night. Maretzek, who made record of the fact, said that the audience numbered only 1,500. Mr. Hackett promptly reduced his prices one-half for the second night, and this price was still further reduced to $1 and kept there till Mr. Maretzek plucked up enough courage to raise it to $1.50. This was the price, I believe, when the high cost of living during the Civil War affected also the cost of giving opera; but it remained at $3 until the advent of the Metropolitan Opera House, I believe. If it was advanced to $5 for the first season of Italian opera, about which I have no time to inquire at this juncture, it was reduced to $4 and remained there throughout the German régime—that is, from 1884-85 to 1890-91. On the return of Messrs. Abbey and Grau, and during the successive administrations from that time down to 1911, the standard price was $5, with $2.50 as the unit at the popular Saturday nights.

I shall publish at the end of this chapter a tabulated statement touching the cost of giving opera at the Metropolitan Opera House during five seasons, from which it will be possible to see to some extent in which departments the cost of giving opera has grown abnormally enormous. Comparisons between the different years can not be made definitely except as regards certain details for the reason that the operatic seasons differed in length, and in the years of Mr. Grau's management (1902-03) and Mr. Conried's (1904-05) the cost of giving opera outside of New York is included. It is equally impossible accurately to appraise past and present artistic results for the reason that while the German seasons developed a list of operas which have remained current for twenty-five years the list has been at least temporarily disarranged by a change of policy caused by the war. Assuming, however, that German operas will some day be restored to the Metropolitan repertory in all their puissance it remains a significant reflection that during the seven years when the owners of the opera house gave opera on their own account, as many if not more permanent additions were made to the Metropolitan list as during the combined consulships of Conried and Gatti. I am omitting works familiar to the public before the Metropolitan Opera House was opened and which might appear in both lists, but as to the quality of new works compare " Fidelio," " Die Meistersinger," " Tristan und Isolde," " Das Rheingold," " Die Walküre," " Siegfried," " Götterdämmerung," and " Königin von Saba " of the Stanton list with " Francesca da Rimini," " Hänsel und Gretel," " Königskinder," " Madame Sans-Gêne," " Prince Igor," " Boris Godounoff," " Rosenkavalier," and " Parsifal," to which I am inclined to allot a measure of endurance in the Conried-Gatti list.

The average cost of giving opera at the Metropolitan Opera House in 1918 I am told was over $10,000 a night. In 1886-87 it was $4,903, which I believe included the cost

WAS THE INCREASE JUSTIFIED? 283

of maintaining the building. In 1887-88 it was $4,432; in 1888-89, $5,224; in 1889-90, $5,386; in 1890-91, $6,480. In all these years, it must be borne in mind, the cost of an orchestra seat was $4 as against the present price of $6. I print the tables referred to given out by Mr. Conried in March, 1906, and three tables showing the cost of opera in as many season during the German régime. It will require some speculation to find points for comparison in some departments, but in others there are some pretty obvious and equally significant. Inside of fifteen years the cost of the orchestra, for instance, was doubled while that of the combined chorus and ballet remained practically unaltered. We may surmise that the cost of principal singers has been largely increased, but we are at a loss for specific information because the salaries of conductors are included in the item "artists and staff" in the later tables. It is saying nothing new, however, to say that conductors, stage-managers, and ballet-masters combined (with men like Anton Seidl and Walter Damrosch wielding the baton) did not cost as much in the German years as any single first conductor since the days of Conried. The royalties account is smaller in the later régime than in the earlier, which would be inexplicable did we not know that Mr. Stanton paid royalties not obligatory under the law for the use of the Wagnerian dramas. The increase in wardrobe and properties is inconsiderable, a fact partly due to the natural accumulation of such assets, but in transportation prodigious —due, of course, to the policy of giving performances outside of New York City.

It is in the light reflected by these figures that the statements made in 1911 to justify the increase in the price of admission must be read. These statements were that the cost of production had grown so high above the receipts as to become a burden on the stockholders of the company because the taste of the public had come to demand not more costly solo singers but more eminent conductors, a better and larger orchestra (though the orchestra was only two-thirds as large after the retirement of Mr. Hammerstein as it was in 1910), a larger and better chorus (though that was reduced one-third in numbers as soon as the rivalry came to an end), more elaborate scenery, more efficient stage management (though Mr. Conried brought such eminent craftsmen as Fuchs and Lautenschläger to his aid) than used to suffice, besides a large increase in the cost of material and labor, an item which is incontestable. The matter of principal singers was waived, but here are two rosters brought into juxtaposition. Mr. Grau's last company: Mmes. Sembrich, Eames, Homer, and Messrs. Burgstaller, Dippel, Reiss, Mühlmann, Scotti, Van Rooy, Blass, Journet, Plançon, and Rossi; Mr. Gatti's company in 1911-12: Mmes. Farrar, Destinn, Fremstad, Gadski, and Matzenauer, and Messrs. Caruso, Amato, Gilly, Burrian, Weil, Witherspoon, Jadlowker, Hinshaw, and Griswold. There is no need to mention artists who were concerned in both régimes.

COST OF OPERA PRODUCTION IN THE GERMAN PERIOD

	1886-87	1887-88	1888-89
Salaries of artists	$121,000.00	$105,182.00	$135,498.32
Orchestra	40,000.00	42,408.75	46,206.00
Chorus	25,000.00	23,962.75	26,295.00
Ballet	19,000.00	16,567.33	17,869.00
Conductors, stage-managers, ballet-masters, etc.	13,000.00	24,067.33	13,176.00
Front of the house	20,000.00	16,423.76	....
Advertising	16,000.00	11,176.47	12,781.13
Transportation	11,000.00	8,317.82	10,481.56
Stage hands	9,500.00	9,244.51	10,174.62
Wardrobe department	6,900.00	3,994.96	....
Property department	4,506.00	4,427.42	9,280.17
Royalties	2,500.00	9,606.52	7,376.59
Totals	$288,406.00	$275,379.62	$289,138.39

COMPARISON OF LATER PERIODS

COST OF OPERA PRODUCTION IN ONE SEASON UNDER MR. GRAU AND ONE UNDER MR. CONRIED

	1902-03	1904-05
Artists and staff	$522,315.13	$544,153.11
Chorus, ballet, and supers	41,386.89	66,212.13
Orchestra and stage-band	85,569.29	95,083.40
Steamship transportation	16,799.60	20,656.07
Railway transportation, transfer of scenery, baggage, hotels, etc.	36,209.52	72,687.30
Costumes, wardrobe department, and wigs	18,110.59	15,953.83
Music and royalties	3,517.16	3,499.67
Commissions and sundries	2,356.62	4,371.54
Advertising	16,566.91	25,167.42
Totals	$743,031.71	$847,783.97

CHAPTER XII

ANOTHER EXPERIMENT WITH ENGLISH OPERA AND A GREAT RUSSIAN WORK

THE SEASON OF 1912-13—ADDITIONS TO THE METROPOLITAN COMPANY—MABEL GARRISON, MELANIE KURT, JOHANNES SEMBACH, LUCA BOTTA, AND ARTHUR MIDDLETON—ROSTAND'S "CYRANO DE BERGERAC" DONE INTO AN ENGLISH OPERA—MOUSSORGSKY'S "BORIS GODOUNOW"—A VISIT FROM THE CHICAGO OPERA COMPANY BRINGS NOVELTIES—ZANDONAI'S "CONCHITA" AND "LES RANZ DES VACHES," A GERMAN VERSION OF KIENZL'S "KUHREIGEN"

THE progress of the season 1912-13 at the Metropolitan Opera House was serene and uneventful, save in the artistic field. Fortune smiled upon it from beginning to end. The mishaps to which operatic institutions are prone were few. If there were contentions in the administrative or artistic ranks the fact was not permitted to reach the public, the old desire to "rush into print" having disappeared with the settlement of the Metropolitan-Manhattan feud, when such a proceeding was "good advertising." The character of the season, artistically, was like that of its predecessors and successors. The popular adoration of a few gifted singers continued, and had much to do with stamping a too familiar physiognomy upon the repertory—and the audience. The management redeemed some of its promises and failed to keep others; but there was nothing new in that, and if the reasons were fit subjects for historical discussion they were not disclosed. There was, however, much rejoicing over the manner in which two promises were kept—the production of an American and a Russian novelty—"Cyrano de Bergerac" and "Boris Godounow"—so much rejoicing, indeed, that the unperformed list was forgotten. If in the distribution of operas between those offered to the general public as distinguished from the general subscribers the action of Mr. Gatti could be looked upon as more significant than ordinary it was because there seemed to be a more heavy leaning than had been wont upon that element of society which was fond of Wagner's dramas; for the relation between Italian and German operas was more than reversed—it was revolutionized. This, however, may better be studied in the record of the season which appears in the Appendix to this book.

As in the case of the two seasons immediately preceding there were subscription seasons also at the Metropolitan Opera House for the Chicago-Philadelphia company—four successive Tuesdays beginning on February 4. In the list of visitors were two novelties, " Conchita " and " Le Ranz des Vaches," of which something must be said presently. The other operas were " Louise " and " Thaïs." Previous to this visit the company came from Philadelphia to bestow upon New York the boon of a performance of " Hamlet " with a sensational baritone, Titta Ruffo, in the titular part. The singer made good his reputation but left no hunger for his continued presence among the patrons of the Metropolitan Opera House. He was speedily forgotten. Significant names among those added to the Metropolitan roster were those of Mabel Garrison, Melanie Kurt, Johannes Sembach, Luca Botta, and Arthur Middleton. Miss Garrison, an American, is a native of Baltimore who had had a short experience in English opera; Melanie Kurt came from Berlin, where she had been dramatic soprano at the Royal Imperial Opera for six years; Johannes Sembach had come into notice by singing in the performances of " Parsifal " and " Die Meistersinger " at the Théâtre des Champs-Elysées; Luca Botta, a youthful tenor, had not attracted large attention then, nor has he since though he remains a member of the company; Mr. Middleton was an American concert baritone who hailed from Iowa.

There remains considerable to say about the novelties. "Cyrano de Bergerac," the text by William J. Henderson after Rostand's play, the music by Walter Damrosch, had its first performance on the evening of February 27, 1913, under the direction of Alfred Hertz. The opera had not had the adventitious help of nation-wide advertising nor a regal prize; yet its advent was heralded as a triumph and, in spite of the criticisms of kindly disposed reviewers, its authors were given to understand that their work was looked upon, officially, as something more and better than a tentative experiment. Yet, like "Mona" it went into the lumber-room at the end of the season. It was not the firstfruit of forced, hot-house culture. The purpose to write it had been formed by Mr. Damrosch ten years before. He had secured the collaboration of Mr. Henderson, and after the latter gentleman had put the libretto into his hands he took up its composition while resting from the labors of conducting. Having composed practically all of the music he applied the Horatian adage to his work and left it alone for nine years. Then he took it up again and gave its first act an improvised trial at his home. Mr. Gatti heard the trial and agreed to produce the opera at the Metropolitan. After Mr. Damrosch had rewritten the fourth act the opera was produced on February 27, 1913. To a *Tribune* reporter the composer had explained that there was more Italian and French influence in the music than German; that in the first act he had harked back to Rameau; that to some extent he had used the Wagnerian system of typical themes and that the musical symbol for Cyrano's celebrated nose was in the whole-tone scale (although he had written it before Debussy was widely known) so that it might stand out in the music as did the huge proboscis from the hero's face. Roxane being a *précieuse*, her music was at first of the florid kind, but became serious and even tragic as her love developed.

There were gladsome incidents at the first performance,

WILLIAM J. HENDERSON
Librettist of "Cyrano de Bergerac"

FIRST PERFORMANCE OF MR. DAMROSCH'S OPERA

including nine curtain calls after the first act for composer, librettist, conductor, singers, and so on. After the balcony scene the composer made a speech and after the final curtain he made another. He said that as his father had been the first to introduce German opera in this country so he hoped he had helped to lay the foundation-stone of a type of opera which should prove as popular as German opera at the Metropolitan Opera House. Perhaps the elation of the moment may be pleaded in extenuation for Mr. Damrosch's faulty history. As a matter of fact German opera in German had been fighting its way toward recognition for nearly thirty-nine years when Dr. Leopold Damrosch began his memorable experiment at the Metropolitan. It was given on extra nights in the Italian seasons of Max Maretzek at the Academy of Music; Bergmann and Anschütz had conducted many performances; Carlotta Patti had traveled through the country at the head of a company that produced " Die Zauberflöte ; " Parepa and Lucca had sung in German performances, and theaters in other cities than New York had echoed to the strains of " Martha," " Stradella," " Fidelio," " Tannhäuser," " Lohengrin," and " Der Fliegende Holländer." " Die Walküre " was performed at the Academy of Music at a Wagner festival in 1877.

Mr. Otto H. Kahn told the newspaper reporters after the performance that he thought the opera would stay in the repertory of the Metropolitan Opera House and that thereafter the Metropolitan Company would produce any American opera which had anything like the merits of " Cyrano." Mr. Henderson's mind preserved its habitually normal temperature. In his review of the season published in *The Sun* newspaper he said that he thought it tolerably certain that no one was better aware of the mistakes made in the composition of the opera than Mr. Damrosch. In its original state it was too long and numerous cuts were found to be necessary in the rehearsals. While these served to reduce the performance to a reasonable time they did unmistakable damage to the structure. If the opera should be retained in the repertory he thought it likely that the third act, which had been robbed of its continuity and dramatic purpose, would be rewritten.

To what extent Mr. Henderson was to blame for the defects of the opera I shall not undertake to appraise. In speaking of the difficulties of declamation I think he assumed too large a share of blame, for in his lyrical paraphrase of Rostand's play I found an admirable measure of that combination of qualities which are essential to the efficiency of a lyrical drama in any language. His book disclosed a knowledge of the art of song, of the demands of the theater, and of the needs of a composer. As a critic of large experience he might, perhaps, have guarded against the diffuseness which he himself condemned so frankly, but he could not know what method the composer would follow in the setting. As for Mr. Damrosch, he showed a common failing of composers, even composers of large experience,—a failure to realize, while writing, how long his work would be in the performance. The operation of reducing a score once it is done is a painful one to a composer. History tells us of the pangs which the revision of " Fidelio " cost Beethoven, and there is a story that Rossini quit attending performances of his " Guillaume Tell " after the director of the Opéra had made some very essential excisions in the score. A friend met the composer walking the streets one night and asked in surprise: " Why aren't you at the Opera? They are giving your ' Tell.' "

" Which act? " laconically inquired Rossini, and walked on.

It was less a marvel that Rostand's " Cyrano de Bergerac " should at last have been turned into an opera than that it should have waited so long for the transformation which every reader or spectator of the play must have seen was inevitable from the beginning. In Europe the play was protected by copyright and no doubt M. Rostand was himself the obstacle in the way of the omnivorous French librettists who have no pity for the literary masterpieces of any people. In the present instance M. Rostand was powerless and though Mr. Damrosch had announced that he intended to divide his royalties with him it is not likely that the French dramatist contemplated with equanimity the fact that his Cyrano was to put on an antic operatic disposition no matter how ingeniously the transmogrification might be accomplished. Least of all was he likely to be pleased to learn that Cyrano was to utter his speeches not only with the alloy of music added to them but sophisticated by a tongue so foreign to their spirit as English. If he had been displeased with English performances of his work he no doubt felt doubly outraged at the fact that his hero's famous nose was to be set to music. And yet it was inevitable. As a matter of fact the work of Messrs. Henderson and Damrosch was not the first operatic version of the drama. In September, 1899, it had a brief career as an opera which had been fabricated to give vent to the ambition of Mr. Francis Wilson to get away from acrobatic musical farce and demonstrate that he could use his mind as well as his legs on the theatrical stage. Unhappily the demonstration involved also the use of Mr. Wilson's voice from the idiosyncrasies of which the genial and scholarly comedian could not divorce himself; and so this first " Cyrano " opera failed miserably. Mr. Wilson made the scenario for his opera himself, Mr. Stuart Reed put it into dramatic shape (that is, he wrote the dialogue and indicated where the music should enter.), Mr. Harry B. Smith concocted the songs, and Mr. Victor Herbert composed the music.

Everybody was quick to recognize that it was a correct instinct which saw the possibility of an opera in " Cyrano," but everybody who saw and heard the opera was equally quick to see that it was a mistake to choose any other medium than frank and broad burlesque for Mr. Wilson, even if he wanted it so. Much of the lyrical celebration of *la panache* seemed provided to order by M. Rostand himself, who had conceived his play on lines which cried out for a musical setting as loudly as a work so profoundly poetical and romantic could. It is sufficient to call the first act to mind, with its merry gathering, its play-scene, the ballad of the duello; the second, with its hungry poets, the rhyming pastry cook and the inditing of the letter to Roxane; the third, with its proxy serenade (for which a prototype is found in "Don Giovanni"), and the song of the cadets of Gascony; the fourth, with its camp-scene before the battle and the battle itself; finally, Cyrano's unconscious confession of his passion, his fight with the phantoms of the things in life of which he had been the implacable enemy—why, they were all conceived, born, and bred for opera! And then the pretty invitation to seventeenth century music—the musette which is the prelude to Montfleury's effort to recite a pastoral, the pavane which was to be played out of tune in case De Guiche should approach the house of Roxane to spoil the love-making—what delightful opportunities these for dainty and ingenious musicianship!

All this seems to be of the opera operatic, and every person in the play also struck out in sharp lines for musical characterization and a transporting interchange of lightsome humor, semi-gravity, and deep passion. Unfortunately there was too much to lend itself to the languid legs of music, and when the authors of the opera undertook the transformation they were not brave enough to make the heroic excisions which, were necessary to bring the play within the operatic framework. Much of the literary sparkle would have to go by the board of course. That Mr. Henderson knew and he labored valiantly and with much success to supply its place with lines which would carry music though they could not reflect the romantic life which was the breath in Cyrano's nostrils. But music came with its clog in spite of him and in spite even of Mr. Damrosch, who had a multitude of pretty conceits which he thought necessary to preserve the joyous vivacity which the hero injects intermittently into the play even though consumed with mournful contemplation of the rôle which he is forced to enact in the eventful history of which he is a part.

There were other drawbacks to a perfect adaptation of the drama to music, but I can not go into them all here. Let it suffice that there was too much action and incident in it to permit a musical expression and illustration and that neither Mr. Henderson nor Mr. Damrosch succeeded in bringing it into reasonable proportions. It is assumed that nobody is sufficiently interested in reading a discussion of the opera who is not familiar with Rostand's play. Mr. Henderson did not depart materially from the French drama except (at the suggestion of the composer) to bring the two closing scenes of the last act closer together in point of time and have the hero die from a wound received at the battle of Arras the day after the incident. There was no serious objection to be urged against this device except that it lessened the psychological interest in Cyrano's character and also measurably that of Roxane by robbing the unvolitional confession of the hero's love and pious fraud of much of its illusion and bringing him nearer the commonplaces of romance than he ever was in the magnificent conception of the poet. It was a more serious defect that not knowing what the composer's method would be Mr. Henderson gave Mr. Damrosch more material to clothe in music than could be compassed within reasonable time by that method. A brave effort was made to obviate this difficulty by liberal excisions in the course of the rehearsals; but the obvious remedy would have been to cut out the scenes which, however brilliant and illustrative of Rostand's genius, were not essential to the presentation of the romantic figure which was uppermost in Mr. Damrosch's mind.

The music of Mr. Damrosch might be approached from

several points of view and always invite more praise than condemnation. As to its style it was most eclectic, so eclectic, indeed, that it can scarcely be credited with marked consistency in style. The opening scene was splendidly effective, full of grace and spirit, and nothing could have been conceived more appropriate in any respect than the measures which begin the pastoral play interrupted by Cyrano. But the interest drooped where it was expected to mount in the duel. Here synchronism of real sword-play and word, a rhythmically piquant melody, and a nice adjustment of music and action would have been of beautiful effectiveness. But they were lacking. It was in the love-music of the third act and in the dramatic finale of the fourth that Mr. Damrosch's skill showed itself at its best. Here there were echoes of the melodic, harmonic, and instrumental idioms of composers who have drawn luminous lines across the pages of operatic history, but enough freshness of inspiration in every department to compel not only respect but admiration. To sum up: a drama which has many external features that lend themselves gracefully to an operatic setting, which might even be said to demand an operatic investiture, but which frequently in all that makes it great and glorious in its original form resents despoliation of any kind, had been turned into an attractive musical drama. With its Gallic *esprit* inseparable from the original text there evaporated so much of its characteristic charm that few of M. Rostand's admirers could approve of the transformation; but saving the defects which were to be found chiefly in the musical settings of portions of its comedy it was yet a notable artistic achievement and one which reflected credit upon its authors and the institution which produced it. It offered nothing pointing to the solution of the problem of English or American opera; yet it was calculated, like "Mona," to encourage native composers to work, and this encouragement would, I think, have been greater had the opera been revived after a careful revision, the need of which was recognized by its

Pasquale Amato
As the Sheriff in "La Fanciulla del West"

A LIST OF THE PERFORMERS

authors, instead of being thrown aside at the end of the season despite the multitude of flattering words which were heaped upon it after the first performance.

The opera was performed with the parts distributed as follows:

Cyrano de Bergerac	Pasquale Amato
Roxane	Frances Alda
Duenna	Marie Mattfeld
Lise	Vera Curtis
A Flower Girl	Louise Cox
Mother Superior	Florence Mulford
Christian	Riccardo Martin
Bagueneau	Albert Reiss
De Guiche	Putnam Griswold
Le Bret	William Hinshaw
First Musketeer	Basil Ruysdael
Second Musketeer	Marcel Reiner
Montfleury / A cadet	Lambert Murphy
A monk	Antonio Pini-Corsi
Four cavaliers	Austin Hughes / Paolo Ananian / Maurice Sapio / Louis Kreidler

"Boris Godounow," owed its first performance in America on March 19, 1913, under the direction of Signor Toscanini, New York, indirectly if not directly, to the success which had been achieved by the work in Paris in a preceding season. From the Parisian capital Mr. Gatti brought the scenery and the proper quantum of *réclame*. It was in effect, if not in fact, an appanage of the Russian ballet the extraordinary, if ephemeral, enthusiasm concerning which had also gone out from Paris and infected London before it reached New York. The opera, thanks to the splendid and enduring merits of its music, though accepted at first with what Mr. Gilbert called "modified rapture" soon won its way to the general public and has remained in the repertory of the Opera ever since it was performed for the first time. The original American cast was as follows:

MOUSSORGSKY'S "BORIS GODOUNOW"

Boris Godounow	Adamo Didur
Theodore	Anna Case
Xenia	Leonora Sparkes
The Nurse	Maria Duchène
Marina	Louise Homer
Schouisky	Angelo Bada
Tchelkaloff	Vincenzo Reschilglian
Pimenn	Léon Rothier
Dmitri	Paul Althouse
(His début)	
Varlaam	Andrea Segurola
Missail	Pietro Audisio
The Innkeeper	Jeanne Maubourg
The Simpleton	Albert Reiss
A Police officer	Giulio Rossi
A Court officer	Leopoldi Mariani
Lovitzki	Vincenzo Reschiglian
Tcerniakowsky	Louis Kreidler

Having presented a critical disquisition on the opera in an earlier work to which I must needs make reference to avoid repetition,* I can do no more here than tell its story, which in its dramatic structure and the sequence of its incident underwent many transformations since it left the hands of its composer.

The opera, which is taken from a story by Pushkin, differs slightly from history. According to the latter Boris Godounow was born about 1551 and rose to be the chief adviser of the Russian Czar Ivan the Terrible, marrying the daughter of the Czar's cruel favorite Walynta Skuratow. Ivan then made Irene, Boris's sister, the bride of his half-witted son Theodore. At Ivan's death Boris became one of the guardians of the young Dimetreus, a son of Ivan by another wife, and at the same time practically the ruler of the empire. Theodore died childless and shortly afterwards Dimetreus also died, murdered some said, though without particular foundation, by Boris. Boris then became Czar and ruled, on the whole wisely. At his death in 1605 he left the throne to his young son, who was shortly afterwards murdered. The opera, however, starts with the hypothesis that Boris has murdered the young Dimetreus (or Dmitri). Boris, overcome with remorse, has sought repentance and seclusion in a convent near Moscow and the curtain

* "A Second Book of Operas." By Henry Edward Krehbiel. New York: Macmillan Company, 1917, p. 209.

Adamo Didur

In "Boris Godounow"

Leon Rothier

rises on the populace assembled in the courtyard appealing to Boris to declare himself Czar. This he at first refuses to do. In this scene the "Gloria" (*Slava*) as sung in the Russian Church is introduced with fine effect.*

The second scene shows us a cell in the Convent of Miracles where Brother Pimenn, an aged monk who is recording the annals of the empire, arouses the imagination of the young novice Gregory, as he relates to him the story of Boris's crime. Strange thoughts are born in Gregory's mind when he learns that the murdered Czarewitch, had he lived to reign, would have been his own age. In the closing scene of the first act Boris, at last yielding to the popular demand, appears to participate in an imposing religious ceremonial. He addresses his people before the cathedrals of the Assumption and the Archangels and then, amid great enthusiasm, enters the former to be crowned.

The second act plays on the frontier of Poland where two vagabonds, Vaarlam and Missail, clad as hermits and followed by Gregory disguised as a peasant, arrive at an inn. A price has been set upon the head of the escaped monk, who has proclaimed himself to be Dmitri, who he says was never killed. Presently the Czar's officers arrive; Gregory looks over the warrant they present, but in reading it changes the description of the fugitive to make it appear to indicate Vaarlam. The latter, although quite drunk, also examines the document and has sufficient intelligence to realize that the warrant is for Gregory, whom he promptly denounces. The False Dmitri, however, is too quick for the officers and dashes from the room. The next scene shows Czar Boris's private apartment in the Kremlin. His children, the young Czarewitch Theodore and his sister Xenia, are there with their nurse. Xenia is grieving over the recent death of her fiancée; the nurse tries to comfort her, the boy amuses himself with games in which the nurse joins him. Boris, entering, advises Xenia to seek distraction with her girl friends and she retires leaving the Czar and his heir alone. Half unconscious of his son's presence, Boris gives way to gloomy meditations and discloses the mental suffering to which the memory of his crime has subjected him. He is interrupted by the announcement that his minister, Prince Schouisky, is arrived to tell him of the uprising of the people in favor of the False Dmitri. Terror seizes the Czar. He insists upon Schouisky's assurance that he really saw the dead body of the murdered Czarewitch. Left alone Boris's emotion overwhelms him; spectre-haunted he sinks upon his chair, crushed and broken, almost bereft of reason.

The next act discloses the garden of the Castle Mischek in Poland. Mischek's daughter, Marina, rejects all other suitors in favor

---

*Lovers of chamber music know this melody from its use in the Allegretto of Beethoven's E minor String Quartet dedicated to Rasoumowsky.

of Gregory. Prompted by love and ambition she urges him to lead the uprising against Boris and seize the throne. The scene following shows a gathering of typical Russian peasants in the forest of Krony. They have captured and are taunting the noble Kroutchow of the False Dmitri's staff. A simpleton furnishes amusement for the urchins. Vaarlam and Missail lead in denunciation of Boris. Monks arrive singing the praises of the False Dmitri. Suspected by the crowd they are attacked and their fate seems perilous, when they are saved by the arrival of Gregory and his troops. In the closing scene of the opera a meeting of the Duma is holding to determine what action shall be taken to crush the False Dmitri. Prince Schouisky, coming in, interrupts the proceedings by describing the agony of Boris, which he had witnessed by eavesdropping. In the midst of his narration Boris himself enters the hall and overhears Schouisky's words. He denounces him bitterly and threatens him with death. At this moment the Monk Pimenn comes in. He has had a mysterious dream in which a venerable shepherd told him how, after having been blind from childhood, he had regained his sight by obeying the order of a miraculous visage of Dmitri, the slain Czarewitch, to offer a prayer at his tomb. The monk's words terrify the Czar; he calls for his son Theodore, feeling that the end is at hand. Declaring Theodore his rightful heir, and begging the mercy of Heaven for his crimes, he sinks into his chair and dies.

The first of the novelties presented by the Philadelphia-Chicago company was "Conchita," the music by Zandonai, which had a performance at the Metropolitan on February 11, 1913, with the principal parts distributed as follows:

Conchita .... Tarquinia Tarquini
Don Maceo .... Charles Dalmorès
Dolores .... Helen Stanley
Ruffina .... Ruby Heyl
Estella .... Minnie Egener
L'Ispettore .... F. A. Prisch
Bandarillo .... Vittorio Trevisan
Madre de Conchita .... Louise Barat
La Gallega .... Rosina Galli
La Danseur .... Luigi Albertieri
Norentio .... Marie Hamilton
Garcka .... Constantin Nicolay
Sereno .... Vittorio Trevisan
Conductor, Cleofonte Campanini

"Conchita" had its first representation in America in San Francisco early in the season. It came East by way of

AN OUTLINE OF THE STORY

Chicago, where it had a single performance, and Philadelphia. On the Pacific coast it was produced by a local troupe, but the representative of the titular rôle was Mlle. Tarquini, who had created the part in London in the previous July and acted it also in Chicago and Philadelphia as well as in New York. The story of the opera exhales the kind of stench which arose from the opera houses of Italy immediately after the success of "Cavalleria Rusticana" and "Pagliacci." It is Spanish so far as its externals and its atmosphere go, and bears close kinship with "Carmen." Like the story of Bizet's opera, too, it was found in a French book, a novel by Pierre Louys. As a reviewer in the *Daily Express* ingeniously observed when the work was produced in London, it seems to have been written to enforce or illustrate the moral contained in the old saw:

> A woman, a dog, and a walnut tree—
> The more you beat them the better they be.

It would not do to put into a relation of its plot all the color used by the novelist or even the librettist. An outline in distemper must serve: The heroine is a cigarette girl whose mother takes money for her shame from a wealthy lover. Learning this Conchita, who, we are asked to believe, wants to be loved for herself alone, compels her mother to return the money and goes away from Seville. Six months later, Maceo, the lover, finds her dancing a lascivious dance for the entertainment of a company of tourists behind the locked doors of a café. There is a violent interruption of the delectable proceeding, which ends in an apparent reconciliation of the lovers, the woman accepting the keys to a house in a secluded part of the city where she agrees to receive Maceo. When he comes, however, she locks the iron gate against him and permits him only the precious privilege of kissing the hem of her dress (or was it her foot?) through the iron bars, and witnessing the sight of herself in the arms of a younger rival. On the next day she mets Maceo again and taunts him with not having kept his threat to blow out his brains. Maddened by rage he hurls her to the ground and gives her a thrashing. When he recovers self-control the man is horrified with what he has done; but now he learns from the woman's cooing and contrite confession that instead of increasing her hatred the physical chastisement has awakened her love.

In adapting "La Femme et le Pantin" for operatic purposes the authors attempted to soften the lines of the story as they have been hurriedly narrated here; but the result has been chiefly to fill the play with contradictions calculated to make a psychologist cudgel his brains to reconcile the utterances and actions of the heroine, which are as far apart as the two poles. If "Conchita" holds its place on the stage (meaning if it lives ten years or so) I shall be strongly tempted to set it down as making a more distinct departure from old Italian ideals than any of the operas of Mascagni, Leoncavallo, or Puccini. Because it is so different in one respect from the work which the younger generation of composers has written, however, it is extremely doubtful if it will so survive. When Dr. von Bülow recovered from the intoxication produced in him by his first hearing of "Cavalleria Rusticana" he tried to make amends to Verdi for a grievous wrong which he had done that master by apologizing to him and writing a letter to Mascagni in which he told the latter that he had found his successor in his great predecessor. Mascagni, Leoncavallo, and all the small fry veritists of Italy, who trod upon each other's heels in their eagerness to exploit the new style set by these pioneers, were the product of an artificially inflated protest against Verdi. To pull him down they set up Wagner only to discover that it was as impossible to imitate their German model as it was to compete with his great Italian contemporary. All that they could do was to seek to lift the dramatic element of their operas into prominence, to which end they plunged their hands into the shambles of Neapolitan life in search for subjects, bespattering the stage with filth and degrading the art which they professed to be raising to a higher potentiality. Undisturbed by their clamors, Verdi kept on his way, keeping step with Wagner in his onward march but unswervingly faithful to the musical ideals of the people from whose loins he was sprung. Puccini, who is not yet within seeing distance of the Verdi who wrote " Aïda," " Otello," and " Falstaff," has won his way by adhering (as he did up to the time when he composed " La Fanciulla del West ") to the principle that vocal melody is the thing most desirable in lyric drama; but it was Bizet who really pointed the way in which German art, typified in Wagner, and Italian art, represented by the early Verdi and his immediate predecessors, might be united.

There was nothing strange that " Carmen " came out of France—that it should have been the product of a people in whom is mixed Teutonic and Latin blood. It is much more surprising that the French have not since produced successors to Bizet and his masterpiece. Some enthusiasts have hailed such successors in Charpentier and " Louise," but it is not likely that they will long be able to press that flattering unction to their souls. Without going any further into the subject it may be said that there can be no permanency of interest in any dramatic representation of the process of making a bawd, and that some of the musical devices which are fascinating in " Louise " will some day be put to a better use. Puccini began to do this in " Madama Butterfly." One of these devices is local color, most appropriate in comedy, but also applicable in the field which lies between comedy and tragedy in the classic sense.

" Carmen " and " Louise "— were they absent five minutes from the minds of the people who saw the new opera? No more than they were absent from the minds of the authors of "Conchita." But before this branch of the subject is taken up something must be said about a third influence—operative in this case—a purely musical one. While the men who made an opera-book out of "La Femme et le Pantin" (Vaucaire and Zangarini) kept "Carmen" and "Louise" in mind Signor Zandonai, the composer, was thinking also of Debussy. From him he drew many of the orchestral devices with which he aimed to produce that effect, so dear to the hearts of critical word-mongers, called atmosphere and mood. Does the lover of fine musical thought, gratifying to the sense, appealing to the emotion and stimulating to the imagination, demand expressive melody and harmony? Immediately he is met by the statement that the essence of a drama is better conveyed in fragmentary phrases, unnatural harmonies, and unwonted instrumental colors. The human voice does not offer the composer an adequate vehicle for conveying these things, so song must needs go by the board and instrumental music take its place. Therefore "Pelléas et Mélisande" had much to do with "Conchita." More than this, Zandonai, I venture to say, was familiar not only with Debussy's opera but also with his "Iberia"—possibly also with Ravel's "Rhapsodie Espagnol," in which work the coiners of pretty phrases would have us recognize not the fine, normal, and natural body of Spain but its flocculent, fleeting, and flimsy soul. "A hot night disturbed by a guitar," said Norman Macleod in characterization of Spanish music; a hot night disturbed by a multitude of orchestral instruments speaking strange idioms mixed with the voices of street vendors is Signor Zandonai's paraphrase of Dr. Macleod's definition. It is a highly spiced ingredient in the Italian composer's operatic decoction, wherefore he employs it again and again, and the instrumental intermezzi become the most significant, as they are the most beautiful, features of his opera.

It is in the subordination of the verbal element to the instrumental that the opera marks a departure even from

A SORDID AND VICIOUS PLAY

those predecessors which it most closely resembles, and which haunted the fancy of its authors while they were making it. Zandonai, we were told, was only thirty years old and "Conchita" his second opera. Of his librettists I know little or nothing, but their book offered ample evidence of their inexperience; only novices would cling so slavishly to their models and thus work their own undoing. The story is not a pretty tale in the original book; on the contrary, it reeks with vulgarity. Professing to purify it of its dross by claiming virtuous conduct for the drab created by the French novelist, the librettists robbed her of all dramatic consistency and every vestige of the psychological trait which some men have professed to find in one type of womankind. They would have us look upon a woman who throws herself into the arms of a man whom she has seen but once and whom she has introduced into her home, who gives him her embraces and kisses, who dances in the nude for patrons who have paid to see her in private behind locked doors of a vulgar cabaret, who locks the man who loves her to distraction out of the house in which he has ensconced her and lets him see her there in the embraces of a rival, who twits him for failing to blow out his brains because of her treatment of him and who finally gives himself to her because he has flogged her, as one who is actuated wholly by "pride of purity under the appearance of vice"— whatever that may mean. Such a woman does not ask, nor does she receive, even that singular sympathy which can go out to such frank sensuality as is personified in the Carmen of Mérimée and Bizet. Neither does the supposed suffering of the heroes of the singular tale kindle a single spark of interest or compassion. It is all sordid and mean, a farrago of nonsense put together for the sake of stage pictures and lurid music of the highly impressionistic kind to be found in portions of "Louise" and the instrumental compositions referred to. For the sake of these pictures and this music large drafts have been made upon Charpentier's opera.

There is a scene in a cigar factory of Seville, with girls at work and gossiping—a parallel to the dressmaking shop in " Louise." Then comes an intermezzo which the authors intended to be played with the scene in which strains of dance music and the sounds of a Spanish street are mingled with the cries of a vendor of fruit and the conversation of the lovers as they walk homeward; but this Mr. Dippel kept veiled by his curtain, thus saving too bald an imitation of the early morning scene on Montmartre. A picture of Conchita's home calls up memories of Charpentier's sewing-girl, but the newer heroine's mother is represented as a wicked foil to an alleged virtuous daughter instead of to the opposite in " Louise." Then comes the cabaret scene, a picturesque one of wild merrymaking culminating in the lascivious dance which, though presented by suggestion rather than literally, was yet as *risqué* as anything that had yet been shown on the operatic stage—more so by far than the dance which brought condemnation on " Salome." There is some beautiful and expressive music in the score, however. The intermezzo already described is such, though it descends to vulgarity in its brazen climax, in which it is somewhat disconcerting and likewise amusing to hear something very like a paraphrase of one of Schubert's " Soirées de Vienne." A narrative by Conchita in the first act has much appositeness and no little beauty, and a languorous interlude between the third and fourth acts is well calculated to take the imagination captive. In the cabaret scene there is much ingenious commingling of rhythms by two bands, and when the noise subsides for Conchita's dance there is a use of local color which falls gratefully into ears which had been rudely assaulted a moment before. All of Signor Zandonai's music of the order which can be called reflective or contemplative is charmingly orchestrated, even if it lacks the merit of originality of idea.

On February 25, 1913, Mr. Dippel brought forward his second novelty, " Le Ranz des Vaches," which, before coming to New York, had enjoyed two performances within four days in Philadelphia. The music was conducted by Signor Campanini, and the principal singers among the many were:

Louis XVI .... Constantin Nicolay
Marquis Massimelle .... Gustav Huberdeau
Blanchefleur .... Helen Stanley
The Chancellor .... F. A. Prisch
Captain Brayole .... Jacques Dury
Marquis de Chery .... Emilio Venturini
Cleo .... Margaret Keyes
Primus Thaller .... Charles Dalmorès
Dursel .... Georges Mascal
Marion .... Eleanor de Cisneros
Favart .... Hector Dufranne
First Chasseur .... Emilio Venturini

The opera, though sung in French and under a French title, is a German work which perhaps would have been happier in a German garb. Its title is not a matter of large consequence, for neither " Le Ranz des Vaches " nor " Der Kuhreigen " conveys a hint of the opera or its story. The French and German terms are identical in meaning and equally vague as to their origin. They stand for the melodies played in Switzerland on the Alpine horn with which cows are called from the pastures, and in this sense are inapplicable, strictly speaking, to the song which provides the dramatic motive for the opera in question. From them we receive suggestions of Alpine herds and lowing kine; in the opera we see signs of sansculottism and bloody revolution. The story of the opera was extracted by Richard Batka from a German novelette entitled " Die kleine Blanchefleur," written by Rudolph Hans Bartsch. Wilhelm Kienzl, who for several years had enjoyed a wonderful degree of popular favor in Germany because of an opera entitled " Der Evangelimann," composed this new opera two years or so before, and for something more than a year it had been sweeping over the German stage like wildfire. It was to the credit of Mr. Dippel that, having brought forward such novelties as the French "Quo Vadis?" and the Italian "I Giojelli della Madonna" and "Conchita," he should also have presented a German novelty. "Der Kuhreigen" was not of very large significance artistically, but it served an excellent purpose as a balance-wheel and as a preservative of good taste in the lyric drama. Its success in Germany, Philadelphia, and New York was at least a handsome tribute to the handicraftmanship of both librettist and composer.

The story of the opera, its romance and its revolution, turns on the singing of a prohibited song by a Swiss volunteer in the French army in the last decade of the eighteenth century. Historically the tale will not bear analysis, but it has a deep psychological foundation. The story goes that the sounds of the Alpine horn used to cause such homesickness and lead to so many desertions in the French army that Bonaparte forbade the singing of a *ranz des vaches* on the penalty of death. Whether or not the story is strictly true does not matter. It has a parallel in the indubitable fact that songs which appeal powerfully to the emotions of a people have frequently been the subject of political regulation. Thus the Austrian Government had had occasion to prohibit the performance of the "Rakotzky March" and confiscate the copies in the music shops because of its effect upon patriotic Magyars; and to cite only one other instance, the Scottish tune of "Lochaber no more" was taboo at the time of the Sepoy mutiny. There is therefore a poetical foundation for the pretty romance utilized in Kienzl's opera, though it is more or less a pity that the novelist, dramatist, and composer were not a little more respectful to the verities in their choice of material. The story of the opera, in brief, is this:

A young Swiss volunteer in the French army, overcome by nostalgia, sings the prohibited song which is called a *ranz des vaches*. The author of the romance being a Ger-

THE STORY OF THE OPERA

man, the Swiss are made to realize that fidelity is typified in the Lion of Lucerne. The singer had quarreled with a French officer because of his treachery to his commander, and the Frenchman seeks revenge by denouncing the Switzer for singing the prohibited song. The wife of the commander intercedes with the king and secures a pardon for the singer. She has looked with favor upon his comely face and figure and dreams a pretty pastoral dream of him playing shepherd to her shepherdess on her estates, but finds herself repulsed by the young soldier because of the fact that she is married. Now the revolutionary storm breaks. The aristocratic commander goes to the guillotine and the romantic wife is condemned to follow him. Circumstances throw the power to save her into the hands of the Swiss soldier, now madly in love with her. But when he suggests a blissful, peaceful life among the cows of Appenzell the lady thinks it so gross a misfit that she chooses to go to her death, after the favor of a minuet.

There is dramatic blood in the story and it flows through the opera, warm and unimpeded. It is too bad, of course, that the song which Primus Thaller, the Swiss hero, sings is not a Swiss song at all, but a German one which describes the fate of a Swiss soldier who was led to desert the French army by sounds from his homeland. The French translation does not disguise it. It is that which all the German world knows and which begins with the stanza:

> Zu Strassburg auf der Schanz,
> Da ging mein trauern an;
> Das Alphorn hört' ich drüben anstimmen,
> Ins Vaterland musst ich hinüber schwinnen,
> Das ging nicht an.

The song is a paraphrase of an earlier one which was no doubt known in some parts of Germany at the time of the French Revolution; but it never was a Swiss song and never a *ranz des vaches*, though it refers to the national type of melody. The familiar tune by Silcher to which it is sung throughout Germany was not composed until 1835, wherefore, no doubt, Kienzl wrote a tune of his own which is the *Leitmotif* of the opera and a most admirable embodiment of the folksong spirit. In harmony with it is the music, which beautifully echoes the melodies of the Alpine horn which invites the Swiss soldier to his offense and which recurs whenever a vision of Alpine scenery is invoked by the dramatic situation or dialogue. Contrasted with this music is the ribald song of the French soldiers about their officer, and the revolutionary airs " Ça ira," " La Carmagnole," and " La Marseillaise," all of which are given savage settings and a pictorial environment which recall Giordano's " Andrea Chenier." It would be foolish to say that there is great music in the opera, but equally foolish to deny much of it splendid effectiveness and emotional as well as æsthetic charm.

CHAPTER XIII

A SEASON PROLIFIC IN INCIDENTS AND OPERAS

OPERAS PRODUCED IN 1913-14—A VISIT FROM THE CHICAGO-PHILADELPHIA COMPANY—DEATH OF PUTNAM GRISWOLD—STRAUSS'S " DER ROSENKAVALIER "—THE THEATRICAL VALUE OF PRURIENCY—BENELLI'S POETICAL DRAMA " L'AMORE DEI TRE RE "—MONTEMEZZI'S MUSIC—ITS RACIAL CHARACTER—CONSTRUCTIVE ELEMENTS BORROWED FROM RUSSIA—SIGNOR FERRARI-FONTANA—LUCREZIA BORI—" MADELEINE "—LIGHT FRENCH COMEDY AND HEAVY MUSIC—" DON QUICHOTTE "—CERVANTES TRAVESTIED—MARY GARDEN AND " MONNA VANNA "—CHARPENTIER'S " JULIEN "—AN ABORTIVE SEQUEL TO " LOUISE "—A COMEDY BY MOLIÈRE DONE INTO A DELIGHTFUL OPERA—WOLF-FERRARI'S " L'AMORE MEDICO "—DEATH OF MME. NORDICA

WHEN Mr. Gatti issued his prospectus for the sixth season of opera at the Metropolitan under his management (the twenty-ninth since the house was opened) he promised five ·novelties, viz.: Charpentier's " Julien," Victor Herbert's " Madeleine," Italo Montemezzi's " L'Amore dei tre Re," Richard Strauss's " Der Rosenkavalier," and Wolf-Ferrari's " L'Amore Medico." Concerning all of these works he redeemed his promise. He also promised revivals of " Carmen," Boito's " Mefistofele," Rossini's " Guglielmo Tell," Saint-Saëns's " Samson et Dalila," and Verdi's " Un Ballo in Maschera." He kept his word only in respect of the last. The fact seemed deplorable only in the case of Bizet's opera, for which it had been announced that Miss Farrar was making studies. There seemed to be something only a little short of amazing in the circumstances that an institution of the magnitude and dignity of the Metropolitan Opera House should not have in its permanent repertory the most perfect opera of the last half-century; but the fact that it was unable to give a satisfactory performance of

"Faust," with which it made one lamentable essay on a Saturday night, was even more amazing. It seemed to illustrate the comment which had often been made touching the lack of proper adjustment between operas and singers. Of the new works Montemezzi's opera achieved the most significant success, one which ranked with that of "Boris Godounow" in the two seasons in which it had been in the Metropolitan repertory. The enthusiastic acceptance of these works was the more gratifying to the intelligent lovers of the lyric drama from the fact that it was due to the works themselves and not to the popular desire to hear admired singers. Caruso and Farrar carried Charpentier's opera through five performances, but the work itself was a bore and Caruso's impersonation a thing of no distinction. Three hours of droning song in moderate tempo to accompany a fantastic allegory which was neither drama, oratorio, nor cantata, and which made one want to shriek for an *allegro* for a change, was a severe test of endurance. It was never heard of after the season. "Der Rosenkavalier" achieved success by its exquisite stage-setting, the beautiful portions of its music, and the splendid singing and acting of Mmes. Ober and Hempel. Wolf-Ferrari's opera came too late in the season to have a fair test, but it proved to be worthy of a permanent place in the Metropolitan list, though it did not achieve it. The Chicago-Philadelphia Company occupied the opera house for four successive Tuesday evenings, beginning February 3, 1914, and gave performances to Massenet's "Don Quichotte," Février's "Monna Vanna," Charpentier's "Louise," and Wolf-Ferrari's "I Giojelli della Madonna," the first two of which were heard in New York for the first time.

The story of the scandal which grew out of the speculation in subscription tickets has been told. A tragic incident of the season was the death on February 26, 1914, of Putnam Griswold, an American basso who had been one of the ornaments of the company since his first appearance with

PASQUALE AMATO
As Cyrano de Bergerac

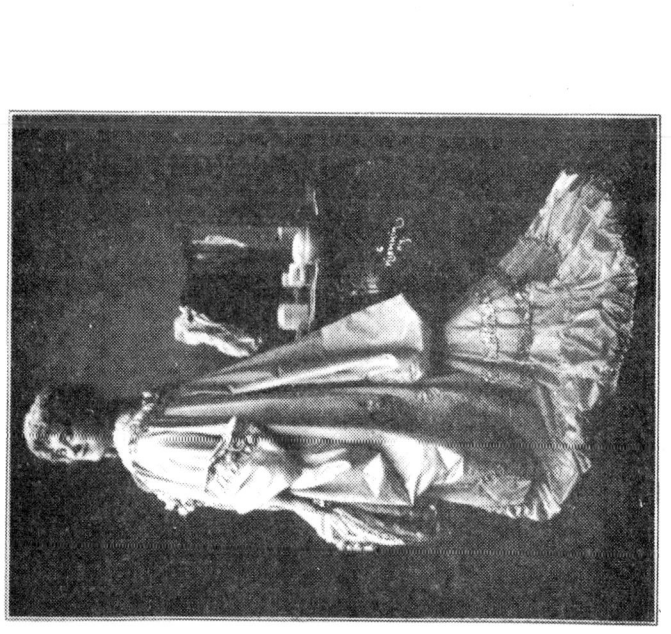

Frieda Hempel. Margarete Ober.

In "Der Rosenkavalier."

it on November 23, 1911. He was only thirty-eight years of age and had made an enviable reputation in America when he sang with the Henry W. Savage Opera Company and afterward in Munich and Berlin. The German Kaiser sent a representative from the Legation at Washington to his funeral. Mr. Griswold was a native of Minneapolis, Minn. The order of the production of the operas new to the New York public, with the discussion of which the rest of this chapter must be concerned, was as follows: "Der Rosenkavalier," "L'Amore dei tre Re," "Madeleine," "Don Quichotte," "Monna Vanna," "Julien," and "L'Amore Medico." Richard Strauss's opera, which after elaborate preparation received its first American representation at a special performance on December 9, 1913, under the musical direction of Alfred Hertz, was given with the following distribution of parts:

Feldmarschallin Fürstin Werdenberg .... Frieda Hempel
Baron Ochs auf Lerchenau .... Otto Goritz
Octavian, genannt Quinquin .... Margarete Ober
Herr von Faninal ....Hermann Weil
Sophie, seine Tochter .... Anna Case
Jungfer Marianna, Leitmetzerin .... Rita Fornia
Valzacchi, ein Intrigant ....Albert Reiss
Annina, seine Begleiterin .... Marie Mattfeld
Ein Polizeikommissär .... Carl Schlegel
Haushofmeister der Feldmarschallin .... Pietro Audisio
Haushofmeister bei Faninal .... Lambert Murphy
Ein Notar .... Basil Ruysdael
Ein Wirth .... Julius Bayer
Ein Sänger .... Carl Jörn
Drei Edelige Waisen .... { Rosina Vandyck
                                                 Sophie Braslau
                                                 Jeanne Maubourg
Ein Lakei .... Ludwig Burgstaller
Ein kleiner Neger .... Ruth Weinstein

Inasmuch as I gave the opera extended critical consideration in my "Second Book of Operas," * I hope I may be

*"A Second Book of Operas; Their Histories, Their Plots, and Their Music." By Henry Edward Krehbiel. New York: The Macmillan Company, 1917. P. 190.

spared a repetition of my views upon that rather unusual work. Those who were informed in advance of its plot probably wondered why the cost of an orchestral stall at this *première* was not set at twice the price exacted. Modern pruriency ought to be more attractive than ancient necrophilism; and if the first glimpse at the delectable " Salome " had been thought to be worth $10 in the holidaytide, then a comedy which deals with the passion more general if not more ancient, but which finds equally frank expression in this lyric play, ought to have been considered worth more to the public which the Metropolitan Opera House, as an agency of education and refinement, is striving to uplift. If I were inclined to go into the question analytically I should say that an opera which begins with the lover kissing the hands of his lady-love extended from the curtains of her bed while the birds are twittering their matin song would be worth, not two-thirds more than the regular price of admission, but at least three times more, provided that the beginning of the dramatic action could have only been made coincident with the instrumental music. There was no question of art involved here; only a question of financial emolument. Herr Strauss is, as the world knows, what the Germans call *ein Pantoffelheld*—the hero of his wife's slipper—though his dramatic poses grow naughtier from day to day for business reasons. When he was in New York he said to one of its best musicians, that he would polish stoves if only the occupation could be made remunerative enough; and there need be no surprise that he was willing to humor the decadent taste of the German stage in his " Rosenkavalier," since by doing so he was able to command larger royalties and enforce more rigorous demands than had ever been heard of before for its production. The conditions explain in part the action of the Metropolitan Opera Company in giving the opera first outside of the regular subscription and in exacting an abnormal fee for the privilege of hearing it.

Without much trumpeting, as if it were a matter of course indeed, the management of the Metropolitan brought forward a new opera on January 14, 1914. It was a new opera in a special sense, for "L'Amore dei tre Re" was scarcely a year old, if it was that, and up to its New York production had been heard only in two opera houses, and those in Italy. This circumstance, associated as it must be with some of the new productions of the five years preceding, indicates a closer relationship than ever existed before between the establishment in Broadway and the composers and publishers of Europe. Montemezzi's "L'Amore dei tre Re" is a tragedy to which the author of the book has given a romantic setting which suggests a historical period and historical peoples without putting a historical clog upon the hearers. In this he has been followed by the composer who, though he uses the musical vehicle which is the characteristic glory of his own country and borrows a device of dramatic expression which is equally characteristic of a different country, yet speaks in the language proper to the proclamation of passions which know no distinction of time or people. The poet's name is Sem Benelli, and he wrote his play not as a drama to be sung, but as a drama to be spoken. To fit it for opera some elisions were made and a scene for chorus added. A fine, strong play it is, in fine, strong verse, picturesque but direct, with a splendid command of the elements which make a drama effective in its appeal to eye, ear, and emotions. It would be difficult to recall another opera in which there is a more puissant exhibit of contrast in character, of conflicting motives, of the devasting result of passions at war with one another, all of which, nevertheless, challenge sympathy in an almost equal degree. To the careless reader there is something misleading in the title. The story is that of the love of three royal personages, but not wholly of the passion which is the burden of mediæval as well as modern romance. A barbarian who has made himself king of an undefined territory in Italy kills the wife of his son because of her adultery. This king's passion is love for his son and the honor of his family. He is old and blind; his reign began forty years before the opening of the story, and there is nothing in the likelihood of nature, his acts, or speeches which indicates the possibility of his harboring a carnal passion for the young native princess who was given to him to be his son's wife by her people as the price of peace. The son is a warrior whose love for his wife is so pure and strong that, confronted with proof of her guilty commerce with another, he can only pity her and love her the more, even to the uttermost of his own undoing. To the old king this trait in the character of his son, whom he had trained in all the virtues of his people, is a weakness; and he takes it upon himself to avenge the wrong done to his son, his house, and his race. Groping in the dark, left to his own devices, and hampered by the treachery of his servant, he yet discovers the unfaithfulness of his son's wife, and, though he can not know who is the partner of her guilt, he throttles her.

The lover is of the people of the princess and was betrothed to her before she became perforce a hostage and a loveless wife. His passion is like that of Tristan, Romeo, and all their fellows who have lived since the human race began. There is pathos in its fierceness and in the fatality which enshrouds it from its first disclosure. There is a greater pathos in the struggle which takes place in the heart of the young wife when she feels the first movings of a love for her husband awakened by recognition of the overwhelming tenderness of his affection; and a still greater pathos in the conduct of the outraged husband who can not take revenge upon the man upon whom his wife has bestowed the boon for which he feels an infinite longing and who follows him into death beside the body of the one who had been so dear to both. And when, at the last, the old man is left alone in the darkness made trebly black by the triple destruction which he has wrought—for lover and husband had both

Italo Montemezzi
Composer of "L'Amore dei tre Re"

sucked death in kissing the lips of the woman whom he had killed and whose mouth he had smeared with poison in the last despairing hope of thus discovering who had wronged his son and his house—there is a pathos which is infinite in his impotent desolation and mute despair.

In this story, but more especially in its presentation, there are many dramatic *motivi* which have done service in other dramas. Involuntarily we think of the tale of Tristram and Yseult, of Romeo and Juliet, of Francesca da Rimini, of Pelléas and Mélisande. There are moments when a cursory glance might almost make one think one or the other of these plays was occupying the stage; for instance, when Fiora, the princess, is seen waving her scarf from the castle terrace, and when Avito, the lover, comes into the crypt of the castle to say farewell to his dead love. But there is a large difference between Benelli's treatment of these episodes and the apparent sources which I have cited. Isolde waves her scarf wildly to call her lover to her side; Fiora waves hers with a breaking heart and heavy arm to speed her parting husband, though she can not but know that his going is only a preface to the coming of Avito. The struggle between love and duty has begun. Here it must be said of the poet, as it must also be said of the composer, that he is so strong and self-reliant in the command of his theme and all its agencies of expression that the parallels only serve to illustrate the aphorism of Fuselli: "Genius may adopt, but it never steals." The remark is, indeed, more significant as applied to Signor Italo Montemezzi than to Signor Benelli. Not only the scene of the scarf but other episodes must have called up memories in his mind of masterpieces which can scarcely be thought of without tempting the creative musician to imitation. The imitation may be unconscious, but it is seldom missing. Echoes of the night of love in the Tristan tragedy have floated down from the stage of the Metropolitan Opera House several times since Wagner's great music first became domiciled there. There are no echoes in "L'Amore dei tre Re" of either the love duet or the music which brings her lover to Fiora's feet. Neither, and for this there might be a special expression of gratitude, are the pallid reflections of Debussy or reverberations of Puccini. Montemessi is proof against temptation. This young composer speaks a speech all his own, and his score, I fancy, would have delighted the soul of Verdi when, seeing the aberrations of his young confrères, he sat himself down in his old age to show them an example of devotion to their country's art.

"L'Amore" is an example of the fine fruit of "Boris Godounow" grafted on an Italian stem. What does that mean? Only this: That Signor Montemezzi has borrowed from Moussorgsky a constructive feature which, though it has a national value in Russian music which it lacks in Italian, is still of fine dramatic effectiveness. Melodically he is all Italian and a legitimate grandson of Verdi; but his melodies, which flow onward like a river, now tumultuously as they carry the passion of the lovers on their current, now gently with wooing murmurs as they float the emotions of the loving and magnanimous Manfredo, and anon interruptedly when they are broken into fragments by the dialogue, are as a rule superimposed on persistently reiterated rhythmical and melodic figures. Sometimes this *ostinato* accompaniment has a delineative purpose, as when we hear in it the coming and going of Manfredo and his warriors; but as a rule the purpose of its employment is purely constructive and the composer's splendid command of the stage and of musical expression enables him to give the figures a dramatic potency which at times reaches the marvelous and approaches his model. He shows equal mastery of the potentialities of harmony and orchestral color by means of which he not only puts a glow into his sustained melody, but also greatly heightens the emotional power of that portion of his dialogue which hovers between speech and song. Though he occasionally makes use of reminiscent phrases, he does not employ musical symbols in the Wagnerian manner. His genius is of the inspirational-creative, not of the reflective order; facts make his successful blending of the Russian device—a folksong element in Muscovite music—with Italian melody all the more admirable.

Poet and composer have left us without clue as to even the approximate period in which the drama plays. But the question of time does not obtrude itself because of the eloquent manner in which poet and composer have given voice to a tale which might be told of any time and any people. The burden of the representation falls upon four persons—the representatives of the old king (Archibaldo), his son (Manfredo), the faithless wife (Fiora), and her lover (Avito). There is but little ensemble singing, and that is confined to the last act, where the poet, to fit his play for operatic treatment, has introduced a hymn and a species of choral dialogue which, like the *ostinato* figures mentioned, has a prototype in Moussorgsky's opera. In this choral there is a brief eruption of the political element, which also plays its part in evoking sympathy for the lovers and saving their conduct from utter condemnation. Like all the other ethical and psychological factors, it is introduced into the drama with great deftness and achieves its purpose without attracting attention to itself or asking for accentuation through local color. If it has a symbol it is the haunting music of flute and horn, which, like the lark's song in "Romeo and Juliet," is the herald of the morn and a sign of parting that comes back like a memory in some other climaxes of the second act.

One of the performers in this first representation of the opera outside of Italy was the original creator of the part of Avito in Milan—Signor Ferrari-Fontana, the husband of Mme. Matzenauer, who was then a member of the Boston Opera Company, but afterward became a member of the New York organization. The opera established a hold upon the admiration of the public and was one of those entitled to special consideration because it had no adventitious helps in the way of popular idols to give it permanency. Its performances were interrupted for a space by the misfortune which overtook Signorina Lucrezia Bori in the next season, but even without that lovely interpreter of the princess its subsequent revival was successful. Signor Toscanini conducted the performances, and the parts in the opera were thus distributed:

Archibaldo	Adamo Didur
Manfredo	Pasquale Amato
Avito	Edoardo Ferrari-Fontana
Flaminio	Angelo Bada
Un Giovinetto	Pietro Audisio
Fiora	Lucrezia Bori
Ancella	Jeanne Maubourg
Una Giovinetta	Sophie Braslau
Una Vecchia	Maria Duchène

How sadly a play based on a conceit which is irradiated by a pretty humor and made mellow and gracious by a sentiment of universal appeal could be spoiled by an attempt to turn it into an English opera was demonstrated on the afternoon of January 24, 1914, when a piece in one act entitled " Madeleine " was performed for the first time. The book of the opera was adapted from the French of Decourcelles and Thibaut by Grant Stewart; the music was composed by Victor Herbert. In the official prospectus of the season Mr. Gatti announced that it was intended to represent " the National Art of Music," which fact may be set down as a deplorable incident in view of the fact that Professor Parker's " Mona," with which the directors of the Metropolitan Opera House made a noble experiment in the line of national art, had been put upon the shelf and the efforts of other American musicians ignored. What the original French play which provided the dramatic framework for " Madeleine " is like I do not know. Certain it is that its story is amiable and that in the hands of a litterateur with poetical instincts and a composer with a light touch, a

A GRACEFUL FRENCH STORY SPOILED

command of gracious and graceful melody, and a knowledge of the essential elements of refined comedy (such a composer as Wolf-Ferrari, for instance), it might have been made into a delightful opera. Its humor is summed up in the conceit that an opera-singer, accustomed to the homage of the world, finds herself unable to get her favored lover, his hated rival, an humble friend of her humble childhood, or even her maid to dine with her on New Year's Day because all have promised to dine with their respective mothers. Sweet and chastened memories are thus forced upon her and in the end she finds happiness and contentment in the companionship of her own mother's portrait.

The dramatic motive is lovely and no doubt was ingeniously and sympathetically developed by the French authors. Its gentle appeal was felt in the operatic transmogrification only for a few moments after the last words had been uttered and the orchestra sang its postlude with the heroine of the play seated at the table bowed before her mother's picture, lost in tender thoughts and emotions to which the instruments gave lovely expression. The rest was futile, far-fetched, frivolous, fuliginous, fumid fustian in the score and inept ill-advised operatic idiom in the text. It did not need the coming of "Madeleine" to demonstrate that if the vernacular is to be greeted with pleasure when used in opera it must neither be the English of every-day speech nor of stilted rhetoric, but the speech of a raised and poetic fancy. It is a little less disturbing to one's equanimity to hear a maid tell her mistress that for dinner she shall have "soup *à la reine,* woodcock, and asparagus," than to have her soliloquize "and still more gifts to swell the sum of those already here"; but there is no difference in the absurdity of the two speeches when they are set to music in the declamatory style which is affected by the new composers and which Mr. Herbert essayed in "Madeleine." Speeches like these were given out in tones prompted by nothing in their contents, separated from each other by gasps and rumbles, squeaks and short phrases with all sorts of efforts at instrumental color. Then came long speeches in which all lyricism is relegated to the orchestra, but which gain nothing in expressiveness from that fact while losing a great deal from strained and unnatural declamation. Of sustained melody, or of the periodic melody with which Mr. Herbert had won favor with his operettas, there are only three examples in the score of the opera. They are a little 6/8 tune which has its model in a hundred English and Irish folksongs, a melody which threatens to become native to its creator by breaking into a waltz, and a suave and lovely melody which is as likable as Massenet's "Ouvre tes yeux bleux," which it recalls on its every repetition. This is the tune which brings solace and delight and works atonement for many of the arid stretches of the score when it rings down the curtain at the close. It is a symbol of the tender emotion which pervades the story and contributes a quota to the Wagnerian system of typical phrases which Mr. Herbert employs. The first melody is used to recall the childhood home of Madeleine and the lover of her youth, while the greatly sophisticated second tune gives musical voice to the aristocratic lover, the Duc d'Estrée. In all these instances Mr. Herbert shows ingenuity in his harmonization, following some latter-day men to the extreme in the employment of dissonances, and also skill in instrumentation. Three times does the composer work up a dynamic climax and each time with as little provocation as suffices Richard Strauss in "Der Rosenkavalier." In this opera a notary closes his portfolio with a noise like the crack of doom. In "Madeleine" all the elements seem to unite in a shriek when the Duc d'Estrée turns Madeleine free and they bolt through a crowd, when my lady flies into a petulant tantrum because no one will dine with her, and finally when her boy-lover, Didièr the painter, kisses her chastely on the cheek. This being a first performance, the cast is appended:

MASSENET'S "DON QUICHOTTE"

Madeleine Fleury, of the Opéra	Frances Alda
Nichette, her maid	Leonora Sparkes
Chevalier de Mauprat	A. Pini-Corsi
François, Duc d'Estrée	Paul Althouse
Didièr, a painter	A. de Segurola

Conductor, Giorgio Polacco

When the Chicago-Philadelphia Opera Company made its visit it continued its perpetuation of the traditions of the Manhattan Opera House, as it no doubt will continue to do as long as Miss Mary Garden is associated with it. This being so, there was nothing surprising in the fact that three of the novelties which that lady introduced to America should have been included in the list of operas performed by the company at the Metropolitan. The first of these was Massenet's "Don Quichotte," which was brought forward on February 3, 1914. The opera was given with this distribution of parts:

La belle Dulcinée	Mary Garden
Don Quichotte	Vanni Marcoux
Sancho	Hector Dufranne
Pedro	Minnie Egener
Garcias	Helen Warrum
Rodrigues	Emilio Venturino
Juan	Edmond Warnery
Le Chef de Bandits	Constantin Nicolay

The conductor was Cleofonte Campanini. "Don Quichotte" was one of the later but not the last work of Massenet, and did not show as great a decay of his powers as operas of his which were brought to the attention of New York through the same industrious agency later. Its book was made by Henri Cain after a French play by M. le Lorraine. To the playwright is due the structure of the piece, the posture and sequence of its incidents. French librettists have no bowels of compassion for classic authors or reverence for their masterpieces. Shakespeare and Goethe were despoiled for Thomas and Gounod, and now Cervantes was made to pay tribute to Massenet. Of the immortal romance I could find little else in the opera besides the names of three characters, Don Quixote's horse, and Sancho Panza's ass; and even horse and ass were calculated to excite commiseration. The great Spaniard's story has haunted the minds of opera-writers for two centuries. There ought to be something in it for a lyrical dramatist, for it contains a world of suggestive beauty for the lover of imaginative comedy literature of the highest type and of the chivalry whose mockery it was written to chastise in a most lovable spirit.

The French creators of the opera found nothing of all this. They used none of the familiar incidents except the lamentable adventure with the windmills, which offered an opportunity for an amusing stage illusion. Don Quixote is seen charging twice across the stage, lance couched, a gigantic windmill waving its arms in the mid-distance. Anon a dummy is seen flying through the air, and just before the curtain closes Sancho leads Dapple across the stage burdened with the wrecked knight and followed by Rosinante with his eye in a bandage. That must recompense the lover of Cervantes for the omission of such episodes as the attack upon the flock of sheep, the battle with the wineskins, the adventure of Mambrino's helmet, Sancho's government on the Island of Barataria, and all the rest of the incidents which have diverted the world ever since Cervantes wrote. Worse than that, the knight is made a farcical figure until his death, and even then the pathos which he ought to challenge is lacking because, while the composer does his best to atone for the invertebrate music with which he has filled the preceding acts, the dramatist knew not how to utilize the simple device with which the novelist grips the heartstrings of his readers. As for Sancho Panza, he is transformed into a conventional buffoon and Dulcinea into a conventional operatic strumpet.

It would try one's patience to tell the story of the opera if it were not so foolish and attenuate. As the audience saw it it is quickly summarized: Act I: People dressed in Spanish costumes sing and dance to Spanish rhythms under Dulcinea's window. Mary Garden appears on the balcony, throws flowers to her admirers, and utters sounds which ought never to be heard in an institution professedly devoted to art. Don Quixote serenades her, fights a duel, and is sent by the lady in quest of a necklace stolen by bandits. Act II: Don Quixote sings fa-la-las, tries to find rhymes for a love-poem, charges a windmill, and a dummy is thrown into the wings. Act III: Don Quixote falls into the hands of the bandits, whose stern natures are melted by his magnanimity and pious prayer, and instead of slaughtering him they give him the necklace and let him go. Act IV: Don Quixote brings back the jewels and claims the hand of Dulcinea as his reward; now she imitates the bandits in having a virtuous fit and dismisses the misguided man with a confession of her wicked character. Act V: The knight dies of a broken heart, bequeathing all his possessions ("the beautiful island of dreams") to his faithful squire.

Thus does an immortal literary masterpiece present itself to the sophisticated operatic eye. As for the music, it discloses Massenet's unfailing mastery of operatic craftsmanship, but also the decay of his melodic inventiveness. Its moments of beauty are few and are confined to the closing scenes. The rest invites a tear of commiseration from the admirers of "Werther" and "Manon."

To the pure all things are pure. In a beautiful sense that is true; but the doings of the purveyors of dramatic entertainments and of some of their show-people have never tempted persons inclined to decency to think that the axiom was the motive which prompts managers to produce pictures of pudicity and lewdness on the stage. Sometimes there is a confession much more convincing than all moral purpose in the simple sequence of theatrical events. After Mary

Garden, under the morally uplifting management of Mr. Hammerstein, had demonstrated the commercial effectiveness of the kind which Phryne's counsel employed in a famous case of antiquity in Massenet's "Thaïs" and Richard Strauss's "Salome," it caused no wonderment when the announcement went forth that the next novelty with which Miss Garden would help the moral uplift would be the operatic version of Maeterlinck's "Monna Vanna." In "Thaïs" she had disclosed herself with as little raiment as a generous law allowed—but only for a moment. In "Salome" she was permitted to divest herself gradually of most of her bodily covering. She did not go quite to the extreme of Istar in her famous descent to the Underworld, but it was at least hinted that she might when it was announced that her next opera would be "Monna Vanna," in which, were she to carry realism to its limit, she would be able to appear before the public clad in a loose cloak, her hair, her cuticle, and nothing else.

Circumstances interfered with that delectable purpose, which, it is needless to say, would never have been carried out literally, until the Chicago Company gave Février's opera on the evening of February 17, 1914. By this time the varnish of sensationalism had been worn off by performances in Boston, Philadelphia, and Chicago. Perhaps elsewhere also. At any rate, New York came in a bad fourth and could not be properly and profitably shocked. Meanwhile only Vincent d'Indy, so far as I know, had conceived the idea of showing a character in its progressive stages of divestment from gorgeous attire to the opposite extreme, and he did it instrumentally by the ingenious device of a downward development from elaborate variations to a simple theme lacking even the covering of harmony. But that device was so artistically sophisticated that it could harm nobody's sensibilities. We are no more shocked by a naked tune than we are by a naked tree. Neither was there anything shocking—except, perhaps, to those keenly susceptible to suggestion—in this performance of Février's opera.

In its primitive estate the theme of Maeterlinck's "Monna Vanna" is that of the old legend of the Lady Godiva; but it has been tricked out with certain elements which make it piquant to the modern taste. The lady, to save her city, goes to the beleaguering enemy's general clad in her virtue and her cloak—no more. She is willing to sacrifice both for her people, but the apparently victorious tyrant is conquered by her innocence and a love dating back to her childhood which makes her person sacred to him. When she returns to the city her husband refuses to believe the story of her chastity and his enemy's magnanimity, so she is forced to practise deception and save the magnanimous man who has again become her lover. A Shakespeare might have whitened the innocency of his heroine as he did in the case of Imogen despite the disclosure of the "mole, cinque-spotted," or a Tennyson have left her purity unquestioned as he did Lady Godiva's. But such a device could not serve the purposes of a modern playwright. Monna Vanna must at the end deceive her husband and run away with the man who had demanded the sacrifice which she was willing to pay but he unwilling to accept.

There is an old story that a good play, especially a good literary play, does not necessarily make a good opera. In fact, it might be stated as a rule that the better the play the poorer the resultant opera, unless it contains moments of sustained lyrical exaltation which invites song—real song. Maeterlinck's "Monna Vanna" is the kind of play which can only be hampered by music so long as it is left in its original state. Its dramatic and literary value would evaporate if paraphrased so that tunes might be adjusted to it, but this not having been done it would have been better to have let it alone than to burden its speeches with music which does not intensify but only clogs them. And it is a play of speeches only. The music which Février has hitched to it is dull—a hindrance, not a help. Cleofonte Campanini conducted the performance and this was the cast:

Monna Vanna	Mary Garden
Prinzivalle	Lucien Muratore
Guido	Vanni Marcoux
Marco	Gustav Huberdeau
Vedio	Edmond Warnery
Borso	Etienne Contesso
Torello	Désire Defrère
Trivulzio	Constantin Nicolay

Charpentier's "Julien," produced on January 27, 1914, came freighted with gloomy forebodings from Paris, where it had received its *première* on the preceding third of June at the Opéra Comique. As a promised sequel to "Louise" and the product of the composer who had been acclaimed by enthusiastic friends as the greatest successor of Gounod, the Parisian public had displayed great interest in it, but the critics had not been deceived. They declared it to be obscure in purpose, undramatic, and much inferior in melodic invention to its predecessors. It turned out to be all these things and more. The natural curiosity of a public which had given a large measure of admiration to "Louise," the desperate need of Mr. Gatti to provide a sensation for the season, the combined popularity of Miss Farrar and Mr. Caruso, all these failed to win for Charpentier's opera what might even be dignified by the term *succès d'estime*. It was a failure, dragged its tedious length through five performances, and sank into the pit of oblivion. It was performed under the direction of Giorgio Polacca, with the following cast:

Julien	Enrico Caruso
Louise, La Beauté, La Jeune Fille, L'Aieule, La Fille	Geraldine Farrar

ENRICO CARUSO
As Julien

GRENVILLE VERNON'S CRITICISM 327

L'Hiérophante Le Paysan Le Mage	Dinh Gilly
La Paysanne	Maria Duchène
Les Filles du Rêve et Chimères	Rosina Vandyck Louise Cox Vera Curtis Marie Mattfeld Sophie Braslau Maria Duchène Lila Robeson
Un Casseur de Pierres Une Voix de l'Abîme Un Camarade	Paolo Ananian
L'Acolyte	Albert Reiss
L'Officiant Une Voix de l'Abîme	Lambert Murphy
Un Ouvrier	Angelo Bada
Un Bucheron	Pietro Audisio
Garçons de Café	Vincenzo Reschiglian Julius Bayer
Trois Fées	Louise Cox Vera Curtis Rosina Vandyck

Concerning its story, Mr. Grenville Vernon, who wrote a criticism on the performance and who made a record of its failure, wrote in the *Tribune,* in my absence from the city, as follows:

It is an allegorical series of tableaux depicting the disintegration of a poet's soul, through disappointment, doubt, spiritual pride, and sensuality. Julien is the same poet who figures in "Louise," and the action opens in his room in the Villa Medici, in Rome. Here he is living in happiness with Louise, his soul aflame with the vision of Beauty with which he is to regenerate suffering, sinning humanity. He falls asleep, and Louise regarding him laments the fact that he is daily becoming more and more enamored of his work, and adds: "What matter, if his genius makes him immortal! My future? His work will tell of it! That is enough for me!"

With this brief scene reality ends, and the rest of the opera, which is Julien's dream, begins.

Julien sets out to redeem the world. His spirit faints a moment at the sight of the band of Poets who have failed, but with Louise at his side, as the symbol of the Beauty that he seeks, he passes on. At the Temple of Beauty the High Priest warns him of the temptations which beset him, but as he persists he is finally crowned by Louise, now become the Spirit of Beauty, who warns him to beware of pride and to love without ceasing.

The next act, laid in a wooded country, finds Julien already doubting in his mission. Louise, or rather her spirit, appears in a young girl, who would have him stay with her and her family, but Julien repulses her and passes on. The third act is on the Breton coast, and here the Poet, pursued by the phantoms of unbelief, vainly seeks refuge. The Grandmother begs him to believe in something beyond himself; but Julien, listening to the voices of the lost, with them curses God.

Lower and lower he sinks, until, a human wreck, he emerges into a riotous crowd on the Place Blanche before the Moulin Rouge. Here he is accosted by a girl of the streets, in whom he recognizes the spirit of his Louise, but who has sunk with his sinking. She drunkenly sings of the pleasure of carnality. For a moment he is roused by a vision of the Temple of Beauty and of the mission to which he has been false—then he sinks in a drunken stupor at the feet of the lost girl.

"L'Amore Medico" came late in the season and so was prevented from having its full quota of representations. Were it the rule with us that artistic merit, and that alone, should give title to permanency, or quasi-permanency, in a repertory, Wolf-Ferrari's ingenious opera might have won an enduring place at the Metropolitan; but it is idle to try to look into the minds of the directors of opera companies. The opera was new. It had its first representation on any stage in Dresden on December 4, 1913, and reached New York as quickly as could have been expected, perhaps, of any opera except one of Puccini's, whose works, for business reasons, now open their eyes on the stage lamps in the American metropolis. Signor Toscanini conducted the work, which was brought forward at the Metropolitan on March 25, 1914, with the parts distributed thus:

Arnolfo	Antonio Pini-Corsi
Lucinda	Lucrezia Bori
Clitandro	Italo Cristalli
Dr. Tomes	Léon Rothier
Dr. Desfonandres	Andrea Segurola
Dr. Macrotom	Robert Leonhardt
Dr. Bahis	Angelo Bada
Uno Notaro	Paolo Ananian

The opera is founded on Molière's "L'Amour Médecin," the book having been prepared for Signor Wolf-Ferrari by Enrico Golisciani. I hope it is not necessary for me to rehearse the plot. Concerning the music, my colleague, Mr. Richard Aldrich, wrote in *The Times* newspaper:

The music of "L'Amore medico" is saturated with the spirit of comedy. It has the mirth and verve of Molière's little piece. There are spots in it that are slow, in which the movement is unduly halted; but they are spots and for the most part it is buoyant, rapid, and graceful. It abounds in fleeting touches of wit, humorous characterization and volatile gayety. The spirit of the rococo period of Louis XIV breathes through it. Much might be said in analysis of the thematic structure of the music. There is a constant preoccupation with thematic work, though Wolf-Ferrari is far from following the procedure of Wagner with "leading motives" and the weaving of a broad and gorgeously colored tapestry from their figures. . . . There is an extended overture based on melodies occurring in the opera, a true foreshadowing of its spirit and outline of the action to follow, an exquisite piece of raillery of reckless pace and airy lightness after the slow introduction. There is an intermezzo played as an introduction to the second act which is a finely conceived development of the love-song of Clitandro—as masterly in its composition as it is continuing in its effect. As for the orchestration it is in some ways the finest and most skilful of anything Wolf-Ferrari has made known here. It is a somewhat richer score than that of "Le Donne curiose" and in the climaxes and most boisterous outbursts the composer has used a fuller complement of orchestral colors.

An incident which belongs to this chapter of history, though it happened after the close of the season of which record has just been made, was the death of Mme. Lillian Nordica, which occurred at Batavia, Island of Java, on May 10, 1914. The lady, of whose early association with opera in New York mention is made in my "Chapters of Opera," to which this book is a sequel, was a passenger on the steamship *Tasmania*, which went ashore on Bramble Cay in the Gulf of Papua on December 28, 1913. She was making a concert tour of the Pacific Islands, and nervous prostration, following her experiences of the shipwreck, produced pneumonia. She was sufficiently recovered to sail for Batavia on April 1, but there she succumbed to the dread disease. It had been her intention to sail for New York from Genoa. Mme. Nordica's real name was Lillian Norton, and she was a granddaughter of a revivalist preacher known in his day as " Campmeeting John Allen." She was born in Farmington, Maine, on May 12, 1859, and her first musical studies were made in Boston. After a somewhat extended concert career she went to Milan to study for the opera, and effected her début at Brescia on April 30, 1879, as Violetta in " Traviata." She was a member of opera companies in Genoa, Novara, and other Italian cities; Moscow, St. Petersburg, Dantzig, Berlin, and Paris. There she married Frederick A. Gower, a representative of American electrical companies, and with him came to New York, where she sang at the Academy of Music on November 26, 1883. She came to the Metropolitan Opera House with an Italian company which, under the management of Abbey and Grau, gave a series of 21 performances after the close of the German season of 1889-90. She was also a member of the company with which Mr. Abbey re-established Italian opera at the Metropolitan in 1901-02, having been engaged for the express purpose of singing the part of Selika in " L'Africaine," but when the time came Mme. Lehmann had to be brought in to make the performance possible. Thereafter she was a familiar figure at the Metropolitan until she joined Mr. Hammerstein's forces for a brief season at the Manhattan Opera House; but her finest success, and it was really a memorable one, was achieved in 1895, when she sang Isolde to Jean de Reszke's Tristan at the Broadway house. Then for the first time it was possible for the reviewer to indulge in something more than praise of her beauty and perfunctory compliments on her voice.

ENRICO CARUSO
In "Samson et Dalila"

CHAPTER XIV

THE YEARS OF THE NEUTRALITY OF THE UNITED STATES IN THE WAR

REDUCTION OF EXPENSES PLANNED—CARUSO AND FARRAR—PHENOMENAL ACTIVITY OF THE COMPANY—NEW SINGERS AND THEIR DÉBUTS—THE SEASON 1914-15—NEW OPERAS—"MADAME SANS-GÊNE"—"L'ORACOLO"—"EURYANTHE"—WEBER AND WAGNER—THE LATTER'S DEBTS TO THE FORMER—DEPARTURE OF ALFRED HERTZ—HIS RECORD AT THE METROPOLITAN—THE LOSS OF TOSCANINI—SEASON OF 1915-16—ARRIVAL OF MME. BARRIENTOS—"PRINCE IGOR"—"GOYESCAS"—SPANISH PIANOFORTE PIECES MADE INTO AN OPERA—FATE OF THE COMPOSER—A GERMAN VERSION OF "THE TAMING OF THE SHREW,"—1916-17—UNNATURAL ACTIVITY—"LES PÊCHEURS DE PERLES"—ITS AMERICAN HISTORY—GLUCK'S "IPHIGENIA AUF TAURIS"—"THE CANTERBURY PILGRIMS"—A SPORADIC BUT IDEAL EFFORT FOR AMERICAN ART—THE SOCIETY OF AMERICAN SINGERS—MOZART'S "BASTIEN ET BASTIENNE" AND "THE IMPRESARIO"

FOR three years after the outbreak of the great war in which at the last Germany found herself in battle with nearly every civilized people of the world there was nothing to compel or even invite a change of policy on the part of the management of the Metropolitan Opera House. It was outwardly, at least, as neutral in thought, word, and deed as it was possible for the President of the United States to wish. In the preparations for the work of the season 1914-15 it was, indeed, necessary for Mr. Gatti to do a great deal of work of an unusual kind, but there was nothing during the season to embarrass him at all comparable with the threatened renewal of Oscar Hammerstein's rivalry which had vexed his soul during the preceding year. The physical obstacles had been overcome even before the annual prospectus was issued in October, and all that the directors had to fear between the day when war was declared and the opening of the season on November 16 was the loss of some of their singers and a possible slump in the subscriptions. The former danger loomed up as the greater of the two.

Many of the singers of the Metropolitan company were foreigners who were accustomed to hurry over to Europe as soon as the New York season was over either to become artistically active in the London season at Covent Garden or to rest in their old homes. With the outbreak of hostilities it became necessary to look after these people—artists, choristers, and instrumentalists—and make sure of their return to New York. All of them were not essential to the season, but Mr. Albert Reiss occupied so unique a position in the artistic economy of the institution that the help of the French Ambassador to the United States had to be invoked to rescue him from a concentration camp in France. Mr. Dinh Gilly, a valuable but less necessary member of the French and Italian contingent, became a prisoner of war in Austria and had to be left to his fate. As for the rest the roster was complete when the prospectus was issued on October 19. It contained, in its German contingent, the names of Emmy Destinn, Johanna Gadski, Frieda Hempel, Melanie Kurt (a newcomer), Margaret Matzenauer, Margaret Ober, Rudolf Berger, Johannes Sembach (a new tenor), Jacques Urlus, Otto Goritz, Robert Leonhardt, Carl Schlegel, Hermann Weil, and Carl Braun.

In the season, which was as like its predecessor as two peas are like each other, except in the size of the artistic pod, there being neither addition nor diminution of the German list of operas performed, the war affected the financial outcome in a twofold manner. The subscriptions fell off (for no reason except apprehension of a possible financial depression, a fear which led to the abandonment of the Boston Opera Company, which had been a losing institution from the beginning, and the bankruptcy at the end of the

Chicago Company, which, however, was reorganized for the following season) and there was a loss of expected revenues from the failure of the promised affiliation with the organizations in Boston and Chicago. No effort had been made to conceal from the public the fact that the demands of a few of the principal singers of the Metropolitan Company had become exorbitant, partly because of the end of the Hammerstein competition, partly because of it, and that the only means which offered to satisfy them was to share their services with Boston and Chicago. With no opera in the capitals of New England and the Middle West, and the concert season ruined by popular apathy and an invasion of foreign artists, an unexpectedly large burden fell upon the Metropolitan Opera Company. How large a loss was entailed I do not know, but the directors, while withholding figures in accordance with their invariable custom, let it be known that the loss was not so large as that of 1910-11.

About the middle of the season Mr. Gatti made it known that the war had brought with it what seemed to him the psychological moment for a reform which should look toward the emancipation of the institution from the exorbitant demands of the singers. What he did in the way of retrenchment it is not in my power to say, nor have I ever been curious to find out; I prefer to confine myself to the artistic doings of the institutions. A great deal of gossip was created by the fact that it was announced early in January that Signor Caruso would cut his season short in order to sing at Monte Carlo. It was, of course, at once concluded that the admired tenor had rebelled against an attempt to reduce his honorarium, notwithstanding the statement of the directors that he was worth to them every cent of the $2,500 a night which he was receiving, and that the projected measure of reform was not aimed at him. In the last week of the season the directors issued a statement to the effect that Signor Caruso would be a member of the company in the entire season of 1915-1916, which compelled the conclusion that the curtailment of his engagement had been an amicable arrangement. Miss Geraldine Farrar, another popular idol, without waiting to learn the intentions of the directors concerning her, executed a strategic movement and placed herself in the hands of Mr. Charles A. Ellis, of Boston, who had been her agent for concerts. It was a shrewd move, but Miss Farrar evidently thought it needed defense, for she put forth some high-sounding phrases about her art as a vocation and the necessity of laying up money against an evil day. This, she intimated, would not be necessary "if we had a government opera house, with the artists cared for during their active careers. With a pension at the close they would not have to haggle over money; all that they would be required to do would be to perfect their art." This sounded well, but would have been a trifle more convincing if Miss Farrar had not deserted the Royal Opera at Berlin, where she might at the last have obtained a pension, and contracted with Mr. Conried to come to America. Also if she had not in an interview sent to the New York *Times* disclosed anything but a patriotic spirit toward her native land. To what measure of success Miss Farrar carried her point I do not know. She did, however, make a contract with the reorganized Chicago Opera Company for a portion of the next season and with the Metropolitan director for the remainder.

Artistically, as I have said, the first season after the beginning of the war was like its predecessor and also like its successors. The old list of German operas was retained. In the susbscription list there were 12 German operas which received 42 performances; in the entire list of performances the same operas received 53 performances. German operas were then relied on for special series and holidays when the general public, not the subscribers, had to be attracted.

There was the conventional complement of 23 weeks in the season of 1914-15 which had become the rule at the Metropolitan Opera House—from November 14 to April

24, inclusive. Within this period of 160 days the company gave 178 evenings and afternoons of opera, besides 23 concerts on Sunday nights, including the performances which had also become the rule in Philadelphia and Brooklyn. Think of the time passed in shunting back and forth between the cities, the hours spent in rehearsals, and reflect upon how many hours the slaves of the opera were permitted to have for rest, reflection, and recuperation! Such statistics do not concern me beyond exciting my sympathy and regret over the inevitable effect which the onerous labors have upon the artistic performances which I have made it my duty to chronicle. In passing, however, it may not be amiss to express a feeling of amazement that Mr. Gatti's harmonious forces should have accomplished so stupendous a labor, and of regret that operatic conditions in New York should have so shaped themselves as to seem to make the labor necessary. This necessity was responsible for all the shortcomings of the season, which I am compelled to overlook, because this is not a critical account of the representations, and which was tempered by admiration for the zeal which Mr. Gatti's people disclosed and the operation of the system which Mr. Gatti's generalship kept alive.

In the previous season Mr. Gatti had done an unprecedented thing in producing five new works. He did not attempt to do so much in the season under review, and even failed in part in what he did undertake. The prospectus had promised three novelties and seven so-called " revivals." The novelties were Giordano's " Madame Sans-Gêne," Borodin's " Prince Igor," and Leoni's " L'Oracolo." The old works which were to be revamped were " Carmen " (with Miss Farrar), " Fidelio," " Mefistofele," " Guillaume Tell," " Samson et Dalila," and Weber's " Euryanthe." " Madame Sans-Gêne " was given and had as large a number of performances as the director's plans made possible, but it failed to create a large interest and the composer did not come to attend the " world *première,*" as it had been announced that he would. " L'Oracolo " was brought forward as a curtain-raiser to " Pagliacci," which Signor Caruso has kept in the repertory. Borodin's Russian opera, for which a warm welcome had been prepared by " Boris Godounow," was abandoned because the chorus had not the time to learn the music. Small wonder. Mascagni's " Iris " was thrust into the place of the promised novelty. Other incidents of the season were the death of one of the German tenors, Rudolf Berger, on February 27; the announcement that Alfred Hertz, the German conductor, would retire from the establishment at the expiration of his contract for the year; and the nervous breakdown, a fortnight before the end of the season, of Signor Toscanini, which compelled the abandonment of two symphony concerts which he had prepared to add to the establishment's laurels. Unhappily, he did not return for the next season. It is also deserving of notice that in this season " Parsifal " was for the first time admitted to the regular list, though it had been in the repertory of the Metropolitan for eleven years.

The occasion of the first performance of " Madame Sans-Gêne " on January 25, 1915, was of considerable moment, but the fact would have been recorded in these memoirs even if this had not been the case. The conductor was Signor Toscanini and the singers were these:

Caterina Huebscher .... Geraldine Farrar
Tonietta .... Leonora Sparkes
Giulia .... Rita Fornia
La Rossa .... Sophie Braslau
Lefebvre .... Giovanni Martinelli
Fouché .... Andrea de Segurola
Vinagre .... Max Bloch
Conte di Neipperg .... Paul Althouse
La Regina Carolina .... Vera Curtis
La Principessa Elisa .... Minnie Egener
Despreaux .... Angelo Bada
Gelsomino .... Riccardo Tegani
Leroy .... Robert Leonhardt
De Brigode .... Vincenzo Reschiglian
Napoleone .... Pasquale Amato
Roustan .... Bernard Bégué

Operatic conditions were not normal in Europe, but that fact had nothing to do with the choice of New York as the place in which Umberto Giordano's opera was to have its first representation. It would have seen its material birth here, even if a war, begun to promote Teutonic notions of civilization, had not intervened to put a clog on artistic culture in Europe. The only effect of the crime committed against culture in the name of *Kultur* was to keep the composer away from the first representation of his work; and that circumstance was entirely inconsequential. The presence of Signor Giordano might have quickened the pulses of the people who heard his opera; it could not have helped the work, which had as admirable a performance as could well be desired, and which could certainly not have been better had the scene of the *première* been laid in Milan, London, Paris, St. Petersburg, Berlin, or Vienna. "Madame Sans-Gêne" is an operatic version of the drama which Sardou developed out of a little one-act play dealing with a partly fictitious, partly historical story of which Napoleon, his marshal Lefebvre, and a laundress were the characters. Whether or not the great Corsican could be justified as a figure in a lyric drama was a moot question when Giordano conceived the idea of making an opera out of the play. It is said that Verdi remarked something to the effect that the question turned on what he was called upon to sing and how he would be expected to sing it. In the palmy days of *bel canto* no one would have raised such a question, as I have set forth in an earlier work already cited.*

In turning Sardou's dramatic people into operatic marionettes a great deal of bloodletting was necessary and a great deal of its characteristic charm was lost, especially in the cases of Mme. Sans-Gêne herself and the Emperor's sister, but enough was left to make a practicable opera; and what more could be asked?

*"A Second Book of Operas." By Henry Edward Krehbiel. New York, 1917.

There were the pictures of all the plebeians who became great folk later concerned in the historical incidents which lifted them up. There were also the contrasting pictures which resulted from the great transformation, and there was also the ingratiating incident of the devotion of Lefebvre to the stout-hearted, honest little woman of the people who had to try to be a duchess. All this was fair operatic material, for music has a strange capacity for purifying stage characters.

Giordano could not do himself justice as a composer without refining the expression of Caterina Huebscher, and so his Duchess of Danzig talks a musical language, at least, which Sardou's washerwoman could not talk and remain within the dramatic verities. Therefore we had "Madame Sans-Gêne" with a difference, but not one that gave any more offense than operatic treatment of other fine plays had accustomed us to.

French revolutionary airs peppered the pages of "Madame Sans-Gêne"—the same airs which had given fierce life to the same composer's "Andrea Chenier." Quite natural, this, for the two operas are allied in subject and period as well as in style of composition. Chenier goes to his death to the tune of "La Marseillaise" and the mob marches past the windows of Caterina Huebscher's laundry singing the refrain of Roget de Lisle's hymn. But Giordano does not make extensive use of the national hymn of France; it appears literally at the place mentioned and surges up with fine effect in a speech in which the Countess of Danzig overwhelms the proud sisters of Bonaparte. Practially that is all. The case is different with the two other revolutionary songs. Their melodies are not so widely known in America now as they were a century and a quarter ago, and so they are reproduced here as a sort of thematic guide to many pages of Giordano's score. The first crash of the orchestra launches us into "La Carmagnole."

"LA CARMAGNOLE"   339

This melody provides the thematic orchestral substratum for practically the entire first scene. It is an innocent enough tune, differing little from hundreds of French vaudeville melodies, but Giordano injects vitriol into its veins by his harmonies and orchestration. With all its innocency, however, it was this tune which came from the raucous throats of politically crazed men and women, while noble heads tumbled into the bloody sawdust, while the spoils of the churches were carried into the National Convention in 1793, and to which " several members, quitting their curule chairs, took the hands of girls flaunting in priests' vestures," danced a wild rout, as did other mad wretches when a dancer was worshiped as the Goddess of Reason in the Cathedral of Notre Dame.

Caterina's account of the rude familiarity with which she is treated by the soldiery (a knowledge of the story of the opera can safely be assumed, since Sardou's play has been acted here by Kathryn Kidder, as well as Mme. Réjane) is set to a melody of a Russian folksong cast, in the treatment of which Russian influences may also be felt, but with the first shouts of the mob attacking the Tuileries in the distance the characteristic rhythmical motif of " Ça ira " is heard muttering in the basses:

Again a harmless tune which in its time was perverted to a horrible use—a lively little contra-dance which graced many a cotillon in its early day, but which was roared and shouted by the mob as it carried the beauteous head of the Lamballe through the streets of Paris on a pike and thrust it almost into the face of Marie Antoinette!

Of such material and a pretty little dance ("La Fricassée"), to which Caterina tells of her rescue by Lefebvre, is the music of the first act, punctuated by cannon shots, made. It is all rhythmically stirring, it flows spiritedly, energetically, along with the movement of the play, never retarding it for a moment, but, unhappily, never sweetening it with a grain of pretty sentiment or adorning it with a really graceful contour. And so with the acts which follow the revolutionary scenes. There is some graciousness in the court scene, some archness and humor in the scene in which the plebeian Duchess of Danzig permits the adornment of her person, some dramatically strong declamation in the speeches of Napoleon, some simulation of passion in the love passages of Lefebvre and of Reipperg; but as a rule the melodic flood never reaches high tide.

Mr. Antonio Scotti's popularity and his success in im-

A CHINESE-AMERICAN OPERA 341

personating the principal character in the opera brought sporadic performances of "L'Oracolo" until the end of the period with which this book deals. Besides this artist's popularity, the opera had in its favor the fact that it was a lyric version of an American play with local color in its story, though not in its music. It was drawn from a play of life in the Chinese quarter of San Francisco. The play was C. B. Fernald's "The Cat and the Cherub," which had been one of the features of the theatrical season of 1897-98. From New York it found its way in the course of the same season to London, and there the Italian librettist, Camillo Zanoni, and the Italian composer, Franco Leoni, turned it into an opera which was performed a few times at Covent Garden in June, 1905, with Miss Donaldo, Mr. Scotti, and Mr. Dalmorès in the cast. At the New York first performance, February 4, 1915, it was sung by these people:

Win-Shee .... Adamo Didur
Chim-Fen .... Antonio Scotti
Hoo-Tsin .... Giulio Rossi
Win-San-Luy .... Luca Botta
Hoo-Chee .... Ella Bakos
Ah-Yoe .... Lucrezia Bori
Hua-Quee .... Sophie Braslau
A Fortune Teller .... Pietro Audisio
Conductor, Giorgio Polacco

There had been an effort made at local color in the incidental music written for the play (for the composer was familiar with the life of the Chinese dwellers in San Francisco), but Mr. Leoni evidently knew too little of the life of the people represented in the play to attempt anything of the sort. He tried at times to be Oriental in expression, especially in the ceremonial parts of the play, but the Orientalism was more like that of Meyerbeer's singular Malagasy music in "L'Africaine" than anything ever heard in China or carried thence to San Francisco. In all else the score was fair Puccini and deftly sugared water.

Weber's opera "Euryanthe" was brought forward at the Metropolitan Opera House at an afternoon performance on December 19, 1914. It was twenty-seven years, almost to a day, since it had had its first hearing at the proud establishment. When Anton Seidl put it into the repertory on December 23, 1887, twenty-four years had elapsed since it had been heard for the first time in New York, that hearing having been provided by a company of German singers who had ventured upon a season of opera under the direction of Carl Anschütz at Wallack's Theater, located then at Broadway and Broome Street. When Mr. Seidl tried to give the opera a home in New York I expressed the conviction in *The Tribune* newspaper that it had been a kind providence which had preserved the work from representation in the interim. On this second resurrection the thought came again. Then the reason was that the generation of opera patrons that had grown up between the tentative efforts of Herr Anschütz and his artistic pioneers could not be prepared for Weber's startling proclamation because they knew too little of Wagner's art. Now the thought which influenced the reviewer was that since the passing of Seidl there had been no conductor at the Metropolitan sufficiently imbued with the spirit of Weber's music to body it forth so that its gracious loveliness, its chivalresqueness, its tragic power would make the irresistible appeal which lies in that music to popular appreciation and affection. That conductor was found in Signor Toscanini, who had performed his most amazing miracles not in the operas of his countrymen, but in the dramas of Wagner.

A year before, when the first intimations were whispered about the opera house that Signor Toscanini contemplated a revival of the opera, it was explained that his reason, outside of his admiration for Weber's score, was that he wished to supply the missing link between operas of the old type and Wagner's lyric dramas and knew that "Euryanthe" was that link. If he really had such a laudable purpose he must have been gratified at the popular reception of the opera. The whisperings and elbow-nudgings in boxes and stalls, the excited between-acts gossip in the corridors, all indicated that an audience that knew Wagner from "Tannhäuser" to "Parsifal" had been fully aroused to a consciousness that from first to last Wagner patterned after the composer who had awakened his musical genius into life as a schoolboy. They found that "Euryanthe," like "Hamlet," was "full of quotations," and no doubt many discriminating minds discovered that Lysiart was a more powerful vessel of wrath than Telramund, Eglantine a more potent personification of malicious wickedness than Ortrud, and Euryanthe a more fragrant flower of chastity than Elsa. Weber set out on a new path when he composed "Euryanthe "—a path more absolutely novel and revolutionary than Wagner had chosen up to the time when he achieved his first popular successes, and a path which he kept in view until he brought his revolutionary labors to an end. He had scarcely hinted at it in "Der Freischütz" and he did not pursue it in "Oberon." There is no clearer or more truthful definition of "Euryanthe" than that which has come to us from Weber himself. It is "a simple, earnest work which strives for nothing save truthfulness of expression, passion, and delineation of character." The words of the composer are only slightly expanded and emphasized by a memorable reply which he made when applied to by a society in Breslau for permission to perform the work in concert form: "'Euryanthe' is a purely dramatic attempt which rests for its effectiveness upon a co-operation of all the sister arts, and will surely fail if robbed of their help."

Romaine Rolland, in his collection of criticisms, has given expression to the belief that, on the whole, the enjoyment of Wagner's Nibelung music is marred by the stage spectacle. I can not subscribe to that notion even when witnessing the faulty representations which are becoming too common, owing to the ignorance or careless attitude of stage-managers and artists; and the soundness of Weber's view is to be commended even in the face of the absurdities of the libretto which the foolish bluestocking von Chezy forced upon him. His attitude toward his idiotically constructed book was sincere at least—even down to the episode of the serpent which nowadays defeats itself and evokes laughter instead of awe. But it is only a ripple, a momentary eddy in the stream of tragic sentiment provided by the music. We are quite as ready to smile at Weber's serpent as at Mozart's monster and Wagner's dragon; but the music soon carries us away from the danger which seems to threaten the drama.

It is the lovely manner and perfection with which Weber has wedded the drama and the music which makes "Euryanthe" an almost ineffable work. There is no groping in the dark such as might have been expected from a pathfinder. Weber was showing the way to thitherto undreamed-of possibilities, yet his hand was steady, his judgment all but unerring. How continent his orchestra! Yet what an eloquence and power does it contain as an expositor of the innermost heart of the drama! Is there another page in operatic literature to be put alongside of the *Largo* episode in the overture and its repeated recurrence when the spectral visitant who haunts the minds of the personages and ruins the fabric of the play makes its appearance? Has Wagner improved the introduction to the third act by his palpable imitations of it in "Siegfried" and "Tristan"? Is there another operatic song of the dewy freshness and fragrance of Euryanthe's first cavatina ("Glöcklein im Thale") or the sweet, gentle, resigned pathos of the second ("Hier, dicht am Quell'") in the last act? Did not the hunt's-up of the last act provoke something like a feeling of impatience with Wagner's imitation in "Tannhäuser"? Will it ever be possible to put loftier sentiment or sincerer expression into a delineation of brave knighthood and its homage to fair women than inspire almost every measure

AMELITA GALLI-CURCI
Of the Chicago Opera Company

DEPARTURE OF ALFRED HERTZ

of the first act? To Wagner's honor be it said that he never denied his indebtedness to Weber, but if he had it would have availed him nothing while the representatives of the evil principle in "Lohengrin" and "Euryanthe" present so obvious a parallel, not to mention so many drafts upon the spiritual as well as physical apparatus in so many parts of the score. The opera was presented as a brilliant spectacle in which pictures and pageantry were successfully and harmoniously blended. The tableau which Weber intended to have exposed during the *Largo* episode in the overture was omitted. We had had it in the performances twenty-seven years before, but it can not be said to shed much light on the play, since its significance becomes apparent only after the drama is developed and then only in part and to those who are willing to endure the brain-racking which the incoherent libretto compels. But we had the *Pas de cinque* in the last act, composed for Berlin, for which Mr. Seidl had substituted the waltz measures from "The Invitation to the Dance." The parts in the opera were distributed as follows:

The King	Arthur Middleton
Adolar	Johannes Sembach
Lysiart	Hermann Weil
Euryanthe	Frieda Hempel
Eglantine	Margarete Ober
Rudolph	Max Bloch
Bertha	Mabel Harrison

The afternoon performance of the season brought an end to the services of Mr. Alfred Hertz as conductor of the German operas at the Metropolitan Opera House. He had been an efficient and faithful (may I say, also somewhat heavy-handed) official at that establishment for thirteen years, had made many friends among the contingent of artists and patrons of the establishment, and his departure was celebrated, or solemnized, with appropriate manifestations of esteem. From the German contingent of the company Mr. Hertz received a magnificent laurel-wreath wrought in gold, and silver, from the directors of the company a massive loving-cup. Mr. Hertz's services at the Metropolitan Opera House began in the last year of Mr. Grau's management. Before he came to New York he, a native of Frankfort, Germany, had received his musical education at the Raff Conservatorium in that city, had been conductor for three years at the Hoftheater in Altenburg, Barmen, Elberfeld, and Breslau. He began his career in New York on November 28, 1892. His associates in New York in his first season were Signor Mancinelli and M. Flon, respectively in charge of the Italian and French lists. With the exception of a single work all of the German operas when Mr. Hertz came belonged to the Wagnerian list firmly established in popular favor, but that exception brought Mr. Hertz into popular notice more emphatically than any operatic incident in the annals of German opera in America. In his first season he conducted the first performance outside Bayreuth of "Parsifal," and every performance which that work received at the Metropolitan Opera House until his departure from New York. After that departure he made his home on the Pacific coast. His monopoly of the German list ceased when Mr. Conried's régime began in the autumn of 1903. Mr. Conried engaged Herr Mottl, who conducted the greater part of the list, leaving only "Tristan," "Parsifal," "Rheingold," and "Götterdämmerung" to his associate. This being the year in which "Parsifal" had eleven representations, however, Mr. Hertz enjoyed a larger share of public attention than his more famous colleague.

The fifth year of his activity was marked by the frustration of Mr. Conried's attempt to place Richard Strauss's "Salome" by the side of Wagner's "Parsifal." Mr. Hertz prepared the unsavory opera and conducted the one representation which the directors permitted for Mr. Conried's benefit. Throughout the season of 1907-08, the last of Mr.

DIVISION OF THE GERMAN REPERTORY 347

Conried's régime, Mr. Hertz shared the German list with Herr Mahler, who was brought over as German director from Vienna. He began his labors on January 1, 1908, and to him were assigned " Die Walküre," " Tristan und Isolde," " Siegfried," and " Fidelio." The Wagnerian list was extended by the inclusion of " Der Fliegende Holländer," which Mr. Hertz conducted, as well as " Das Rheingold," " Götterdämmerung," and " Meistersinger." With the advent of Signor Gatti-Casazza and Mr. Dippel in the management, the German field was shared by three conductors. Signor Toscanini's sympathies were not circumscribed by the Italian list. He had produced " Götterdämmerung " at La Scala in Milan, and leaving the old-fashioned Italian operas to his compatriot, Spetrino, he took charge of the final drama in the Nibelung tetralogy here, though it was again placed in Mr. Hertz's hands at the special serial performances.

Mr. Mahler took over " Tristan und Isolde " and " Fidelio," and Mr. Hertz was left with " Walküre," " Siegfried," " Parsifal," " Tannhäuser," and " Meistersinger." The German novelties of the season were d'Albert's " Tiefland," conducted by Hertz, and " The Bartered Bride," conducted by Mahler.

In 1910-11 the entire Wagnerian list (save " Tristan " and " Die Meistersinger " yielded to Mr. Toscanini) reverted to Mr. Hertz, who also took over " The Bartered Bride," and gave Humperdinck's " Königskinder " its world *première* under the eyes of the composer. Thuille's " Lobetanz," Blech's " Versiegelt," and Professor Parker's prize opera " Mona " were Mr. Hertz's contributions to the season of 1911-12, and Walter Damrosch's " Cyrano de Bergerac " to the season of 1912-13. The last novelty which he brought forward was the opera with which he ended his local service, " Der Rosenkavalier." In all, Mr. Hertz conducted twenty-seven operas during his term at the Metropolitan, of which eleven were novelties.

I have given much space to the incident of Mr. Hertz's departure from the Metropolitan Opera House, largely because of his long association with it and his identification with its most progressive activities. A greater loss was suffered by the establishment when Signor Toscanini did not return for the season of 1915-16. I coupled an anticipatory expression of the extent of that loss with an estimate of his genius in Chapter III of this book. Various explanations were offered for his non-appearance in the autumn of 1915, among them the state of his health at the end of the preceding season and his desire to do service for his country in the artistic field after Italy had become embroiled in the war with Germany and Austria. His loss to opera in America has never been made good. His services in the production of novelties were not more notable than those bestowed upon operas long familiar to the local list and perhaps even less remarkable in behalf of the works of his native land than those bestowed upon the masterpieces of Wagner and Weber's " Euryanthe."

There was little for the newspapers to chronicle about the opera season of 1915-16. The accounts which in the romantic days of storm and stress, told of shipwrecks with managerial hulks strewn along the beach, of ceaseless conflicts between singers, conductors, and impresarios, were absent from the story of the season. Through a year of universal strife Mr. Gatti steered the operatic ship over a serene sea into a harbor of prosperity and reaped his reward in an extension of his contract before its expiration. It may be that there was a little too much placidity, a little too much consonantal harmony prevalent in the big theater. Critical historians with ideals are hard to please. Perhaps the striving for higher things would have been more profitable for art even if accompanied by some discordant sounds. But the complacent progress maintained by the establishment seems to have been invited and encouraged by the people who make opera possible. There had for years been utterances to the effect that Mr. Gatti and the public-spirited gentlemen for whom he acted had always had immortal longings in them—had, indeed, hungered and thirsted for ideal things in art; but the voice which speaks from the box-office had forbidden the realization of such longings and ambitions. That voice is one of awful authority and not to be disobeyed with impunity. A generation before, when the occupants of the boxes and stalls of this season were cutting their eye-teeth on Wagner, there used occasionally to be strivings toward the artistic heights; but the enjoyment of them was too frequently troubled by the apprehension that the tenure of the delightful entertainment would not be a long one:

> 'Tis man's perdition to be safe
> When for the truth he ought to die;

and opera's also. One could not quarrel with the management of the opera without quarreling also with the public whose tastes it served.

The season was three weeks shorter than its immediate predecessor, the term of twenty weeks having been set in the preceding autumn to give the use of the opera house to the Diaghileff Ballet, which was to occupy it during the month of April while the opera company gave a season of three weeks in Boston and one week in Atlanta, Ga. The contemplation in retrospect of what had been accomplished from an artistic point of view does not call for loud encomiums. It was one of the consequences of the rut into which the Opera had fallen, in which in truth it had wallowed for years, that there was no stability in the repertory except in respect of the most hackneyed operas (preserved by the presence in the company of Mr. Caruso and Miss Farrar) and the Wagnerian list essential when an appeal was to be made especially outside of the subscription list. The success of the Wagnerian dramas and such works as "Boris Godounow" and "L'Amore dei tre Re," in which there was no exploitation of the favorite singers, might have been pursued farther than it was had it not been for the fact that the policy, no doubt based on the fancies of the people of influence with the management, compelled the distribution of the services of singers like Caruso, Farrar, and (for want of a better) Madame Barrientos, who made her début on January 31, 1916, in "Lucia di Lammermoor," as extensively as possible over the subscription dates of the season. Another newcomer, Giuseppe de Luca, baritone, made his first appearance in America in "Il Barbiere di Siviglia" on November 25, 1915.

The one addition to the season's repertory which met with real warmth was "Samson et Dalila," with which the season opened, and which had been heard but once before at the Metropolitan Opera House many years before, and then in a slipshod performance; but it was in no sense a novelty. Its music was familiar from concert-room performances and it had been given in a fairly satisfactory manner by Mr. Hammerstein's people at the Manhattan Opera House. To the subscribers "Rheingold," which this year found itself in the subscription list for the first time since the German régime, was quite as much of a novelty. A long lapse of time between its first English production in New York and its revival in the original German version of Goetz's "Taming of the Shrew" prevents that opera from being put in the same category. The only real novelties were the Russian opera "Prince Igor" and the Spanish "Goyescas." The conditions of the latter production were so unusual that they can not form a precedent, nor is it likely that the opera will be heard of again. With all the charm of its Spanish dance rhythms it is too sadly lacking in dramatic quality to have vitality. It was a singular conceit that a set of pianoforte pieces might be transformed into an opera by orchestrating them and imposing solo and ensemble songs upon them. Liszt made symphonic poems out of some of his pianoforte studies, but Señor Granados's

Maria Barrientos
As Lakmé

efforts went beyond that. Borodin's "Prince Igor" was handicapped by the success won by "Boris Godounow," a much finer work also inspired by the spirit of Slavic folksong. Nevertheless it was well worth producing and would be well worth preserving in the standard list of the Metropolitan Opera House if conditions were not those which have already been discussed, one of which compelled this Russian work, like its companion, to be sung in Italian when common-sense suggested that if a translation must be made it ought to be into English. The temporary loss of "L'Amore dei tre Re" was deplorable and equally the circumstance which brought it about. This was the illness of Mlle. Bori, who had rightly been hailed as a valuable acquisition to the Metropolitan forces by critics and public alike. She represented the element upon which the betterment of our operatic conditions largely depends. Goetz's opera "Der Widerspänstigen Zähmung" came too late in the season to receive fair judgment from the public. As a contribution to the Shakespearean tercentenary it came too late to be of real consequence and a more welcome tribute would have been a fine revival of either "Otello" or "Falstaff"; but these are works which have always frighted the souls of the Metropolitan management. Nevertheless Goetz's opera is worthy of careful study and shall receive it.

Borodin's "Prince Igor," the first of the season's novelties, had its production on December 30, 1915. The performance was conducted by Giorgio Polacco and the people concerned in the cast were these:

Yaroslavna	Frances Alda
Konchankovna	Flora Perini
Nurse	Minnie Egener
Prince Igor	Pasquale Amato
Prince Galitzky } Khan Konchak }	Adamo Didur
Vladimir	Lucca Botta
Eroshka	Angelo Bada
Skoula	Andrea Segurola

The opera was Borodin's child of sorrow. Though he had had it in mind for years he never finished it and heard public performances of only portions of it. The story was drawn by his friend Stassow from an epical poem of the Russians which deals with the adventures of the prince in an expedition against a nomadic people allied to the ancient Turks called Polovitzi, who, according to ancient tradition, invaded Russian territory about the twelfth century. As in the Russian poem there is a conflict between Russian influences and manners and those of the farther East, so Borodin made essay to preserve the same element in his music. He saturated himself with the old literature on the subject and also made a study of the songs of the people who now live on the steppes once occupied by the Polovitzi. The opera was completed after Borodin's death by Glazounow, and Rimsky-Korskow and other friends used their influence in having it published. Portions of it had been sung and the ballet music (which became one of the features of the Diaghileff productions) played in New York at a concert of the MacDowell Chorus under the direction of Kurt Schindler on March 3, 1911. I was not present to witness the first performance of the opera and can not speak of its reception. My assistant, Mr. Grenville Vernon, writing in *The Tribune,* remarked that it was the wonderful Slavic choruses and the Tartar dances which raised " Prince Igor " from the level of dull Italian opera. " Whenever," said he, " Borodin attempts to wax lyrical his soul undergoes a momentous change, loses its Slavic color, and drifts helplessly across the Alps into the vineyards and gardens of Italy. Here he begins to dote on love and pipes dolefully in the manner of Tuscan or Lombard amorists. Whether it be Igor or Yaraslovna, Vladimir or Konchankovna who pour out their souls dulcetly they invariably do so in the Italian manner. But when Borodin turns to the scenes of carousal he turns full-heartedly. Give him a chance to sing of the joys of vodka and he sings with all the spirit of the

Russian race. Here he bases himself on the firm rock of Slavic folksong, and how high does Bacchus stand in their old lays!" My colleague, William J. Henderson of *The Sun,* recording the fact that at the rehearsal the third act had been voted a bore and eliminated, thought that the opera lacked in dramatic continuity and could endure further pruning. He praised the choruses and the ingeniously developed scenes of barbaric revel in the camp of the Khan. Concerning some of the music he said: " To be sure we may shrug an impatient shoulder when we find our ears choked with flattened seconds, but we are in the musical Orient where the flat second and the flat sixth dwell together in loving fraternity. But there is other material and most of it is serviceable and some of it newly disposed in captivating patterns. Borodin has written a long and elaborate development of a choral dance. The music allotted to the chorus in this scene is highly effective and the variety of figure in the whole dance is good. The glitter of costumes and the agility of dancers do not constitute the entire value of this scene. It is musically successful."

The story of " Goyescas " would have had a sentimental, perhaps a diverting, character had it not terminated so tragically as to become an incident of world-wide significance in the war. Through the efforts of Emilio de Gorgorza, a singer, and Ernest Schelling, a pianist, some of the salon music of Granados had been favorably received by American audiences. Though he had written an opera entitled " Maria del Carmen " which had been dignified by a performance at Madrid in 1898 and another called " Lilian " in Barcelona in 1911, it can not be said that he had won his operatic spurs when the feelings aroused by the war led his friends to use their influence to bring him to America. Out of a set of pianoforte pieces written to illustrate some of the paintings by Goya, a librettist named Periquet concocted an opera. Of action the play was comparatively guiltless. The people met twice in the midst of as many terpsichorean whirls. At the last there was an invisible duel and the play came to an end with a heartbroken woman lamenting the killing of her lover. The reason for the beginning, middle, and end of the tragedy was never made clear to the spectators. The listeners were treated to much Spanish music most of which they were familiar with in its original pianoforte dress and some of which was re-orchestrated by others than the composer after the score was placed in the hands of the director of the opera. The work had five performances, the first on January 28, after much kindly propaganda had been made for the composer. Giovanni Bavagnoli conducted the representation and the parts were assumed by the following artists:

Rosario	Anna Fitziu
Pepa	Flora Perinin
Fernando	Giovanni Martinelli
Paquiro	Giuseppi de Luca
A Public Singer	Max Bloch

After hearing his opera Señor Granados visited other American cities, Washington at the last, with his wife, and then started for his home in Spain in March, 1916. Both fell victims to the fiendish crime of the Germans in torpedoing the steamer *Sussex* while she was crossing the English Channel.

The German version of "The Taming of the Shrew" ("Der Widerspänstigen Zähmung"), the book by Joseph Viktor Widmann, the music by Hermann Goetz, was performed at the Metropolitan on March 15, 1916, under the direction of Mr. Bodanzky and with this cast:

Baptista	Otto Goritz
Katharina	Margarete Ober
Bianca	Maria Rappold
Hortensio	Robert Leonhardt
Lucentio	Johannes Sembach
Petruchio	Clarence Whitehill
Grumio	Basil Ruysdael

SHAKESPEARE AND OPERA 355

A Tailor .... Albert Reiss
Majordomo .... Max Bloch
Housekeeper .... Marie Mattfeld

The opera was new to the vast majority who attended the representation, though it had had five performances at the Academy of Music a little more than thirty years before. In its operatic form the comedy was first given in New York in an English translation, and the wish must have lain close to many minds that the vernacular might have been used in the revival. But unhappily, our singers are foreigners. It was with the purpose of helping opera to emancipate itself from its Tuscan trammel that the American Opera Company had been called into being and that this work and Nicolai's " Merry Wives of Windsor " were incorporated into its repertory.* The promoters of the enterprise, which started out bravely but came to a woeful end in a short time, believed that the time was come to put aside an old affectation and do honor to the vernacular. Their belief found expression in the creation of an institution which was to strive to habilitate the English language on the operatic stage and to do for the United States the national work France, Germany, and Russia had accomplished for themselves. To this end nothing seemed to be more appropriate and dignified than a choice of operas with Shakespearean subjects, which seemed at least to assure a better knowledge of the plays and a more sympathetic interest in their settings on the part of performers and public than was generally prevalent at the time. But the effort went to waste. Since then the noblest attempts which the world has seen to give Shakespearean plays an operatic dress have been put forth by two of the finest geniuses of the operatic stage. Boito and Verdi collaborated in " Otello " and Falstaff." Tendencies and methods which were only beginning to ripen in the days of Goetz,

* See the author's " Chapters of Opera." New York: Henry Holt and Co.

who died without having seen the success of his masterpiece, have reached a marvelous fruition and yet the problem of a Shakespearean opera in English has not been solved and nothing can be more obvious than the fact that its solution waits upon the coming of a great musical dramatist born to the English manner.

The German book of "The Taming of the Shrew" is an admirable piece of operatic work; but it is Shakespearean only in its externals. Perhaps not even in these, for it uses only the framework of the plot which the English poet himself borrowed. So much of the humor as could be preserved by the chief incidents of the comedy's action, its satirical purpose and a few of its psychological elements, have found their way into the opera; but all have suffered a sea-change. In part the transformation was the inevitable consequence of the introduction of music. The swift movement of comedy is necessarily clogged by music, as I have often argued. The witty verbal plays of the original had to go by the board in a literary paraphrase and the effervescent vitality of the play's people had to be submerged in the music. Widmann did not attempt to translate Shakespeare's play. He took the characteristic scenes between the shrew and her rude tamer as he found them, set them off for musical as well as dramatic purposes against the secondary plot of Bianca's wooing of Lucentio and Hortensio, and invented new speeches for all, going to his original only for suggestions. In a way he may be said to apply an emollient to the characters of Katharine and Petruchio. The former is more plainly conquered by her love for the masterful man in the German libretto than in the English comedy, and the latter has a loftier motive for his uncouth courtship. After the first encounter between the two, Shakespeare's Katharine thinks of Petruchio only as "one-half lunatic, a madcap ruffian, and a swearing Jack that thinks with oaths to face the matter out"; but the German Katharine has already lost her heart when Petruchio rapes her lips of the first kiss. Till then she has shown none of the weaknesses which may be discovered in Shakespeare's heroine—her susceptibility to flattery, her vanity—she would not have Petrucio even think that she limps in her walk, and she can not withstand the allurement of promised finery. But now that she has found a man whom she can not outface she confesses that her heart is already lost to him. It is the first of her songs which is not accompanied by a musical tempest, of which there is much too much in Goetz's score, that betrays the fact. She is sorely torn between conflicting passions when she confesses to herself that, though she would like to tear him in pieces, she would yet like to call him her own; that so long as he draws breath she needs must hate him, and if he were dead she could not hate him; that if she had bow and arrow she would shoot him dead and call him back to life with tears of love. This is a pretty touch of the librettist, and the composer has emphasized its significance by recurring to the fundamental motive of the song when at the last Katharine confesses her love for Petruchio, which she does frankly, open-heartedly, unreservedly, instead of veiling it under a speech of wifely submission as Shakespeare's shrew does. Shakespeare's Petruchio is not half so bad as he sounds. We suspect that, though he starts out with the appearance of being a mercenary wretch, bent only on "wiving it wealthily at Padua," he puts on most of the antic disposition after he has caught sight of the beauteous Katharine and that she inspires him with an admiration quite likely to develop into something more passionate and loftier. Mr. Furnival says of him in his introduction to the comedy that "he is one of those men who like a bit of devil in the girl he marries and the mare he rides." The German librettist is not willing to leave Petruchio's real feelings to surmise. His man has met the lady before and loves her; the corrective motive of his ruffianly behavior is to win her love, for he sees through her nature, and fit her to be the helpmeet of a man of the world who recognizes that the time is come for him to settle down to a life of quiet domesticity. When she confesses her love and defeat he is quite as ready as she to join in a conventional operatic duet. On this duet the stage-manager closed the last curtain, but librettist and composer bring in all the other characters that they may express their wonderment at the shrew's conversion.

The other characters in the play underwent no changes at the hands of the opera-makers, though Mr. Goritz, unable apparently to withstand his desire to create a laugh, indulged in some foolish horse-play and thus outraged the character of Baptista and spoiled some of Goetz's music. Lucentio, in the hands of Mr. Sembach, was also robbed of some of the dignity which it might have preserved along with its native sentimentality. Grumio is little more than a voice in the musical ensemble, but the Tailor is turned into a Frenchman speaking German with an accent to meet the German conception of humor. This conception finds expression in a pairing of much boisterous music with the boisterous conduct of Petruchio. Goetz's score is frequently beautiful, frequently graceful (in a German way), and always scholarly and refined. What it lacks from beginning to end is the true *vis comica,* the lightness of touch, the effervescent sparkle essential to comedy. What I said of it thirty years before seems sufficiently apposite to be repeated:

> It is polite music which occasionally threatens to carry off the play on a flood of excitement, but at the critical moment retires with an apology for the intrusion and finds entire satisfaction in flowing along between flower-embroidered lyrical banks, rippling entrancingly as it goes, but scarcely floating the comedy which it should buoyantly uphold. Yet it is noble music, the creation of an artist fully conscious of the changed relations of book and music since the decadence of Italian singsong, and most erudite in his handling of the elements of composition.

It cannot be amiss to call attention to some of the unquestioned beauties of the score. Lucentio's serenade at the beginning is a gracious bit of melody which flows easily and charmingly into the love-duet with Bianca after the first interruption of Baptista's servants in revolt. Hortensio is also provided with a serenade, but an instrumental one in which the character of the band and the style of the music recalls the kind of compositions which were variously called serenades, divertimenti, and cassationi in the time of Mozart and Haydn. The duet between Hortensio and Lucentio is one of the few instances in which the comedy style is approached—capital throughout. The heavy Teutonic hand does not appear until Petruchio's entrance, and with him come occasional intimations that it is something only a little less than the crack of doom that is impending. Goetz's orchestra takes Petruchio's masquerading altogether too seriously, and the song in which Katharine first discloses that the blind boy's bow-shaft has struck her comes as a welcome relief to the orchestral turmoil. Petruchio's song, which ends the act, is from Wagner of the " Lohengrin " vintage. The entire scene of Lucentio's instruction of Bianca in Latin and Hortensio's music lesson is delightful in its ingenuity and musical effectiveness. Widmann has Lucentio affect to translate the opening lines of Virgil's " Æneid " instead of the verses from Ovid's " Epistolæ Heroidum " which served Shakespeare's turn, and when the operatic Hortensio teaches Bianca the gamut he does so in a song in which, like Guido d'Arezzo's " Hymn of St. John " (" Ut queant laxis "), every line begins on a consecutive note of the scale ascending. The concluding duet, with its significant echo of Katharine's soul-conflict, in the second act is good dramatic music, if somewhat too tragic for the situation. There are suggestions of Wagner which militate against the conviction of Goetz's originality as a melodist, but the method throughout is Wagner in his " Lohengrin " period rather than that of " Die Meistersinger." The system of leading motives is not employed, and that of reminiscent phrases sparingly.

The record of the next season, 1916-17, was more extraordinary than praiseworthy from the artistic point of view which I have labored to uphold as against that of mere, sheer physical accomplishment. But the world is growing more and more strenuous in proportion as it seems to conservative observers to be growing more indifferent to excellence in any field of art. From November 13, 1916, to April 21, 1917, there was not a single secular day on which the singers and orchestral musicians of the Metropolitan Opera House were not employed in operatic representations. As for the orchestra, there was no respite even on Sundays. Seven operatic performances a week was the rule, and to make this practicable there had to be sixteen visits to Philadelphia and eleven to Brooklyn. There is no operatic institution in the world of the Metropolitan Opera Company's pretensions to artistic dignity which would not think such a labor not only monstrous, but destructive of good art. In European opera houses—like that of Dresden, for instance—so much consideration is had for the players of the woodwind instruments that, as Herr Schuch told me when he visited New York in the Conried period, an oboe player was never expected to play two days in succession. But even seven performances a week did not suffice the management. Thirteen times in the season there were eight performances a week, and in the second week of February nine besides the Sunday concert. Under such circumstances is it to be wondered at that many of the representations were marked by lassitude and many more by perfunctoriness? The wonder is, rather, that there were not frequent breakdowns of the huge machine into which the company had been developed.

I can not but believe that the season was financially more successful than any of its predecessors under the management of Mr. Gatti; but it was not greater in artistic achievement. In this respect it fell short of that of the first year of the war. In that season there were 151 opera performances in New York City against 149 in the season now in

NEW OPERAS AND REVIVALS 361

mind. The attempt made in the latter year to freshen the repertory was energetic and commendable; but even in this regard the season was not quite the equal of that of 1913-14, when five absolute novelties were brought forward. There were six works in the repertory of 1916-17 which had not been heard before at the Metropolitan Opera House under Mr. Gatti's management; but of the six only four were new to the New York public. The real novelties were " Les Pêcheurs de Perles," " Iphigenia auf Tauris," " Francesca da Rimini," and an English, or American, opera, " The Canterbury Pilgrims." " Thaïs," though new to the Metropolitan repertory, had been heard in an earlier day at the Manhattan Opera House, while " Lakmé " had been performed at the Metropolitan by Mme. Patti and her company at a special season in April, 1890, and afterward formed a feature of the regular seasons of 1891-92 and 1906-07. It also had one performance at the Manhattan Opera House in March, 1910. The predecessors in the titular rôle of Mme. Barrientos were Mme. Patti, Miss Van Zandt, Miss Nevada, Mme. Sembrich, and Mme. Tetrazzini. Bizet's " Pêcheurs de Perles " must be set down as having made a complete fiasco. It was performed three times between the opening night and December 13, but never again. Gluck's " Iphigenia " and Reginald De Koven's " Canterbury Pilgrims " ran the complete gamut of subscription meetings and were given an extra representation besides. Mr. De Koven's opera received greater consideration than that given to any of its predecessors before or since, but was then shelved in spite of the changed situation brought about by the succeeding year. Righteously from an artistic point of view, I make no doubt. Zandonai's " Francesca da Rimini " was a brave show, but its musical beauty was largely confined to its first act, in which there was no dramatic interest, and to its spectacular interest to the second, in which the music was reduced to its lowest estate. Particularly disappointing was the scene of the reading of the

Arthurian romance, which, of all the scenes of the play, calls most loudly for sensuous beauty and lofty passion of musical expression. Gluck's "Iphigenia auf Tauris," though beautifully mounted and performed with evident sincerity, failed to make a deep enough impression to justify the expectation that it would remain a fixture in the Metropolitan repertory. Some of the reasons were obvious from the beginning. The work, which is one of the finest examples of French classicism, was too much Teutonized, not only in its language, but also in the manner of its performance. If it was impracticable to perform it in French, it ought to have been given in English; but for English performances such as this work calls for the Metropolitan company had not been made ready. A translation into the vernacular would have done no greater violence to the genius of the French language as Gluck conserved it in his setting than did the German; and we might have been spared some of the bad vocalization with which we were frequently overwhelmed in this and previous seasons.

Before proceeding with the story of other incidents of the operatic season in New York let me dispose of the Metropolitan's novelties. The first was Bizet's "Les Pêcheurs de Perles," which was given on the opening night, November 13, 1916. The performance was conducted by Giorgio Polacco, and the characters in the opera were thus distributed:

Léila .... Frieda Hempel
Nadir .... Enrico Caruso
Zuriga .... Giuseppe de Luca
Nourabad .... Léon Rothier

It was officially given out by the management of the Metropolitan Company that the opera, save for the first two acts, in which Mme. Calvé had once sung the part of Léila, was new to this country. Statements of this kind are often lightly but honestly made, and I am not inclined to attach a large measure of obliquity to them when they prove to be er-

Enrico Caruso
In "Les Pêcheurs de Perles"

roneous. Who can know all about the doings of the opera companies which spring up in America overnight? Companies are wrecked annually in South America, Cuba, and Mexico. Their flotsam and jetsam are cast upon the shores of the United States. Hunger and desperation drive the singers into the hands of a manager—and lo! somewhere there appear flamboyant announcements of the coming of a Royal, or Imperial, or Milanese, or La Scala Grand Opera Company which gives performances in the metropolis for two or three days, or even one week, and sinks again into the bubbling depths. Opera companies came and went on the East Side of New York ever and anon during the decade whose story I am trying to tell, and for aught I know to the contrary Bizet's divers for pearls may have fished in local waters under my very nose without my getting a whiff of their activities. It would be a useless book which should seek to give an account of them. Permanency in the repertory, or what passes for such in the operatic world, is only gained by performances by organizations which maintain a local habitation and a name. Many French operas which New Yorkers only learned to know in the period of which I have tried to be the historian were familiar as household words to the patrons of the French Opera in New Orleans when they reached New York.

Twenty-five or more years ago the critics of New York whose knowledge of new operas could not be satisfied at home occasionally ran over to Philadelphia, where the Hinrichs Grand Opera Company was wont to shake a novelty out of its sleeve every week or two. From Mr. Hinrichs and his industrious singers came our first knowledge of "Cavalleria Rusticana," "Pagliacci," "L'Amico Fritz," "Manon Lescaut," and several other operas, and it was at the Grand Opera House in Philadelphia on August 25, 1893, that "Les Pêcheurs de Perles" had what may have been its first performance in America, with such well-known singers as Guille and Campanari in the cast. If the performance of two acts of the opera on January 11, 1896, did not find firm lodgment in the minds of the Metropolitan's patrons the fact need not cause much wonderment. The acts were precipitated on the stage to oblige Mme. Calvé and to serve as a curtain-raiser for "La Navarraise," a blood-curdling little opera which the lady sang and acted in so realistic a manner as to send her audience home to nightmares instead of restful sleep. Afterward it was because Mme. Sembrich wanted to sing Léila's airs that the two acts were given and then put away among forgotten things until Mr. Gatti dragged them forth again to make a holiday for Signor Caruso and Mme. Hempel. No doubt it was because Mme. Tetrazzini had produced the opera in 1904 in San Francisco.

But it was not necessary to impute such purely transient motives to Mr. Gatti for including the opera in his repertory in the season now reviewing. Partly it may have been because it had become almost a mania for managers to rummage among the early works of composers who had achieved a masterpiece in the hope of finding among them some of the stepping-stones which had led to the higher things. Such a proceeding is always fraught with danger. It implies an extravagant estimate of every excellency which may be found in the work, to say nothing of a reflection on the judgment of contemporary criticism. Had there been no "Carmen," it is not likely that we should ever have heard of "Les Pêcheurs de Perles" after it had had its trial and been found wanting in Paris. "La Jolie Fille de Perth" and "Djamileh" came later; there has been no thought of producing them here, though it is reasonable to suppose that they are riper products of Bizet's genius.

In the case of Mr. Gatti's exhibition of interest in the work it is probable that an amiable bias in favor of Italian opera led to the belief that "Les Pêcheurs" bears evidence to a spiritual affiliation between Bizet, a representative French composer, and Verdi, the highest embodiment of the best modern Italian manner. On Bizet's return to Paris after his sojourn in Rome as a winner of the government's finest prize he belonged to the coterie of musicians that contemned the Conservatoire and its methods and lauded Wagner—Wagner and Verdi. To Jouvin, who refused to swing the censer under the nose of the great German, Bizet once said: " You love Verdi's music? Very well; Wagner is Verdi with style!" Now there is nothing inconsistent in liking or even in loving the music of both Wagner and Verdi; but it seems to me to require a great stretch of the imagination to find either Verdism or Wagnerism in the music of " Les Pêcheurs de Perles " or even " Carmen." The dramatic language of the latter where it is most eloquent is most individually Bizetesque. The dramatic language of the former, of which there is little, is a hotchpotch of empiricism. It ranges from Hérold through Gounod to Meyerbeer and Verdi at their worst. We think of both of the latter two in the finale of the first act (" Dans le ciel " and " Ah, chante, chante encore "), which is about the paltriest music to which the walls of the Metropolitan have resounded, except at a Lambs' gambol. We have a premonition of " Carmen " in the cavatina of the first act (" Comme autrefois dans la nuit sombre "), even down to the horn melody, but it is only because both cavatina and Micaëla's romance belong to a type with the creation of which Bizet had nothing to do, and because for the time being the chaste priestess of the earlier opera slips into the skin of the insipid maiden of the later, who was created only that there might be a little admixture of virtue in the viciousness of the fierce Spanish story.

Had there been the faintest stirring of the genius which created " Carmen " in Bizet when he was writing " Les Pêcheurs "—anything beyond the love of an occasional piquancy of harmonization or orchestration—it is inconceivable that he would have undertaken to set so commonplace and foolish a play as this. He who treated local color in so masterly a manner in " Carmen " and " L'Arlésienne " does not seem even to have taken the trouble to study the palette of Félicien David while setting an Oriental story. His efforts at Orientalism are almost infantile and show maturity only in the ballet music of the last act, which he wrote—so, at least, it is said—for the opera " Noé " of his father-in-law, Halévy, though why antediluvian women should have danced like Gaditanian I do not know. The recurrence ever and anon of a melody (slightly suggestive of the " Ave Maria " wrongly accredited to Arcadelt) which is associated with the love of Léila and Nadir, and which is ecstatically sung by the lovers when they leave the scene for the last time, was probably considered *Wagnerisme* when it was first heard; but such dramatic reminiscences were an old device when Wagner set out on his career as a composer.

The story of " Lakmé " has a bit of " Norma " in it in that a vestal virgin is discovered to be not all that a vestal virgin should be, though Léila does not seem to have gone to the extreme of the Druidic priestess. She, who has sworn not to love a man or show her face to one, is discovered to have loved the tenor and to have been loved by both him and the baritone. Wherefore the implacable Ceylonese pearl-fishers to whom she has to bring luck by singing in the Meyerbeerian manner condemn her to death by fire. Their chief, however, who is the sworn friend of her lover, though his rival, discovers at the last moment by means of a string of beads (like those of the blind woman in " Gioconda ") that she had once saved his life. So to save hers he sets fire to a village and tells her and her lover to run away from there while the Ceylonese are saving their household goods. They escape slowly to the opera's *Leitmotif*. Books and stage-managers do not agree as to what happens after that. Originally, I believe, the Ceylonese, wanting to burn somebody, burn Zurga, their chief, who had been *particeps criminis* in the escape. But at the Metropolitan performance Nourabad, the high-priest, put a knife into Nadir's back, which seemed as good a way as any to bring the curtain down.

Gluck's "Iphigenia auf Tauris" (to adopt its German title) was brought forward at an afternoon performance under the direction of Mr. Bodanzky on November 25, 1916, with the people of the play represented as follows:

Diana	Marie Rappold
Iphigenia	Melanie Kurt
Orestes	Hermann Weil
Pylades	Johannes Sembach
Thoas	Carl Braun
First Priestess	Marie Sundelius
Second Priestess	Alice Eversman
A Temple Attendant	Robert Leonhardt
A Greek Slave	Leonora Sparkes

The lyric drama of today, as it reflects the careless tastes and idle desires of the times, is immeasurably distant from the tragedy with music as Gluck conceived it; yet note a fact of big and lovely purport: for half an hour of this representation a matinee audience of whose character I have been inclined to make light sat spellbound—not like a gathering of pleased pleasure-seekers, but more like a congregation of religious worshipers—listening to songs and witnessing a mimicking of ancient rites connected with the consecration of a human sacrifice; listening, too, to music which a village choir today might think too simple for its consideration and looking upon the pantomimic posturing of a dancer as if upon such song and movement hang everlasting things. And so they do; for in what Iphigenia chanted, the orchestra sang, and Rosina Galli expressed in exquisite pose and eloquent movement in the second act of the opera there lies the essence of all that inspired the drama at its birth and will live in it till its death. I must assume a reasonable familiarity on the part of the reader with the antique story of Iphigenia as told in the tragedy of Euripides of which the original French tragedy is a paraphrase. For those who do not know it—or, knowing, have no sympathy with its sentiments and teachings—there can be no interest in Gluck's wonderful art-work, which is a perversion of the original, albeit a respectful one; nothing in its music, which is all foreign to the taste of today; nothing in its action, which is simple in the extreme, and little in its scenic outfit, although an American artist, Mr. Monroe Hewlett, had wrought for the play beautiful pictures in a reverent mood. If I have singled out a moment for comment which seemed to me of supremest beauty it is because in it I found the most perfect realization of the classic ideal. In Iphigenia kneeling at the altar in the temple of Diana invoking a blessing upon a deed against which her gentle heart rebelled, pouring out a libation for a brother whom she was unknowingly consecrating to a sacrificial death, while the vestal virgins chanted a requiem and a priestess vitalized speech and tone with gestures of exquisite grace and loveliness, there was a dramatic consummation which put to shame all the efforts that had but recently been made in academic circles to humanize the old tragedy by an attempt to mimic it in the commonplace pose and action of today, and all the choreographic platitudes and conventions of the Ballet Russe which had for a period become a fad. In the things which the audience saw and heard within the significant half-hour they were made conscious of the beauty and eloquence of Hellenic art. Much of the dialogue, Teutonized to the extinction of its declamatory grace and fitness, and much of the song vulgarized by a style foreign to its spirit, could with difficulty be brought into harmony with the genius of the old ritual drama which Gluck and his poet tried to fit to the lyric stage. There was much rude singing, but when, to the exquisite music which Mr. Bodanzky borrowed from "Orfeo," Signora Galli spoke the language of ritual "with woven paces and waving arms" eternal conceptions of beauty and truthfulness were made manifest.

Listeners familiar with the French language regretted that the tragedy was not sung in its original tongue; sticklers for purity in the musical classics deplored that it should have been thought necessary to introduce into the score the sophistications of Richard Strauss, some of which, especially a short chorus at the close of the work, were in bad taste; but every lover of a noble type of lyric drama felt grateful to Mr. Gatti, Mr. Bodanzky, and the German contingent of the Metropolitan company for having enabled them to get acquainted with a work of which it can be said as truthfully as it can of anything of its kind that it was not born to die.

Mr. Gatti's third novelty, " Francesca da Rimini," was presented on December 22, 1916. At this *première* and that of Mr. De Koven's " Canterbury Pilgrims " on March 8, 1917, I was not able to be present because of absence from the city. The former opera, conducted by Giorgio Polacco, had the following cast:

Francesca	Frances Alda
Samaritana	Edith Mason
Istasio	Riccardo Tegani
Giovanni	Pasquale Amato
Paolo	Giovanni Martinelli
Malatestino	Angelo Bada
Biancofiore	Mabel Garrison
Garsenda	Leonora Sparkes
Altichiara	Sophie Braslau
Donella	Raymonde Delannois
A Maid of Honor	Queenie Smith
The Slave	Flora Perini
A Notary	Pietro Audisio
A Jester	Pompilio Malatesta
An Archer	Max Bloch
A Torchbearer	Vincenzo Reschiglian

Of Zandonai's " Conchita " I have spoken at considerable length. The composer had a more attractive subject in this work, but it did not reveal his talent of inventiveness in so favorable a light. I have already spoken of its most noticeable weakness. " Francesca " was first performed at Turin on February 18, 1914, and had a production at Covent Garden, London, on July 16 of the same year. The drama on which the libretto by D'Annunzio was based had been played in America by Eleanora Duse, so there was nothing novel about its treatment of the old theme. It was abridged and adapted by Tito Ricordi, the publisher, but the language was that of the poet. The plot needs be told only in outline: For reasons of state Francesca is to be married to the physically and morally deformed Giovanni Malatesta. Knowing that she would refuse to marry him if she saw him, a trick is played upon her, Giovanni's handsome brother Paolo being passed off upon her as her destined husband. In a second act, during a fight on the battlements of the castle of Malatesti, Francesca reproaches Paolo for the fraud. He protests his innocence and reveals his love, but leaves the place for Florence, where he has been elected Captain of the People. In the third act comes the famous scene as told by Dante, where Paolo and Francesca read together the story of Lancelot and Guinevere. Love overcomes them and their lips meet in their first kiss. In the last act Malatestino, Giovanni's youngest brother, who is also in love with Francesca, betrays Paolo, and the outraged husband kills the lovers while they are enfolded in each other's arms.

"The Canterbury Pilgrims," an English opera by Percy Mackaye and Reginald De Koven, was performed for the first time on March 8, 1917. Mr. Bodanzky conducted, and the cast was as follows:

Chaucer	Johannes Sembach
The Knight	Robert Leonhardt
The Squire	Paul Althouse
The Friar	Max Bloch
The Miller	Basil Ruysdael
The Cook	Pompilio Maletesta
The Shipman	Maria Laurenti
The Summoner	Carl Schlegel
The Pardoner	Julius Bayer
The Host	Giulio Rossi
Man of Law	Robert Leonhardt
Joannes	Pietro Audisio
King Richard II	Albert Reiss
Herald	Riccardo Tegani

Alisoun, The Wife of Bath	Margaret Ober
Margarete, The Prioress	Edith Mason
Johanna	Marie Sundelius
Two Girls	{ Maria Tiffany { Minnie Egener

I shall let the author of the libretto give his own account of how the opera came to be written. Said Mr. Mackaye:

> In writing "The Canterbury Pilgrims" one of my chief incentives was to portray for a modern audience one of the greatest poets of all times in relation to a group of his own characters. As a romancer of prolific imagination and dramatic insight Chaucer stands shoulder to shoulder with Shakespeare. For English speech he achieved what Dante did for Italian, raising a local dialect to a world language. Yet the fourteenth century speech of Chaucer is just archaiac enough to make it difficult to understand in modern times. Consequently his works are little known today except by students of English literature. To make it more popularly known I prepared, a few years ago (with Prof. J. S. P. Tatlock), "The Modern Reader's Chaucer," published by Macmillan; and I wrote for Mr. E. H. Sothern in 1903 my play "The Canterbury Pilgrims," which since then has been acted at many American universities by the Coburn Players and in published form is used in numerous Chaucer classes. In the spring of 1914, at the suggestion of Reginald De Koven, I remodeled the play in the form of opera, condensing in characters to the more simple essentials appropriate to operatic production.

There was also a great deal of thundering in the index touching the new English opera on the part of the composer, and it received remarkable consideration on the part of the management of the Opera House. The conditions of the next season should have been propitious to it had the critical judgment of management, press, and public spoken with sufficient loudness in its favor. But it did not; and the work went the way of much better operatic flesh.

A few incidents of the season which can not be discussed as fully as those connected with the history of the Metropolitan Opera Company remain to be put on record. For a week after November 6, 1916, there were nightly performances of opera by an organization calling itself the Boston

National Grand Opera Company, of which Max Rabinoff was general manager and Roberto Moranzoni principal conductor, at the Lexington Theater, as the house was now called which Mr. Hammerstein had built to be the home of the institution which he had planned to set up in opposition to the Metropolitan Opera House. There were a number of artists in the company who had established themselves in good repute and some of whom, like the conductor, later joined Mr. Gatti's forces. The operas performed were "Andrea Chenier," "Madama Butterfly," "L'Amore dei tre Re," "Iris," and La Bohème." Cursory comment on such seasons have sometimes been made in these memoirs, but oftener omitted, since they exerted no permanent influence upon operatic development in New York at least, whatever they may have accomplished in other parts of the country.

An enterprise which disclosed idealistic aims quite beyond the ordinary had preceded it by a short time, having been called into existence by Mr. Albert Reiss and other artists who had the promotion of a national art as their purpose. Under Mr. Reiss's management and the musical direction of Mr. Sam Franko, a pair of performances was given at the New Empire Theater to Mozart's youthful opera, "Bastien et Bastienne," in an English version by A. Mattulath, and to an operetta called "The Impresario," whose music dated from the heyday of Mozart's genius and which had been woven into an amiably satirical comedy by the writer of these memoirs. The singers concerned in these performances were Miss Mabel Garrison, Miss Lucy Gates, Mr. Reiss, and David Bispham. Out of this experiment, which proved phenomenally successful, there grew a Society of American Singers, which in the following May gave a longer season at the Lyceum Theater. By this time an organization had been effected on a co-operative basis which enlisted a number of excellent artists and to the two Mozart pieces were added English versions of Gounod's "Le

Médecin malgré lui" ("The Mock Doctor"), Pergolesi's "La Serva padrona" ("The Maid Mistress"), and Donizetti's "Il Campanello" ("The Night Bell"). In the season 1818-19 the organization, now under the presidency of William Wade Hinshaw, gave a season from early fall till spring at the Park Theater; but its personnel had meanwhile undergone a change as had also its ideals. It became an English opera company of the type with which the country has been familiar for generations, and its financial integrity was saved by a reversion to performances of the operettas of Gilbert and Sullivan.

A vast amount of puzzled comment was mingled in the newspapers with enthusiastic praise which greeted the production of the two thitherto unknown works of Mozart at the New Empire Theater. Why had this music, which proved to be so charming, never been heard in public in New York before? The answer was not difficult. Comparatively only an infinitesimal portion of the music which Mozart composed in his short life has survived in our theaters and concert-rooms. Of his forty-nine symphonies only three are familiar,—though there are others which the public could and would enjoy if opportunity offered. Two or three of his seventeen string quartets are in the repertories of our chamber music organizations. A Papal edict has banished his masses from the Catholic church, and it was the irony of fate that the most popular of these compositions, "Mozart's Great Mass in C" as it was called, was not his composition at all but a clever piece of music made, I believe, in England, to which a conscienceless publisher attached Mozart's name. Amateur players delight in a few of his sonatas for violin, and pianoforte teachers prescribe two or three of his pianoforte sonatas for young pupils. Of his twenty-three operas we know more or less well three: "Don Giovanni," "Le Nozze di Figaro," and "Die Zauberflöte." The Mozart tradition is departing from our stage, nor will it return until popular taste compels a reform in the manner of writing for the voice and greater thoroughness in vocal instruction.

Several reasons might be found for the absence from the local stage of the work which was performed under the title of "The Impresario." "The Impresario" is not an opera at all, though it is always listed among Mozart's operatic compositions. Its music for the greater part is incidental music for a comedy containing a scene in which two opera singers, after being engaged by a distracted theatrical manager, fall to quarreling about their rank in the company, each insisting that she is the prima donna. This number, turned into a trio by the introduction of a buffo tenor who seeks to make peace between the women, is the gem of the work and the immediate cause of its preservation for the stage. The other music composed for the original comedy consists of the overture, two arias in which the singers exhibit their skill, and a finale for three voices in which there is a preachment touching the attitude which artists ought to assume toward each other for the good of art. The comedy would not bear reviving, though I believe it was attempted fifty years ago in an English version which was performed a few times at the Crystal Palace.

When Louis Schneider created the operetta which is current in Germany under the title "Der Schauspieldirektor," he used all of the original music and supplemented it with three songs and another trio of Mozart's composition; and these were orchestrated by Taubert. The plot of Schneider's operetta, in which Mozart was introduced along with Schikaneder, was used as a basis by the maker of the book for the operetta as produced by Mr. Reiss, though the English author proceeded with a free hand in the construction of the dialogue, aiming to direct its satirical shafts at some of the idiosyncrasies of opera people as they seem always to have existed, exist today, and will probably continue to exist *in sæcula sæculorum*. He also presented a few historical elements, including the circumstance that Mozart and Schikaneder were compelled by one of their rivals to change the plot of " Die Zauberflöte " on which they are supposed to be at work in the progress of the comedy. Mr. Krehbiel also made historical people out of the women of the play. The success of the first performance was so instantaneous and emphatic that before Mr. Reiss had left the theater he was overwhelmed by demands for a greater number of performances and arranged some for the following week at the Garrick Theater.

CHAPTER XV

CONCERT MUSIC AND THE OPERA IN WAR-TIME

GRADUAL CHANGE IN SENTIMENT AFTER THE OUTBREAK OF HOSTILITIES—MR. BODANZKY—A BOYCOTT DECLARED BY GERMANY AGAINST AMERICAN OPERA HOUSES — ENGAGING GERMAN SINGERS IN THE OLDEN TIME—DRAW-POKER AS AN EMOLLIENT—FIRST DEMONSTRATIONS OF PATRIOTIC FEELING AT THE METROPOLITAN—THE QUESTION OF ENEMY ALIENS IN THE COMPANY—HANS TAUSCHER AND HIS WIFE MME. GADSKI—A PLEA FOR NATIVE SINGERS—CHANGES IN THE CONCERT-FIELD—FOREIGN ARTISTS—KUNWALD AND MUCK INTERNED—A TAX ON ENTERTAINMENTS—THE OPERA PROSPECTUS FOR 1917-18—DISMISSAL OF GERMAN SINGERS— THE HISTORICAL NARRATIVE RESUMED—A VISIT FROM THE CHICAGO COMPANY—ITS NOVELTIES—" ISABEAU "—" AZORA "—" LE SAUTERIOT "—MME. GALLI-CURCI—NEW WORKS AT THE METROPOLITAN—" MARÔUF "—" SAINT ELIZABETH "—" LODOLETTA "—A REVIVAL OF " LE PROPHÈTE "—" LE COQ D'OR "—" SHANEWIS "—WHAT OF THE FUTURE?

THE United States did not become embroiled in the war until within a fortnight of the end of the third season after the beginning of the universal upheaval. During these seasons, after the first flurry of financial apprehension and the slight reorganization to which I alluded in the preceding chapter of these memoirs, for which the general condition of affairs offered occasion if not an excuse, there was no appreciable change of policy on the part of the management of the Metropolitan Opera Company and nothing in the attitude of the public to suggest the need of one. The repertories were predominantly Italian, but the dramas of Wagner had more numerous representation than those of any other composer and were relied on particularly for the performances outside of the subscription because of their attractive power with the general public. The list of Ger-

THE COMING OF MR. BODANZKY

man singers was kept full and received a few acquisitions. Mr. Artur Bodanzky, a new German conductor, came in 1915-16, though his coming had nothing to do with war conditions. He came to replace Mr. Alfred Hertz, who at the end of the preceding season had resigned a post which he had held for thirteen years. To bring Mr. Bodanzky, an Austrian, from Mannheim, where he was conductor of the Opera, required the consent of both the British and French governments, which was obtained without difficulty through diplomatic channels. By the end of the season, I am told, he had made up his mind that his future home should be America and though he was forced to face an emotional ordeal when a popular demonstration in the midst of a performance greeted the intelligence that President Wilson had asked the Congress of the United States to declare that a state of war existed between our country and Germany, he did not flinch but conducted an impromptu performance of " The Star-Spangled Banner." Mme. Destinn, absent from the season of 1915-16, returned for the next. To the standard list of German operas, which included all of Wagner's works from " Tannhäuser " to " Parsifal " inclusive, there were no additions which could be reckoned as significant, but no subtractions. Goetz's " Der Widerspänstigen Zähmung " (" The Taming of the Shrew ") was toyed with rather half-heartedly, I thought, in the season of 1915-16 and Gluck's French " Iphigénie en Tauride " was performed in German in the next season. All this with appropriately illuminating gloss already has been set forth in this book. The important point to be kept in view is that the German operas not only kept their places in the first three years of the war but also their predominance in the popular representations. There was some falling off in the subscriptions but no complaint of a large loss in general receipts. That was accounted for by the widespread prosperity brought to some classes of the population by the war. In the next season the loss in subscriptions was much larger owing to the departure from the city of many subscribers and the loss by death suffered in the families of the wealthy supporters of the institution.

A change, however, was impending, and though it may have had no influence upon either management or public an incident, the first in the summer which followed the entrance of the United States into the war, to which public attention was drawn deserves to be recalled here, if for no other reason than to throw light upon that strange thing called German psychology, which came up often for discussion in the progress of German military and diplomatic methods.

While Mr. Gatti was resting in undisturbed contemplation of a coming season like that which had ended in April, 1917, there came an intimation that Germany was preparing to prevent her singers from having that "place in the sun" which engagements at the Metropolitan Opera House offered them. In the first days of June of that year there was a meeting of the German Stage Society, as the cable dispatches described it, at which without a dissenting vote a resolution offered by Count Seebach, director of the Royal Theater at Dresden, was unanimously adopted which bound the members of the society to grant no leave of absence to any singer who wished to go to America and not to engage any singer who accepted an American contract, the agreement to last for five years. The action, Count Seebach said, had nothing to do with the war, but was only a measure of self-protection on the part of German theaters. In fact, he professed to want it understood as directed against German artists rather than American managers. It was intolerable, he said, that German artists after having been trained in their own country should at the maturity of their powers make themselves over to American contractors, spend their best years abroad, and come back to Germany with an accession of conceit as well, I suppose, of dollars. Artists should therefore be compelled to chose between America and Germany. Frankly he admitted that no injury could result to

ARTUR BODANZKY
Conductor at the Metropolitan Opera House

German influence in America, for Germany no longer had any influence there and it would be vain to try to win Americans by civilities and sentimentalities. There had not as yet been the slightest exhibition of hostility toward German art in America, and the German singers were as indifferent as was the management of the Metropolitan to the Berlin pronunciamento. Mr. Edward Ziegler, the executive secretary of the Metropolitan Company, declared the action to be purely academic, inasmuch as it did not affect the German singers of the company whose contracts had not expired while those whose contracts had expired would be glad to renew them, since they would be unable to return to their homes so long as the war lasted.

The matter was left to repose on the knees of the gods, and there it still lies. I recall the incident partly to indicate how liberal was the American attitude toward the German operas and German singers, as latė as two months after the United States had formally declared that a state of war existed between herself and Germany and because I want to tell the story of a boycott similar to that declared by the German managers against German singers who came to New York and its consequences thirty years before. If the tale is not particularly relevant to the present history, it is at least diverting and somewhat illuminative of the ethics of German managers. It was an open secret during the seven years of the German régime at the Metropolitan Opera House that though the laws of the German *Cartellverband* were stringent as against the breaking of contracts singers who wanted to accept engagements in New York found no difficulty in doing so. Mr. Edmund Stanton, who acted for the owners of the Metropolitan, had a plan which worked to a charm. He engaged the singers from the *Intendanten* and *Direktoren,* royal and municipal officials, direct, and paid salaries of such generous proportions that the officials could retain a large percentage for themselves and yet leave the lure large enough to attract the singers that Mr. Stanton wanted. Only two of the singers ever suffered in consequence. Emil Fischer, the original representative of Hans Sachs in America (and, as old admirers of "Die Meistersinger" think, the best), who spent his last years in New York, was engaged by Mr. Stanton before his plan had been evolved. He had to begin legal proceedings against the King of Saxony when on his return to Germany he sought reinstatement as a member of the Court Theater at Dresden. Whether or not he won his case I do not remember, but our opera having been Italianized he became a theater manager in Holland until he felt again the irresistible call to New York. Mme. Lilli Lehmann broke her contract with the Royal Opera at Berlin and of her own volition paid the prescribed penalty, or *conventional Strafe*. Nevertheless she was boycotted by the *Cartellverband* for several years until the Royal Intendant found that the Opera's need of her was greater than her need of the Opera.

Apropos of Mr. Stanton's methods, it used to be told with amusement by some of the inner brotherhood in the days of the German régime that the American director, in order to become *persona grata* to his German confrères, used to play draw-poker with them with an understanding between himself and his American companions, who were also associates in the New York enterprise, to permit themselves to be bluffed out by their adversaries or to bet heavily on weak hands. It was some time before Mr. Stanton learned that Count Perfall, of Munich, was as keen a hand at the game as any of the Americans and could hold his own in the winning without having the latter generously throw the game to him. They only added to the percentage which came his way when the contracts were signed.

Considering the popular indignation at the manner in which Germany, arrogantly confident of victory, conducted her warfare from the beginning of hostilities it is almost inconceivable now that the public permitted three seasons to

THE ABSENCE OF CHAUVINISM 381

pass by without a word of protest against the artistic policy of the management. It is a record of honor. Not even the unparalleled outrage against humanity exemplified in the sinking of the steamship *Lusitania* with her hundreds of innocent men, women, and children created a chauvinistic feeling among the music-lovers against German art. It was not for want of patriotism. That fact was made plain by a demonstration which followed the receipt of the intelligence that the President of the United States had asked Congress to take action recognizing that a state of war existed between Germany and the United States. The news was brought into the audience-room of the opera house in the midst of a performance of " The Canterbury Pilgrims." It came just before the third act. Immediately a wave of excitement rose which quickly ran through the audience and broke in a foaming crest when the orchestra, conducted by Mr. Bodanzky, played the melody of " The Star-Spangled Banner." Mr. James W. Gerard, who, as ambassador at the Kaiser's court, had heard the threat of the unspeakable Hohenzollern that after he had finished with his then enemies he would " have no more nonsense from the United States," arose in a box and called for cheers for the President. They were given with a roar and followed by cheers for the American army and navy and calls for " La Marseillaise." Mme. Ober, who had come on the stage in the character of The Woman of Bath, was overcome with emotion and had to be carried off the stage by her German colleague, Johannes Sembach, who was impersonating Chaucer. Yet on the afternoon of Good Friday, April 6, when Congress adopted the momentous resolution which eventually sealed the fate of Germany, Wagner's " Parsifal " was listened to as decorously and reverently as ever it had been and within the few remaining days of the season there were representations of " Die Meistersinger," " Tristan und Isolde," and " Iphigenia auf Tauris " which awakened not a word of protest.

The nation was seething with excitement, but the season of 1916-17 closed with an unofficial announcement that in 1917-18 German opera would again be in the repertory and be sung by German singers in the language native to them and the works. Against the first contention I could then feel no desire to raise a voice of objection; nor do I now. It was in accord with American notions of fair play as well as with the lofty artistic principles which had always been professed and to a large extent practised at the Metropolitan Opera House, that the beautiful and good in art had neither geographical nor political boundaries. That German art should be recognized as generously as Italian (though it never had been), and as French, English, and American ought to be, seemed obvious to every fair-minded lover of music. There had never been a spirit of artistic chauvinism in the United States, nor did there seem to be a place for it in a nation which in matter if not in spirit represented an amalgam of all the peoples of the civilized world. The plan which gave recognition to all schools of composition and presented their products so far as possible in the languages in which they were created seemed not only wise but even imperative in an institution of such magnitude and dignity as the Metropolitan Opera Company.

But now the question arose: did a liberal policy toward German art as exemplified in its creations carry with it a continued obligation to German artists who were become alien enemies? As a rule the conduct of the members of the German contingent in the Metropolitan company had been unexceptionable during the period of the country's neutrality. There were exceptions, and around two of these a storm had blown up before the United States had become a belligerent country. One of these was Mme. Gadski. Her husband, Hans Tauscher, who, during her many years of service at the Opera (she had come to America to join Mr. Walter Damrosch's company in 1895 and had belonged to the Metropolitan forces since 1900-01), had been an active agent of German manufacturers of military arms—the Mauser and Krupp companies. Tauscher had been an officer in the German army, but was obliged to resign his commission by reason of having married a woman of the stage contrary to the German military rules, or the etiquette of the German military courts. His relation to the German army after that was that of a reservist. At the outbreak of the war he was in Germany and, as he told his friends in New York, had immediately offered his military services to his country, but they had been declined because he could be of greater service in another, and unexplained, capacity. Earlier than in any preceding year he appeared in New York, having escaped capture by the British by sailing as a minor officer on a Dutch steamship. In the summer of 1916 he was arrested by officers of the Secret Service of the United States on the charge of having violated the laws of the country in conspiring with agents of the German Government to wreck the Welland Canal. On his trial General Crozier, Chief of Ordnance of the United States Army, was guilty of the amazing indiscretion, to make use of mild and diplomatic language, of sending a letter to the Federal Judge who was trying his case. The letter was ruled out as incompetent evidence (it was a certificate of character) but not until after it had been read to the jury. Two of General Crozier's aides also testified to the general good character of the prisoner, and Tauscher was acquitted. Nevertheless the prosecuting attorney of the United States denounced him in open court as one who had escaped punishment because of the credulity of the jury that had tried the case. Protests against Mme. Gadski's appearance at the Opera poured in to the management and the newspapers. She continued her activities, however, appearing at the Opera for the last time on April 13, a week after the United States had entered the war, and was cordially greeted at her farewell performance, which was in "Tristan und Isolde." When Count von Bernsdorff, Germany's ambassador to the

United States, having received his passports, sailed for Europe Tauscher sailed with him. In connection with another member of the company the story was told that at a convivial gathering on New Year's Eve, 1916, held in Mme. Gadski's home a parody on a popular romance from "Der Trompeter von Säkkingen" had been sung containing sarcastic allusions to the fate of the Americans who had gone down with the torpedoed *Lusitania*.

Mr. Gatti did not wait till the end of the season before permitting it to become known that Mme. Gadski would not be a member of the next season's company, but his intention to continue an unchanged policy with reference to repertory and singers remained unaltered. While I believed at the time, and still believe, that there should be no elimination of operas from the Metropolitan Opera House simply because they were composed by Germans, so far as the recruiting of the company was concerned I thought that the time was come for a more generous treatment of native artists than had been hitherto practised. The changed conditions brought about by the war had placed upon the management an obligation toward our own people which, if fulfilled, might advance native art more rapidly than any amount of listening to foreign singers. There were many American artists singing in German theaters in the early months of the war, because they found there opportunities to gain a routine in their profession which was denied them in our proud establishment accustomed to pick what it wanted from the talent of the world. Many of these singers would be thrown back upon our shores by the new conditions, and it seemed to me that they were entitled to consideration to the full amount of their artistic ability. By recruiting its forces from these artists it was obvious that the way would be paved for a fitting representation of English and American operas in the repertory. When the contest between the champions of Italian and German opera was raging in the early period of the Metropolitan's existence, *The Tribune* newspaper stood up stoutly in favor of the German form of the art not because of a want of appreciation of Italian and French art but because it saw a needed education toward seriousness in the popular attitude towards the lyric drama which the broader and more cosmopolitan attitude of the German régime then under the direction of the owners of the opera house themselves would advance but which a one-sided Italian policy would not promote. It also saw in German opera a bridge over which opera in the vernacular might come into the artistic economy of the country. In a retrospect of the season 1888-89 I wrote:

> In the nature of things the United States must soon follow the example of France, Germany, and Russia and establish a national opera, or opera which like the drama shall use the vernacular. From German opera to opera in English, the step is feasible; from Italian opera dependent on compositions which have no consonance with the dramatic taste of the American people and the present time, the step is impossible. Progress in the arts means life; stagnation means death. Music in America must strive for an ideal in which the impulses and feelings of the American people can find expression. Operas on German lines will build a road to that ideal; Italian opera will open a chasm.

In the murderous struggle in progress when I urged the employment of native singers at the conclusion of the season of 1916-17, I saw a breaking-out of the desire of peoples for racial and national expression in politics and government. It had been preceded by strenuous endeavor on the part of several of these peoples, notably the Russians, to give racial expression to their music also. It seemed imperative that the Metropolitan Opera Company should perceive that it was confronted with a larger duty than the maintenance of a company, no matter how admirable, of exclusively foreign artists, and yet I was unwilling to sacrifice the future good of art to a prejudice against a people with whom we were at war. What *The Tribune* printed thirty years ago was a glimpse into a future for which the vista is opening now.

I resume my historical narrative. The summer of 1917 wore on, and though a growing detestation of all things German became more and more manifest there were still no signs of ferment indicating a change of attitude towards art or artists about the Opera House or elsewhere. From May to the middle of October, so far as anything of real musical significance is concerned, New York enjoys a dead season. Summer concerts of many kinds there are in profusion, but if they offer much, it is as a pleasant stimulus to the enjoyment of the people who flock to the public parks, the recreation piers, and other places for which generous provision is annually made by the municipality and the philanthropy of private citizens. As the time for the opening of the concert season in the fall of 1917 approached, however, there were indications that the feeling of liberal toleration toward music and musicians of Teutonic origin was giving way before a prejudice which eventually became as unreasonable as the earlier attitude had been honorable and amiable. Some of the means used to stimulate the prejudice was of a nature which I shall not dignify by either definition or description. The first manifestations of this feeling that attracted more than local attention broke about the head of an artist who had enjoyed popular favor in a greater measure and for a longer period than any of his colleagues. This was Mr. Fritz Kreisler, the violinist, and the reason, no doubt, was because he, an Austrian, had in the previous year served for a brief period (and suffered a slight wound) in the military service of his country. The circumstance had redounded to his credit rather than against him in the season of 1916-17. Mr. Kreisler's was a conspicuous case and deserves to be discussed more fully than others, but, after all, in the last instance it illustrated a changed attitude of the United States toward European artists in general, meaning those

THE CASE OF FRITZ KREISLER 387

of great and those of no eminence. As soon as the war broke out the United States was called upon not only to alleviate want and suffering among the warring peoples but also to give hospitality and support to a horde of invading musicians, performers, singers, and teachers who had hitherto earned their livelihood in Europe. What was at first looked upon as a temporary haven had now become the home of hundreds, not to say thousands, who were not likely to return to their devastated and impoverished homes for a long time at least. Whether their sojourn was to work for the cultural good of America was a question not to be answered in the summer of 1917 and not to be answered yet.

The fact that a large number of foreign *virtuosi* of high rank took up a residence in this country in 1914 and remained here was not looked upon with disfavor at the time, though it was feared that it would lead to a plethora of concerts which might militate to some extent against their educational value. The apprehension was fulfilled, and there is no gratification to be derived from the fact that some of those who have intrenched themselves here bear Slavic instead of Germanic names. Their names and their willingness to crook the pregnant hinges of the knee that thrift might follow fawning distinguished them from the Austrian Kreisler; but not to his discredit. The storm of opposition, as I have said, broke first over Mr. Kreisler. Whether or not he should be permitted to play before a club in Sewickley, Penn., kept the people of that suburb of Pittsburgh and Pittsburgh itself in a ferment during the latter part of the summer of 1917. The concert was canceled and in Pittsburgh the Director of Public Safety called on the chief of police to prohibit a concert which was to be given there. Trouble arose in other cities, and Mr. Kreisler, acting with commendable dignity and frankness, canceled all the concerts for which he had been booked except those which had charitable objects. Of such concerts, it may be well to state there were a great many in the ensuing season, as there had been in the preceding, since it was found easy to throw the cloak of charity over many an enterprise in which selfish purpose was disguised as patriotism. Especially was this the case after the imposition by the Government of the United States of a war tax of ten per cent. upon the price of all tickets of admission to places of amusement. Concerning this more presently. After the belated declaration of war against Austria Mr. Kreisler publicly stated that he asked no consideration beyond that to which he was entitled as a well-behaved alien enemy. I am far from contending that he should have been permitted to continue his career as a concert-giver, but am giving unusual attention to his case partly because it was the first that excited wide public notice, and partly because during the period of excitement which culminated in action directly connected with the history of opera in New York he conducted himself with decorum and dignity, showing no rancor when the treatment which he received from the newspapers and even the pulpit compelled him to withdraw from his projected charity concerts. He thus preserved his self-respect and the respect of all his friends and many of his political enemies.

This is more than can be said for all other foreign artists who found themselves similarly situated. Mr. Josef Stransky, conductor of the Philharmonic Society of New York, soon found himself and his society in the vortex of a storm. He too was an Austrian subject, and there were musicians in his orchestra who had never become American citizens by naturalization. Mr. Stransky weathered the gale. The orchestra was purged of its alien-enemy element; the Musical Union of New York impeached and deposed its German president; Mr. Stransky defended himself against attacks made against his loyalty to the United States by public proclamation of the fact that he had opened the series of Philharmonic Concerts with a performance of

"The Star-Spangled Banner," which, without official sanction, had come to be looked upon as the national anthem; that he was a Bohemian of Czecho-Slavic parentage; that Bohemia was favorable to the Allies and fighting for her independence; that he had renounced his native country and declared his intention to become a citizen of the United States; that he had given his services to war charities, etc., etc. He held his position and though he did not eliminate the music of the German classics from his programmes, he placed a tabu upon the music of living German composers. Dr. Ernst Kunwald, conductor of the Cincinnati Symphony Orchestra, was less diplomatic. He, too, was an Austrian, and I believe had served in the Austrian army before coming to this country. He fell under suspicion, and was arrested by officers of the United States Government in December, 1917, freed for a time, but rearrested in January, 1918, and condemned to internment at Fort Oglethorpe, Ga., during the period of the war.

The evidence on which Dr. Kunwald was imprisoned was never divulged; neither was that which sent Dr. Karl Muck, who had been conductor of the Boston Symphony Orchestra since the fall of 1912, to be his companion. Dr. Muck's case caused the greater sensation because of its graver consequences and the length of time within which it was kept before the public mind. Dr. Muck's troubles, indeed, began almost as early as those of Mr. Kreisler. At the first concert of 1917-18 in Providence, R. I., a request was handed to the manager of the orchestra, Mr. Charles A. Ellis, that the music begin with a performance of "The Star-Spangled Banner." Mr. Ellis compared the list of signatures, that of representative women of the city, with a list of subscribers, and finding few if any of them there, took it upon himself to ignore the request. Intelligence of the incident was sent broadcast throughout the country at once. A storm blew up which was measurably appeased by the fact that at the next concert in Boston and at every concert thereafter the patriotic music was played under the guidance of the conductor. Stories of Dr. Muck's intense Germanism pursued him, however, and were not nullified by an attempt on his part to take refuge behind an old certificate of Swiss citizenship. The regular concerts were given in Boston, New York, Philadelphia, and other cities, but a score of the members of the orchestra were Germans, and citizens of the enemy country being prohibited from entering the national capital the concerts usually given there had to be abandoned. A concert booked for Chicago was also canceled. The protests against the presence of Dr. Muck in New York became very vigorous when the last two concerts of the season were reached, and though they resulted only in creating counter demonstrations for him, Major Higginson, who had founded the orchestra and maintained it for nearly a generation, in the following summer turned it over to a body of trustees. He had been obliged to accept the inevitable, for though he had stoutly refused to believe that Dr. Muck had in any way violated the laws of the United States, he was permitted to examine some documentary evidence which had convinced the Department of Justice that his conductor was a dangerous alien and had been subjected to the humiliation of seeing the man, whose cause he had manfully championed, arrested on March 25, 1918, and sent to Fort Oglethorpe for internment. Needless to say the staunch patriotism of Major Higginson was never in question for a moment.

A few more words must be added to the history of the concert season before the operatic record is taken up and the story of its external features completed. On November 1, 1917, there went into effect a federal law which imposed a tax on tickets for amusements. A fear that this tax would work havoc in the concert-field was not realized. The field had been greatly overworked in the years immediately preceding and continued to be overworked down to the end of 1917-18, which marks the conclusion of these studies. In the department of recitals by singers and instrumentalists the maintenance of the plethora was not difficult of explanation. Concerts by newcomers in New York are largely advertising affairs. Those who give them in the great majority of cases seek to get metropolitan publicity for exploitation in other localities. Audiences and newspaper notices are essential to them. The former are secured by the distribution of free tickets. The fear justified by the nature of the habitual "dead-head" that such audiences would not be willing to pay even the tax of ten per cent. on the price of the tickets was overcome to a great extent by the device of having the tax paid by the concert-giver. It added to the cost of the advertisement—that was all. Upon the public the tax was not felt as a burden except in the case of artists of established reputation and undoubted merit. In cases where subscriptions had been paid for series of concerts and for the opera before the tax law had been enacted the tax was paid in advance by the management and, where the justice of such a course was obvious, collected from the government in the form of a rebate.

The feeling of intolerance toward German music and musicians was apparent in the concert-rooms before public recognition of it was reflected in any action by the directors of the Opera Company. A great many singers quickly banished all German songs from their programmes; others sang the songs in English translations. Local orchestras in some of the small cities eliminated the music of even the classics, and this folly which could but result in the debasement of taste found some men and women, fortunately not many, who justified it. As if the music of Haydn, Mozart, Schubert, Schumann, Brahms, and Wagner, all dead long before the war was even a dream in the wicked minds of the German rulers and people, could in any wise be connected with the authors of the most monstrous crime of a millennium. In January, 1918, the Philharmonic Society, finding it doubly desirable to repair fortunes already somewhat decayed and now threatened by the controversy over its conductor, proclaimed a policy which left the classic repertory intact but eliminated the compositions of living German composers. This seemed a proper expedient and one akin with the proscription of German singers at the Metropolitan Opera, of which I am now called upon to speak.

During the rising tide of anti-German feeling in the summer and early autumn of 1917, no suggestion of a change of policy at the Metropolitan Opera House found record in the newspaper press so far as I know. If there was any thought of a possible impending change in the minds of the directors, which must have been actively occupied with the subject, it was scarcely discernible in the prospectus for the approaching season, which was published, as usual, about the middle of September. There was, indeed, in the document an absence of emphasis upon the subject of the German repertory; but to that the public were accustomed. The prospectus called attention to the proposed production of two American works (an opera, "Shanewis," and a ballet, "The Dance in Place Congo," by Henry F. Gilbert) and also of Liszt's oratorio "St. Elizabeth," which was to be given in the form of an opera in English; but mention was made of the retention of a stage-manager for the German repertory, all the familiar German names appeared in the list of singers and the list of operas contained all those of Wagner which had been strong props of the repertory for many years.

Ten days before the opening of the season of 1917-18 the directors made it known to the public that there would be no German performances. This decision had not been arrived at hastily, but after ample discussion prompted by a study of public opinion. When the fact was announced in the newspapers of November 2, 1917, it was given out

CHARLES WAKEFIELD CADMAN
Composer of "Shanewis"

MELANIE KURT
In "Fidelio"

that the decision was not of recent date nor had it been influenced by the recent experience of the Boston Symphony Orchestra at Providence. The directors, it was said, had reached the conclusion that to continue the giving of German opera might hearten the people of Germany because of the exaggerations with which the story of the German performances might be accompanied. Such a risk, however remote, the directors did not intend to take. Nothing was said about any German operas in particular, but the brief announcement was made that when the repertory of the opening week should be announced the public might rest assured that it would contain "nothing that could cause the least offense to the most patriotic Americans." A fortnight later it became known that the general manager had canceled the contracts with Margarete Ober, Melanie Kurt, Johannes Sembach, Carl Braun, and Hermann Weil—all singers engaged for the performance of German operas. The contracts with these artists contained a clause that they might be abrogated "by reason of war, fire, flood, epidemic, or any other act of God"—a familiar formula in contractual obligations. Mme. Ober's contract was said to have been modified by correspondence after its signing, and she therefore stood in a somewhat different relation towards the Opera Company than her companions. However this may be, she began legal proceedings against the company for damages and the case was settled by agreement out of court a little more than a year afterwards. Mme. Gadski's contract had not been renewed. She was permitted to remain in the country after the departure of her husband. She kept herself in the public eye for a space, sang at a celebration of the anniversary of Luther's birth in New York, also at a concert of the German Männergesangverein Arion, and then so far as New York was concerned went into silence. Four of the men singers whose usefulness at the opera had ended formed a concert organization and in seeking to promote their own interests by giving concerts did more to perpetuate a prejudice against German music, I am inclined to think, than did the misguided and narrow-minded patriots who kept up an agitation against the German classics and tried, in vain, to put the United States on a lower scale of intelligence than France, where there was no cessation of the performance of the German classics, or England, where Wagner's dramas held their own in the repertory albeit in English versions of the texts.

There was a visit to New York in the season of 1917-18 by the Chicago Opera Company, which came not in its old affiliatory relationship but as an energetic rival. To it under the circumstances I must devote a little more space than I would feel disposed to give an ordinary itinerant troupe. Taking time by the forelock Mr. Cleofonte Campanini caused the concluding strains of the Metropolitan season of 1916-17 to commingle with the announcement that he had leased the Lexington Theater "for a year" in order that he might produce grand opera in it for four weeks in the next season. In a spirit of magnanimity he added: "I do not wish to crush the Metropolitan; I am coming to develop my own season." The explanation of this remark was to be found in the fact that it had been recognized that Chicago was unable to support a season of more than ten weeks and that inasmuch as it was not practicable to make contracts for singers of such short duration it was necessary to add a month's performances in New York and a fortnight's in Boston to make the existence of the Chicago company possible. He set his prices of admission at the same rate as those of the Metropolitan and continued in effect the same policy that had been made familiar by Mr. Hammerstein years before. Miss Mary Garden was his chief reliance, though he found a more potent attraction in Mme. Galli-Curci, concerning whom much ado, not altogether unjustified, was made. She had made a modest effort to enter Mr. Gatti's forces before going to Chicago

Rosa Raisa
Of the Chicago Opera Company
as Aida

REPERTORY OF THE CHICAGO COMPANY

and turned out to be the subject of a sensational episode even greater than that which had attended the coming of Mme. Tetrazzini to the Manhattan Opera House. Of this something more may be said later. The majority of Mr. Campanini's singers were familiar to New Yorkers from the old Manhattan days. Among them were Miss Garden, Mme. Louise Bérat, Gustave Huberdeau, Charles Dalmorès, Hector Dufranne, and Vittorio Arimondi; in the list were also Georges Baklanoff, and Riccardo Stracciari. The season began on January 23, 1917, and ended on February 15, 1918. The operas performed were "Monna Vanna," "I Giojelli della Madonna," "Thaïs," "Roméo et Juliette," "Dinorah," "Manon," "Aïda" (in which a fine dramatic soprano, Rosa Raisa, effected her début), "Lucia di Lammermoor," "Faust" (in which Mme. Melba effected a re-entry on February 1), "Il Barbiere di Siviglia," "Louise," "Le Jongleur de Notre Dame," "Traviata," and three novelties, viz.: Mascagni's "Isabeau" (February 13, 1918), Henry Hadley's "Azora" (January 28, 1918), and Sylvio Lazzari's "Le Sauteriot" (February 11, 1918). Not one of the novelties excited more than a modicum of interest, although there was a pretty general expression of astonishment that "Isabeau"—whose story is founded upon the legend of Lady Godiva and whose heroine is supposed to begin and end her famous ride in unconventional costume in the presence of the public—was not among Miss Garden's list but was permitted to fall to the lot of Miss Raisa. The music of the opera in an attempt to give expression to the spirit of mediæval chivalry is frequently pompous and strident only, though much superior to the novelty by the same composer, "Lodoletta," which was brought out as if in opposition at the Metropolitan Opera House. The story of "Le Sauteriot" was taken from the play of E. de Keyserling by Henri, Pierre Roche, and Martial Pérrier. Its music, by a native of the Italian Tyrol who had been a pupil of Guiraud in

Paris, was found to contain some Slavic elements and considerable charm and made a deeper impression than that of Mascagni. "Azora" had a story of ancient Mexico at its base, and its life on the stage, limited to a single performance, was unusually brief even for an American work.

Concerning the artistic merit of the principal women of Mr. Campanini's company I am the less disposed to make a large discussion because extravagant eulogy of both filled columns of the newspapers in this season and that which followed. To the class of opera-goers and commentators whose experience was bounded by a decade or two there seemed to be no limit to the admiration to which Miss Garden was entitled as an actress and Mme. Galli-Curci as a singer. Characteristic of the absence of a standard of knowledge based on knowledge, experience, and taste was the constant coupling of the latter's name with that of Mme. Adelina Patti. They made a sorry confession of unfitness for judgment who placed the two singers on a plane—unfitness by reason of ignorance of what Mme. Patti's voice and art had been and want of knowledge concerning the art of vocalization itself. Mme. Galli-Curci is a delightful singer, with so beautiful a natural voice and such exquisite skill that she deserves high admiration despite a woeful blemish in her art which obtruded itself in nearly every one of her performances. This blemish, that of incorrect intonation (she generally sang flat in the early part of every one of her performances), seems to be due to imperfect training rather than faulty instinct, but that fact neither banished nor excused it. More than that, she had had several peers as a lyric artist within the memory of persons whose experience is measured by the span of history covered by the Metropolitan Opera House, while Mme. Patti has had none. Nilsson, Gerster, Sembrich, Melba—were they to be forgotten because rivalry had broken out between the Metropolitan and

ROBERTO MORANZONI
Conductor at the Metropolitan Opera House

Chicago companies? That seemed to be a popular attitude. Few names of new singers appeared in the list published in the prospectus of the Metropolitan Opera House of 1917-18, and of these the most were in what may be called the junior list. The most significant were those of Florence Easton, John McCormack, Hypolito Lazaro, a tenor, Thomas Chalmers, a baritone who had won favorable opinion at English performances with the Century Company, and José Mardones, a bass who came from the wreck of the Boston National Opera Company, as did the new Italian conductor, Roberto Moranzoni. Mme. Easton, of English birth and an artist of fine stature, was among the singers of foreign birth who had acquired not only a fine routine which stood her in good stead but also made an enviable reputation at the Royal Opera in Berlin before the war. She effected her début at the Metropolitan in " Cavalleria Rusticana " on December 7, 1917, and more than held her own against rivals established in favor throughout the season, carrying off chief honors, such as they were, in Liszt's " St. Elizabeth." Mr. McCormack, who had become one of the idols of the concert-rooms and was not new to the opera, sang only three times—in " La Bohème," " Madama Butterfly," and " Tosca." Hypolito Lazaro sang for the first time at the Metropolitan in " Rigoletto " on January 31, 1918. José Mardones, who proved to be an admirably serviceable bass, sang often during the season, the first time on the opening night on November 12, as Ramfis in "Aïda." Signor Moranzoni, who replaced Giorgio Palacco as principal conductor of the Italian list, was active throughout the year. Adolf Bolm was specially engaged to supervise the production of Rimsky-Korsakow's brilliant opera " Le Coq d'Or," which, in obedience to a foreign precedent which I can not pardon, had been changed to what was called an " opera pantomime," which meant that the acting was done by one set of artists and the singing by another. A governmental order which commanded the closing of all places of amusement on Monday nights was liberally construed to the advantage of the Metropolitan Opera House by the officials in Washington (there being no Tuesday performances) and did not interfere with the regular sequence of subscription representations. The novelties of the season in the order of their production were "Marôuf" on December 19; "St. Elizabeth" on January 3; Mascagni's "Lodoletta" on January 12; "Le Coq d'Or" on March 6; "Shanewis" and a ballet, "The Dance in Place Congo," on March 23. There was a revival of Meyerbeer's "Le Prophète" on February 7. Concerning each of these incidents comment seems imperative for the sake of the integrity of this critical record, though they were of very unequal artistic importance. I take them up in their order:

"Marôuf," an opéra comique in four acts and five scenes, has for the author of its libretto Lucien Nepoty and for its composer Henri Rabaud, with whom the lovers of serious music in the Eastern cities of the country made excellent acquaintance a year later when he came to the United States as conductor of the Boston Symphony Orchestra. The performance was conducted by Pierre Monteux, also a newcomer, and the cast was as follows:

Marôuf	Giuseppe de Luca
The Princess	Frances Alda
The Sultan	Léon Rothier
Fatimah	Kathleen Howard
The Vizier	Andreas de Segurola
Ali	Thomas Chalmers
A Pastry Cook	Robert Leonhardt
The Fellah	Angelo Bada
Chief Sailor	Albert Reiss
Two Merchants	{ Angelo Bada { Pompilio Malatesta
The Cadi	Giulio Rossi
Two Muezzins	{ Max Bloch { Angelo Bada
A Donkey Driver	Pietro Audisio
Sheik-al-Islam	Mr. Burgstaller

HENRI RABAUD
Composer of "Marôuf"

THE OPERATIC BARBER OF BAGDAD

How many opera stories are there still locked up in the "Arabian Nights" tales? I do not know; I cannot guess. Only Allah (extolled be his name!) knows. The thesaurus has been opened scores of times, hundreds of times, probably, but the uncut gems still lie heaps upon heaps. There have been English, French, German, and Italian operatic Aladdins, even a Swedish, but they have long ago gone into the limbo of things forgotten. A Bohemian Ali Baba lived once on the lyric stage and had namesakes who were begotten by composers whose names and some of whose music have a familiar sound—Bottesini, Cherubini, Lecocq; but our boyhood friend, who had been the friend of a score of generations before us, has gone with the Forty Thieves into the cave of oblivion, whose door will no more swing open to our "Open, sesame!" We never saw Marôuf till Mr. Gatti presented him to us, and never even heard of him unless it was he who used to frequent the German stage under the disguise of "Der lustige Schuster." Possibly, but the matter doesn't signify; we have the Cairene cobbler now and we hope for his continued acquaintance for years to come.

But I remember, and with much grateful kindness, another fellow of infinite jest and excellent fancy, who journeyed to our opera house from Bagdad, though he came to us from that center of German culture (not *Kultur*), Weimar, fragrant with memories of Goethe, Schiller, Herder, and Liszt. The "Barber of Bagdad," by Peter Cornelius, was a feature of the Metropolitan in its German period. That was a long time ago, yet his embodiment in the acting of Emil Fischer came back to occupy memory and fancy when we listened to Rabaud's delightful opera. Again we listened to the gabble and the Gilbertian patter of the prototype of all loquacious, prying, intermeddling barbers. We heard him hurl his terrible name, Abu Hassan Ali Ebe Becar, amid orchestral thunderings at Noureddin's affrighted servants. Saw them attack him, throw him on a divan;

poultice, plaster, rub, bandage, phlebotomize, and dose him to the verge of death, because when called on to shave their master he insisted on casting his horoscope and chattering half an hour about his own paucity of speech and the garrulity of his six brothers before he even honed his razor. We saw the lovelorn hero enduring the torture, with bursting gall bladder and crumbled liver, till the call of the muezzin summoned him to his tryst with the Cadi's daughter though his head was but half shaved and he dashed off only to suffer new adventures, because of the barber's dilatoriness and pertinacity.

In the music of Rabaud's "Marôuf" there are only the Oriental arabesques of the muezzin's call to matin prayer, which trace kinship with Cornelius's setting of his own dramatic version of the tailor's story in "The Thousand Nights and A Night." Rabaud's composition is saturated with the languorous colors and odors of the East. Cornelius's is German music. There is no effect in which they meet, unless, as we thought when hearing "Marôuf" for the first time, it is that dry cackling of wood-wind instruments in dissonant chords which accompanies Bostana, the female pendant of the barber, and which Rabaud uses to characterize the virago who drives Marôuf into good fortune.

But this is an all but negligible feature in the French opera and not one of its charming traits. The chief fascination comes from the use of Oriental themes; perhaps not so much from the idioms themselves as from the manner in which they are employed. We can imagine that ears accustomed to only melody of the Occidental types might become weary of the dialogue in "Marôuf" (for of set song there is nothing except an air in the third act which does not belong to the score and was interpolated by the composer to oblige Mme. Alda), but it was an uninquisitive ear and a stagnant fancy that was not arrested, lured, and seduced by the woven voices of the orchestra. Here the

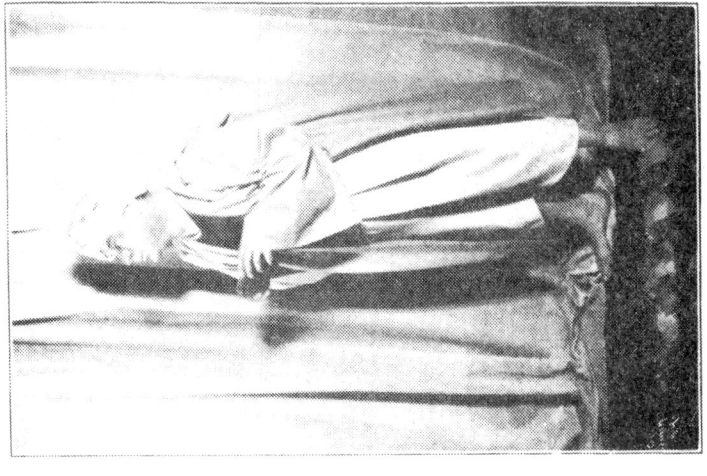

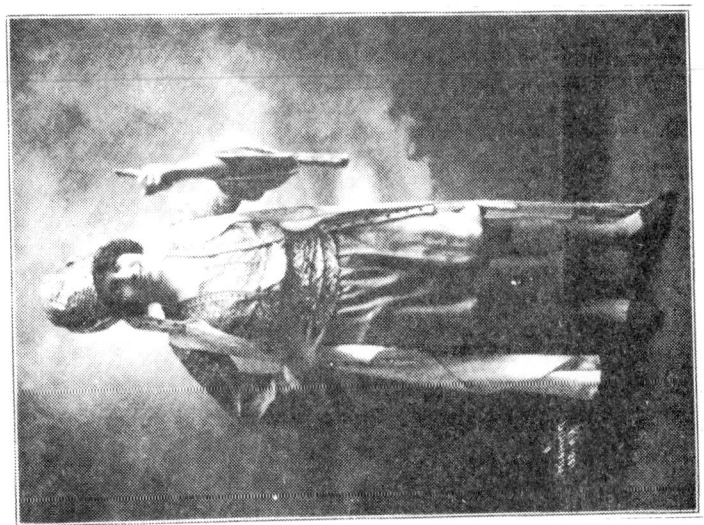

Frances Alda   Giuseppe De Luca

In "Marôuf"

idiom of the East is transmuted into a speech which belongs to the world of exalted fancy—exalted yet altogether ingenuous. The score is wonderfully transparent. There is not an opaque measure in it, not one in which instruments are multiplied or colors mixed till the utterance becomes turgid, not one in which one voice invalidates another, not one in which even the most exotic of tones and combinations does not seem native because of its fitness to scene or situation.

There are throbbings of Arab drums and the reedy tones of oboes which might bring up memories of the Streets of Cairo in the big show in Chicago in 1893, if they were not refined and sublimated by the atmosphere in which they float, the atmosphere of the land of romance through which we walked when we put our hands in the long ago within the irresistible fingers of Scheherazade, where they still remain and whence they shall never be withdrawn.

Faint tintinnabulations of golden-toned gongs float through the air, and the ear, enslaved by the imagination, absorbs them, not wonderingly, but as if they were the natural food of hearing, as the pale blue, starless sky, with its faraway domes wreathed and crowned with lights, seems the only picture that ought to fill the vision.

The dialogue in "Marôuf" is carried on not in set melodic formularies, but in a species of musically heightened and emotionally colored speech. It ought to have been intelligible to all, and would have been if it had been sung in the vernacular, or to all knowers of French, if the pronunciation and diction of all the persons concerned in the performance had been what they ought. The composer did nothing to obscure it. In part it makes use of the intervallic idioms of Oriental music and is burdened with the *remplissage* of ornament peculiar to Oriental song. But the characteristic racial element is found chiefly in the orchestral stream upon which the dialogue floats. There are a few exceptions to the rule. Marôuf's first song, "Il est

Musulman," is plainly a Cairene folksong, shorn of some of its redundancy of ornament, which Villoteau preserved for us. The song of the muezzin, which calls the faithful to prayer, as we hear it first from two solo voices in the second scene of the second act, and which is woven through the later contrapuntal ensemble, is another quotation from that learned musical Egyptologist. Villoteau was one of the savants whom Bonaparte sent into Egypt in 1798, and he wrote the chapters on music in the monumental "Description de l'Egypte." Rabaud is only one of many composers who have studied him, though he has done so to better purpose than any of his predecessors, save, possibly, Félicien David, who makes fine use of the chant of the Muezzin in his "Désert." Cornelius uses this music, or another transcription of the call, in his "Barber of Bagdad," where it is the only bit of local color introduced, but where it is also most skilfully treated.

There are, no doubt, many other quotations in Rabaud's score which escaped our recognition, and themes which had their inspiration in melodies noted down by Villoteau. There is a suggestion of a traditional Egyptian march in the militant theme which introduces the Sultan and accompanies him through the scenes in which he figures. This device of characterization is frequently employed by Rabaud. The cobbler is a shameless liar and impostor. Why do all the characters in the play who know him give him their sympathy? Why does he bewail himself and his neighbors echo the commiserating strain? Why is he a colossal liar without forfeiting our regard? The injustice which prevails in all the "Arabian Nights" stories is flagrantly proclaimed in the final punishment of the only farseeing personage of the play.

We smile while seeing the Vizier punished; yet it was he who saw through the false pretence of the rascally cobbler who is rewarded for his domestic truancy with a wife, beautiful as the moon, and immeasurable treasure, while

AN ORATORIO DONE INTO OPERA

the servant of the Sultan who sought to save his master goes to the bastinado. *Kismet.* "What will happen, will happen." No harm. It is all of the very essence of the "Arabian Nights," Scheherazade distilled it in her recital to her lord the King; Rabaud has given it to us again out of his alembic. *Bismillah!* With Liszt's German oratorio turned into an English opera, I found little patience. Mr. Bodanzky conducted the performance and a generous effort was made to put it upon the stage with pictures in the new manner, which affects to believe that the imagination provides better subjects for illustration than poor Dame Nature, who has some respect for cause and effect in the matter of lights and shadows, the habits of trees and so forth. The parts were distributed as follows:

Saint Elizabeth	Florence Easton
Landgrave Ludwig	Clarence Whitehill
Landgrave Hermann	Carl Schlegel
Landgravine Sophie	Margarete Matzenauer
The Seneschal	Robert Leonhardt
A Hungarian Magnate	Basil Ruysdael
Elizabeth, as a child	Constanze Bitterl
Ludwig as a child	Margarete Belleri

"St. Elizabeth" as an oratorio had been last heard in New York on December 11, 1911, at a concert of the MacDowell Chorus. That was announced as a first performance in New York; but the good people who put forward the announcement were not blessed with either long memories or interest in the musical doings of the past. A glance at local records would have taught them that the oratorio was performed first by the Deutscher Liederkranz in 1870, repeated by the same society two or three years later, revived by Mr. Theodore Thomas and the Brooklyn Philharmonic Society on February 28, 1885, and performed by the same society, as a memorial to the composer, who had died in the preceding summer, on December 17 and 18, 1886.

There are a few points, historical and legendary, connected with "St. Elizabeth" and its subject-matter which may be taken up with possible profit before a description of the work is entered upon. It is generally supposed that the oratorio was composed at the instance of the Grand Duke of Weimar (though the score bears a dedication to King Ludwig II of Bavaria) for a festival held at the Wartburg on August 28, 1867, in commemoration of the eighth centenary of its foundation and in honor of the restoration of the famous castle, then just completed. In a general way this is true, but the oratorio had previously been performed in Pesth, as well as in Eisenach, two years before the Wartburg festival. The Wartburg, it will be recalled, was the scene of the contest of minstrelsy celebrated in Wagner's "Tannhäuser" and Luther's hiding-place while he was engaged in translating the Bible into German and creating a literary language for the German people. The Wartburg had been enriched after its restoration by six frescoes by Moritz von Schwind, illustrating as many episodes in the historical and legendary account of Elizabeth of Hungary, and these pictures were the starting-point of Litzt's inspiration, or, let us say, they gave the suggestion for his oratorio. Otto Roquette put the pictures into words, and Liszt, grouping the text into two divisions, set it to music of a partly dramatic, partly epical kind. The scenes may be briefly described thus:

I. Arrival of Elizabeth as a child at the Wartburg. She is accompanied by magnates of her native Hungary, and is received with joy by a group of children, who are to be her playmates, and by the Thuringian nobility.

II. Elizabeth has grown to maturity and been married to Ludwig of Thuringia, to whom she had been betrothed as a child and who had succeeded his father, Hermann, as Landgrave. On a hunting expedition Ludwig detects her carrying bread and wine to the poor, contrary to his commands. He upbraids her, but, though she confesses her pious guilt, when her basket is opened it is discovered that the viands have been miraculously changed to roses.

III. The miracle turns the Landgrave's mind to piety, and at the head of his vassals he starts out on a crusade to the Holy Land.

Florence Easton
In "Saint Elizabeth"

A HUNGARIAN SAINT AND TANNHÄUSER

IV. There he dies, and his mother, Landgravine Sophie, usurps Elizabeth's rights and drives her out of the Wartburg.

V. Elizabeth dies surrounded by the poor whom she had befriended and with whom she shares her last crust of bread.

VI. She is buried with solemn pomp in the Cathedral in the presence of the Emperor Frederick II of Hohenstaufen, a magnificent company of German and Hungarian bishops and a large concourse of people.

The circumstance that the scene of the oratorio or opera (Liszt called it a "Legend," though it mixes historical and mythical material) is the Wartburg, near Eisenach, and that two of the characters bear the names of people who figure, as does the scene, in Wagner's "Tannhäuser," is calculated to cause a little confusion in the minds of some people touching the relationship existing between the two works. "Tannhäuser" deals with a contest of minstrelsy held in the Wartburg at the instance of Hermann, Landgrave of Thuringia, and the heroine in the play is Elizabeth, who loves Tannhäuser and whose saintly intercession is invoked by the knight with his dying words. Wagner's Landgrave is historical, and supposedly the same Hermann who figures in Liszt's oratorio; but the heroine of the opera is Wagner's creation, while the Elizabeth of Liszt's work is an historical personage who still holds a place in the calendar of saints. If they were contemporaries at all, however, it cannot have been under any such conditions as are set forth in either opera or oratorio, for the contest of minstrels at the Wartburg is said to have taken place A.D. 1207, in which year St. Elizabeth was born at Pressburg. At four years of age she was betrothed to Ludwig IV, Landgrave of Thuringia, and taken to the Wartburg to be educated under the direction of Ludwig's parents. Stimulated by the example of her mother's sister, Hedwig, wife of Henry VI, Duke of Silesia (who was also canonized), she sacrificed all her childish pleasures to religious duty and charity. At the age of fourteen she married Ludwig, over whom, according to the historical accounts, she acquired such influence that he became her zealous helper in the dispensation of alms. The legendary story is that told in the pictures of Schwind and Liszt's oratorio. Returning from a hunt, Ludwig met his wife carrying food to the poor contrary to his wishes. He sternly commanded her to open the bundle which she was carrying, and when she did so it was found to be filled with roses. The miracle led him fully to accept the Christian faith.

Thus the legend; now to return to what may be considered fairly substantiated history: Ludwig died A.D. 1227, and Elizabeth was robbed of the regency by his brother on the pretext that she was wasting the estate by her almsgiving. She was driven out of the Wartburg with her three children in poverty, being allowed to carry away with her scarcely enough to sustain life. She found asylum, however, with her maternal uncle, the Bishop of Bamberg, and after a space the regency was again offered to her through the intervention of some of the Thuringian barons, and her son Hermann was declared heir to the Landgraviate. She chose a life of seclusion to the exercise of her powers, and continued her lavish distribution of charity under the care of her father confessor, Conrad of Marburg, a bigoted, persecuting prelate, until her death in November, 1231. Four years later she was canonized by Pope Gregory IX.

The difference between legend, or myth, and history is apparent from a comparison of this exposition and the summary printed above explanatory of Moritz von Schwind's frescoes. The discussion was scarcely necessary to an appreciation of the work of Roquette and Liszt, but it can do no harm and may save some hearers of the work inclined to take a serious view of lyric drama from the singular blunder into which a New York critic fell in his discussion of the first performance of "Parsifal," when, knowing nothing of the mediæval German epics, he jumped to the conclusion that Kundry was Lohengrin's mother. He had

MASCAGNI'S "LODOLETTA"

seen Kundry enter the Temple of the Holy Grail after her absolution, and heard Lohengrin proclaim that Parsifal (or Parzival) was his father. That sufficed his ingenuous soul! The latest of Mascagni's operas, "Lodoletta," was produced for the first time in America under the direction of Signor Moranzoni on January 12 with the following cast:

Lodoletta	Geraldine Farrar
Flammen	Enrico Caruso
Franz	Andreas de Segurola
Gianotto	Pasquale Amato
Antonio	Adamo Didur
A Mad Woman	Lila Robeson
Vannard	Cecil Arden
Maud	Minnie Egener
A Voice	Max Bloch
A Letter Carrier	Sante Mandelli
An Old Violinist	Mr. Burgstaller

It seemed to me that Mascagni never wrote a weaker score than this. Obviously the opera was chosen for the sake of Mr. Caruso and just as obviously Mr. Caruso will not be able to save it. Its story is that of the little romance by Ouida entitled "Two Little Wooden Shoes." A French poet meets a little girl in Holland and she falls innocently in love with him. Her guardian is killed, and as the poet stops to paint his portrait evil tongues slander the girl. The poet goes to Paris and there lives the gay life that poets will if they can; but in the midst of his gaieties he is unable to forget the little girl in her wooden shoes. She follows him to the capital and dies on his doorstep in a snowstorm. That is all that need be said about play or music.

"Le Prophète" was revived under the direction of Mr. Bodanzky on February 7, 1918, with the following cast:

Jean of Leyden	Enrico Caruso
Fidés, his Mother	Margarete Matzenauer

Bertha, his Bride	Claudia Muzio
Jonas	Max Bloch
Mathisen	Carl Schlegel
Zaccharia	José Mardones
Count Oberthal	Adamo Didur
An Anabaptist	Louis d'Angelo
An Officer	Pietro Audisio
A Captain	Basil Ruysdael
A Peasant	Vincenzo Reschiglian

It is one of the anomalies in the history of "Le Prophète" that till this period it was not to the Italian or French performances but to the German the opera owed the greatest part of its life on the stage of the Metropolitan Opera House. The opera was given nine times in the first German season and until this season the majority of the performances heard in New York were in the German language. When Dr. Leopold Damrosch produced it, it rivaled the Wagnerian operas of his list in popularity. Since Mr. Abbey brought it forward in the season of 1883-84, when the theater was new, New Yorkers had heard three representatives of the titular character in Italian (Stagno, Tamagno, and Jean de Reszke), five in German (Schott, Sylva, Niemann, Perotti, and Gudehus), and two in French (Alvarez and Caruso). That the opera had never been popular in the sense that Puccini's operas are popular is no doubt due to the great difficulty of finding adequate representatives of its two principal characters and the depressing effect of the singing of those three black crows, the Anabaptist missioners, unless the parts are carried by vocal artists of the first rank; the only instance of which that I can recall was in the performances under Mr. Grau, when men like Edouard de Reszke and Plançon were called into service.

"Le Coq d'Or," a Russian opera, the book after Poushkin by Vladimir Bielski, the music by Rimsky-Korsakow, adapted as an "opera-pantomime" by Michael Fokine, staged by Adolph Bolm and conducted by Pierre Monteux, was produced with the following double cast:

The Princess	Maria Barrientos	Rosina Galli
The King	Adamo Didur	Adolph Bolm
Amelfa	Sophie Braslau	Queenie Smith
The Astrologer	Rafaello Diaz	Giuseppe Bonfiglio
The Prince	Pietro Audisio	Marshall Hall
The General	Basil Ruysdael	Ottokar Bartik
A Knight	Vincenzo Reschiglian	Vincenzo Loucelli
The Golden Cock	——	Marie Sundelius

When Mr. Rimsky-Korsakow, a man of intellect and a composer of genius and experience, wrote "Le Coq d'Or," he thought he had created an opera. So did the Russian censor who, for political reasons, suppressed it till after the composer's death. So did the manager of the private theater at Moscow who produced it in May, 1910. So did the composer's widow, who protested, though in vain, when the work was presented as a sort of glorified Punch and Judy show in Paris and London in 1912. Yet it was in this form that Mr. Gatti thought fit to bring it out. The excuse offered for the transmogrification of the work is that its action offers insuperable difficulties to operatic singers. There is nothing novel in such a contention; it stands as against every lyric drama that is a trifle remote from the old-fashioned concert in costume. As a rule opera singers are not actors. They wear costumes sometimes of historic appositeness, wave their arms about, attitudinize, and make more or less pleasing and intelligible sounds with their voices. That is acting as they conceive it to be.

I cannot quite accept the explanation of the transformation of "Le Coq d'Or" as authentic, when I recall the genesis of the change. It was made in a period of the world's history very like that in which Dryden said he lived:

> A very merry, dancing, drinking,
> Laughing, quaffing, and unthinking
> Time.

The world had been dance-mad for several years; it was in very truth "dancing on a volcano." The neurologists of ·

the next generation will no doubt give some attention to the subject and associate the phenomenon with the world-war. I should not wonder; although unlike the nervous disorder which followed the plague in the fourteenth century our mania preceded our war. It was a precursory instead of a sequential symptom. Our foxtrotting and tangoing had little to do with the revival of pantomimic dancing by Loie Fuller, Isadora Duncan, and the Russian Ballet, but a good deal to do with that popular frame of mind which refuses to demand seriousness in the theater and is content with a stimulation of the senses. "But, perhaps, 'twere to consider too curiously to consider so." There is nothing more to be said until "Le Coq d'Or" in its present form shall have run its course and the public shall have spoken its judgment—not on Rimsky-Korsakow's opera but on Fokine's fantoccini capering to the composer's delightful and frequently brilliant music. I shall take the liberty to add, however, that, as it is, "Le Coq d'Or" suggests the coming of "movie" operas just as it recalls the drama of the Javanese, the Chinese shadow-plays, and the old English moralities in which puppets played to musical sounds. Turn about is fair play, I presume, in the opera house. Don Giovanni had his fling on the puppet stage before Mozart composed him and Faust before Goethe immortalized him; while the passion of Pelléas and Mélisande was designed by Maeterlinck to be exhibited in a marionette theater. Debussy wrote his opera in spite of the Belgian poet's protest, just as Fokine made a pantomime with song out of "Le Coq d'Or" against the wishes of the composer's widow, when the composer could no longer protest. There is no reason obvious to me why Mr. Gatti's singing and dancing forces should not have been united to bring out the dramatic conceit in the minds of Poushkin and Rimsky-Korsakow. There would have been no loss in the pageantry, no sacrifice of the choreographic side of the entertainment saving, and excepting always, the witchery

Rosina Galli
In "Le Coq d'Or"

THE PLOT OF "LE COQ D'OR"

of Rosina Galli's person and miming, of which, indeed, there was too much.

The story of "Le Coq d'Or" is supposed to be charged with political satire, but to that I prefer to pay no heed in these troublesome times. Let it be told in the conventional parlance of the theater: In the first scene we are introduced to a hall in the palace of King Dodon where he is holding a council with his boyars. He tells them that he is weary of royal responsibilities and especially of the perpetual warfare with his hostile neighbors. He longs for rest. He asks the advice of his heir, Prince Guidon, who says that instead of fighting on the frontier he should withdraw his troops and let them surround his capital after well provisioning it. Then while the enemy is destroying the rest of the country the King might rest, and think of some new way of circumventing him. General Polkan, however, disapproves of the project. Very soon the assembly is in violent disagreement when an astrologer arrives upon the scene and offers to King Dodon the gift of a Golden Cock which shall always give warning of approaching danger. The King, at first skeptical, is converted when the Cock being brought in cries: "Kikeriki, kikerikou! Be on your guard, mind what you do!" In the second act Dodon and the Voyovode Polkan with their army come to a narrow pass among the rocks which has evidently been the scene of a battle. Here Dodon comes upon the dead bodies of his two sons, who have apparently killed each other. Amidst his grief he perceives under the shelter of the hillside a large tent whence emerges a beautiful woman and sings a song to the dawn. She is the Queen of Shemakha, who allures the old King with her beauty and consents to go to Dodon's capital and be his bride. There the Astrologer appears and demands his reward, which is the Queen. King Dodon refuses. The Cock utters a threatening cry and with a blow of his beak pierces the skull of the King.

"Shanewis," an American opera, the book by Nellie Richmond Eberhard, the music by Charles Wakefield Cadman, conducted by Mr. Moranzoni, was produced with the parts distributed as follows:

Shanewis	Sophie Braslau
Mrs. Everton	Kathleen Howard
Amy	Marie Sundelius
Lionel	Paul Althouse
Phillippe	Thomas Chalmers

There were also Indians, high school girls, a pianist who had to play an accompaniment to a song, and an Indian girl in the cast; but they signified little. The plot of the opera was generally voted about the stupidest that could be conceived for such a purpose and the dramatic construction of the score betrayed the hand of the apprentice. What made the opera tolerable was its melodiousness, in the sentimental salon style, and the use of Indian color in some of the music. Mr. Henderson, reviewing the season, said in *The Sun* newspaper: "Mr. Cadman's little opera contains the elements of dramatic sincerity and force; and these have commended it to the public attention. It is always melodious, and of course that counts for much, and the first act has a duet of really meritorious quality. It has the character of the composer's songs and it does not rise to the higher levels of lyric style, but it has temperament and dramatic feeling." This was a verdict prompted by a desire to be as kind as possible to a native work because it was a native work. An American ballet associated with it in performance was the "Dance in the Place Congo," originally composed by Henry F. Gilbert as a free rhapsody on Creole melodies to which attention had been called many years before by a series of magazine articles written by George W. Cable. Choreographic scenes with a conventional plot of jealousy and murder were grafted onto the music by Mr. Ottokar Bartik. The music was voted good, even admirable, in its way, but the dramatic scenes were neither

SOPHIE BRASLAU
As Shanewis

varied nor significant enough to justify the title ballet, and the work lived a shorter life than it would probably have enjoyed had it been reserved for the concert-room, for which it was designed. This brings the record of the effect of the war upon music in the United States and opera at the Metropolitan Opera House, with which the last chapters of these memoirs are particularly concerned, to an end. There remains what I must look upon in the light of an obligation, since my purposes have been critical as well as historical from the beginning, to discuss the æsthetic principles which have been brought into court by the facts presented. I do not care to indulge in speculation or prophecy touching the future, in which matters will inevitably adjust themselves. Throughout the period of political turmoil the public mind seemed to be sadly muddled as to the attitude which our concert and operatic institutions ought to adopt toward German music and German musicians. There was little effort to differentiate between the art and its practitioners; between an expression of the beautiful which in its very nature is both guiltless and incapable of the political sentiments now abhorred by nearly all the civilized peoples of the world; the masters who created it with neither knowledge nor premonition that those who came after them would revert to moral savagery, and the practitioners who lived under that savagery and in some cases sympathized with it and upheld it. Yet such a distinction ought to be instinctive in every intelligent child. To banish Wagner's dramas from the stage of America can as little serve the cause for which the nation pledged its wealth, honor and life, as to bedaub the statues of Goethe and Schiller as was done in some places. The people set up a statue of Heine in New York years ago, largely as a protest against the attitude of the German Emperor, who would not tolerate a memorial of that uncompromising democrat in Berlin. Why should it have been thought patriotic to dishonor the symbols of our veneration for the genius of Goethe, who refused to hate France and its literature even while Germany was striving to throw off the Napoleonic yoke? Or of Schiller, who hymned freedom in what is now called the "Ode of Joy," which Beethoven, a hater of German political institutions and a lover of the British constitution, helped to make immortal? Why should Wagner's dramas have been banished from the stage of the Metropolitan Opera House? Because of the political beliefs of their composer? Assuredly not; for he was a revolutionary against the monarchical state while living and after his death left no preachments which could bring comfort to those who attempted to destroy the political ideals for which America went into battle. He wrote a silly lampoon on the French Government after the Franco-Prussian War, but its banality avenged itself on his fame. He wrote a march to glorify William I, but his political reputation wrought its rejection at the function for which he had designed it. He also wrote a march to celebrate the centenary of American Independence, but with it he garnered as little artistic glory as with his foolish French farce.

Should Wagner's dramas be banished from our stage because of the doctrines which they inculcated? The world has learned to smile at Wagner as a philosopher. Even Bernard Shaw breaks down in his elucidation of the doctrines of socialism, which he assumes to be the basis of "The Ring of the Nibelung" when he reaches "Götterdammerung"; wherefore he proclaims that drama to be mere opera and poor opera at that. But the underlying purpose of the tetralogy is to teach that selfish egoism, finding its expression in brute force, must give way to a dispensation of justice and love; the selfish will of Wotan is broken by the willing self-sacrifice of Brünnhilde. Shall we quarrel with such an ethical conception? Or with that which lies at the base of "Tannhäuser"—that salvation comes to humanity through the love of pure womanhood? Then must we also condemn the uplifting fable of Alkestis and empty our vessels of contumely not only upon the eighteenth-century Austrian Gluck and his French librettist but also upon Euripides, in whose favor the statute of limitations may surely be pleaded. Is there aught of political or moral obliquity in " Parsifal," whose fundamental thought is that it is the enlightenment which comes through compassionate pity that brings salvation? Perhaps " Die Meistersinger von Nürnberg " falls under the ban because it is in its externals so peculiarly German. But it is a comedy which admirably illustrates the classical definition, " Ridendo castigat mores," and has no other purpose than to illustrate the conflict between the regulative and creative impulses in art—between classicism and romanticism rightly understood, between conservatism and radicalism. " Lohengrin? " Alas for proud and too feminine Elsa! Alas, also, for her classic prototype Psyche! The Knight of the Grail ought not to have consumed so much time apostrophizing the balmy zephyrs of his wedding night, giving his bride opportunity to grow inquisitive; but he came in chivalric pity to rescue a damsel in distress. Is there harm in our contemplation of his dilatoriness and its consequences? Besides though unfortunate himself in his adventure he rights a great wrong and sets the machinations of the wicked at naught.

The man Wagner, then, can not be to us a rock of offense, nor can the ethical aims of his artistic creations. What remains? Only the language of his vocal music which has become hateful because of the conduct of the people to whom it is the vernacular. Because of this hatred we were asked and obliged to suffer not only the loss of Wagner's dramas but also the songs of Schubert, Schumann, Brahms, Franz, and other German lyricists—some of the most exquisite music of composers who wrote long before German materialism and lust of material conquest created by German imperialism had crushed out the creative spirit from German music. Let it not be forgotten that the days of Germany's greatness in literature and music were antecedent to her political greatness. The soil of Prussia, and Prussianized Germany, has produced little in art which we can not spare. The last truly great German composer in the line of succession to Haydn, Mozart, Beethoven, Schubert, and Schumann who lived in the days of the modern empire was Brahms; and he was a son of the once free city of Hamburg. His predecessors, who had laid their hands on his head in apostolic benediction, were all sons of petty states. The Great Dead owed nothing to Germany united under the yoke of Prussia—neither the poets who were destroyed by those whom they had compelled to emancipate themselves, nor the composers who sang in blissful indifference to the political conditions which surrounded them. Only one among them all took an interest in politics—Beethoven, who loomed up in his own day as a democrat, willing to be estranged from the Rhineland in which he was born, chafing under the bonds which held him in Vienna, damning the régime which gave him of its bounty that it might share his glory, and admiring the English and their constitution with undisguised admiration. "You have heads on your shoulders in England," said he to one of his English visitors, and on his deathbed he called for a reading of the entire speech of Canning advocating a recognition of the South American Republics. But in 1917-18 we were prohibited from listening even to Beethoven's celebration of conjugal love and fidelity, because "Fidelio" was composed to German words, though even its plot was borrowed from the French.

In the season which has last been passed under review the public of New York heard "Martha" sung in Italian, as they had been accustomed to hear it for so many years that the fact that it is a German opera was scarcely known to the listening generation, and Liszt's "St. Elizabeth" sung in English. The exigencies of grim war, therefore, compelled a change from the policy which had been followed

WHAT OF THE FUTURE?

with reasonable consistency (there being such exceptions as the Russian " Boris Godounow " and " Prince Igor " sung in Italian and " Le Coq d'Or " in French). One result, therefore, may be an approach, at least, to " national opera." Putting aside the question of language, it was sound and sensible as well as proper and practical to put a tabu upon enemy aliens as far as possible in our opera house, for the simple reason that by retaining and remunerating them Americans were putting money into their hands which would in time be turned into aid and comfort for our enemies. In a sense it was merely a part of the commercial warfare which must follow the end of the military. If it involves something of a sacrifice of artistic excellence for a period it will not be for long and will in the end bring profit in the recognition and development of our own resources. The just claims of our native talent, creative and re-creative, will be met.

APPENDIX

RECORDS OF THE LAST TWO SEASONS AT THE MANHATTAN OPERA HOUSE AND TEN SEASONS, 1908-18, AT THE METROPOLITAN

RECORD OF THE LAST TWO SEASONS AT THE MANHATTAN

SEASON 1908-1909

Twenty weeks from November 9, 1908, to March 27, 1909. Under the sole management of Mr. Oscar Hammerstein.

TABLE OF PERFORMANCES

Opera	First Performance	Times
"Tosca"	November 9	5
"Thaïs"	November 11	7
"Samson et Dalila"	November 13	6
"Il Barbiere di Siviglia"	November 14	3
"Lucia di Lammermoor"	November 18	7
"Gli Ugonotti"	November 20	2
"Carmen"	November 26	2
"Le Jongleur de Notre Dame"	November 27	7
"Cavalleria Rusticana"	December 4	5
"Pagliacci"	December 4	5
"Rigoletto"	December 5	5
"Traviata"	December 12	5
"La Bohème"	December 14	5
"Les Contes d'Hoffmann"	December 16	7
"Otello"	December 25	6
"Pelléas et Mélisande"	January 6	4
"Crispino e la Comare"	January 9	3
"Salome"	January 28	10
"Aïda"	February 10	2
"La Sonnambula"	February 13	3
"Louise"	February 19	5
"I Puritani"	February 26	2
"Il Trovatore"	March 1	1
"Princesse d'Auberge"	March 10	3
"La Navarraise"	March 20	1

APPENDIX

SUMMARY

Total number of performances 111
Number of representations 104
Total number of operas produced 25
Operas composed in Italian 14
Operas composed in French 9
Opera composed in German 1
Opera composed in Flemish 1

The difference between the number of representations and the total number of performances of the different operas is due to the fact that on some occasions two or more works were produced in the same evening.

SEASON 1909-1910

Mr. Hammerstein's last season, for an account of which see Chapter V. The regular season began on November 8, 1909, and ended on March 26, 1910. There had been a preliminary season from August 30 to October 30, 1909. The record embraces the regular season only:

Opera	*First Performance*	*Times*
"Hérodiade"	November 8	6
"Traviata"	November 10	4
"Aïda"	November 12	3
"Thaïs"	November 13	6
"Cavalleria Rusticana"	November 13	4
"Pagliacci"	November 13	8
"Lucia di Lammermoor"	November 16	7
"La Fille de Madame Angot"	November 16	2
"Sapho"	November 17	3
"La Fille du Régiment"	November 22	4
"La Mascotte"	November 23	1
"Carmen"	November 25	6
"Tosca"	November 26	3
"Les Dragons des Villars"	November 27	2
"Le Jongleur de Notre Dame"	December 4	5
"Les Cloches de Corneville"	December 4	3
"Faust"	December 8	3
"Tannhäuser"	December 10	3
"Les Contes d'Hoffmann"	December 25	8
"Trovatore"	January 8	2

APPENDIX

Opera	First Performance	Times
"La Bohème"	January 14	5
"Grisélidis"	January 19	4
"Samson et Dalila"	January 28	2
"Elektra"	February 1	7
"Rigoletto"	February 11	4
"Louise"	February 23	2
"La Navarraise"	February 28	2
"Salome"	March 5	4
"Pelléas et Mélisande"	March 11	3
"Lakmé"	March 21	1
Mixed Bill	March 25	1

After the conclusion of the season Mr. Hammerstein sold his Philadelphia Opera House, which had been opened a week after the performances began in New York, to a company of gentlemen largely interested in the Metropolitan, and entered into an obligation with them not to give grand opera in New York City for ten years. It seems appropriate, therefore, to print the following tabular record of his performances during his four years' management of the Manhattan Opera House:

FOUR SEASONS AT THE MANHATTAN

Opera	1906-1907	1907-1908	1908-1909	1909-1910
"Aïda"	12	9	2	3
"Andrea Chenier"	0	1	0	0
"Ballo in Maschera"	2	4	0	0
"Barbiere di Siviglia"	2	0	3	0
"Bohème"	4	0	5	5
"Cavalleria"	8	4	3	4
"Carmen"	19	11	2	6
"Contes d'Hoffmann"	0	11	7	8
"Cloches de Corneville"	0	0	0	3
"Crispino e la Comare"	0	3	3	0
"Damnation de Faust"	0	3	0	0
"Dinorah"	1	1	0	0
"Don Giovanni"	4	3	0	0
"Dragons des Villars"	0	0	0	2
"Elektra"	0	0	0	7
"Elisir d'Amore"	3	0	0	0
"Ernani"	0	1	0	0

APPENDIX

Opera	1906-1907	1907-1908	1908-1909	1909-1910
"Faust"	7	4	0	3
"Fille de Mme. Angot"	0	0	0	2
"Fille du Régiment"	0	0	0	2
"Fra Diavolo"	4	0	0	0
"Gioconda"	0	4	0	0
"Grisélidis"	0	0	0	4
"Hérodiade"	0	0	0	6
"Huguenots"	5	0	2	0
"Jongleur de Notre Dame"	0	0	7	5
"Lakmé"	0	0	0	1
"Louise"	0	11	5	2
"Lucia di Lammermoor"	6	8	7	7
"Martha"	4	0	0	0
"Mascotte"	0	0	0	1
"Mignon"	3	0	0	0
"Navarraise"	2	5	1	2
"Otello"	0	0	6	0
"Pagliacci"	10	9	5	8
"Pelléas et Mélisande"	0	7	4	3
"Princesse d'Auberge"	0	0	3	0
"Puritani"	2	0	2	0
"Rigoletto"	11	5	5	4
"Salome"	0	0	10	4
"Samson et Dalila"	0	0	6	2
"Siberia"	0	3	0	0
"Sapho"	0	0	0	3
"Sonnambula"	3	0	3	0
"Tannhäuser"	0	0	0	3
"Thaïs"	0	7	7	6
"Traviata"	3	5	5	4
"Tosca"	0	0	5	3
"Trovatore"	6	5	1	2

TEN SEASONS AT THE METROPOLITAN OPERA HOUSE

SEASON 1908-1909

Twenty-fourth of the regular subscription. Twenty weeks beginning on November 16, 1908, and ending on April 19, 1909. Under the joint management of Giulio Gatti-Casazza and Andreas Dippel. An extra week was added for performances of the Wagnerian tetralogy, " Aïda " and " Madama Butterfly," and this week is included in the table.

Opera	First Performance	Times
"Aïda"	November 16	8
"Die Walküre"	November 18	5
"Madama Butterfly"	November 19	8
"La Traviata"	November 20	5
"Tosca"	November 21	6
"La Bohème"	November 21	7
"Tiefland"	November 23	4
"Parsifal"	November 26	5
"Rigoletto"	November 28	3
"Carmen"	December 3	6
"Faust"	December 5	7
"Götterdämmerung"	December 10	5
"Le Villi"	December 17	5
"Cavalleria Rusticana"	December 17	7
"Lucia di Lammermoor"	December 19	2
"Il Trovatore"	December 21	5
"Tristan und Isolde"	December 23	4
"L'Elisir d'Amore"	December 25	2
"Pagliacci"	December 26	5
"La Wally"	January 6	4
"Le Nozze di Figaro"	January 13	6
"Die Meistersinger"	January 22	5
"Manon"	February 3	6

Opera	First Performance	Times
"Tannhäuser"	February 5	7
"The Bartered Bride"	February 19	6
"Fidelio"	February 20	1
"Falstaff"	March 20	3
"Don Pasquale"	March 24	1
"Il Barbiere di Siviglia"	March 25	2
"Siegfried"	March 27	2
"Das Rheingold"	April 5	1

Summary

Subscription weeks	20
Extra week	1
Regular performances (afternoons and evenings)	120
Special representations of the drama in "The Ring"	4
Special benefit and holiday performances	10
Italian operas in the repertory	17
German operas in the repertory	10
French operas in the repertory	3
Bohemian opera	1
Italian representations	79
German representations	45
French representations	19
Oratorio performance on an opera night	1
Double bills	2
Novelties produced	4

Fifteen performances were also given in Brooklyn, twenty-four in Philadelphia and four in Baltimore. The last city and Brooklyn were privileged to hear "Hänsel und Gretel," which was denied the metropolis. The operas given in the Borough of Brooklyn were: "Faust," "Rigoletto," "Die Walküre," "Tiefland," "Mma. Butterfly," "Il Trovatore," "Carmen," "Cavalleria Rusticana" and "Pagliacci," "Le Nozze di Figaro," "Hänsel und Gretel," "Meistersinger," "La Traviata," "The Bartered Bride," "Aïda," and "La Bohème."

SEASON 1909-1910

Twenty-fifth regular subscription season. Twenty weeks beginning November 15, 1909, ending April 2, 1910. Giulio

APPENDIX

Gatti-Casazza, General Manager, Andreas Dippel, Administrative Director. There were also a subscription season of twenty representations in Brooklyn, two performances each week at the New Theater, many special performances and subscription seasons in Philadelphia, Baltimore, and Boston. Because of this unexampled activity, New York never having been so overburdened with opera in its history before or since, I make a detailed tabulated statement.

SUBSCRIPTION SEASON AT THE METROPOLITAN

Opera	First Performance	Times
"La Gioconda"	November 15	5
"Otello"	November 17	6
"La Traviata"	November 18	3
"Madama Butterfly"	November 19	6
"Lohengrin"	November 20	6
"La Bohème"	November 20	6
"Tosca"	November 23	6
"Cavalleria Rusticana"	November 24	7
"Pagliacci"	November 24	7
"Il Trovatore"	November 25	6
"Tristan und Isolde"	November 27	5
"Aïda"	December 3	6
"Tannhäuser"	December 4	4
"Manon"	December 6	3
"Siegfried"	December 16	2
"Orfeo ed Eurydice"	December 23	5
"The Bartered Bride"	December 24	1
"Faust"	December 25	5
"Rigoletto"	December 25	2
"Die Walküre"	January 8	3
"Il Barbiere di Siviglia"	January 15	3
"Germania"	January 22	5
"L'Elisir d'Amore"	January 27	1
"Hänsel und Gretel"	January 29	1
"Don Pasquale"	February 2	2
"Stradella"	February 3	2
"Fra Diavolo"	February 5	3
"Falstaff"	February 16	2
"Das Rheingold"	February 24	1
"Werther"	February 28	2
"Götterdämmerung"	March 4	1
"Pique Dame"	March 5	4

APPENDIX

Opera	First Performance	Times
"Der Freischütz"	March 11	2
"The Pipe of Desire"	March 18	2
"Die Meistersinger"	March 26	2
"La Sonnambula"	April 2	1

SUMMARY

Weeks in the season 20
Subscription performances 120
Number of operas produced 36
German operas 11
Bohemian opera 1
Russian opera 1
English opera 1
Italian operas 18
French operas 4
German performances 34
French performances 13
Italian performances 79
English performances 2
Double bills (including ballets and divertissements) 23
Number of ballets 2
Performances of complete ballets 6

EXTRA REPRESENTATIONS AT THE METROPOLITAN OPERA HOUSE

"Parsifal," Thanksgiving matinee, November 25.
"Hänsel und Gretel," special matinees, December 21 and 28.
"La Bohème," benefit of Italian charities, January 4.
"Manon," benefit of French charities, January 18.
"Das Rheingold," serial matinees of "Der Ring," January 24.
"Die Walküre," serial matinees of "Der Ring," January 27.
"Siegfried," serial matinees of "Der Ring," January 28.
"Götterdämmerung," serial matinees of "Der Ring," February 1.
"Stradella," benefit of German Press Club, February 15.
"Vienna Waltzes," ballet, benefit of German Press Club, February 15.
"Parsifal," special matinee on Washington's birthday, February 22.
"La Gioconda," benefit of Italian charities, February 22.
Mixed bill, benefit of Opera House Pension Fund, March 1.
"Aïda" and ballet divertissement, benefit of the Legal Aid Society, March 15.
"Hänsel und Gretel" and "Coppelia," ballet, special matinee, March 15.
"Parsifal," Good Friday matinees, March 25.

APPENDIX

Summary

Total number of extra performances 16
German operas 7
German representations 11
French opera 1
French representation 1
Italian operas 3
Italian representations 3
Miscellaneous programme 1
Double bills (operas, ballets, and divertissements) 5

PERFORMANCES AT THE NEW THEATER

Opera	First Performance	Times
"Werther"	November 16	4
"The Bartered Bride"	November 17	2
"Il Barbiere di Siviglia"	November 25	3
"Czar und Zimmermann"	November 30	4
"Il Maestro di Capella"	December 9	3
"Cavalleria Rusticana"	December 9	3
"La Fille de Madame Angot"	December 14	4
"Don Pasquale"	December 23	3
"Pagliacci"	January 6	2
"Fra Diavolo"	January 11	2
"Manon"	February 3	1
"L'Elisir d'Amore"	February 4	1
"L'Attaque du Moulin"	February 8	4
"La Bohème"	February 17	2
"Stradella"	February 22	1
"Madama Butterfly"	March 4	1
"Tosca"	March 22	1
"La Sonnambula"	March 23	1
"The Pipe of Desire"	March 31	1

Summary

Number of performances 40
Number of operas produced 19
German operas 2
Bohemian opera 1
English opera 1
Italian operas 9
French operas 9
French operas 6
German representations 7
French representations 15

APPENDIX

Italian representations 20
English representation 1
Double bills (including ballets and divertissements) 15
Pantomime 1
Ballets 3

THE BROOKLYN SEASON

Opera	Date of Performance
"Manon"	November 8
"Tannhäuser"	November 15
"Madama Butterfly"	November 22
"Tosca"	November 29
"Lohengrin"	December 6
"Martha"	December 13
"Il Trovatore"	December 20
"Il Maestro di Capella" and "Pagliacci"	January 3
"Aïda"	January 17
"Faust"	January 27
"Fra Diavolo"	January 31
"Stradella" and divertissement	February 7
"L'Attaque du Moulin"	February 13
"La Bohème"	February 21
"Otello"	February 28
"La Gioconda"	March 7
"Il Barbiere" and divertissement	March 14
"Rigoletto"	March 21
"Der Freischütz"	March 29
"Madama Butterfly" and "Hungary" (ballet)	April 4

The following table offers an analytical summary of the entire season:

Subscription performances 160
Total performances 197
Operas produced 41
German operas produced 13
Italian operas produced 18
French operas produced 7
Bohemian opera produced 1
Russian opera produced 1
English opera produced 1
German representations 56
Italian representations 115
French representations 23
English representations 3
Double bills (including ballets and divertissements) 48
Performances of complete ballets 12

APPENDIX

SEASON 1910-1911

Twenty-sixth season of the subscription. Twenty weeks beginning November 14, 1910, and ending on April 15, 1911. Table including extra performances, a subscription by the Philadelphia-Chicago Company, and performances in Brooklyn:

REGULAR METROPOLITAN SUBSCRIPTION PERFORMANCES

Opera	First Performance	Times
"Armide"	November 14	3
"Tannhäuser"	November 16	5
"Aïda"	November 17	6
"Walküre"	November 18	4
"Madama Butterfly"	November 19	5
"La Bohème"	November 21	5
"Gioconda"	November 23	6
"Rigoletto"	November 24	3
"Cavalleria Rusticana"	November 25	5
"Pagliacci"	November 25	7
"Lohengrin"	November 28	5
"Trovatore"	December 1	5
"Faust"	December 10	4
"Orfeo ed Eurydice"	December 10	5
"La Fanciulla del West"	December 26	7
"Königskinder"	December 28	7
"Tristan und Isolde"	January 4	4
"Roméo et Juliette"	January 13	2
"Siegfried"	January 14	1
"Meistersinger"	January 20	4
"Germania"	February 1	2
"Traviata"	February 2	2
"Tosca"	February 8	5
"The Bartered Bride"	February 15	4
"Otello"	February 27	5
"Ariane et Barbe-Bleue"	March 29	4
"Hänsel und Gretel"	April 6	6
Mixed Bill	April 6	1

There were ten Saturday evening subscription representations at regular prices, one of which, "Thaïs," was given by the Chicago Company. Also twenty-six performances outside of the subscription, at which " Parsifal " (on November 24), " Das Rheingold " (February 2), and " Götterdämmerung " (February 22), which were not in the subscription list, and twelve other operas and a mixed bill were given.

GRAND SUMMARY OF THE METROPOLITAN COMPANY

Total representations (including double and mixed bills) 141
Italian operas 14
German operas 7
French operas 3
Bohemian opera (sung in German) 1
Performances in Italian 77
Performances in German 40
Performances in French 11

The Metropolitan Opera Company also gave fourteen representations, one of a double bill, bringing forward the following operas: " Il Trovatore," " Orfeo," " Tannhäuser," " Cavalleria Rusticana " with " Pagliacci," " Lohengrin," " Königskinder," " La Bohème," " Rigoletto," " Butterfly," " Tosca," " Aïda," " Otello," " Parsifal," and " The Girl of the Golden West," in the Borough of Brooklyn.

There was an extra subscription season by the Philadelphia-Chicago Company at the Metropolitan Opera House which made the following showing:

SUBSCRIPTION SEASON OF THE PHILADELPHIA-CHICAGO COMPANY

Opera	First Performance	Times
" Thaïs "	January 24	1
" Louise "	January 31	2
" Pelléas et Mélisande "	February 7	1
" Les Contes d'Hoffmann "	February 14	1
" Carmen "	February 21	1
" Natoma " (once in double bill)	February 28	3
" Il Segreto di Susanna " (in double bill)	March 14	2

APPENDIX 433

Opera	First Performance	Times
"Le Jongleur de Notre Dame" (in double bill)	March 14	1
"Quo Vadis"	April 4	1

Eleven subscription evenings, one extra, nine operas, three double bills.

SEASON 1911-1912

Twenty-seventh subscription season, twenty-two weeks from November 13, 1911, to April 13, 1912. There were 110 subscription representations and thirty-nine extra performances, included in which were three representations of " Parsifal " on Thanksgiving Day, New Year's Day, and Good Friday. " Das Rheingold " and " Götterdämmerung," which were not included in the subscription season, were included in the cyclical representation of " The Ring of the Nibelung." Two other German operas which were in the subscription repertory had special performances: " Hänsel und Gretel," 5, and " Königskinder," 3.

METROPOLITAN SUBSCRIPTION SEASON

Opera	First Performance	Times
"Aïda"	November 13	5
"Königskinder"	November 15	4
"La Fanciulla del West"	November 16	5
"Tristan und Isolde"	November 17	5
"Lobetanz"	November 18	5
"Madama Butterfly"	November 20	5
"Faust"	November 22	3
"Götterdämmerung"	November 23	2
"Cavalleria Rusticana"	November 24	3
"Pagliacci"	November 24	6
"Lohengrin"	November 25	4
"Gioconda"	November 29	5
"Trovatore"	November 30	3
"Hänsel und Gretel"	December 4	2
"Tosca"	December 11	4
"Armide"	December 16	4

Opera	First Performance	Times
"La Bohème"	December 23	5
"Orfeo ed Eurydice"	December 25	5
"Lucia di Lammermoor"	December 27	3
"Siegfried"	December 30	2
"Le Donne curiose"	January 3	5
"Rigoletto"	January 11	2
"Versiegelt"	January 20	4
"Ariane et Barbe-Bleue"	January 31	3
"Tannhäuser"	February 17	3
"Otello"	February 21	4
"The Bartered Bride"	February 23	2
"Die Walküre"	February 26	4
"Meistersinger"	March 6	3
"Mona"	March 14	4
"Manon"	March 30	3

GRAND SUMMARY

Total representations	148
Italian operas	19
German operas	11
French operas	4
English opera	1
Bohemian opera	1
Total operas	36
Performances in Italian	77
Performances in German	58
Performances in French	13
Performances in English	4
Double bills	4
Mixed bill	1

There were also performances by the Metropolitan Company in Brooklyn as follows: "Madama Butterfly," "Il Trovatore," "Hänsel und Gretel," "Cavalleria Rusticana" and "Lobetanz," "Lohengrin," "La Bohème," "Tannhäuser," "Faust," "Pagliacci," "Siegfried," "Tosca," "The Bartered Bride," "Otello," "Königskinder," "Aïda," "Die Walküre."

Also performances by the Philadelphia-Chicago Company at the Metropolitan. For an account of these performances see **Chapter X**.

APPENDIX

SEASON 1912-1913

Twenty-eighth subscription season, twenty-three weeks beginning November 11, 1912, and ending April 19, 1913. Giulio Gatti-Casazza, General Manager. Table of the subscription and general lists together with the operas given in Brooklyn:

THE SUBSCRIPTION SEASON

Opera	First Performance	Times
"Manon Lescaut"	November 11	5
"Tannhäuser"	November 13	5
"Gioconda"	November 14	3
"Madama Butterfly"	November 15	5
"Götterdämmerung"	November 16	3
"Königskinder"	November 18	5
"Cavalleria Rusticana"	November 20	3
"Pagliacci"	November 20	5
"Faust"	November 21	3
"Die Zauberflöte"	November 23	5
"La Fanciulla del West"	November 25	4
"Trovatore"	November 27	3
"Bohème"	November 28	5
"Hänsel und Gretel"	November 30	2
"Meistersinger"	December 6	4
"Aïda"	December 9	3
"Il Segreto di Susanna"	December 13	3
"Die Walküre"	December 14	4
"Orfeo ed Eurydice"	December 19	2
"Gli Ugonotti"	December 27	5
"Tristan und Isolde"	December 30	5
"Il Barbiere di Siviglia"	January 1	3
"Tosca"	January 4	5
"Otello"	January 6	3
"Les Contes d'Hoffmann"	January 11	5
"Siegfried"	January 17	1
"Manon"	January 22	4
"Traviata"	January 29	3
"Le Donne curiose"	February 5	3
"Cyrano de Bergerac"	February 27	5
"Lohengrin"	March 17	2
"Boris Godounow"	March 19	4
"Don Pasquale"	April 5	2

To arrive at the sum total of the season's activities there must be added the customary list of benefit and holiday performances together with those arranged for what used to be called the Metropolitan Opera House's pension fund. Of these performances, numbering thirty-seven, eighteen were in German, seventeen Italian, and five in French. The Grand Summary for the season barring the performances of the Chicago Company, which will be found discussed in their proper places, and fourteen performances in Brooklyn from the conventional list, reads as follows:

GRAND SUMMARY

Regular subscription performances	115
Subscription Saturday Nights	12
Subscription "Nibelung" performances	4
Special benefits	7
Extra performances	14
Total performances	152
Total number of operas performed	36
Operas composed in Italian	17
Operas composed in German	12
Operas composed in French	4
Opera composed in English	1
Opera composed in Russian	1
Italian performances	86
German performances	54
French performances	16
English performances	5
Double bills	13
Mixed bills	2

SEASON 1913-1914

Twenty-ninth subscription season. Twenty-three weeks from November 17, 1913, to April 25, 1914. Giulio Gatti-Casazza, sole manager.

THE SUBSCRIPTION SEASON

Opera	First Performance	Times
"La Gioconda"	November 17	4
"Zauberflöte"	November 19	5

APPENDIX 437

Opera	First Performance	Times
"La Bohème"	November 20	5
"Lohengrin"	November 21	5
"Un Ballo in Maschera"	November 22	5
"Madama Butterfly"	November 24	4
"Lucia di Lammermoor"	November 26	1
"Manon Lescaut"	November 27	4
"Boris Godounow"	November 28	5
"Siegfried"	December 4	3
"Cavalleria Rusticana"	December 5	2
"Pagliacci"	December 5	5
"Les Contes d'Hoffmann"	December 6	2
"Aïda"	December 8	4
"Tannhäuser"	December 12	2
"Der Rosenkavalier"	December 18	5
"Tosca"	December 19	6
"Die Walküre"	December 20	5
"Tristan und Isolde"	December 24	4
"Manon"	December 31	4
"La Traviata"	January 1	4
"L'Amore dei tre Re"	January 2	5
"Königskinder"	January 8	5
"Die Meistersinger"	January 15	4
"Madeleine"	January 24	4
"La Fanciulla del West"	February 4	3
"Don Pasquale"	February 5	2
"Julien"	February 26	5
"Götterdämmerung"	February 28	2
"Orfeo ed Eurydice"	March 2	3
"L'Amore Medico"*	March 25	4
"Hänsel und Gretel"*	March 26	2
"Il Segreto di Susanna"*	March 30	3

*Operas given only in double bills.

As indicative of the manager's differentiation between the taste of his subscribers and that of the general public invited to patronize the representations outside of the subscription, a record of the extra performances must be examined. The subscription compassed 115 representations, in 11 of which there were double bills. There were, therefore, 126 operatic performances—69 in Italian, 42 in German, 11 in French, and 4 in English. "Parsifal" was reserved for the holidays as in the preceding seasons. "Der Rosenkavalier," a novelty, had its first performance on December 9 and was

APPENDIX

then incorporated into the subscription repertory and had two later representations in the extra list. "Hänsel und Gretel," withheld this season from the subscribers, had four performances. "Das Rheingold" figured only in the customary "Nibelung" cycle. "Faust" had a single performance on a Saturday evening at popular prices. The remainder of the extra 39 representations were of operas in the subscription list.

GRAND SUMMARY

Regular subscription representations 115
Extra representations 39
Double bills 15
Mixed bills 2
Total operatic performances 167
Performances in Italian 88
Performances in German 63
Performances in French 12
Performances in English 4
Operas by Italian composers (including Gluck) 17
Operas by German composers 13
Operas by French composers (including Offenbach) 4
Opera by American (naturalized) composer 1
Opera by Russian composer 1

The activities of the Chicago Company in New York may be studied in their proper place. The operas performed in Brooklyn were fourteen, viz.: "Bohème," "Faust," "Les Contes d'Hoffmann," "Traviata," "Tannhäuser," "Königskinder," "Madeleine," "Pagliacci" (double bill), "Der Rosenkavalier," "Aïda," "Tosca," "Lohengrin," "Gioconda," "Die Walküre," and "Orfeo ed Eurydice."

SEASON 1914-1915

Thirtieth subscription season, twenty-three weeks from November 16, 1914, to April 24, 1915. Giulio Gatti-Casazza, general manager.

APPENDIX

THE SUBSCRIPTION SEASON

Opera	First Performance	Times
"Un Ballo in Maschera"*	November 16	2
"Lohengrin"	November 18	4
"Carmen"	November 19	5
"Rosenkavalier"	November 20	5
"La Bohème"*	November 21	6
"Die Zauberflöte"	November 23	5
"La Gioconda"	November 25	2
"La Traviata"	November 26	4
"Boris Godounow"	November 28	5
"Madama Butterfly"	November 30	5
"Tristan und Isolde"	December 3	4
"Tosca"	December 4	5
"Cavalleria Rusticana"†	December 5	2
"Pagliacci"†	December 5	6
"Die Walküre"	December 11	5
"Euryanthe"	December 19	4
"Aïda"	December 23	5
"Manon"	December 24	3
"Tannhäuser"	December 25	4
"Les Huguenots"	December 30	3
"Manon Lescaut"	January 1	3
"Siegfried"	January 9	2
"Madame Sans-Gêne"	January 25	5
"Fidelio"	January 30	5
"L'Oracolo"†	February 4	5
"L'Amore dei tre Re"	February 11	5
"Il Trovatore"	February 20	5
"Die Meistersinger"	March 12	3
"Götterdämmerung"	March 18	1
"Iris"	April 1	4

* Once in a double bill. † In double bills only.

The operas which had performances only in the extra list were "Parsifal" (four times), "Das Rheingold" (once), and "Hänsel und Gretel" (four times).

GRAND SUMMARY

Regular subscription performances	115
Extra performances	36
Double bills	12
Mixed bills	2

APPENDIX

Total number of performances 151
Total number of representations of different operas 165
Operas by Italian composers 15
Operas by German composers 13
Operas by French composers (including Meyerbeer) 3
Opera by Russian composer 1
Performances in Italian 92
Performances in German 58
Performances in French 12

At the Opera House in Brooklyn the operas performed were " Manon Lescaut," " Cavalleria Rusticana " and " Pagliacci," " Lohengrin," " La Bohème," " Die Zauberflöte," " La Traviata," " Euryanthe," " Carmen," " Tosca," " Aïda," " Tannhäuser," " Madama Butterfly," " L'Oracolo," and " Hänsel und Gretel."

SEASON 1915-1916

Thirty-first subscription season at the Metropolitan Opera House. Twenty weeks of opera from November 15, 1915, after which the house was given over till April 29, 1916, to the Diaghileff Ballet Russe. The season under the sole management of Giulio Gatti-Casazza.

TABLE OF THE SUBSCRIPTION PERFORMANCES

Opera	First Performance	Times
"Samson et Dalila"	November 15	5
"Boris Godounow"	November 17	5
"Götterdämmerung"	November 18	2
"La Bohème"	November 19	4
"Der Rosenkavalier"	November 20	5
"Il Barbiere di Siviglia"	November 25	3
"Lohengrin"	November 26	4
"Tosca"	November 27	3
"Tristan und Isolde"	December 1	4
"Cavalleria Rusticana"	December 2	2
"Pagliacci"	December 2	3
"Trovatore"	December 4	3
"Die Zauberflöte"	December 8	4
"Aïda"	December 9	3
"Marta"	December 11	4

APPENDIX

Opera	First Performance	Times
"Manon"	December 15	1
"Die Walküre"	December 16	3
"Traviata"	December 22	2
"Prince Igor"	December 30	5
"Madama Butterfly"	December 31	2
"Un Ballo in Maschera"	January 1	2
"Manon Lescaut"	January 6	3
"Meistersinger"	January 7	3
"Siegfried"	January 15	2
"Hänsel und Gretel"	January 19	2
"Goyescas"	January 28	4
"Lucia di Lammermoor"	January 31	4
"Rigoletto"	February 11	5
"Carmen"	February 17	5
"Das Rheingold"	February 18	2
"La Sonnambula"	March 3	2
"Der Widerspänstigen Zähmung"	March 15	2
"Madame Sans-Gêne"	March 17	2

There were 100 subscription representations and 106 performances in all, two of them offering double bills. The performances in Italian, German, and French respectively were 58, 33, and 11 in number. The representations outside of the subscription numbered 28, two of them made up of double bills and one of a mixed bill, which was the customary offering at the representation for the benefit of the emergency fund. "Parsifal," which had two performances, was the only opera in the extra list not included in the subscription.

GRAND SUMMARY

Italian composers represented	8
German composers represented	6
French composers represented	3
Russian composers represented	2
Spanish composer represented	1
Performances in Italian	72
Performances in German	47
Performances in French	11
Performances in Spanish	5

Double bills presented 8
Mixed bills presented 1
Total number of operas presented 34
Total number of evenings and afternoons 128
Total number of full operatic performances 136

The operas given in Brooklyn were "Il Trovatore," "Boris Godounow," "Die Zauberflöte," "La Bohème," "Il Barbiere," "Aïda," "Tristan und Isolde," "Manon," "Die Meistersinger," and "Lucia di Lammermoor."

SEASON 1916-1917

Thirty-second subscription season; twenty-three weeks from November 13, 1916, to April 21, 1917—115 representations. Giulio Gatti-Casazza, General Manager.

TABLE OF SUBSCRIPTION PERFORMANCES

Opera	First Performance	Times
"Les Pêcheurs de Perles"	November 13	3
"Tristan und Isolde"	November 15	5
"Manon Lescaut"	November 16	2
"Der Rosenkavalier"	November 17	3
"Prince Igor"	November 18	2
"Aïda"	November 18	4
"Die Zauberflöte"	November 20	2
"Trovatore"	November 23	4
"Samson et Dalila"	November 24	3
"Iphigenia auf Tauris"	November 25	6
"Boris Godounow"	November 27	3
"Traviata"	November 29	2
"La Bohème"	November 30	4
"Lohengrin"	December 1	4
"Tosca"	December 4	5
"Fidelio"	December 9	3
"Cavalleria Rusticana"	December 15	2
"Pagliacci"	December 15	4
"Francesca da Rimini"	December 22	5
"Marta"	December 25	3
"L'Elisir d'Amore"	December 30	5
"Madama Butterfly"	January 1	3
"Das Rheingold"	January 4	1
"Carmen"	January 5	5

APPENDIX 443

Opera	First Performance	Times
"Die Meistersinger"	January 17	4
"Siegfried"	January 20	2
"Le Nozze di Figaro"	January 24	3
"Rigoletto"	February 7	4
"Die Walküre"	February 8	2
"Thaïs"	February 16	5
"Il Barbiere"	February 22	1
"Lucia di Lammermoor"	February 28	1
"Madame Sans-Gêne"	March 2	3
"The Canterbury Pilgrims"	March 8	5
"Lakmé"	March 24	3
"L'Oracolo"	March 31	2

Besides the subscription performances there were 34 representations for benefits, etc., and the annual cyclical representation of the dramas composing "The Ring of the Nibelung," besides "Parsifal" and "Hänsel und Gretel." Including these extra performances we arrive at the following

GRAND SUMMARY

Italian composers represented	9
German composers represented	6
French composers represented	4
Russian composers represented	2
American composer represented	1
Operas by Italian composers	16
Operas by German composers	13
Operas by French composers	5
Operas by Russian composers	2
Opera by American composer	1
Performances in Italian	78
Performances in German	45
Performances in French	25
Performances in English	6
Double bills	5
Mixed bill	1
Total number of operas presented	39
Total number of performances of different operas	154
Total number of representations	149

The operas given in Brooklyn were "Boris Godounow," "La Bohème," "Cavalleria," and "Pagliacci," "Lohen-

grin," " Tosca," " Aïda," " Carmen," " Tristan und Isolde,"
" Lucia di Lammermoor," " Marta," and " Thaïs."

SEASON 1917-1918

The war wrought so great a change in the character of the repertory of the Metropolitan Opera House in this, the thirty-third, subscription season, that it was thought unnecessary, because uninstructive touching the public taste, to distinguish in the tabulation of the performances between the regular subscription performances and those given for benefits and on special occasions. The season covered the usual twenty-three weeks, began on November 12, 1917, and ended on April 6, 1918. Mr. Giulio Gatti-Casazza was the sole manager.

Opera	First Performance	Times
" Aïda "	November 12	8
" Boris Godounow "	November 14	6
" L'Elisir d'Amore "	November 15	5
" La Bohème "	November 16	5
" Faust "	November 17	6
" Traviata "	November 17	3
" Tosca "	November 19	6
" Marta "	November 21	5
" Madama Butterfly "	November 22	6
" Samson et Dalila "	November 23	4
" Francesca da Rimini "	November 24	4
" Carmen "	November 29	7
" Prince Igor "	November 30	2
" Trovatore "	December 1	3
" Manon Lescaut "	December 5	4
" Cavalleria Rusticana "	December 7	5
" Pagliacci "	December 7	5
" La Figlia del Reggimento "	December 17	5
" Marôuf "	December 19	6
" Nozze di Figaro "	December 22	2
" L'Oracolo "	December 22	6
" Rigoletto "	December 29	5
" Saint Elizabeth "	January 3	5
" Thaïs "	January 5	6
" Lodoletta "	January 12	5
" Le Prophète "	February 7	5

APPENDIX

Opera	First Performance	Times
"I Puritani"	February 18	4
"Il Barbiere"	February 22	4
"Madame Sans-Gène"	March 2	3
"Le Coq d'Or"	March 6	6
"L'Amore dei tre Re"	March 14	5
"Shanewis"	March 23	5
"The Dance in Place Congo" (ballet)	March 23	4

SUMMARY

Subscription performances 115
Extra performances (including benefits) 26
Total performances 141
Double bills 7
Triple bill 1
Mixed bill 1
Operas by Italian composers 19
Operas by German composers (including Meyerbeer and Liszt). 4
Operas by Russian composers 3
Operas by French composers 5
Opera by American composers 1
Ballet by American composers 1
Performances in Italian 102
Performances in French 40
Performances in English 10

There were performances in Brooklyn as follows: " Tosca," " Le Nozze di Figaro," " Il Trovatore," " La Figlia del Reggimento," " Aïda," " Rigoletto," " Cavalleria Rusticana " with " Pagliacci," " La Bohème," " Thaïs," " I Puritani," and " Carmen."

INDEX

Abbey, Henry E., and Abbey, Schoeffel and Grau, 15, 16, 66, 67, 281, 330, 408
Aborn, Milton and Sargent, 177, 179
Absolute pitch, 264
Académie Royale, 133, 200
Academy of Music, New York, 14, 15, 228
Adaberto, Ester, 39
"Addio O miei sospiri," 148
Addison, 7, 129, 184
Adkins, Morton, 177
"Aeneid," 359
"Africaine, L'," opera by Meyerbeer, 330, 341
Agostinelli, soprano, 96
"Aïda," opera by Verdi, 42, 48, 48, 55, 177, 178, 178, 178, 243, 301, 395 (*see* Appendix)
Alboni, Marietta, 252
"Alceste," opera by Gluck, 144, 147
Alda, Frances, 31, 39, 50, 140, 274, 295, 321, 351, 398; *portrait*, 400
Aldrich, Mariska, 96, 141, 164
Aldrich, Richard, 329
Alkestis, 415
Alpine music, 53, 305, 306
Alten, Bella, 144, 248, 253
Althouse, Paul, début, 286; 321, 336, 370, 411
Altruism professed by managers, 95
Alvarez, tenor, 408
Amato, Pasquale, 29, 39, 39, 50, 51, 60, 140, 149, 204, 210, 266, 284; *portrait*, 294; 295, *portrait*, 310; 318, 336, 351, 407
American Company, The (theatrical), 189
"American Indian, The," 189

"Americano, L'," 189
American Opera House, planned by Hammerstein, 88
American opera, the first, 191
"Americans in England, The," 192
"Americana in Europa," 189
"American Adventurers, The," 189
"Americans in England," 192
American school of composition, 45 *et seq.*; how a school may be created, 186
American slave music, 212
American theatrical companies, early, 73, 186
American tunes in "The Girl of the Golden West," 209
"Amico Fritz, L'," opera by Mascagni, 363
"Amore dei tre Re," opera by Montemezzi, 309, 310, 311; first performance, 313; criticism, 313 *et seq.*; 349, 351, 372 (*see* Appendix)
"Amore medico, L'," opera by Wolf-Ferrari, 309, 310, 311; first performance, 328; criticism, 328 (*see* Appendix)
"Amour de Tzigane, L'" (*see* "Zigeunerliebe")
"Amour Médecin, L'," 329
Ananian, Paul, 39, 158, 248, 295, 327, 328
"Andrea Chenier," opera by Giordano, 97, 308, 338, 372 (*see* Appendix)
Andrews, Lyle D., 83, 84
Anschütz, Carl, 145, 342
Anselmi, conductor, 112
"Arabian Nights Entertainments," 399
Arcadelt, 366

INDEX

"Archers, The," opera by Carr, 229
Arden, Cecil, 407
Arditi, Luigi (see "Spia")
Ariadne, story of, 217
"Ariane et Barbe-Bleue," opera by Dukas, first performance, 216; criticism, 216 et seq.; a satire on woman, 223, 225 (see Appendix)
Arimondi, Vittorio, 96, 235, 395
Arion, Männergesangverein, 393
"Aristeo," opera by Gluck, 149
"Arlesienne, L'," 365
"Armide," opera by Gluck, 144; first performance, 190; criticism, 199 et seq.; 226 (see Appendix)
Arne, Dr., 190
Arnold, Samuel, 190
Aronson, Rudolph, 25, 92
"Askold's Tomb," opera by Verstowsky, 158
"Asrael," opera by Franchetti, 55, 150
Associazione Italiana di Amici della Musica, 266
Astor, John Jacob, 33
Atlanta, Ga., 138, 349
Atmosphere in opera, 212
"Attaque du Moulin, L'," opera by Bruneau, 139; first performance, 154; criticism, 155 et seq. (see Appendix)
Auber, 53 (see "Muette di Portici" and "Fra Diavolo")

Bada, Angelo, 38, 204, 210, 248, 296, 318, 327, 328, 336, 351, 398
Bagehot, Walter, 46
Baird, Edward Kellogg, 174, 176, 176
Baker, George F., 33, 60
Bakos, Ella, 341
Baklonoff, Georges, 194, 395
Balfe (see "Bohemian Girl"), 186
Ballets in Gluck's operas, 201
"Ballo in Maschera, Un," opera by Verdi, 97, 309 (see Appendix)
Baltazarini (see "Circe")
Baltimore, Md., 22, 74, 137, 138, 190, 191, 193, 273, 274, 360
Baracchi, Aristide, 149
"Barbe-Bleue," operetta by Offenbach, 221, 222
Barber, Donn, 33
"Barber of Bagdad," opera by Cornelius, 399
"Barbiere di Siviglia, Il," opera by Rossini, 127, 198, 395 (see Appendix)
Barilo, Rita, 149
Barker, stage manager, 186
Barnay, Ludwig, 25
Barney, Charles T., 33
Baron, Alice, 118
"Bartered Bride" (see "Verkaufte Braut")
Bartik, Ottokar, 409, 412
Barton, Andrew, 191
Barton, George Edward, 167
Barrientos, Maria, début, 350; portrait, 350; 361, 409
Bartsch, Rudolph Hans, 305
Bascom, Inc., ticket agents, 270
Bassi, Amadeo, 250
"Basso Porto, A," opera by Spinelli, 108
"Bastien et Bastienne," opera by Mozart, 372
Bates, Blanche, 206
Battle of Leipsic, 152
Bavagnoli, Giovanni, 354
Bayer, Julius, 40, 56, 213, 311, 327, 370
Baylies, Edmund L., 22, 33, 176, 178, 179, 277
"Béatitudes, Les," oratorio by Franck, 124
Beauty, appreciation of, 123; stability of principles, 11
Beck, William, 112
Beethoven, criticism of, 10; 123, 162, 252, 264, 290, 297, 414, 416; his republicanism, 416 (see "Fidelio")
Bégué, Bernard, 40, 158, 210, 216, 336
Belasco, David, his "Girl of the Golden West," 204; directs an opera production,

INDEX

204, 206, 212; on opera singers as actors, 209
Belleki, Lamberto, 210
Belleri, Margarete, 403
Bellini (see "Sonnambula," "Puritani," and "Norma")
Belmont, August, 33
Bendix, Max, 141
Benelli, Sem, 313
"Benvenuto Cellini," opera by Berlioz, 156
Bérat, Louise, 250, 251, 395
Berger, Rudolph, 332; death of, 336
Bergman, Gustav, 177
Bergmann, Carl, 289
Berlin, opera in, 134
Berlioz (see "Troyens" and "Benvenuto Cellini"), 148
Bernard, John, 192
Bernstorff, Count von, 383
Bertoni, 148
Bickerstaff, 190
Birchpfeiffer, Charlotte, 53
"Birichino, Il," opera by Mugnone, 54
Bishop, Cortlandt Field, 33
Bispham, David, 173, 372
Bitterl, Constance, 403
Bizet (see "Carmen," "Pêcheurs de Perles," "Fille de Perth," "Djamileh," "Arlesienne"), 58
Blass, Robert, 40, 56, 140, 274, 284
Blech, Leo (see "Versiegelt")
Bloch, Max, 336, 345, 354, 370, 398, 407, 408
Blockx, Jan (see "Princesse d'Auberge")
Bluebeard, 218 et seq.
"Boabdil," opera by Moszkowski, 92
Boadicea, 260
Boccacio, 125
Bodanzky, Artur, 354, 367, 368, 370; portrait, 378; 403
Boehm, Clara, 39
"Bohème, La," opera by Puccini, 97, 117, 179, 198, 212, 372, 397 (see Appendix)
Bohemian Club, San Francisco, 247

"Bohemian Girl," opera by Balfe, 113, 179, 180
Bohemians in New York, protest against Austrian hymn, 49; dance in "Verkaufte Braut," 56
Boileau, 129
Boito (see "Iago," "Nerone," and Mefistofele")
Bolm, Adolf, 397, 408, 409
Bonci, Alessandro, 31, 39, 40, 50, 60, 140, 274
Bonfiglio, Giuseppe, 409
Bori, Lucrezia, portrait, 318; 318; illness of, 318; 328, 341
"Boris Godounow," opera by Moussorgsky, 108, 159, 233, 282, 286; first performance, 295; criticism, 295 et seq.; 310, 316, 336, 349, 351, 417 (see Appendix)
Borodin (see "Prince Igor")
Boston—Boston Opera Company, 28, 317, 332; Hammerstein gives up performing operas, 80; protests against "Salome," 106, 137; early opera in, 190; 273, 274, 364, 349; National Grand Opera Company, 371, 397; conductor of orchestra interned, 389; orchestra turned over to trustees, 390
Botta, Luca, 287, 341, 351
Bottesini, 399
Bouilly, 189
Bourgeois, Georges, 210, 216
Boyce, 190
Bozzano, Enzo, 39
Brahms, 415, 416
Braslau, Sophie, 311, 318, 327, 336, 341, 409; portrait, 412; 412
Braun, Carl, 332, 367, 393
Brema, Marie, 146
Brescia, 330
Bressler-Gianoli, Clotilde, 227, 235
Breton (see "Dolores")
Bréval, Lucienne, 126
Brignoli, Pasquale, 9
Bristow, George F. (see "Rip Van Winkle")

Brooklyn, opera in, 138, 273, 336; Philharmonic Society, 403 (see Appendix)
Bruneau (see "Attaque du Moulin") and Wagner, 156
Bucholz, Robert, stage name of Conried, 25
Buck, Dudley, 159
Buckreus, Stefen, 248
Buononcini (see also Bononcini), 7, 126
Burgstaller, Aloys, 40, 284
Burgstaller, Ludwig, 311, 398, 407
Burney, Dr. Charles, 111, 200
Burrian, Carl, 40, 105, 284
Byrom, John, 126

Cable, George W., 412
Cadman, Charles Wakefield (see "Shanewis"); portrait, 392
Cain, Henri, 126, 235, 251, 321
"Ca ira," 308, 339, 340
Cairo, folksongs of, 402
Calvé, Emma, 48, 67, 98, 136, 146, 362, 364
"Camilla," opera by Paër, 142
Campanari, Giuseppe, 40, 51, 60, 363
"Campanello, Il" (see "Night Bell")
Campanini, Cleofonte, 80, 96, 112, 226, 235, 250, 251, 305, 321, 326, 394
Campanini, Italo, 9
"Campmeeting John Allen," 330
"Camptown Races," 208, 211
Canning, 416
"Canterbury Pilgrims, The," opera by De Koven, 365; first performance, 370 (see Appendix)
Carew, Miss, 114
Carey, Henry, on rival singers, 8, 190
"Carmagnole, La," 308, 338, 339
"Carmen," opera by Bizet, 43, 67, 108, 113, 117, 179, 183, 198, 225, 231, 301, 302, 309, 335, 365 (see Appendix)
Carr, Benjamin (see "Archers, The"), 229
Carré, French librettist, 127
Carrillons in the Netherlands, 111
Cartellverband, German, 379
Carter, Thomas, 189
Cartier, 112
Caruso, Enrico, 9; under contract to Grau, 25; engaged by Conried, 25; supports Dippel in controversy, 29; 32, 40, 60, 61, 64; illness of, 63, 194; 140, 149; in "Armide," 203; 204, 205, 274, 284, 310; portraits, 326, 330, 362; 274, 284, 310, 326, 326; honorarium, 326; 333; re-engaged for 1915-16, 333; 336, 349, 350, 362, 364, 407, 407, 408
Case, Anna, 141, 266, 296, 311
Catalani (see "Wally" and "Dejanice"), 51, 55
"Cat and the Cherub, The," 341
Cavalieri, Lina, 77, 99; quarrel with Mary Garden, 100, 102; 112, 114
"Cavalleria Rusticana," opera by Mascagni, 48, 54, 67, 92, 108, 113, 143, 145, 363 (see Appendix)
Cavan, Marie, 235, 251
"Cendrillon," opera by Massenet, 111, 113; first performance, 251; criticism, 251 et seq.
"Cenerentola," opera by Rossini, 252
"Cenerentola," opera by Wolf-Ferrari, 250
Centanini, "Count," 26, 27
Century Opera Company, 164, et seq.; repertory, 178; abandons exclusive use of English, 179; losses of, 179; analysis of financial report, 179; competition with Metropolitan Opera Company, 181; 214, 397
Century Theater (Opera House), 33, 87; two seasons

of popular opera at, 164 *et seq.*
Cervantes despoiled, 321
Chadwick, George W., 171
Chalmers, Thomas, 177, 397, 398, 412
Changelings, 961
"Chapters of Opera," book by H. E. Krehbiel, quoted, 1, 4, 13, 54, 66, 84, 92, 102, 176, 329, 355
Characterization by keys, 261
Charlestown, S. C., 73, 190
Charlier, conductor, 112
"Charlotte Temple," author of, 192
Charpentier (*see* "Louise" and "Julien")
Chaucer, 371
Chavannes, Puvis de, 147
"Chemineau, Le," opera by Leroux, 139
"Cherokee, The," opera by Storace, 189
Cherubini, 390
Chicago, 60, 299, 324; Chicago Opera Company, 28, 77, 80, 93, 226, 333, 394; Chicago-Philadelphia Opera Company, 80, 81, 193, 224 *et seq.*, 287, 310, 321 (*see* also Philadelphia-Chicago Opera Company)
"Children of the Don," opera by Holbrooke, 83
Chinese shadow plays, 410
Chopin, 162, 187
"Chopin," ballet, 139
"Chute de la Maison Usher, Le," opera by Debussy, 141
"Cid, Le, opera by Massenet, 116
Cilea (*see* "Tilda")
Cincinnati, orchestra leader interned, 389
Cinderella, story of, in opera, 251
"Circe, ou le Ballet Comique de la Reine," 200
Cisneros, Eleanora, 235, 305
City Club, opera project, 87, 89, 92, 173, 177
Civini, C., 204

Clément, Edmond, 141, 158, 158
Clément et Larousse, dictionary of operas, 252
"Cloches de Corneville, Les," operetta by Planquette, 83 (*see* Appendix)
"Coal Oil Tommy," 208
Coburn Players, The, 371
Coini, Jacques, 83, 118
Coke, Lord Chief Justice, 276
"Columbus, or a World Discovered," 189
Collier's Weekly, newspaper, quoted, 134
Composers and long operas, 290
"Conchita," opera by Zandonai, 287; first performance, 298; criticism, 298; 306
Conried, Heinrich, his administration of the Metropolitan Opera House, 3, 16 *et seq.;* failures of his management, 18; treatment of German opera, 19; retirement of, 20 *et seq.;* the Conried Metropolitan Opera Company, 22, 23; resignation as director, 22; system of profit sharing, 23; profits of the company, 24; sells his shares, 24; illness and death, 24; his career, 24; change in organization of the company, 29; manager of Irving Place Theater, 32; plans New Theater, 32; approves of plans, 33, 37; anecdote, 38; abandons "Salome," 103; 103, 135, 136; fails to appreciate Renaud, 194; 197, 214, 224; cost of opera under his management, 282, 346
Constantino, tenor, 112, 194
"Contes d'Hoffmann, Les," opera by Offenbach, 111, 113, 114, 139, 178, 226 (*see* Appendix)
Contesse, Etienne, 326
Converse, Frederick (*see* "Pipe of Desire")
"Coq d'Or, Le," opera by Rimsky-Korsakow, 397, 398;

first performance, 398, 408; criticism, 408 et seq.; 417 (see Appendix)
Cornelius, Peter (see "Barber of Bagdad")
Cornwell, William C., 174, 176
Cortez, Hernando, his horses in Mexico, 213
"Cortez, Hernando," opera by Spontini, 213
Cottenet, Rawlins L., 20
Cotrelly, Mathilde, 25
Covent Garden Theater, London, 82, 369
Cox, Louise, 295, 327, 327
Crabbe, Armand, 98, 107, 112, 114, 229, 235
Cravath, Paul, 33, 86
"Cricket on the Hearth," opera by Goldmark, 38, 139, 195
"Crispino e la Comare," opera by the brothers Ricci, 113 (see Appendix)
Cristali, Italo, 328
Criticism, need and value of, 9 et seq.
Crozier, General, U. S. Chief of Ordnance, 383
Curtis, Vera, 295, 327, 336
Cuyler, T. De Witt, 80, 277
Cuzzoni, 8
"Cyrano de Bergerac," opera by Damrosch, 286; first performance, 288; criticism, 288 et seq. (see Appendix)
"Cyrano de Bergerac," opera by Herbert, 291
"Czar und Zimmermann," opera by Lortzing, 142 (see Appendix)

Daddi, Francesco, 107, 233, 250, 251
Dalayrac, 189
D'Albert (see "Tiefland"); parentage and education, 45; a man without a country, 45
Dalmorès, Charles, 77, 81, 96, 105, 112, 114, 115, 124, 227, 235, 305, 395
D'Alvarez, Molle, 115
"Dama di Picche" (see "Pique Dame")

"Damnation de Faust, La," by Berlioz, 202, 225 (see Appendix)
Damrosch, Frank, 64, 249
Damrosch, Dr. Leopold, 2, 15, 289, 408
Damrosch, Walter (see "Scarlet Letter" and "Cyrano de Bergerac"); 45, 63, 64, 171, 174
"Dance in Place Congo, The," ballet by Gilbert, 398, 411 (see Appendix)
Dance mania, the world's, 409
D'Angelo, Louis, 408
D'Annunzio, "Francesca da Rimini," 370
Dante, 371
Dantzig, 330
"Darby's Return," 192
Dargomischky, 159
David, Félicien (see "Desert"), 366
"Dead Alive, The," 189
Debussy (see "Chute de la Maison Usher," "Diable dans le Beffroi," "Pelléas et Mélisande," "Légende de Tristan," "Les Sirènes"); 10, 111; his operas, 155; 288, 302, 316
"Decameron," 125
Declamation in opera, 157
Decourcelles, 318
Defrère, Désire, 229, 251, 326
"Dejanice," opera by Catalani, 54
De Koven, Reginald (see "Canterbury Tales"), 173
De la Fuente, conductor, 112, 114, 118, 123
Delna, Marie, 141, 149, 158, 158
De Luca, Giuseppe, 354, 362, 398; portrait, 400
Delwary, Stefen, 40
Denton, Stanley, 84
Denza, "Funiculi, funicula," 211
De Reszke, Edouard, 136, 408
De Reszke, Jean, 9, 66, 72; on translations, 131; 136, 330, 408
"Description de l'Egypte," 402

INDEX

"Desert, Le," cantata by David, 402
"Déserteur, Le" (see "Deserter, The")
"Deserter, The," opera by Monsigny, 190
Desmond, Miss, 118
De Staël, Madame, 130, 166
Destinn, Emmy, 39; career in Berlin, 38; a Bohemian patriot, 39; detained in Austria, 49; *portraits*, 40; 44, 48, 51, 55, 56, 140, 149, 160, 210, 266, 273, 284, 332, 377
"Deutschland über Alles," 49
Devaux, Leo, 158
Devries, singer, 101
"Diable dans le Beffroi, Le," opera by Debussy, 141
Diaghileff Ballet, 349, 352
"Diane von Solange," opera by the Duke of Saxe-Coburg, 55
Diaz, Rafaello, 409
Dibdin, C., 190
Didur, Adamo, 39, 39, 56, 60, 60, 140, 160, 210, 213, 248, 274, 296; *portrait*, 298; 318, 341, 407, 408, 409
"Die kleine Blanchefleur," 305
D'Indy, Vincent, 324
"Dinorah," opera by Meyerbeer, 395 (*see* Appendix)
Dippel, Andreas, conflict with Gatti-Casazza, 3, 21, 29 *et seq.*; appointed a joint manager of the Metropolitan Opera House, 22; his general usefulness as a singer, 23; service to German opera, 25; has support of principal singers, 29; *portrait*, 32; declines dinner offered by German Liederkranz, 31; made administrative director, 31; organizes Chicago Opera Company, 32; 36, 48, 60, 60, 61, 64, 78, 138; début in New York, 151; 155, 176, 195; interest in English opera, 196; 233; 214, 225, 284, 304, 306
"Disappointment, The," 191
Dodge, Allen and Campbell, 190
"Dolores," opera by Breton, 97
"Don Carlos," opera by Verdi, 55
"Don Giovanni," opera by Mozart, 67, 68, 198, 292, 373 (*see* Appendix)
Donizetti (*see* "Don Pasquale," "Lucia," "Fille du Régiment," "Linda di Chamounix," and "Night Bell")
"Donne Curiose, Le," opera by Wolf-Ferrari, first performance, 247; 250, 329 (*see* Appendix)
"Don Pasquale," opera by Donizetti, 60 (*see* Appendix)
"Don Quichotte," opera by Massenet, 310, 311; first performance, 321; criticism, 321 *et seq.*
Doria, Augusta, 95, 112
"Dragons de Villars, Les," opera by Maillart, 139 (*see* Appendix)
Draper, Eben S., 106
Drury Lane Theater, London, 82, 189
Dryden, 409
Duchène, Mme., 118, 123, 266, 296, 318, 327, 327
Dufau, Jenny, 250, 251
Dufault, 118
Dufranne, Hector, 96, 98, 107, 112, 115, 124, 229, 235, 251, 305, 321, 395
Dukas, Paul (*see* "Ariane et Barbe-Bleue")
Duncan, Isadora, 410
Dunlap, William, 192, 229
Dury, Jacques, 305
Duse, Eleonora, 48, 370

Eames, Emma, 9; supports Dippel in controversy, 29; retires from operatic stage, 31, 32; 40, 49; *portrait*, 66; career, 66; repertory of, 67; adds German operas to her list, 67; 136, 284
Easton, Florence, 397, 403

Eberhard, Nellie Richmond, 412
"Echo et Narcisse," opera by Gluck, 149
Educational opera, 112
"Edwin and Angelina," opera by Pelissier, 229
Egener, Minnie, 229, 321, 336, 351, 371, 407
"Electra," tragedy by Sophocles, 119
"Elektra," opera by Richard Strauss, 111; Hammerstein buys performing rights, 111; 113, 113; criticism, 117 (see Appendix)
" Elisir d'Amore, L'," opera by Donizetti (see Appendix)
Ellis, Charles A., 334, 389
Engel, Louise, 213
English opera (and opera in English) 141, 165; exclusive use of language abandoned by Century Opera Company, 179; in competition with Italian, 181; need of good diction in, 185; in America, 188; and Dippel, 196; notes on its history, 226
Epine, Margareta de l', 7
"Epistolae heroidum," 359
"Erastus," 191
"Ernani," opera by Verdi, 97 (see Appendix)
"Ero e Leandro," opera by Mancinelli, 68
"Esmeralda," opera by Goring Thomas, 175
Euripides's "Iphigenia," 367
"Euryanthe," opera by Weber, 43, 128, 335; appreciation of, 342; 348 (see Appendix)
"Evangelimann, Der," opera by Kienzl, 305
Eversman, Alice, 367
Ewell, Lois, 177

"Fanciulla del West, La," opera by Puccini, 195, 197; first performance, 204; fate of, 204; criticism, 204 et seq.; 215, 249 (see Appendix)
Farrar, Geraldine, 5, 8; selected by Grau, 25; supports Dippel in controversy, 29; 32, 40, 61, 64, 101, 139, 140, 195, 213, 215, 216; interprets "Ariane et Barbe-Bleue," 218; 220, 222; *portrait*, 214; 248, 273, 284, 310, 326, 326; her thoughts on German engagements, 334; unpatriotic sentiments, 334; contract with Chicago Company, 334; 335, 336, 349, 350, 407
"Falstaff," opera by Verdi, 48, 55, 59, 67, 97, 201, 365 (see Appendix)
"Familie Americaine, La," 189
"Faust," opera by Gounod, 67, 67, 113, 179, 225, 246, 310, 395 (see Appendix)
"Faust" as puppet play, 410
Feinhals, Fritz, 39, 44
Female librettist, an early, 191
Female suffrage in opera, 217
"Femme et la Pantin," 300
Fenton, Lavinia, 8
Fernald, C. B., 341
Ferrara-Fontano, Eduardo, 317, 318
Ferrara, gives opera at Academy of Music, 113
"Feuersnot," opera by Richard Strauss, 111, 113
Février (see " Monna Vanna ")
Fichte, 152
"Fidelio," opera by Beethoven, 92, 143, 189, 282, 289, 290, 335, 416 (see Appendix)
Field, William B. Osgood, 33
"Figlia del Reggimento" (see "Fille du Régiment")
"Fille de Madame Angot," operetta by Lecocq (see Appendix)
"Fille du Régiment, La," opera by Donizetti, 198 (see Appendix)
Finch, Edward R., 174, 176, 177
Finley, John H., 35
First performances of operas in New York, "Tiefland," 44; "Le Villi," 50; "La Wally," 51; "Verkaufte Braut, Die," 55; "Jongleur

INDEX

de Notre Dame, Le," 98;
"La Princesse d'Auberge,"
106; "Elektra," 114, 117;
"Hérodiade," 114; "Sapho,"
115; "Grisélidis," 123; "Germania," 146; "L'Attaque du
Moulin," 154; "Pique Dame,"
158; "The Pipe of Desire,"
164; "La Fanciulla del
West," 204; "Königskinder,"
213; "Ariane et Barbe-
Bleue," 216; "Armide," 199;
"Il Segreto di Susanna,"
234; "Quo Vadis?" 235;
"Lobetanz," 243; "Le Donne
Curiose," 247; "I Giojelli
della Madonna," 250;
"Mona," 255; "Cendrillon,"
251; "Conchita," 298; "Ranz
des Vaches," 304; "Rosenkavalier," 311; "L'Amore
dei tre Re," 313; "Madeleine," 318; "Don Quichotte,"
321; "Monna Vanna," 324;
"Julien," 326; "L'Amore
Medico," 328; "Madame
Sans-Gêne," 336; "L'Oracolo," 341; "Prince Igor,"
351; "Goyescas," 354; "Iphigenia auf Tauris," 367,
"Francesca da Rimini," 370;
"The Canterbury Pilgrims,"
370; "Maroûf," 398; "Lodoletta," 398, 407; "St. Elizabeth," 398
First performances of operas
which pass unnoticed, 362
Fischer, Emil, 380, 399
Fish, a symbol of Christianity,
238
Fitziu, Anna, 354
Flahaut, Marianne, 39
Flemish elements in "Princesse d'Auberge," 107
"Fliegende Holländer, Der"
(see "Flying Dutchman")
"Flying Dutchman, The," opera by Wagner, first production in Italy, 26; 289
Fokine, Michael, 408
Folksong idioms in national
schools of music, 187
Forbes-Robertson, 35

Fornaroli, Lucia, 216
Fornia, Rita, 40, 44, 248, 265, 266, 311, 336
Forsell, John, 160
"Forza del Destino, La," opera by Verdi, 55
Fosetta, Nicolo, 107, 250
Foster, Stephen C., 211
"Fra Diavolo," opera by Auber, 225 (see Appendix)
France, Anatole, 101
"Francesca da Rimini," opera
by Montemezzi, 282, 361; first
performance, 369; criticism,
369 et seq. (see Appendix)
"Francesca da Rimini," by
d'Annunzio, 370
Franchetti (see "Asrael" and
"Germania"); sketch of,
150
Franck, César, "Les Béatitudes," 124
Franco-Prussian war, 157
Franko, Sam, 372
Franz Joseph, Emperor of
Austria, 25
Franz, Robert, 415
Freeholder's Journal, The, 126
"Freischütz, Der," 343 (see
Appendix)
Fremstad, Olive, 8, 40, 105, 139, 140, 203, 204, 274, 284
French opera, taken up by
Hammerstein, 71; under
Gatti, 72; against Italian
(anecdote), 72; French
ideals in art, 125; French religious music, 124; in New
York, 224
"Fricassée, La," 340
Frick, Henry Clay, 33
Fry, W. H., 165, 228
Fuchs, Anton, 19, 284
Fuller, Loie, 410
"Funiculi, funicula," 211
Furnival, 357
Fuselli, 315

Gade, 187
Gadski, Johanna, 40, 140, 144, 253, 274, 284, 332, 382, 393
Galetti-Gianoli, 198
Gallet, Louis, 156

Galli, Rosina, 250, 367, 409, 411
Galli-Curci, Amelita, 28; *portrait,* 344; 395, 396
Galuppi, 190
Garden, Mary, 5, 77, 81, 96, 98, 99; quarrel with Cavalieri, 100; 102, 104, 105; her disrobing act, 105; 112, 115, 115, 123, 124, 229, 230, 251, 253, 321, 323, 324, 326, 394, 395, 395, 306
Garibaldi, Gatti's father one of his "Thousand," 27
Garrison, Mabel, 287, 345, 372
Garrick Theater in New York, 375
Gary, Elbert H., 33
Gates, Lucy, 372
Gatti-Casazza, Giulio, conflict with Andreas Dippel, 3, 20; 21, 29 *et seq.; portrait,* 22; engaged as director of the Metropolitan Opera House, 22; sketch of his career, 27; his taste in music, 28; his contract extended, 30, 36; estimate of public taste in New York, 41; 42, 50, 51, 60; attitude toward French opera, 72, 225; 78, 78, 138, 170; on repetition of operas, 180; sole manager of the Metropolitan Company, 193; rejects "Natoma," 196; 282, 284; "Madeleine," 318; 348
"Gaudeamus igitur," 153
Gauthier-Villar, 118
Gay, Maria, 39
"Geierwally," 53
Geminiani, 190
"Genius may adopt but it never steals," 315
Gentle, Alice, 118
Gerard, J. W., 381
"Germania," opera by Franchetti, 139; first performance, 149; criticism, 149 *et seq.;* 248 (*see* Appendix)
Germania Theater, 92
German, Kaiser, honors Griswold, 311; language comes to be hated, 41, 415; managers boycott America, 379; music,

attitude of public toward, 2, 382 *et seq.;* opera under Conried, 19; Toscanini's devotion to, 36; attitude of Metropolitan Opera Company, 79, 382 *et seq.;* seasons of opera at Metropolitan Opera House, 165, 284, 334; opera helped by Caruso's illness, 194; history of opera in America, 289; future of in New York, 413 *et seq.*
German operettas given by Conried, 18
German Press Club, 49, 139
Germany, modern, not artistically creative, 416
Gerster, Etelka, 9, 396
Gerville-Réache, Jeanne, 96, 107, 112, 114, 118; *portrait,* 118
Giardini, 190
Gilbert, Henry F. (*see* "Dance in Place Congo"), 412
Gilbert and Sullivan, 175, 373
Gilder, Richard Watson, 35
Gilibert, Charles, 77, 81, 96, 107, 112; death of, 198; memorial, 198; *portrait,* 196
Gilly, Dinh, 141, 158, 204, 210, 274, 284, 327, 332
"Gioconda, La," opera by Ponchielli, 54, 178 (*see* Appendix)
"Giojelli della Madonna, I," opera by Wolf-Ferrari, 249; first performance, 250; 306, 310, 398
Giordano, Umberto (*see* "Mala," "Andrea Chenier," "Siberia," "Madame Sans-Gêne"), 53; kept from coming to New York, 337
"Girl of the Golden West," melodrama by Belasco, 204, 207
Glazounow, 352
Glinka (*see* "Rousslan et Ludmilla"), 187
Gluck, Alma, 141, 144, 147, 160, 204; *portrait,* 144
Gluck (*see* "Orfeo," "Armide," "Iphigenia," "Echo

INDEX 457

et Narcisse," "Alceste," "Aristeo"), 166, 186; dancing in his operas, 201; 415
Godiva, Lady, 325, 395
Goethe, his Mephistopheles, 127; 321, 399, 410, 413, 414
Goetz, Hermann (see "Widerspänstigen Zähmung")
Gogol, 159
Gogorza, Emilio de, 64, 353
"Götterdämmerung," opera by Wagner, first performance in Italy, 26; 243, 265, 282, 414 (see Appendix)
Goldmark, Carl (see "Cricket on the Hearth," "Merlin")
Golisciani, Enrico, 329
Gordon, George A., 106
Goritz, Otto, 40, 44, 140, 213, 153, 311, 332, 354, 358
"Gott erhalte unser Kaiser," 49
Gould, Curtis, 106
Gould, George J., 33
Gounod (see "Faust," "Roméo et Juliette," "Mock Doctor," and "There Is a Green Hill"), 125, 156, 321
Gounsberg, Raoul, 202
Gower, Frederick A., 330
Goya, 353
"Goyescas," opera by Granados, 350, 353; first performance, 354 (see Appendix)
Granados (see "Goyescas," "Maria del Carmen," and "Lillian"); loses his life on steamer Sussex, 354
Grand Duke of Weimar, 404
Grassi, Rinaldo, 39
Grau, Maurice, 2; his management of the Metropolitan Opera House, 15; 16, 18, 21; engagement of Caruso, 25; selects Farrar for New York, 25; 67, 83, 126, 175, 198, 224, 245, 284, 408
Greek ideals outraged, 119
Gregory, Eliot, 33
Gregory IX, Pope, 406
Grenville, Lillian, 229, 235
Grétry (see "Richard Cœur de Lion"), 168

Grieg, 187
"Griselda," opera by Bononcini, 126
"Grisélidis," opera by Massenet, 97, 111, 113, 123; first performance, 123; criticism, 124 et seq. (see Appendix)
"Grisélidis, Le Mystère de," 125
Grisi, 281
Griswold, Frank C., 30
Griswold, Putnam, début, 243; 265, 274, 284, 295; death of, 310
Grizel, The Patient, 125
Grogan, Larry, 190
Guard, William A., 70
Guardabassi, Mario, 235
Gudehus, Heinrich, 408
"Gugelino," opera by Thuille, 247
"Guglielmo Tell" (see "Guillaume Tell")
Guido d'Arezzo, 359
"Guillaume Tell," opera by Rossini, 290, 309, 335
Guille, tenor, 363
Guimera, Angel, 44
Guiraud, Ernest, 395
"Gypsy Baron" (see "Zigeunerbaron")

"Habanera," opera by Laparra, 38, 139
Hackett, James H., 281
Hadley, Henry K. (see "Azora")
Halévy (see "Juive" and "Noé")
Hall, Glenn, 160, 164, 210
Hall, Marshall, 409
Hall, Thomas, 191
"Hamlet," opera by Ambroise Thomas, 287
"Hamlet," Shakespeare's, 343
Hammerstein, Arthur, son and agent of Oscar Hammerstein, 76; appointed attorney in fact by father, 80; agrees that his father shall retire from management, 80; 88
Hammerstein, Oscar, 3; plans opera in Boston, 21; in

458 INDEX

Philadelphia, 21; rivalry with Metropolitan Opera House, 19, 39, 69 *et seq.*; 70; attitude of newspapers towards him, 70; agrees to abandon opera, 70; courts society, 71; led into giving French opera, 71, 73; his first season, 73; the Philadelphia Opera House, 74, 77 (*see* Philadelphia); borrows money from E. T. Stotesbury, 75; seasons, 1909-10, 75; foresees failure, 75; offers to combine with Metropolitan Company, 75; season 1910-11, 77; threatens to abandon Philadelphia 77; his losses in that city, 79; receives advances from Stotesbury, 79; claims the money as gifts, 79; sells out his interests, 79; remarks on the losses of himself and rivals, 80; plans for season 1910-11, 80; conceives invasion of London, 81; attacks ticket speculators in New York, 81; enters operetta field, 82; builds theater in London, 82; cost of the London house, 82; the London adventure, 82 *et seq.*; conducts an operetta, 83; financial embarrassment relieved by Lord Howard de Walden, 83; refuses to continue performances of an opera, 84; mortgage on the London house foreclosed, 84; sale of the theater, 84; new plans for New York, 84; asks consent of Metropolitan Opera Company in vain, 86; builds theater in Lexington Ave., 87, 88, 93; terms of his contract with the Metropolitan Company, 88; threatens renewal of competition, 89; injunction obtained by Metropolitan Opera Company, 91; death of three sons, 92; death of, 92 (footnote); his Harlem Opera House, 92; first Manhattan Opera House, 92; his last two seasons at the Manhattan, 94 *et seq.*; flamboyant advertising, 96; fight with newspaper writers, 102; his French performances, 111; "educational opera," 112; gives *opéra bouffe*, 113; essays Wagner's operas, 29; English opera, 170; 224; his Chicago scheme, 225; 226; his attempts at reform of ticket speculation, 269; 394; picture of his London Opera House, 82

Handel, 126, 190
"Hans the Flute Player," 82
"Hänsel und Gretel," opera by Humperdinck, 20, 178, 197, 214, 251, 253, 282 (*see* Appendix)
Hapgood, Norman, 172
Hargreaves, Charles, 248
Harlem Opera House, 92
Hartman, Richard J., 274, 278
Harvey, George B. M., 45
Hastreiter, Helene, 145
Haydn, 391, 416
Haymarket Theater, London, 190
"Heimchen am Heerd" (*see* "Cricket on the Hearth")
Heine, Heinrich, 413
Heliane, Christine, 149, 158
Hempel, Frieda, *portrait*, 310; 310, 311, 332, 345, 362, 364
Henderson, William J. (*see* dedication of this book, and "Cyrano de Bergerac"); on his own libretto, 289; 353; on "Shanewis," 411; tribute to Sembrich, 62; *portrait*, 288
Henri III, of France, 200
Henry VI, Duke of Silesia, 405
Hensel, Heinrich, début, 243
Herbert, Victor (*see* "Natoma," "Cyrano," and "Madeleine")
Herder, 399
"Hernando Cortez," opera by Spontini, 213
Herman, Landgrave of Thuringia, 405

INDEX

Hermann, Carl, 25
"Hérodiade," opera by Massenet, 111, 113; first performance, 114; 116 (see Appendix)
Hertz, Alfred, 29, 39, 44, 79, 141, 171, 213, 253, 265, 273, 273, 274, 288, 311; retirement from Metropolitan Opera House, 336; departure from New York, 345; career, 346; conducts first performance of "Parsifal" in America, 346; goes to San Francisco, 346; conducts first performance of "Salome," 346; other novelties conducted by him, 347; 377
Hewlett, Monroe, 368
Hibbard, George A., 106
Higgins, Henry V., 21
Higginson, Major, retires from support of Boston Orchestra, 390
Hillern, Baroness von, 52
Hinckley, Allan, 39, 44, 140, 274
Hinrichs Grand Opera Company, 363
Hinshaw, William Wade, 193, 213, 265, 284, 295, 373
Hofmannsthal, Hugo von, 118, 119, 125
Hogarth, George, 130
Holbrooke, Josef (see "Children of the Don")
Holt, Roland, 174
Homer, Louise, 40, 64, 140, 144, 147, 164, 204, 213; portrait, 262; 265, 274, 284, 296
Hooker, Brian, his libretto of "Mona," 172 et seq.; 256
Horses on the stage in "Hernando Cortez," 213
Howard, Kathleen, 177, 398, 412
Huberdeau, Gustave, 115, 118, 124, 126, 229, 235, 251, 305, 326, 395
Hughes, Austin, 295
Hughes, Charles E., Governor of N. Y. State, 34, 35
"Huguenots, Les," opera by Meyerbeer, 178, 260 (see Appendix)
Huillier, Madame l', 44, 51, 56
Humboldt, 152
Hume, Miss, 107
Humperdinck (see "Hänsel und Gretel" and "Königskinder"), 187; visits New York, 197; 251
Huntington, Archer M., 33
"Huron, Le," 189
Hyde, James Hazen, 21, 33

"Iago," opera by Boito, 54
"Iberia," by Debussy, 302
"Iliad," Homer's, 11
Illica, librettist, 51, 150
"I'm a Pilgrim," 111
"Impresario, The," operetta with Mozart's music, 374
Indian music in "Fanciulla del West," 209, 211
"Inglesi in America, Gli," 189
International Ballet, The, 178
"Invitation to the Dance," Weber's, 345
Ioncelli, Vincenzo, 409
"Iphigenia," by Euripides, 367
Iphigenia, 377
"Iphigenia auf Tauris," opera by Gluck ("Iphigenia en Tauride"), 144, 361, 362; first performance, 367; criticism, 367 et seq.; 381 (see Appendix)
"Iris," opera by Mascagni, 68, 108, 336, 372 (see Appendix)
Irving Place Theater, 25, 32, 214
"Isabeau," opera by Mascagni, 395
Isouard, 252
Istar, 324
Italian opera, advent of, in New York, 74
Italy, Wagner's influence in, 53
Iteration in Russian folksong, 316

Jadlowker, Hermann, 141, 213, 248, 253, 284
Jake Wallace, 208

James, Bernice, 39
Javanese drama, 410
"Jean-Christophe," 252
"Je crains de lui parler de nuit," 163
"Jewels of the Madonna" (see "Giojelli della Madonna")
Job, 128
Jörn, Carl, 39, 56, 311
Johnstone, Miss, 118
"Jolie Fille de Perth, La," opera by Bizet, 364
"Jongleur de Notre Dame, Le," opera by Massenet, 97, 98; criticism, 98 et seq.; 101, 116, 124, 125, 395 (see Appendix)
Jordan, Eben D., 21, 22
Jordan, Mary, 177
Journet, Marcel, 284
Jouvin, 365
Juch, Emma, 145
"Juive, La," opera by Halévy, 112, 113
"Julien," opera by Charpentier, 309, 310; first performance, 326 (see Appendix)

Kahn, Otto, H., 22; introduces "Count" Centanini, 27; supports Gatti in controversy with Dippel, 30, 30; one of the founders of the New Theater, 33, 33; cablegram to Toscanini, 43; 80, 86, 169, 171, 174, 176, 176, 176; portrait, 176; 226, 289
Kaiser, German, 311, 381, 413
Kalbeck, Max, 233
Kaschowska, Felice, 39, 39
Kauffman, Alfred, 177, 184
"Kde domov muj," 49
Keene, Thomas M., 191
Keyes, Margaret, 305
Keyserling, 3, 395
Keys used in characterization, 263
Kidder, Kathryn, 339
Kienzl (see "Ranz des Vaches" and "Evangelimann")
King of Saxony, sued by a singer, 380

"King's Children" (see "Königskinder")
Kingston, Morgan, 177
Kingsway, London, Theater in, 82; sold, 84
Klaw and Erlanger, 225, 226
Klink, Gabrielle, 229
Klopstock, 264
Koch, Walter, 309
"Königskinder," opera by Humperdinck, 38, 139, 178, 195, 196, 197, 206; first performance, 213; criticism, 213 et seq.; 282 (see Appendix)
"Königin von Saba," opera by Goldmark, 282
Körner, Theodor, 152, 153
Koster and Bial's Music Hall, 92
Kountze, W. DeLancey, 33
Krehbiel, portrait, frontispiece; "A Second Book of Operas," quoted, 115, 206, 214; "Chapters of Opera," quoted, 1, 4, 13, 54, 66, 84, 92, 176; remarks at Sembrich banquet, 64; the libretto for Mozart's "Impresario," 375
Krehbiel, Mrs. H. E., 64
Kreidler, Louis, 177, 295, 296
Kreisler, Fritz, 386
"Kuhreigen" (see "Ranz des Vaches")
Kurt, Melanie, 287, 332, 367; portrait, 392; 393

Labia, Maria, 96, 97, 107
"Lakmé," opera by Delibes, 361 (see Appendix)
Lamont, Thomas W., 177
Language, original and translations in opera, 19, 38, 42, 129, 143, 165 et seq.; 182 et seq.; 195
Laparra (see "Habanera")
La Scala, Teatro alla, in Milan, Wagner's operas at, 26; Gatti becomes director, 27
Laurentini, Maria, 370
Lautenschläger, Carl, 19, 284
Lavarenne, Mlle., 101
Lawrence, Bishop, 106
Lazaro, Hypolito, 397

INDEX

Lazarri, Sylvio (see "Sauteriot")
Lecocq (see "Fille de Madame Angot"), 399
Lefebvre, Marshal of France, 337
Legal Aid Society, 49
"Légende de Tristan," opera by Debussy, 141
Lehar (see "Zigeunerliebe")
Lehmann, Lilli, 9, 380
Leitmotive as symbols, 264
Le Lorraine, M., 321
Lena, Maurice, 99
Leoncavallo (see "Pagliacci," "Zaza"), 300
Leonhardt, Robert, 328, 332, 336, 354, 370, 398, 403
Leoni, Franco (see "Oracolo"), 336
Lermontoff, 159
Leroux, singer, 115
Leroux, Xavier (see "Chemineau")
Lewis, Earl, 277
Lexington Avenue Theater, built by Hammerstein, 93; used for vaudeville, 93; occupied by Chicago Opera Company, 93; sold to pay mortgage, 372, 394
Librettos, early publications of in America, 188
Liederkranz, German, offers banquet to Dippel, 31, 403
"Linda di Chamounix," opera by Donizetti, 97
Lipkowska, Lydia, 194
Liszt (see "St. Elizabeth"); 399
"Lobetanz," opera by Thuille, first performance, 243; criticism, 243 *et seq.* (see Appendix)
Local color in opera music, 53, 108, 109, 211, 365, 400
"Lochaber no more," 306
"Lodoletta," opera by Mascagni, 398; first performance, 407 (see Appendix)
Loeffler, Charles Martin, 171
Loewe, 152
"Lohengrin," opera by Wagner, first performance in Italy, 26; 54, 58, 67, 67, 113, 129, 178, 183, 243, 264, 289, 345, 359, 415 (see Appendix)
London, opera season compared with New York's, 133; Hammerstein's Opera House in, *picture*, 82 (see Hammerstein)
Longfellow, H. W., 230
Long, John Luther, 206
"Lord of the Manor, The," 190
Lortzing (see "Czar und Zimmermann")
Los Angeles, 262
"Louise," opera by Charpentier, introduced in Italy by Gatti, 28; 113, 178, 180, 198, 226, 287, 301, 302, 303, 304, 310, 326 (see Appendix)
Louisenbund, 151
Louise, Queen of Prussia, 151, 153
"Love in a Village," 190
Low, Seth, 61
Lubricity in opera, 312
Lucca, Pauline, 289
"Lucia di Lammermoor," opera by Donizetti, 179, 183, 350, 395 (see Appendix)
Ludwig, Anna, 160
Ludwig II, King of Bavaria, 404
"Lützow's wilde Jagd," 152, 153
Lully, 130, 166, 199
Lusitania, steamship sunk by Germans, 381
"Lustige Schuster, Der," 399
Luther, Gadski sings at celebration of, 393; 404
Lyceum Theater, New York, 372
Lydig, Philip M., 177

McManeny, George, 177
McBride, John, 270, 272
McClellan, Mayor of New York City, 34
McCormack, John, 81, 112, 194, 229, 397
MacDowell Chorus, 352, 403

Mackay, Clarence H., 33, 80, 176, 177, 196, 225, 226
Mackaye, Percy, 35, 370, 371
Macleod, Norman, on Spanish music, 302
"Madama Butterfly," opera by Puccini, 48, 108, 178, 178, 178; history of, 206; 208, 301, 372, 397 (see Appendix)
"Madame Chrysanthême," 206
"Madame Sans-Gêne," opera by Giordano, 282; first performance, 336; criticism, 336 et seq.; 335 (see Appendix)
"Madeleine," opera by Herbert, 309, 311; first performance, 318; criticism, 318 et seq. (see Appendix)
"Mademoiselle Wagner," 206
"Maestro di Capella," opera by Paër, 139, 142 (see Appendix)
Maeterlinck, 216, 220 (see "Monna Vanna")
"Magali," song of, 116
"Magic Flute, The" (see "Zauberflöte")
Mahler, Gustav, 19, 23, 25, 29, 31, 39, 55, 56, 140, 141, 160, 163, 347
"Maid Mistress, The," opera by Pergolesi ("La Serva Padrona"), 373
"Maitre de Chapelle" (see "Maestro di Capella")
Malatesta, Pompilio, 370, 398
"Mala Vita," opera by Giordano, 54
Mancinelli (see "Ero e Leandro")
Mandelli, Sante, 407
Manhattan Life Insurance Company, 90
Manhattan Opera House, Hammerstein (first), 92; (second), 70 et seq.; mortgaged to Stotesbury, 79; 82; seasons 1908 to 1910, 94 et seq.; season 1909-10, 11; record of all seasons at (see Appendix)
Mannheim, costly scenery in, 200

"Manon," opera by Massenet, 48, 97, 116, 117, 179, 225, 323, 395 (see Appendix)
"Manon Lescaut," opera by Puccini, 51, 197, 363 (see Appendix)
"Manru," opera by Paderewski, 108
Mapleson, Helen, 40
Maran, Ernst, 213
Marcoux, Vanni, 321, 326
Mardones, José, 397, 408
Maretzek, Max, 281, 289
Mariani, Leopoldo, 296
Marie Antoinette, 200
Mario, 281
Markoe, Peter, 191
Marlow, opera singer, 56
"Marôuf," opera by Rabaud, 398; first performance, 398; criticism, 398 et seq. (see Appendix)
"Marseillaise, La," 308, 338, 381
"Marta of the Lowlands," 44
"Martha," opera by Flotow, 179, 289, 416 (see Appendix)
Martin, Riccardo, 40, 51, 140, 164, 165, 265, 274, 295
Martinelli, Giovanni, 354
Mascagni (see "Cavalleria Rusticana," "Iris," "Amico Fritz," "Isabeau," and "Lodoletta"), 300
Mascal, Georges, 305
"Maschenka," Russian folksong, 162
"Mascotte, La," operetta (see Appendix)
Mason, Edith, 371
Massenet, 115, 116; "Mademoiselle Wagner," 124; 150, 252, 321 (see "Manon," "Werther," "Grisélidis," "Jongleur de Notre Dame," "Hérodiade," "Sapho," "Navarraise," "Cendrillon," "Thaïs," "Cid," "Portrait de Manon," "Ariane," and "Don Quichotte")
Massiglia, Count, 45
Materna, Amalia, 9

INDEX 463

Matinee audiences in New York, 245
Mattfeld, Marie, 44, 55, 149, 149, 160, 210, 213, 253, 295, 311, 327
Mattulath A., 372
Matzenauer, Margarete, début, 243; 274, 284, 317, 332, 403, 407
Maubourg, Jeanne, 204, 216, 248
Maxwell, George, 208
Mazarin, Marietta, 118; *portrait*, 118; 119
"Médecin malgré lui, Le" (*see* "Mock Doctor")
"Mefistofele," opera by Boito, 309, 335
Mehul, 168
"Meistersinger von Nürnberg, Die," opera by Wagner, first performance in Italy, 26; 67; 68, 113, 129, 140, 246, 255, 282, 287, 359, 380, 381, 415 (*see* Appendix)
Meitschik, Anna, 160
Melba, Nellie, 9, 67, 67, 96, 97, 194, 395, 396
Melis, Carmen, 101, 194
Meltzer, Charles Henry, 266
Mendelssohn (*see* "Walpurgis Night")
Mendès, Catulle, 131, 217
Mérimée, Prosper, 303
"Merlin," opera by Goldmark, 146
"Merry Widow, The," operetta, 64
"Merry Wives of Windsor," opera by Nicolai, 365
Metropolitan English Grand Opera Company, 175
Metropolitan Opera Company, plans for extension, 21; a season in Paris, 22; leases Metropolitan Opera House, 22; reorganized, 23; Gatti and Dippel appointed joint managers, 23; abolishes abuses, 23; conflict between managers, 29; extends Gatti's contract, 30; appoints Dippel administrative manager, 31; joint managers, 36; forces increased, 37; 59; rivalry with Hammerstein in New York and Philadelphia, 69 *et seq.;* policy of expansion, 73, 78; establishes opera in Baltimore, 74; foregoes guarantee in Philadelphia, 77; Dippel resigns as administrative manager, 78; courts German opera patrons, 79; affiliates with Chicago, 77; refuses Hammerstein's offer of merger, 76; stockholders interested in purchase of Hammerstein's properties, 79; Cuyler and Stotesbury enter directorate, 80; losses in season 1909-10, 80; refuses to permit Hammerstein to reenter operatic field, 86; secures injunction against him, 91; rivalry with Manhattan, 94 *et seq.;* speculation in tickets, 95; Debussy's operas announced, 111; alliances, 133; losses, 135, 136; cost of singers, 136; increase of personnel, 140; influence of Puccini's publishers, 155; English opera considerations, 169; offer of prize for English opera, 141, 169 *et seq.;* affiliated with Century Opera Company, 175; 177; Gatti appointed sole manager, 193; in Philadelphia, 193; reduces forces, 193; activity during years of neutrality, 331; bringing back singers from Europe, 332; Reiss and Gilly, 332; roster of German singers, 332; falling off of subscriptions, 332; end of affiliation with Boston and Chicago Companies, 332; Gatti proclaims reforms, 333; Caruso's honorarium, 333; attitude toward German singers, 382
Metropolitan Opera House, vicissitudes of first twenty-five years, 2; German period,

3, 15, 165; under Conried's administration, 3; German language banished from, 4; periods in its history, 13; rivalry with the Academy of Music, 14, 15; pension fund, 18; rivalry with Manhattan Opera House, 19, 69 et seq. (see Hammerstein and Metropolitan Opera Company); leased to Metropolitan Opera Company, 22; directors' benefits, 18; season 1908-09, 48; season 1909-10, 133; season, 1910-11, 193; season 1911-12, 242; prices of admission increased, 267, 272; ticket speculation scandal, 267 et seq.; cost of giving opera at various times, 282 et seq.; season 1912-13, 286 et seq.; German opera versus Italian, 287; season 1913-14, 300 et seq., season 1914-15, 331, 334 et seq.; season 1915-16, 348 et seq.; season 1916-17, 359 et seq.; season 1917-18, 382 et seq.; obligation to American singers, 384; ten seasons of opera tabulated (see Appendix)
Metropolitan Real Estate and Opera Company, 16; leases house to Metropolitan Opera Company, 22; improvements in the building, 40; 59
Metropolitan Trust Company, 274
Meyer, Charles, 251
Meyerbeer (see "Huguenots," "Prophète," "Africaine," "Dinorah")
Middleton, Arthur, 287
Mifflin, Thomas, 191
"Mignon," opera by Ambroise Thomas, 178 (see Appendix)
Milda, Miss, 118
Mildenberg, Albert, 173
Military operas, 154
Missiano, Eduardo, 39, 149, 210
Mistral, Frédéric, 116
"Mock Doctor, The," opera by Gounod, 373

Molière (see "Amour Médecin")
"Mona," opera by Parker, 171, 242; first performances, 255; criticism, 256 et seq.; 294, 318 (see Appendix)
"Monna Vanna," opera by Février, 310; first performance, 324; 395
Monsigny (see "Deserter")
Montemezzi, Italo, portrait, 314 (see "Amore dei tre Re")
Monteverde (see "Orfeo")
Monteux, Pierre, 398, 408
Morand, Eugène, 126
Moranzoni, Roberto, 372; portrait, 396; 397, 407, 412
Mordkin, 139, 198, 201
Morena, Berta, 40
Morgan, J. Pierpont, 33, 35
Moscow, 330
Moszkowski (see "Boabdil")
Mottl, Felix, 19, 346
Mozart (see "Nozze di Figaro," "Zauberflöte," "Don Giovanni," "Impresario," and "Bastien et Bastienne"); and Smetana, 58, 123; his music in New York, 373, 391, 410, 416
"Mozartiana," by Tschaikowsky, 162
Mühlmann, Adolph, 40, 56, 160, 284
"Muette de Portici," opera by Auber, 53
Muezzin, call to prayer, 400, 402
Mugnone (see "Birichino"), 78
Mulford, Florence, 295
Municipal opera, 174 et seq.
Muratore, Lucien, 326
Murphy, Lambert, 248, 265, 295, 311, 227
Muzio, Claudia, 408

Napoleon Bonaparte, 337, 402
Naprawnik, 162
National music and nostalgia, 306
National Opera Company, 159

National schools of composition and folksongs, 187
"Natoma," opera by Herbert, 101, 113, 170, 179; rejected by Gatti, 196; 226; first performance in Philadelphia, 237; in New York, 229; criticism, 229 et seq. (see Appendix)
"Naughty Anthony," 206
"Navarraise, La," opera by Massenet, 108, 116, 146, 364 (see Appendix)
Nepoti, Ludovico, 149
Nepoty, Lucien, 398
Nero, as a singer, 236 et seq.
"Nero," opera by Rubinstein, 159, 237
"Nerone," opera by Boito, 54
Netherlands, bell-ringing in, 111; people and languages, 107
Neuendorff, Adolf, 92
"Neugirige Frauen, Die" (see "Donne curiose")
Nevada, Emma, 361
Nevin, Arthur (see "Twilight")
New Empire Theater, New York, 372
Newspapers, their frivolous attitude toward music, 4, 96
New Theater, The, 4; planned by Conried, 32; foundation of, 33 et seq.; land bought, 33; architects' plans approved, 33; purposes of founders, 33; cornerstone laid, 34; dedicated, 35; cost of, 35; 87, 135; losses at, 137; season at, 137; 138, 193, 273
New York, Opera Season, one compared with European cities, 133; cost of opera in, 270 et seq.; rivalry with Philadelphia, 74; Hammerstein agrees not to give opera in, 80; early opera in, 190; society and opera, 14
Nicolai (see "Merry Wives of Windsor")
Nicolay, Constantin, 114, 118, 229, 235, 251, 305, 321, 326

Niemann, Albert, 408
Nielsen, Alice, 141, 194
Nielson, Francis, 206
Niessen-Stone, Matja, 39
"Night Bell, The," opera by Donizetti, 373
Nilsson, Christine, 9, 396
"Noé," opera by Halévy, 366
Noguès (see "Quo Vadis?")
Nordica, Lillian, 9, 140, 274; death and career of, 320, 330
Noria, Jane, 27, 158
"Norma," opera by Bellini, 260
Note, Jean, 39
"Nozze di Figaro," opera by Mozart, 48, 59, 199, 373 (see Appendix)

Ober, Margarete, portrait, 310; 310, 311, 345, 354, 371, 381, 393
"Ode to Joy," Schiller's, 414
Odilion, Helene, 25
"O, du Deutschland, ich muss marschiren," 152
Offenbach (see "Contes d'Hoffmann" and "Barbe-Bleue"), 111
O'Keefe, John, 190
"Old Dog Tray," 211
Open-air theaters, 247
Opéra bouffe, 138
Opéra Comique, Paris, 133
"Oracolo L'," opera by Leoni, 335, 336; first performance, 341; criticism, 341 (see Appendix)
Oratorio Society of New York, 98, 249
Orefice, Prof., 266
"Orfeo," opera by Monteverde, 243, 265
"Orfeo et Eurydice," opera by Gluck, 144 et seq.; 199, 204, 368 (see Appendix)
Osborne, Hannah Jane, 141
"Otello," opera by Verdi, 55, 67, 97, 301, 355 (see Appendix)
Otto, Wilhelm, 160
Ouida, 407
"Ouvre tes yeux bleux," 320
Ovid, "Espistolæ heroidum," 359

Paderewski, Jan, 62 (see "Manru")
Paër (see "Léonore," "Maestro di Capella," and "Camilla"); "Pagliacci," opera by Leoncavallo, 54, 108, 113, 146, 179, 253, 336, 363 (see Appendix)
Palm, Nuremberg bookseller, 151, 152
"Paradise Lost," 11
"Pardon de Ploërmel" (see "Dinorah")
Parepa, 289
Paris, Meropolitan Opera Company's season in, 22; opera activities compared with New York, 134; 330
Park Theater, 373
Parker, Horatio W., 4 (see "Mona," "Hora Novissima," "A Wanderer's Psalm"); wins prize, 171; sketch of, 172; honored by Cambridge University, 172; 173, 246; portrait, 256; 256; his compositions, 262
"Parsifal," opera by Wagner, 20, 20, 48, 48, 168, 178, 185, 246, 282, 287, 336, 343, 377, 381, 406, 415 (see Appendix)
Paterna, Coreto, 39
Patterson, George J., 106
Patti, Adelina, 9, 361, 396
Patti, Carlotta, 289
Pavlova, dancer, 139, 197, 201
"Pêcheurs de Perles, Les," opera by Bizet, 97, 361, 361, 362; criticism, 362 et seq. (see Appendix)
Pelissier (see "Edwin and Angelina")
"Pelléas et Mélisande," opera by Debussy, 221, 226, 302, 410 (see Appendix)
"Pelléas et Mélisande," Maeterlinck's puppet play, 410
Pendleton, Judge, grants injunction against Hammerstein, 91; sustained on appeal, 91
Penzano, singer, 96

Perfall, Count, 380
Pergolesi (see "Maid Mistress")
Périer, M., 227
Perini, Flora, 351, 354
Periquet, 353
"Per la gloria," 125
Perotti, Julius, 408
Pérrier, Martial, 395
Peter the Great, 142
Petrarch, 125
Petronius, 237
Philadelphia-Chicago Opera Company (see also Chicago-Philadelphia Opera Company), 80, 170, 193, 243, 298 (see Appendix)
Philadelphia (see Hammerstein), 22; 72 et seq.; history of opera in, 73; 190, 101; Hammerstein builds opera house, 74, 77; his losses, 79; opera house sold, 79; privilege of giving opera abandoned for ten years, 80; alliance with Chicago, 80; Kahn, Mackaye, and Vanderbilt join directorate, 80; 81, 137, 138, 273, 324, 335, 360, 363; Metropolitan Opera Company in, 19, 227
Philharmonic Society of New York, 140, 388
Philidor, 190
Phryne, 6, 324
Piccini, 189
Pierre Loti, 206
Pini-Corsi, Antonio, 143, 149, 210, 213, 248, 295, 321, 328
"Pipe of Desire, The," opera by Converse, 38, 139, 141; first performance, 164; criticism, 164 et seq.; 228 (see Appendix)
"Pique Dame," opera by Tschaikowsky, 38, 139, 140, 158; first performance, 160; criticism, 160 et seq. (see Appendix)
Pittsburgh, Pa., 387
Plançon, Pol, 136, 408
Planquette (see "Cloches de Corneville")

INDEX

Pocahontas, 189
Podesti, Vittorio, 141
Pointed music, 214
Poker in musical diplomacy, 380
Polacco, Giorgio, 326, 341, 351, 362, 397
Polesi, Giovanni, 112
Ponchielli (see "Gioconda")
"Pop Goes the Weasel," 208, 211
Porter, Horace, 45
"Portrait de Manon, Le," opera by Massenet, 116
Possart, von, German tragedian, 25
Post, Laura J., 59
Pouschkin, 160, 408, 410
"Précieuses ridicules, Les," opera by Goetzl, 139
Preisch, Frank, 229
Press, the New York newspaper, fight between its editors and Hammerstein, 102
Prima donnas, quarrels about, 6
"Prince Igor," opera by Borodin, 108, 282, 335, 350; first performance, 351; criticism, 352; 417 (see Appendix)
"Princesse d'Auberge, La," opera by Blockx, 97; first performance, 106; criticism, 107 et seq. (see Appendix)
Prisch, F. A., 305
Prize offer for English opera, 169 et seq.
"Prodana Novĕsta" (see "Verkaufte Braut")
Progressists in Italy, 53
"Prophète, Le," opera by Meyerbeer, 112, 113, 113, 398, 407; performances in New York, 408 (see Appendix)
Providence, R. I., 389
Prussia and music, 416
Puccini (see "Edgar," "Manon Lescaut," "Bohème," "Tosca," "Fanciulla del West," "Villi," "Madama Butterfly"); a family of musicians, 51; 53; influence at Metropolitan Opera House, 155; visits to the United States, 197; portrait, 204; reception in Metropolitan Opera House, 205; 300, 301, 316
"Puppenfee" ballet, 139
Puppet plays and operas, 410
Purcell, Henry, 185, 187
"Puritani, I," opera by Bellini, 113 (see Appendix)

Quarti, Ariodante, 39
Quinault, 130, 199, 201, 203
"Qui facit per alium facit per se," 276
"Quo Vadis?" opera by Noguès, 83; first performance, 235; criticism, 235 et seq.; 306 (see Appendix)

Rabaud, Henri (see "Marôuf"); portrait, 398; 398
Rabinoff, 225
Raisa, Rosa, portrait, 394; 395, 395
"Rakoczy March," 306
Rameau, 288
Randa, Mme., 44
Rantzenberg, Mary, 39, 51
"Ranz des Vaches," opera by Kienzl, 287; first performance, 304; criticism, 304 et seq.
Rappold, Marie, 40, 204, 354, 367
Rasoumowsky, the E minor quartet by Beethoven, 297
Ravogli, Sophia and Giulia, 146
"Reconciliation, The," 191
Redding, Joseph, 196, 226, 227, 231
Reed, Stuart, 291
Reger, Max, 10
Régis, George, 158
Reinagle, Alexander, 192
Reinagle, Alexander Robert, 192
Reiner, Marcel, 213, 253, 295
Reiss, Albert, 40, 44, 56, 140, 204, 210, 213, 265, 284, 295, 296, 311, 327, 332, 370, 372, 375, 398

INDEX

Réjane, French actress, 339
Renaud, Maurice, 77, 81, 96, 98, 99, 112, 114, 194, 235
Republic Theater, 82
Reschigliani, Vincenzo, 107, 210, 248, 296, 327, 336, 408, 409
"Retrospections in America," 192
Revision of new operas, 294
Revolutionary airs, French, 338 et seq.
"Rhapsodie espagnole," 302
"Rheingold," opera by Wagner, first performance in Italy, 26; 282, 350 (see Appendix)
Ricci, the Brothers (see "Crispino e la Comare")
"Richard Cœur de Lion," opera by Grétry, 163
Ricordi, Tito, and his publishing house, 55, 85, 172, 172, 173, 196, 208, 249
"Ridendo castigat mores," 415
Riegelman, Mabel, 250, 251
"Rienzi," opera by Wagner, first performance in Italy, 26
"Rigoletto," opera by Verdi, 97, 113, 179 (see Appendix)
Rimsky-Korsakow (see "Coq d'Or"), 352
"Ring des Nibelungen, Der," tetralogy by Wagner, 178, 414 (see Appendix)
"Rip Van Winkle," opera by Bristow, 228
Ritter, Alexander, 247
Robeson, Lila, 327, 407
Robinson, Anastasia, 8, 126
Roche, Henri Pierre, 395
Roget de Lisle, 338
Rolland, Romaine, 343
Rolli, 126
"Roméo et Juliette," opera by Gounod, 67, 179, 198, 225, 246, 385 (see Appendix)
Roosevelt, Theodore, President of the United States, 34
Root, Elihu, 35
Roquette, Otto, 404

Rosa Opera Company, 176
"Rosalie the Prairie Flower," 208
Rose, Johann Wilhelm, 189
"Rosenkavalier, Der," opera by Richard Strauss, 282, 309, 310; first performance, 311; 329 (see Appendix)
Rossi, Giulio, 39, 51, 56, 149, 210, 248, 284, 296, 341, 370, 398
Rossini (see "Barbiere," "Guillaume Tell," "Cenerentola," "Signor Bruschino"), 142, 290
Rostand (see "Cyrano de Bergerac")
Rothier, Léon, 193, 216, 222, 274; portrait, 296; 296, 328, 362, 398
Rothmeyer, Adolph, 61
Rousseau, 201
"Rousslan et Ludmilla," opera by Glinka, 159
Rowson, Mrs., 192
Rubinstein (see "Nero"); lack of nationalism in his music, 159
Ruffo, Titta, 287
Rullman, Fred, 270; ticket agency, 271, 274
Russell, Henry, 22, 78
Russian ballet, 81, 243, 410
Russian operas in the United States, 158
Ruysdael, Basil, 194, 216, 253, 265, 266, 295, 311, 354, 370, 403, 408, 409

Sachetto, Rita, 143
"Saint Elizabeth," oratorio by Liszt, 397, 398; first performance as an opera, 398; as an oratorio, 403; 403, 416 (see Appendix)
Saint Elizabeth of Hungary, 405
St. Petersburg (Petrograd), 85, 134, 330
"St. Peter's," hymn-tune, 192
Saint-Saëns' little known operas, 155 (see "Samson et Dalila")

INDEX 469

"Salome," opera by Richard Strauss, 17, 94, 96, 97, 102; rejected at Metropolitan Opera House, 103; abandoned by Conried, 103; purchased by Hammerstein, 103; in French, 105, 106; perversity in, 105; in Philadelphia and Boston, 106; 114, 120, 178, 212, 312, 324 (see Appendix)
"Salome," by Oscar Wilde, 119, 125
Sammarco, Mario, 96, 112, 229, 230, 233, 250
"Samson et Dalila," opera by Saint-Saëns, 97, 98, 179, 309, 335, 350 (see Appendix)
Sanderson, Sybil, 124
San Francisco, 61, 298
San Martino, Count, 21
"Sapho," opera by Massenet, 111, 113, 114, 115 (see Appendix)
Sapio, Maurio, 295
Sardou (see "Madame Sans-Gêne"), 337
"Sauteriot, Le," opera by Lazzari, 395
Savage, H. W., and English Opera Company, 27, 39, 125, 176, 177, 207, 311
Scalchi, Sofia, 146
"Scarlet Letter, The," opera by Damrosch, 228
Scenic splendor in old operas, 200
"Schauspieldirektor, Der" (see "Impresario")
Schikaneder, 374, 375
Schiller, 399, 413, 414
Schindler, Kurt, 352
Schmedes, Erik, 39, 44
Schlegel, the brothers, 152
Schlegel, Carl, 311, 332, 370, 403, 408
Schneider, Louis, 374
Schönberg, Arnold, 10, 11
"Schöne Galatea, Die," operetta by Suppé, 139
Schott, Anton, 408
Schratt, Kathi, 25
Schubert, Erik, 39

Schubert, Franz, "Soirées de Vienne," 304; 391, 415, 416
Schuch, Hofrath von, 360
Schumann, 10, 62, 391, 415, 416
Sconamiglio, conductor, 112
Scott, Henri, 118, 124
Scotti, Antonio, 32, 40, 60, 60, 64, 140, 248, 274, 284, 340, 341
"Second Book of Operas, A," by H. E. Krehbiel, quoted, 115, 206, 214, 148, 251, 296, 311
"Secret of Susanne" (see "Segreto di Susanna")
Seeler, Edgar V., 33
Seebach, Count, 378
"Segreto di Susanna, Il," opera by Wolf-Ferrari, 179, 226, 233; first performance in New York, 234; criticism, 234; 249, 250 (see Appendix)
Segurola, Andrea, 98, 158, 204, 210, 214, 248, 248, 251, 296, 296, 311
Seidl, Anton, and Wagner's operas in Italy, 26; 283, 342
Seligman, Isaac N., 174
Sembach, Johannes, 287, 332, 345, 354, 367, 370, 381, 393
Sembrich, Marcella, retirement of from opera, 3; supports Mr. Dippel, 29; 40; farewell to operatic stage, 59 et seq.; gifts to, 61; benefactions to orchestra, 61; speech of thanks, 61; musicians give her a banquet, 62; repertory waltz, 65; Mr. Henderson's poetic tribute to, 62; activities after retirement, 66; 125, 136, 284, 361, 364, 396
"Serenade for Strings," by Tschaikowsky, 162
"Serva Padrona, La" (see "Maid Mistress")
Severina, singer, 96, 107, 118
Sewickley, Pa., 387
Sexual perversity in "Elektra," 119
Shakespeare, "Hamlet," 35; "Antony and Cleopatra," 35; "Cymbeline," 128; 321, 325;

his subjects in opera, 355; 356, 371
"Shanewis," opera by Cadman, 398; first performance, 398; 411 (see Appendix)
"Siberia," opera by Giordano, 97, 108, 113 (see Appendix)
"Siegfried," opera by Wagner, 282, 344 (see Appendix)
Sienkiewicz, 235
"Signor Bruschino," opera by Rossini, 139
Silcher, 307
Singers, cost of, 136
Singspiel, 138
"Sirènes, Les," 222
"Six francs for an E-string!", 168
Skroup, 149
"Slaves in Algeria," 192
Slezak, Leo, 141, 160, 163, 274
Smareglia, Anton (see "Vassal von Szigeth"), 151
Smetana (see "Verkaufte Braut"); Mozart's style in his music, 58; Wagner's influence, 58; 187
Smirnoff, Dmitri, 193
Smith, Captain John, 189
Smith, Elihu Hubbard (see "Edwin and Angelina")
Smith, Harry B., 291
Smith, Queenie, 409
Snelling, Lillia, 164
Society and opera, 103
Society for the Promotion of National Opera, 228
Society of American Singers, 372
Society for the Promotion of Opera in English, 173
"Sonnambula, La," opera by Bellini (see Appendix)
Sonneck, O. G., 188, 189, 190, 191
Sonnenthal, German actor, 25
Soomer, Walter, 39
Sophocles, 119
Sothern, E. H., 371
"So viel' Stern'," 173
Sparkes, Leonora, 39, 149, 160, 164, 204, 216, 296, 321, 336, 367

Speculation in theater tickets, 81, 95; a scandal, 267 et seq.; attempts to reform, 269; large subscriptions by agents, 270; introduction of system at Metropolitan Opera House, 270; Grau and Rullman, 270; Tyson and Company's purchases in 1913, 274; Rullman's purchases, 274; Richard J. Hartman obtains control of Tyson and Company, 274; tickets pledged as collateral, 275; Metropolitan Trust Company advances loan, 274; Metropolitan Opera Company denies that agency purchasers are subscribers, 275, 276; subscribers offered an opportunity to repurchase, 276; Mr. Baulies alleges that Tyson and Company have no title, 277; Mr. Cuyler denies knowledge of hypothecation, 277; indignation meeting of subscribers, 277; the District Attorney intervenes, 278; Hartman arrested, 278; criminal charge not pressed, 278; Hartman imprisoned on another accusation, 278; Metropolitan Company invites direct subscription, 271
Spetrino, conductor, 347
"Spia, La," opera by Arditi, 228
"Spoil'd Child, The," 190
Spontini (see "Hernando Cortez")
Stagno, Roberto, 408
Stahlschmidt, Arthur E., 174
Stanley, Helen, 305
Stanton, Edmund C., 83, 151, 379, 380
"Star-Spangled Banner, The," 35, 49, 377, 389
Stassow, 352
Steibelt, 252
Stewart, Grant, 318
Stillman, James, 33
Storace, 189
Stotesbury, E. T., lends Ham-

INDEX

merstein money, 75, 79; he and others buy out Hammerstein's interests, 79, 80, 82
Stracciari, Riccardo, 395
"Stradella," opera by Flotow, 289 (see Appendix)
Stransky, Josef, 388
Strauss, Johann (see "Fledermaus" and "Zigeunerbaron")
Strauss, Richard (see "Salome," "Feuersnot," "Elektra," "Rosenkavalier"), 10, 112; and Wagner, 120; 187, 247, 312, 369
Streets of Cairo, Chicago Exposition, 401
Sturani, conductor, 112
Subscriptions to opera easily obtained, 195
Sugana, Luigi, 250
Sun, The, newspaper, quoted, 289, 353, 412
"Sulamita, La," opera by Wolf-Ferrari, 250
Sundelius, Marie, 367, 371, 409, 412
Suppé, Franz von (see "Schöne Galatea")
"Susanna's Geheimniss" (see "Segreto di Susanna")
Sussex, steamer torpedoed by the Germans, 354
Swann, District Attorney of New York, 269
Swift, Jonathan, lampoons singers, 8
Symbolism in opera, 221
"Sylphides, Les," ballet, 139
Sylva, Eloi, 408
Sylva, Marguerite, 227
"Sylvia," ballet, 139
Sylvestre, Armand, 126
Szendrei, Alfred, 179

"Tales of Hoffmann" (see "Contes d'Hoffmann")
Tamagno, Francesco, 98, 408
"Taming of the Shrew" (see "Widerspänstigen Zähmung")
Tancredi, Miss, 107

"Tancredo," opera by Bertoni, 148
Tango, Egisto, 141
"Tannhäuser," opera by Wagner, first time in Italy, 26; 58, 67, 67, 113, 129, 168, 178, 244, 289, 343, 377, 404, 405, 414 (see Appendix)
Tatlock, J. S. P., 371
Tato-Lango, Mlle., 118
Taubert, 374
Tauscher, Hans, activities in behalf of Germany, 382
Taylor, H., 190
Tecchi, Giuseppe, 40
Tegani, Riccardo, 336, 370
Tennyson, 262, 325
Terpnos, 237
Tetrazzini, Luise, 96, 112, 361, 395
Teyte, Maggie, 251
"Thaïs," opera by Massenet, 100, 101, 114, 116, 124, 178, 178, 226, 287, 324, 361, 395 (see Appendix)
Theater tickets, speculation in, 81, 95, 267 et seq.
Theatrical companies, early in America, 73
"Theuerdank," opera by Thuille, 246, 247
Thibaut, 318
Thomas, Ambroise, 321
Thomas, Augustus, 35
Thomas, Goring (see "Esmeralda")
Thomas, Theodore, 145, 149, 150, 403
"Thousand Nights and a Night, A," 399, 400
Thuille, Ludwig (see "Lobetanz," "Theuerdank," "Gugelino"); 243, 246; his music in America, 249
Ticket speculation in New York, 81, 95, 267 et seq.
"Tiefland," opera by D'Albert, 28, 38; first performance in America, 44; criticism, 44 et seq.; 48, 179 (see Appendix)
Tiersot, 148
Tiffany, Maria, 371

"Tilda," opera by Cilea, 54
Times Building Ticket Agency, 270
Times, The, newspaper, quoted, 329, 334
Timotheus of Miletus, banished from Sparta, 120
Toedt, Mrs. Theodore J., 64
Tofts, Mrs., 7, 8
"Tosca," opera by Puccini, 97, 113, 178, 198, 206, 397 (see Appendix)
Toscanini, Arturo, 20; engaged for the Metropolitan Opera House, 22; appointed musical director, 23; introduced to the New York press, 22; taste in music, 28; fondness for Wagner, 28; devotion to German opera, 36; described in prospectus, 37; 39; his conducting, 42; career, 43; retirement from Metropolitan Opera House, 43; cablegram sent by Kahn, 43; 59; 78, 79, 140, 141, 144, 146, 147, 200, 204, 210, 216, 247, 273, 273, 274, 295, 318 328; breaks down in health, 336, 342; attitude toward German opera, 347; departure from New York, 348
Train, Arthur C., 269
Translations (see Language, etc.), 166, 178
"Traviata," opera by Verdi, 60, 113, 178, 194, 330, 395 (see Appendix)
Trentini, Emma, 96, 112
Tribune, The New York, newspaper, quoted, 1, 9, 26, 27, 42, 45, 165, 210, 220, 288, 327, 342, 352, 385
"Tristan und Isolde," opera by Wagner, 20, 31, 58, 120, 131, 140, 178, 243, 245, 282, 330, 344, 381 (see Appendix)
"Trompeter von Säkkingen, Der," opera by Nessler, 384
"Trovatore, Il," opera by Verdi, 113 (see Appendix)

"Troyens, Le," opera by Berlioz, 116, 156
Tschaikowsky (see "Pique Dame," "Serenade for Strings," "Mozartiana"); his melancholy, 161; and Wagner, 161; and Mozart, 161, 162; and Naprawnik, 162
Tugendbund, 151
"Twilight," opera by Arthur Nevin, 196, 228
"Two Little Wooden Shoes," 407
Twombly, Hamilton McK., 33
Tyson and Brother, 272
Tyson and Company, 270, 274, 276
Tyson Company, 270

"Ugonotti" (see "Huguenots")
United Booking Company, 90
United Theater Ticket Corporation, 270
Urlus, Jacques, 332

Valerie, Odette, 97
Vallez, Louis, 98, 107
Vallier, 114
Van Cortlandt, Robert B., 33
Vanderbilt, Cornelius, 33
Vanderbilt, William K., 30, 80, 86, 176, 226
Vanderlip, Frank A., 177
Van Duyse, Prudens, 110
Van Dyck, Rosina, 216, 311, 327
Van Rooy, Anton, 284
Van Zandt, Marie, 361
"Vassal von Szigeth," opera by Smareglia, 55, 151
Vaucaire, 302
Verdi (see "Falstaff," "Aïda," "Manzoni Requiem," "Traviata," "Trovatore," "Otello," "Forza del Destino," "Rigoletto," "Don Carlos," "Ballo in Maschera," "Ernani"), 54, 59, 300; and Wagner, 301; 365; on how a Napoleon should sing, 337
"Verkaufte Braut, Die," opera

INDEX 473

by Smetana, 28, 38, 48, 49;
first performance, 55; criticism, 56 et seq. (see Appendix)
Vernon, Grenville, 327, 352
"Versiegelt," opera by Blech, 139; first performance, 253; criticism, 253 et seq. (see Appendix)
Verstowsky (see "Askold's Tomb")
Venturini, singer, 107, 114, 118, 235, 250, 305, 305, 321
Vestris family, 201
Vestvali, Felicita, 145
Victoria Theater, New York, 82, 84, 84
Vienna opera season compared with New York's, 134
"Vienna Waltzes," ballet, 139
Vieulle, 98
Villa, 115, 124
"Villi, Le," opera by Puccini, 28, 31, 38, 48; first performance, 50; criticism, 50; 53, 160, 248 (see Appendix)
Villoteau, 402
"Violin Maker of Cremona, The," 111, 113
"Vita Nuova," oratorio by Wolf-Ferrari, 235, 249
Von Bülow, Hans, 300
Von Chezy, Frau, 344
Von Schwind, Moritz, 404

Wagner, Richard (see "Parsifal," "Ring des Nibelungen," "Tristan und Isolde," "Rienzi," "Fliegende Holländer," "Tannhäuser," "Lohengrin," "Meistersinger," "Rheingold," "Walküre," "Siegfried," "Götterdämmerung"); criticism, 10; first performance of his operas in Italy, 26; influence in Italy, 54; and Greek chorus, 120; at the Manhattan Opera House, 129; 166, 186; at Metropolitan Opera House, 287; relation to the Italian veritists, 300; influenced by Weber, 342 et seq.; and Verdi, 365; 391; his dramas after the war, 413 et seq.; ethics of his dramas, 413 et seq.
Wakefield, Henrietta, 40, 55, 216, 266
Walden, Lord Howard de, 83, 84
"Walküre, Die," opera by Wagner, 26, 38, 68, 289 (see Appendix)
Wallace, 186
"Wally, La," opera by Catalani, 28, 38, 48, 50, 51; first performance, 51; criticism, 51 et seq.; 160, 248 (see Appendix)
"Walpurgis Night," 265
Walter, Edna, 213
Walters, Henry, 33
Walter-Villa, Mme., 115, 118, 123
War, the struggle of 1914-1918, influences changes in conditions, 1, 41; during years of neutrality, 331 et seq.; 376 et seq.; how it affected the Metropolitan opera, 376; German opera in early part of period, 377; Bodanzky, 377; German operas and singers retained, 377; managers in Germany forbid American contracts, 378; announcement of the declaration at opera house, 381; protests against Mme. Gadski, 382, 383, 384; effects of America's entrance, 386 et seq.; taxes on amusements, 388, 390; compels changes in Philharmonic Society, 388; president of Musical Union impeached, 388; Kunwald and Muck interned, 389; Boston Symphony Orchestra turned over to trustees, 390; growth of intolerance toward German music, 391; German language banished from song recitals, 391; Philharmonic Society of New York elimi-

nates music of living German composers, 392; Metropolitan Opera Company abolishes German performances, 392; cancels contracts with German singers, 393; probable effects on the future, 413; righteousness of the dismissal of German singers, 417
Warburg, Paul M., 177
Warnery, Edmond, 227, 250, 321, 326
Warrum, Helen, 321
Wartburg festival, 404
Washington, D. C., 274
Weber (*see* "Euryanthe," "Freischütz," and "Invitation to the Dance"), 152, 153, 154; influence on Wagner, 342 *et seq.*
Weil, Hermann, début, 243; 253, 266, 284, 311, 332, 345, 367, 393
Weinstein, Ruth, 311
"Werther," opera by Massenet, 116, 124, 225, 323 (*see* Appendix)
Wheeler, Arthur and Walter, 235
White, Caroline, 233, 250
White, Stanford, 33
Whitehill, Clarence, *portrait*, 140; 141, 164, 167, 354, 403
Whitman, Governor of New York State, 269, 270
Whitney, Henry Payne, 33, 176, 177
Whole note scale, 288
Wickham, Florence, 149, 160, 213, 216
"Widerspänstigen Zähmung, Der," opera by Goetz, 350, 351, 354; history and criticism, 355 *et seq.*; 377 (*see* Appendix)
Widmann, Joseph Viktor, 354
Wilde, Oscar, 101, 105, 119, 125
"Wilhelmus von Nassauen," 111

William I, German Emperor, 152
Williamsburg, Va., 73
Willis, N. P., 152
Wilson, B. Orme, 33
Wilson, Francis, 291
Wilson, Woodrow, President of the United States, 377
Winthrop, Henry Rogers, 33, 177
Witherspoon, Herbert, 39, 140, 164, 265, 266, 274, 284
Wittkowski, Marta, 250
Woehning, Paula, 40
Wolf-Ferrari (*see* "Segreto di Susanna," "Donne curiose," "Vita Nuova," "Amore Medico," "Sulamita," "Cenerentola"), 233; *portrait*, 234; visits America, 248; 249, 319
World premières, doubtful value of, 215
Wulman, Paolo, 149

"Yankee Doodle," 191

Zandonai (*see* "Francesca da Rimini," "Conchita")
Zangarini, G., 204, 302
Zanoni, Camillo, 341
"Zauberflöte," opera by Mozart, 68, 162, 289, 373 (*see* Appendix)
"Zaza," opera by Leoncavallo, 111
Zenatello, Giovanni, 96, 112, Zepilli, Alice, 96, 107, 235
Zerola, tenor, 112
Ziegler, Edward, 379
"Zigeunerbaron" (also "Gypsy Baron"), operetta by Johann Strauss, 20; staged by Conried, 25
"Zigeunerliebe," operetta by Lehar, 139
Zola, Emile, 156, 157
Zoppet, open-air theater at, 247
"Zu Strassburg auf der Schanz," 307

LIBRARY OF DAVIDSON COLLEGE

Books on regular loan may be checked out
nted at the Circulation Desk in